RAILWAY RENAISSANCE

In Memory of Trefor David (1930–1999)

Inspiration for my life-long interest in railways

Cymmer Afan had become the temporary terminus for trains from Bridgend and Maesteg, following closure of the Rhondda Tunnel and the link to Treherbert in 1968. Shortly before closure in 1970, the author stands alongside a Class 121 'bubble car' with his late father, Trefor, and an unknown driver. Photo: Derek Short

RAILWAY RENAISSANCE

Britain's railways after Beeching

Gareth David

PEN & SWORD
TRANSPORT

First published in Great Britain in 2017 by
Pen & Sword Transport
an imprint of
Pen & Sword Books Ltd
47 Church Street
Barnsley
South Yorkshire
S70 2AS

ISBN 978 1 47386 200 5

A CIP catalogue record for this book is available from the British Library

Typeset in Ehrhardt by
Mac Style Ltd, Bridlington, East Yorkshire
Printed and bound in China by Imago

Pen & Sword Books Ltd incorporates the imprints of Pen & Sword
Archaeology, Atlas, Aviation, Battleground, Discovery, Family History,
History, Maritime, Military, Naval, Politics, Railways, Select, Transport,
True Crime, Fiction, Frontline Books, Leo Cooper, Praetorian Press, Seaforth
Publishing and Wharncliffe.

For a complete list of Pen & Sword titles please contact
PEN & SWORD BOOKS LIMITED
47 Church Street, Barnsley, South Yorkshire, S70 2AS, England
E-mail: enquiries@pen-and-sword.co.uk
Website: www.pen-and-sword.co.uk

CONTENTS

Introduction   1

Chapter 1   Beeching and the Aftermath   17

Chapter 2   The Making of a Modern Railway   52

Chapter 3   Re-openings across England   91

Chapter 4   Rebuilding Scotland's Railway   130

Chapter 5   Revival in the Welsh Valleys and Beyond   161

Chapter 6   A High Price for High Speed   191

Chapter 7   Rails across London   209

Chapter 8   Still to Come   231

Chapter 9   Longer Shots   255

Chapter 10 On Reflection   278

Appendix I: Lines opened or re-opened since Beeching   301
Appendix II: Stations opened or re-opened since Beeching   304
Appendix III: Bibliography   318
Appendix IV: Campaign and Promotional Groups   320
Acknowledgments   322
Index   323

Gareth David developed his life-long interest in railways while growing up in Cheltenham Spa during the 1960s and early 1970s, then moved to London, where he read Modern History at University College (UCL). On graduating in 1979 he trained as a journalist, before joining *The Times* as Stock Market Reporter in early 1982. He went on to work on the business section of *The Observer* and later *The Sunday Times*, where he was Deputy City Editor from 1988–90. A highlight of his subsequent career in public relations consultancy was to support Ian Yeowart for 12 years in battling to launch 'Open Access' operator Grand Central Railway Company.

Gareth now lives at Haslemere in Surrey and has been a commuter to Waterloo for nearly 25 years. He is married, with four grown-up children, and spends some of his limited spare time working as a volunteer booking clerk or buffet car steward on the Mid-Hants Railway (Watercress Line). To learn more, please visit www.railwayworld.net

INTRODUCTION

Half a century ago, on the morning of Sunday 2 July 1967, a small boy stands beside the railway line on the south side of Basingstoke station, opposite the shed where a few steam locomotives stand in idle silence, awaiting their final days in service and then the cutter's torch. It is the last week of steam in southern England and the boy and his father are there to witness a commemoration of this sad day. There had been plans to run no less than five steam specials from London to Bournemouth to mark the end of Southern Region steam, but the fare of £4 return to Bournemouth from Waterloo (equivalent to £67.25 today) had put many enthusiasts off, with the result that only two of the five were run, hauled respectively by Merchant Navy Class locos 35008 *Orient Line* and 35028 *Clan Line*. The *Bournemouth Belle*, another victim of electrification, was hauled that day by a Brush Type 4 (later Class 47) diesel, but there was one other steam special, hauled on its outward journey by West Country Class 34025 *Whimple*.

Move ahead just over a year and that same small boy and his father are standing outside Moses Gate station near Bolton on the afternoon of Sunday 11 August 1968. The father has a tear in his eyes as Class 5 locos 44781 and 44871 come into view, heading the Carlisle to Manchester leg of the famous *15 Guinea Special* – this time it really is the end of steam on the whole of British Railways. Witnessing this sad day for father and son had followed a couple of trips from Cheltenham to Preston in early summer 1968 to experience the last outpost of British steam working – including a last ever steam-hauled trip on BR – from Preston to Kirkham on a service for Blackpool – and visits to the last remaining steam sheds in the area, nearby Lostock Hall (shed-code 10D), as well as Springs Branch, Wigan (8F) and Speke Junction in Warrington (8C)

For many August 1968 was a black time in the history of our railways. Steam was at an end and the spate of closures initiated by the 1963 Beeching Report was at its peak – 300 miles of line were closed in 1967 and a further 400 miles in 1968. Widespread

The 1968 Ian Allan 'ABC' was my first spotting 'bible' and last in this famous series to have steam locomotives at the front. Besides the three Vale of Rheidol narrow gauge locomotives, it lists a total of 430 steam locomotives that were still in service (all confined to northwest England), based on numbers checked to 2 December 1967. The cover photo is of now-preserved Class 52 D1062 *Western Courier* approaching Acock's Green near Birmingham on 11 June 1963.

Two memorable souvenirs from the trainspotting years: a Midland Railtourer ticket and a footplate pass, arranged for me by Tom Greaves, a legendary figure in BR management at the time and friend of my late father. Note Tom's endorsement – which secured me a trip from York to Kings Cross in the cab of D9021 *Argyll and Sutherland Highlander*.

motorway construction threatened to marginalise what would remain of the national network, which had long been starved of investment. As that small boy who had been at Basingstoke and Moses Gate, it was an inauspicious time to be developing a life-long passion for railways, but trainspotting ran in the family, and if I were to be deprived of seeing any more Merchant Navys, Jubilees or Britannias in action then the first generation of diesel – the Peaks, Warships, the Westerns and Deltics – would have to do.

So began a life-long interest in all things railway – a journey that has taken me to every corner of Great Britain and places abroad stretching from Albania to Zimbabwe. Besides unforgettable footplate experiences on steam locomotives in Poland and Zimbabwe, notable milestones along the way were a cab ride in one of the last Deltics from York to London (1981), being arrested in Poland for photographing an Ol49-class steam locomotive on a passenger train at Sierpc (1990), leading a successful campaign to save buffet cars on the Waterloo–Portsmouth Line (1996) and being a founder director of Grand Central Railway Company at the time it launched services from Sunderland to London in 2007.

But for all the many facets of my railway interest, one that really captures my imagination is that of railway re-openings. Lines and stations that fell under the Beeching axe, and others that had closed even before the Doctor did his worst, but have been resurrected decades later and have successfully brought rail services back to places as far afield as Alloa and Galashiels in Scotland, Aberdare and Ebbw Vale in Wales, Mansfield and Melksham in England.

If there was a single moment when I felt inspired to write this book, it was on a visit to the small Scottish borders village of Stow in February 2015. Stow is mid-way along the the reopened Borders Railway route from Edinburgh to Galashiels and Tweedbank and had not originally been earmarked as a station re-opening in the £350 million project. But local pressure had won the day, and I was looking down from a road bridge at the newly rebuilt line – it is double track at this point – and recalled seeing pictures of the station before its closure in 1969 and of a house built across the line in the decades since then.

Forty-six years on and the station was almost ready for its first new trains, with contractors even working to refurbish the old station building, which had been acquired as part of the revival process. Today the citizens of Stow enjoy hourly trains to Galashiels and Edinburgh – the best service the station has ever seen since it first opened in 1848 – and after less than six months, passengers numbers at Stow were running at double what had been forecast prior to re-opening. The 35-mile long Borders Railway has become the longest of the routes proposed for closure in Dr Beeching's 1963 report *The Re-shaping of British Railways* to be re-opened to passenger service, albeit representing little more than one third of the full Waverley Route from Edinburgh to Carlisle, which had succumbed to closure in 1969, amid howls of protest.

Paying a return visit to Stow in late September 2015, only three weeks after the line had re-opened (on 6 September 2015) and the locals were already complaining that they only had an hourly day-time service, with the other train each hour passing the station non-stop. First impressions of the Borders Railway itself were of a system that could quickly reach the capacity of the new infrastructure. Some of the two-coach services were already running full to capacity, while on a Sunday morning Borders Railway journey from Newtongrange to Edinburgh my four-coach train was already full and standing by the time it reached the station, with around 25 of us boarding at Newtongrange and some 50 more people trying to squeeze on at Eskbank.

Passenger numbers for the first six months of the new line confirmed that there was more than just novelty factor behind its success. In the period between September 2015 and March 2016 almost 700,000 passengers were recorded, which was 22% ahead of forecast. Stow was among a number of stations on the route to have massively exceeded forecast numbers, recording total journeys of 24,365, or almost five times the anticipated number of 5,129. Galashiels, too, saw five times more passengers (104,593) than the forecast 18,979, while at the route's terminus, Tweedbank, the clearest evidence of how inadequate forecasts can be was a journey count of 183,918, which was almost ten times larger than the first six month forecast of 18,978 journeys.

The heart of the matter

At its peak in 1950, the British Railway network had extended to some 21,000 miles, but by the time of Beeching (1963), the network had already been reduced to 17,830 route miles, on which were some 7,000 stations. Beeching identified 5,000 further miles of railway line and 2,363 stations for closure. In the decade following publication of the his 1963 report, some 4,100 miles of line were closed, and, by its low point in 1975, the British Railway network had shrunk to 12,000 miles of track and around 2,000 stations.

The Borders Railway re-opening has brought the total length of lines where passenger services have been opened or restored to almost 550 miles, as listed in Appendix (i). The extent of these openings and re-openings ranges from High Speed One, the 68-mile long link from London to the Channel Tunnel, to important strategic curves, such as those at Bicester, Todmorden and Manchester (the long-awaited Ordsall Chord), each less than a mile in length, but each opening up major new journey opportunities as new direct services are introduced. Along with these have come new airport links, cross-city connections and a host of freight or diversionary routes returned to regular passenger use.

Across the rail network, the post-Beeching era has also seen almost 370 stations openings or re-openings (see Appendix ii), around 7.5% of the number that succumbed to closure following Beeching. Like the revived lines, these cover a huge range of places and populations, from major and now well-established main line stations such as Bristol Parkway, Milton Keynes Central and Birmingham International, through large numbers of new suburban stations in major conurbations such as Strathclyde,

A British Rail poster from 1967 announces launch of the Waterloo to Bournemouth electrification, which spelled the end of steam in the South of England.

LONDON-
SOUTHAMPTON
& BOURNEMOUTH
ELECTRIFIED - JULY 10
MORE SPEED, MORE COMFORT, MORE TRAINS

The sane way to travel
British Rail Inter-City

Merseyside, the West Midlands and West Yorkshire, to stations serving new communities, airports, and those in rural areas, which were often the fruits of successful local campaigning.

But we are still only scratching the surface of potential future openings and re-openings. Committed future developments, notably High Speed Two, East–West Rail, Crossrail (Elizabeth Line) and Bristol–Portishead represent another 375 miles to be added to the existing network, and are due to be delivered from 2018 onwards. Equally exciting are the large number of other projects featured in Chapters 8 & 9 which add up to almost 400 miles of route that have viable and often compelling cases for re-opening and, in some cases, are close to being formally adopted, so bringing the prospect of improved transport links to many more communities across Great Britain.

While most revived routes have been re-opened to passengers after surviving many years of freight use, the Borders Railway was unusual in being a complete rebuild of the long closed line, although fortunately able to re-use many surviving bridges, viaducts and tunnels. What its re-opening clearly demonstrates is the belief of Scottish politicians in the power of a railway line to act as the catalyst for the revitalisation of what is an economically deprived area, and one which was further from a railway link than almost anywhere else in Scotland, England or Wales. Passenger traffic has built up rapidly and is far exceeding the forecasts made at the time re-opening was being planned.

Devolved governments in both Scotland and Wales have been at the forefront of railway re-openings, as the later chapters of this book will outline in more detail. In the case of Scotland,

Redoubling of the 13 miles from Swindon to Kemble in 2014, at a cost of £45m, brought an end to a bottleneck caused by a Beeching-inspired rationalisation that could have seen the whole Golden Valley Line from Swindon to Standish Junction, near Gloucester, reduced to single track. On 25 January 2016 an HST service for London Paddington heads onto the restored up line, with power car 43148 in 'Bristol 2015' livery at the rear.

the Borders Railway followed a number of earlier re-openings, which began as early as 1975, when the route from Perth to Ladybank was re-opened to passenger traffic, continued with the 1979 creation of the cross-city Argyle Line in Glasgow and has more recently included the highly successful revival of services between Edinburgh, Bathgate and Airdrie to create a fourth rail link between Edinburgh and Glasgow, as well as the equally successful reconnection of Alloa to the Scottish network at Stirling.

Not to be left behind, Wales has also shown how the focus of a devolved administration on improving transport links can lead to new stations and re-opened lines. That has been particularly true in South Wales, where the post-Beeching era has seen re-opening of Valleys Line services to Aberdare and Ebbw Vale, the City Line in Cardiff, the Vale of Glamorgan line from Barry to Bridgend and the route from Bridgend to Maesteg. Add to that a swathe of new stations between Cardiff and Swansea and a revived local service from Carmarthen to Fishguard Harbour and it is clear that the Welsh Assembly Government too has a lot to be proud of when it comes to reversing the Beeching cuts.

England has seen revivals on a more modest scale – significant examples being the Robin Hood Line from Nottingham to Mansfield and Worksop, Kettering to Corby and Oakham, Walsall to Rugeley and Chippenham to Trowbridge – but the most significant developments have been in cross-city links within a number of major cities, the successful development of the London Overground network, and building of High Speed One, the 68-mile link between St Pancras station in London and the Channel Tunnel at Folkestone.

Cross-city links have transformed links across a number of provincial cities in both England and Scotland, as their respective chapters will explain. In Scotland, the Argyle Line project was one of the earliest instances of route opening and re-opening following the Beeching cuts, while in England major cross-city developments have transformed the fortunes of rail in Birmingham and Liverpool. Meantime, tram or metro schemes have transformed Manchester, Newcastle, Sheffield and Nottingham. Trumping all of these are the huge and nearly-completed Thameslink and Crossrail projects in London, which promise to bring a step change in north–south and east–west links across the capital. Then, on another scale altogether is the £55+ billion HS2 project to bring high speed rail from London to Birmingham and the north.

A far cry from the '60s and '70s

Growing up as a teenager and a trainspotter in the 1970s, the picture on Britain's railways looked bleak. While on the one hand there were bright spots, like completion of the West Coast Main Line electrification to Glasgow in 1974, elsewhere the scene was pretty dismal. The aftermath of Beeching cuts – largely completed by the early 1970s – had left a truncated rail network where there seemed no end to the cycle of declining traffic and increasing fares. My overriding memories of that time are of a sense that things were only heading in one direction: a process of managed decline; and the notion that things might one day look very different was hard to imagine.

A few teenage memories will hopefully give a flavour of how things felt in those far off times to a generation which has grown up in an age when capacity constraints and over-crowding have become more familiar descriptors of our rail network. I grew up in Cheltenham, so like scores of my school friends, would spend a week at a time travelling far and wide across the West Midlands using the marvellous Midland Railtourer ticket, which in the early 1970s cost £1.25 (child fare) for a week's unlimited travel across a region bounded by Gloucester, Hereford, Shrewsbury, Stafford, Matlock, Oakham and Northampton.

While much of our time would be spent watching the shiny new electrics from platform ends at Rugby and Stafford, we would also venture to lesser known lines, two of which particularly spring to mind for what has become of them since. One was the remaining section of the former Great Western mainline from Paddington to Birkenhead that connected Wolverhampton (Low Level) with Birmingham (Snow Hill). It had somehow survived, but was operated as an isolated stretch of line by single 'Bubble Car' Class 121 units, with the sparse service operating from the south end of Wolverhampton's Low Level station, at a time when the rest of it had been given over to a parcels depot, into a deserted Snow Hill, which had earned a dubious accolade as the 'world's largest unstaffed halt'!

That service lasted until 1972 and freight continued to use part of the route until 1994, but 27 years after its closure to passengers the line was reborn as Line One of the Midland Metro scheme, which now connects Wolverhampton town centre with Birmingham city centre, creating a new link between Snow Hill and New Street stations. While Wolverhampton (Low Level) sees trains no more, Birmingham Snow Hill has undergone a Lazarus-like revival, now being served by both the trams of Midland Metro, but also the frequent cross-city services and longer distance Chiltern Railways trains to London Marylebone that began serving the station following its re-opening in 1987. Visiting the hectic city centre station at a peak time today it is hard to believe that it was ever a little-used unstaffed halt, and even harder to believe that could have been closed for 15 years.

Another destination in the Midland Railtourer area that has seen a total transformation is Redditch. Back in the early 1970s the surviving five-mile stub of the former Midland Railway route from Barnt Green to Evesham and on to Ashchurch was served by no more than a handful of weekday peak-time trains, of little use to us Midland Railtourers from further afield, but there was a single return trip around lunch-time on Saturdays. Even then there were a good number of shoppers making use of the service to get to Birmingham city centre, but at one train a week, it was hardly the frequency to have mass appeal!

Since 1978, however, the cross-city line has been developed beyond recognition, initially by linking up what were diesel multiple unit-operated routes to Lichfield City and Redditch, with new stations opened at Five Ways, University and Longbridge, followed by electrification and extension to Lichfield Trent Valley and, most recently, by capacity improvements on the Redditch branch to enable services to operate at a 20-minute frequency and planned extension of services to a new £24m station at Bromsgrove. The route now has the distinction of being the busiest commuter route in the UK outside London.

Of course, many places have not been so lucky as the citizens of Redditch New Town. During a visit to grandparents in Bridgwater, I recall travelling aboard a three-coach multiple unit on the line from Barnstaple Junction to Ilfracombe, shortly before its closure in October 1970. What I remember was the general air of decay – signalling removed, the route singled and stations unstaffed, with all track at the once busy seaside terminus removed, apart from a basic run-round loop. Had it survived just a few more years then, like the remaining line from Barnstaple to Exeter, there is little doubt that it would never have closed, and would doubtless have prospered in the way that the development of 'community railway' projects involving local people has stimulated huge growth in traffic on all the surviving branch lines in Devon and Cornwall.

Speaking to the BBC back in 2008, Richard Burningham, Manager of the Devon and Cornwall Rail Partnership, a promotional body jointly funded by the local authorities in the two counties and the rail industry, pointed out that a quarter of all the holidaymakers visiting Ilfracombe in 1962 had arrived by train. Beeching assumed that these people would simply arrive by bus if there was no longer a rail service. 'This was one of the big mistakes', Burningham told the BBC, 'and it cost places like Ilfracombe and other seaside towns dear because people simply stopped coming.'

While Ilfracombe looks unlikely to ever be revived – the loss of the curving railway bridge across the River Taw at Barnstaple in 1977 dealt a final blow to the lingering hopes of preservationists – another line which once ran from Barnstaple does look like a viable candidate for re-opening. This is the nine-mile stretch of line which linked Barnstaple Junction with Bideford, where the trackbed is largely intact, albeit converted to a cycleway, and with a preserved station at Bideford that is well located for the town and surrounding area (see Chapter 9).

Casting my mind back even further than that visit to North Devon, I recall a summer holiday to West Wales in August 1967

The Exeter to Barnstaple 'Tarka Line' has hugely benefited from its designation as a community railway and seen substantial growth in passenger numbers. On Sunday 26 June 2016 the driver of 143603/143612, the 13.23 from Barnstaple, hands over the single line token for the section from Eggesford to the Crediton signaller, who stands in front of the 1875-vintage London & South Western Railway signal box.

when, armed with a ten shilling note to pay my fare to the 'paytrain' guard, my father put me on a train at a deserted Narberth station and drove to the branch line's terminus at Pembroke Dock to meet me. It was at the height of the Beeching closures and, although not one of the lines to have featured in the original report, it had also failed to feature in British Railways' *Network for Development* document, published in March 1967, meaning its days were numbered at the time of my trip. The passing loop at Narberth had just been lifted, while the next station down the line, Templeton, had closed three years previously, although the redundant station, loop and signal box all remained.

But, by contrast to the fortunes of branch lines serving such places as Caernarfon, Bewdley, Keswick and St Ives (Cambridgeshire) – all of which did feature in that planned *Network for Development*, but which subsequently lost their services, closure of the Pembroke Dock line was thankfully averted. Today the branch remains a key part of the local transport infrastructure, with the *Pembroke Coast Express* continuing to provide a seasonal direct link between London Paddington the popular resort of Tenby – the line's principal intermediate station – as well as Pembroke and Pembroke Dock.

Making a return to the line, 49 years after my childhood visit, it was reassuring to see that Narberth station building is still standing and now used as a sawmill and joinery – making for a rather noisy wait on the platform for a train! Templeton station has been razed to the ground, although this growing village could surely justify re-opening as another of the many request stops. Further along the line there are numerous halts for the train to

Having survived threatened closure in 1967/8, the Whitland–Pembroke Dock branch enjoys a basic two-hourly service, with additional HST services in the summer. On 19 April 2016, Class 150 unit 150285 departs from Whitland with the 'feather' lighting on the signal indicating that the points are set for the branch line.

The place where my West Wales travels began in summer 1967. Narberth is one of five request stops on the Pembroke Dock branch, and its station building survives for use as a sawmill. No. 150285 is about to depart for Pembroke Dock on 19 April 2016.

inch across ungated level crossings, while at each station the HST stop boards some considerable distance from platform ends are a reminder that, like the Par–Newquay line in Cornwall, this is a branch where even eight coach HSTs must stop and give way to road traffic!

Tenby station remains the heart of the line and sole crossing place for the regular two-hourly Class 150-worked services, with drivers accessing the single line tokens not from a signaller, but from the large Arriva-liveried cupboards on each platform, that are also a feature of crossing places on the Heart of Wales Line. There is no sign now of the passing loop and signal box at Pembroke station, another busy intermediate station with fine views of the nearby castle, while at journey's end, Pembroke Dock station building has found a welcome new use as the Station Inn, but the former line onwards to the Dock has been built on and the second platform has recently had its track removed.

One final childhood reminiscence that deserves a place in these pages, is of days spent with my father at Yeovil Junction, watching the West Country and Merchant Navy class locomotives speeding past with expresses from Waterloo to Exeter and onward to far-off seaside towns in the South West – places like Sidmouth, Ilfracombe, Bude and Padstow. The South Western route was one of those duplicate routes identified by Beeching in his report and I distinctly remember reading in youthful disbelief a poster outside Yeovil Junction station outlining drastic rationalisation plans, which saw the removal of all express services and route itself downgraded to a largely single track secondary line.

An account of the rationalisation plans in the May 1967 issue of *Railway World* magazine offers a stark reminder of how drastic the plans were and how they were a prelude to plans for wholesale singling of routes across the Western Region (WR). 'Yeovil Junction is likely to consist of nothing more than one platform facing a single track line' read the report. However, operational difficulties led to a 45-year reprieve for the signal box (which finally closed in 2012) and last minute retention of the double track between Yeovil Junction and Sherborne, so maintaining a double line section all the way from Yeovil Junction to the recently-closed Templecombe station. But *Railway World* went on to say that WR management would be closely watching the new method of operation, with plans already for singling the Swindon–Gloucester and Princes Risborough–Aynho Junction lines (both now redoubled) and named the Berks & Hants Main Line (Newbury–Taunton) and Plymouth–Penzance among other potential routes to be singled.

Community pressure led to the re-opening of Templecombe station in 1983, 17 years after it had closed, along with the Somerset & Dorset Line. At re-opening the signal box doubled up as a ticket office, but services now use a new platform on the south side of the line, where a new station building and ticket office have been provided.

Yeovil Pen Mill's semaphore signals are due to be replaced imminently. On Bank Holiday Monday, 30 May 2016, Class 159 set 159008 departs with the 12.58 to Yeovil Junction, one of the summer services introduced that month, with support from Dorset County Council, to provide a direct link from stations between Salisbury and Yeovil Junction to Weymouth.

Yeovil Junction station is two miles south of the town it serves (it is even in a different county – Dorset) but in the mid-1960s there was a convenient auto-train which shuttled between the now-closed Yeovil Town station and Yeovil Junction on which I secured my first ever cab ride! That service ceased in 1966 with closure of Town station, but a shuttle service ran for another couple of years to the town's other station, Yeovil Pen Mill, which is also some distance from the town centre – though not as far out as the Junction station – on the former Great Western route from Weymouth to Bristol.

For almost half a century Yeovil's two remaining stations had no connecting train service, despite the connection remaining *in situ* and seeing regular week-end use as a diversionary route for Great Western and South West Trains services between Exeter and London, when engineering work was affecting either the former Great Western route via Taunton or the section of the former Southern route between Yeovil Junction and Salisbury. Past plans have envisaged restoring a west-to-south curve at Yeovil Junction, enabling trains from Weymouth to reach the station then reverse and continue on to Yeovil Pen Mill, but these have never come to fruition and, since 1968, travellers wishing to get between the two stations have had to rely on a bus or taxi.

Fast forward some 50 years and the picture is very different. After years as a 'Cinderella' route, the former London and South Western Railway mainline from Salisbury to Exeter has seen substantial new investment, with a second section of double track restored near Axminster, to permit the operation of an hourly frequency of service from Waterloo to Exeter, while no less than four stations along the route have been opened or re-opened –

Clear evidence of how quickly good rail services can attract custom. On 19 December 2015, less than a week after it had opened, a crowd of around 20 people waits at Cranbrook station in East Devon for the 12.29 service to Exeter St David's.

Templecombe, Feniton (formerly Sidmouth Junction), Cranbrook (very close to the site of the former Broad Clyst station) and Pinhoe. Perhaps even more remarkably, in December 2015 the franchised operator of the line, Stagecoach-owned South West Trains, began running trains between Yeovil Junction and Pen Mill stations, the first service between the two stations since 1968.Going one step further, the May 2016 timetable saw a summer Saturday service launched from Waterloo to Weymouth via Yeovil Junction and

The summer 2016 service from Waterloo to Weymouth via Yeovil Junction – operating on Saturdays and Bank Holidays – created new interchange opportunities at Yeovil Pen Mill. On 30 May 2016 South West Trains 159008 arrives from Yeovil Junction to connect with a Great Western Railway service to Weymouth, formed of Great Western Railway unit 150263.

Yeovil Pen Mill. It was sponsored by Dorset County Council but despite its popularity, and attractive £5.00 return fare, was not repeated in 2017.

Reversing the Beeching cuts and more

Much has been written about the rights and wrongs of Beeching and his legacy of communities isolated from the railway network that have unquestionably suffered economically from having lost their rail services. This book will outline the dramatic changes to the railway network brought about by implementation of closures planned in that 1963 report, and consider how lines which had been slated for closure have fared since they managed to escape the axe. Notable examples of this being the Far North and Kyle of Lochalsh lines radiating from Inverness in Scotland, in Wales the branch line from Llandudno Junction to Blaenau Ffestiniog and the Heart of Wales Line from Llanelli to Shrewsbury and, in Northern England, the famous Settle to Carlisle line.

What I hope to be able to convey is the scale and future potential of the railway revival that has taken place since that dark decade between the publication of Beeching's original report and a low point for British Railway in the early 1970s and the 50 years that have passed since the end of steam in 1968. Across England, Scotland and Wales that half century has seen a remarkable turning of the tide, both in terms of lines re-opened and of new stations replacing ones that had been long-closed or brand new ones

Britain's newest steam locomotive is A1 60163 *Tornado*, built at Darlington and completed in 2008. On 20 March 2016, it heads a 13-coach special train to Exeter through Andover. M8Y on the smoke-box door was a tribute to former National Railway Museum Operations Director, Ray Towell (nicknamed 'Matey'), who had recently died.

that were developed to serve new or expanding communities. In almost every case, initial traffic forecasts have been substantially exceeded, with service frequencies subsequently increased and lines in some cases electrified post re-opening.

Increasing or restoring capacity on many routes has been another feature of the railway network's steady recovery since its low point in the late 1960s/early 1970s. Singling of double track main lines, for example, was one way in which British Rail sought to cut costs, presumably in the curious belief that a single line would not require twice as much maintenance as a double tracked route. As pressure on the network has grown, the folly of singling has become all too apparent, with the result that there have been costly and expensive redoubling of many routes, notably the Chiltern Line between Princes Risborough and Banbury, the North Cotswold line between Hanborough and Evesham and the Golden Valley or South Cotswold Line between Swindon and Kemble.

HS2: a vital scheme or a vanity project?

Major new capacity in London is about to be delivered, with completion of both the Crossrail and Thameslink projects promising to transform cross-London connectivity. Meanwhile the biggest and most divisive project of all, High Speed Two, continues to dominate the infrastructure debate, with opinion divided between its many supporters in the political and railway worlds and the many who question whether the £55+ billion commitment it represents is the right way to enhance our railway network.

Here I have to declare an interest, having made my modest contribution to the debate in a comment piece I wrote for *The Guardian* on 10 July 2013 entitled 'HS2 will not deliver a better rail service. Here is a radical alternative'. In this I questioned whether this hugely costly new line really was the only way to solve the perceived lack of future capacity on the West Coast Main Line, Britain's busiest railway route, which was the reason for its promotion.

My argument was in part prompted by my involvement in the launch of the Grand Central's 'Open Access' passenger services from Sunderland to London Kings Cross (see Chapter two), where the company was constantly told by Network Rail that space could not be found on the busy East Coast Main Line for more services. Yet when experts employed by Grand Central persistently challenged Network Rail's methodology, it eventually proved that there was capacity after all, not only for the services which Grand Central wanted to run, but also for improved frequencies between Leeds and London being sought by the then franchised operator on that route, GNER.

Given my first-hand experience of seeing how flawed rail capacity studies really are, I put forward a radical alternative vision for creating capacity on the WCML. My solution was to make Paddington the new London terminus for fast services to the West Midlands – making use of the terminal's extra capacity, which is being freed up by the opening of Crossrail in 2018, and by further upgrading the route from Old Oak Common (just west of Paddington) to Birmingham via Banbury and Leamington Spa. One section of this route – from Old Oak Common to its junction with the line from Marylebone at South Ruislip – had a service of just one train a day, so no capacity issues there!

In my *Guardian* comment, I pointed out that this was one of the main routes to Birmingham until electrification of the line to Euston was completed in 1967, when it was relegated to the role of a secondary and partly single-track route. But it has been significantly upgraded by its current franchised operator, Chiltern Railways. Potential capacity issues could be solved by reinstating fast through lines at stations that once had them – Gerrards Cross, Beaconsfield, High Wycombe, Bicester North – and diverting north–south freight trains – currently using this route north of Banbury – on to the soon-to-be-reopened East–West Route from Oxford to Bletchley, where they could join the West Coast Main Line, or on to Bedford, for the Midland Main Line.

Further investment would be required on the sections of route from Leamington Spa to Birmingham as well as between Leamington Spa and Coventry, but the cost of these improvements would be small change when set against the colossal bill for HS2. Making Paddington the focus for services from the West Midlands would avert the devastating impact of HS2 on the Euston/Camden area in London, where 600 homes are likely to be demolished – as well as on communities and countryside along the proposed line of route. One real bonus would be to give users of these services a direct connection at Paddington or Old Oak Common to Heathrow Airport and across London via Crossrail.

In conclusion, I argued that instead of giving a blank cheque to HS2, government could instead commit perhaps £10 billion to these enhancements of the existing infrastructure and then set aside another £10 billion to finance a programme of route re-openings around the country, which could deliver a wide range of long sought after schemes such as Uckfield–Lewes, Bristol–Portishead, Skipton–Colne, Stratford-upon-Avon–Honeybourne, Southampton–Hythe, and Bere Alston–Okehampton, all of which are featured elsewhere in this book. Two years later, on 11 October 2015, it was pleasing to see a report published by the right wing think tank, the Bow Group, entitled *Reviving Britain's Railways*, which came to exactly the same conclusion!

Chapter 1

BEECHING AND THE AFTERMATH

When a 49-year-old physicist and former director of chemicals giant ICI stood up inside the British Railways Board headquarters at 222 Marylebone Road on the morning of Wednesday, 27 March 1963, he was, according to the following day's *Times* lead story 'looking pale but completely at ease'. The bombshell delivered by Dr Richard Beeching to the assembled press that day was his draconian solution to spiralling losses on Britain's outdated railway network, a plan which was to usher in a new age of diesel and electric traction, but which was to spell isolation and economic stagnation for scores of communities across England, Scotland and Wales.

Beeching had been brought in as first Chairman of the newly created British Railways Board in 1961 with a remit to fix the railways in a way which a Modernisation Plan of 1955 had failed to do. He had no background in the railway industry, so could be dispassionate in the grim assessment and the solutions proposed in his 148 page report, *The Reshaping of Britain's Railways*. Faced with a system losing £200 million a year (equivalent to around £3.8 billion today) Beeching's answer was to close 5,000 miles of track, almost a third of the network, as well as more than 2,000 stations, to eliminate some 70,000 jobs, all with the aim of returning the network to profitability by 1970.

Launching his nervously awaited report, Beeching declared that the British Railways Board hoped to carry out the plan as rapidly as possible. A substantial backlog of projected closures was ready for submission to the Transport Users' Consultative Committees immediately after the report had been debated in the Commons towards the end of April and in the Lords on 1 May, he added. Closures could start later in the year and increase rapidly in 1964. Increases in London suburban fares were expected. At the same time there was a familiar warning that fares would rise: 'we would like to make a fairly substantial increase fairly soon', he announced.

In the foreword to his report, Beeching noted that in 1961 (all the report's traffic surveys were undertaken in the week ending

Beeching not surprisingly made headline news in The Times on 28 March 1963, which highlights the prospect of fare rises along with the wholesale closures, and quotes Beeching as saying 'we are not anxious to have subsidies' when stating his hope that there would not be a widespread retention of rural lines.

BEECHING PLAN SHUTS 2,000 STATIONS

CLOSURE OF 5,000 MILES OF PASSENGER TRACK URGED

SUBSTANTIAL FARE RISES IN LONDON SOON

In a 148-page report—on sale to the public at £1 a copy—Dr. Beeching, chairman of the British Railways Board, yesterday presented his eagerly awaited proposals for the reshaping of Britain's railway system.

The plan recommends drastic changes in the hope of making the railways, at present losing nearly £200m. a year, nearly self-supporting by 1970. Among the controversial proposals are: —

The closing of more than 2,000 stations and 5,000 miles of track to passenger traffic as a first step. This would deprive substantial parts of Scotland, Wales, and north-eastern and south-western England of passenger services.

A reduction in jobs on the railways amounting possibly to 70,000 in the next five years.

A concentration of freight services so far as possible into bulk train loads, with the introduction for general merchandise of a fleet of fast-scheduled liner trains carrying containers.

MODERN NEEDS

Dr. Beeching said yesterday that the British Railways Board hoped to carry out the plan as rapidly as possible. A substantial backlog of projected closures was ready for submission to the transport users' consultative committees

the lines now proposed was essential, Mr. Marples said. It was not possible to have effective and efficient coordination of transport without, as a basis, a twentieth-century railway system.

Dr. Beeching introduced his plan at a press conference at the Marylebone headquarters of British Railways yesterday morning. Looking pale but completely at ease, he met a battery of cameras with good-natured calm and responded to a barrage of questions with masterly lucidity.

"EMOTIONAL UPSURGE"

The proposed closures he took easily in his stride. "There is a great emotional upsurge every time we propose to close a service. A week afterwards, it has all died away." This time, he added with a smile, it might take a little longer.

He hoped there would not be a widespread retention of rural lines. "We are not anxious to have subsidies." Subsidies might arise in some cases to retain a minimum level of service. But this would probably be a transitional phase; the railway was a very expensive way of carrying a small volume of traffic.

The effect of rail closures on road congestion would be beneficial. Dr.

23 April 1961, so conveniently missing the seasonal traffic that was a feature of so many lines in holiday areas) the network's total route mileage was 17,830, on which there were about 7,000 stations, or one for every two and a half miles of route. It noted the huge discrepancy between the most heavily loaded parts of the system and the least loaded, with one third of the route mileage carrying only 1% of the total passenger miles and half of the total route mileage carrying just 4% of total passenger miles.

That discrepancy was also reflected in passenger receipts, where one third of the stations produced less than 1% of total revenue and half of all stations accounted for only 2% of British Railways' revenue. At the opposite end of the spectrum, Beeching noted that the busiest 34 stations – less than 1% of the total – produced 26% of passenger receipts.

Beeching acknowledged that the wholesale closures he was proposing would cause some hardship, but pointed out that the Transport Act 1962 had made its consideration the responsibility of Transport Users' Consultative Committees. 'For the purpose of judging the closure proposals as a whole, however, it is necessary to have some idea of the scale and degree of hardship which they are likely to cause' he wrote. The report asserted that: 'with the exception of northern Scotland and parts of central Wales, most areas of the country are already served by a network of bus services more dense than the network of rail services which will be withdrawn, and in the majority of cases these buses already carry the major proportion of local traffic.'

Buses were the answer to loss making rural rail services, argued, Beeching, whose major failing, with the benefit of hindsight, was in not realising how few rail passengers would actually be willing to switch to bus. Instead he saw an opportunity to revive the fortunes of an industry that had seen steadily declining revenues: 'With minor exceptions, these bus services cater for the same traffic flows as the railways on routes which are roughly parallel… they have enough spare capacity to absorb the traffic which will

Like other post-war steam locomotives, the Standard Class 9Fs had very short working lives. Swindon-built 92212 was one of the final ten, entering service in September 1959 and being withdrawn from Carnforth shed just eight years later (January 1968). On Boxing Day 2015 the 2-10-0 arrives up the gradient at Medstead & Four Marks station on the Mid-Hants Railway, with a service for Alton.

be displaced from the railways, which will do no more than replace the bus traffic which has been lost over the last decade, and which will provide a very welcome addition to the revenue of bus operators.'

Reaction to Beeching

In a leader comment the following day (28 March 1963) simply headed 'Beeching', *The Times* thundered that Dr Beeching's plan was of 'heroic proportions' and welcomed its boldness:

> 'The arguments in support of it are so unanswerable that implementation to some extent there must be. It is a plan which envisages the transformation of Britain's railways from a relatively backward system to one of the most advanced in the world in the space of a bare ten years. If it amounts to shock treatment, this is not because of the nature of the prescription but because of the size of the dose.
>
> 'Dr Beeching has shown brilliantly how the railways may be made to pay. But there are social and economic implications to his proposals which are not his concern. The most painful part of the process and that which will be most fiercely opposed is the closure, as a first instalment, of 5,000 miles of track and over 2,000 stations to passenger traffic. Even allowing for the fact that the first batch contains many unanswerable cases there must be some also which will cause real hardship, some which could conceivably be operated more efficiently and more economically than they are at the moment, and some which would have important repercussions on comprehensive regional transport plans for rail and road if such existed. The trouble is that they do not.'

XXXXXX

Having lamented the lack of any joined up transport planning at the time, *The Times'* leader comment concluded with what appears to have been a side-swipe at Transport Minister Ernest Marples, whose personal business was to be a major beneficiary of the forthcoming motorway construction programme: '...we cannot claim to have got transport into perspective until the social and economic consequences of what is now proposed have been fully assessed and until a Beeching type of approach for the whole of the transport system has been completed. If road users were to be inspected with the same severity as Dr. Beeching has applied to rail travellers, there is no knowing what the results would be.'

Contemporary reaction to Beeching's proposals was distinctly mixed. In the House of Commons, however, Transport Minister Ernest Marples described it as 'a major contribution to the Government's policy of providing an efficient, economic, and well-balanced transport system for Great Britain as a whole.' The

A busy scene at Gloucester Eastgate on 6 May 1961, as BR Standard Class 4MT 75002 on a Bristol-bound service is about to be overtaken by Class 5 44944 on *The Devonian*, a service from Bradford Forster Square to Paignton. The former Midland Railway Eastgate station closed in December 1975, when all services were routed into what was then known as Gloucester Central. Photo: Trefor David

Government agreed that extensive reshaping on the lines now proposed was essential, he added, saying it was not possible to have effective and efficient coordination of transport without, as a basis, a twentieth century railway system. For the Labour opposition, Ray Gunter MP, the shadow Minister of Labour and president of the Transport Salaried Staffs Association, said the nation should be grateful to Beeching, whose plan was 'one of the bravest efforts I have known in industry to face the economic facts of life'.

But Beeching was predictably denounced by the National Union of Railwaymen (NUR), which published a clever take-off of the Report, a four page document designed in the style of the original and entitled *The Mis-shaping of British Railways – Part 1: Retort*. It opened by describing Beeching's work as 'Bristling with statements and figures that cannot be checked; cemented with academic argument and polished by much skilled handling' and went on to point out that, by basing its conclusions on a single week's traffic studies, 'this gives only a one in fifty-two chance of the figures being truly representative.' The NUR estimated that implementation of the plan would leave vast areas of the British Isles without any railways at all – 5,000 sq. miles in N and NW Scotland, 3,600 sq. miles in NE Scotland and 3,500 sq. miles in South Wales being its principal examples.

A key element in Beeching's justification for wholesale branch line closures was an analysis of movement costs, which claimed to show that, even with the lower cost operation of diesel multiple units in place of steam, a passenger density of 10,000 per week was necessary for a stopping passenger service to cover its costs, even when there was freight traffic capable of absorbing a share of the route cost. 'Where there is no other traffic, routes carrying up to 17,000 passengers per week may barely pay their way' added Beeching. But this reasoning was challenged in an article for *The Guardian* by Oxford University's Reader in Economics and Organisation of Transport, D.L. Munby, who questioned Beeching's numbers and suggested that 'It is almost as if a target of 10,000 passengers per week has been chosen arbitrarily as the target for closures and the figures produced to prove the case.'

Munby's argument was that it was possible to have paying passenger services at lower densities of traffic than those predicated in the Beeching Report, and maintained that it should have been more focused on the loading of individual trains than the total flow of passengers on a particular service. Beeching had suggested that a diesel multiple unit stopping service carrying 17,000 passengers a week might not be profitable if no other services are sharing the overheads – based on an hourly service for 15 hours a day along a single line with stations 2.5 miles apart and an average of 74 passengers per train. Munby, however, demonstrated in his article that, on the basis of the same data used by Beeching, a two-hourly service could break even with just 13,200 passengers a week. If railbuses were used, he concluded – something dismissed by Beeching on grounds of their high initial cost – the breakeven point for these rural services would be even lower.

A leader comment entitled 'The Beeching arithmetic' published in *The Guardian* on the same day as Munby's evaluation (9 May 1963) pulled no punches:

> 'The Transport Users' Consultative Committees which will consider objections to railway closures will decline to hear arguments about the costs of railway operation, and there will be no opportunity to cross-examine representatives of the Railways Board on their case for closure. The underlying assumption seems to have been that Dr Beeching's cost accountants do not make mistakes. And it is true that so far the arithmetic of the Beeching Report has not been seriously challenged.
>
> '…Mr Munby's conclusions are important because they suggest that the Beeching calculation of operating costs of passenger stopping services is unnecessarily pessimistic…. He questions all the main assumptions in the Beeching equation, and arrives at a totally different conclusion – that, given economies on station, track, and signalling operations, a service of four trains a day (two each way) loaded with sixty passengers at two pence a mile could breakeven. But how is this argument to be communicated to the Railways Board and the Minister? And what assurance is there that it will be seriously considered? The TUCCs are disbarred and both Houses of Parliament have had their debate. Once again the inadequacy of the procedure for considering the case for closures and their consequences is exposed.'

Another aspect of Beeching's report attracting contemporary criticism was its lack of focus on improving the speed and comfort of inter-city passenger services. A leader comment in the July 1963 edition of the respected *Modern Railways* magazine entitled 'Now a passenger plan is needed' chastised Beeching for paying so little attention to the future development of express passenger traffic. The magazine noted that the only reference in the report were the words 'Improvements have and are being made and will continue', and there is brief commendation of the recently launched Blue Pullman services from London to Birmingham, Manchester and Swansea as well as the hourly diesel-hauled services from the capital to Newcastle, some of which were timed to cover the 268.5 mile journey in four hours.

'Is the BR Board as devoid of any co-ordinated plan for the development of express passenger services as this cursory dismissal of the subject suggests,' asked *Modern Railways*...'True we have recently seen evidence in mock-up of a new era in British passenger coach design [the prototype XP64 vehicles which were the forerunners of Mark II coaches]...But much more than new rolling stock, however elegantly furnished and smoothly riding, will be required to retain and improve express passenger train carryings in the late 1960s and 1970s.... We have the greatest respect for the East Coast achievement, which has produced a combination of speed and *frequency* of main-line service unequalled in the Western world. But the averages of its fastest trains make more impact on British minds because the standards prevailing on some other trunk routes in this country are still deplorably low.'

A botched Modernisation Plan

Beeching's report had been commissioned after the failure of an earlier attempt at sorting out the many problems of the post-war railway network. This was a document published in 1955 by the British Transport Commission (forerunner of the British Railways Board) entitled 'Modernisation and re-equipment of British Railways, but better known as the 1955 Modernisation Plan, a modest 36-page document which had heralded the end of steam by recommending a huge expenditure of £1.2 billion (equivalent to around £22 billion today) on new equipment. This included £210 million on new signalling, £345 million on replacing steam with diesel and electric locomotives, £285 million on new passenger rolling stock, including both diesel and electric multiple units as well as new passenger coaches, and £365 million on new marshalling yards for freight traffic.

The 1955 Plan failed to restore the financial fortunes of the railways for a number of reasons. It marked a fundamental switch away from steam towards diesel and electric traction, but diesel technology remained unproven and in the haste to order new locomotives, many designs proved hopelessly unreliable, so

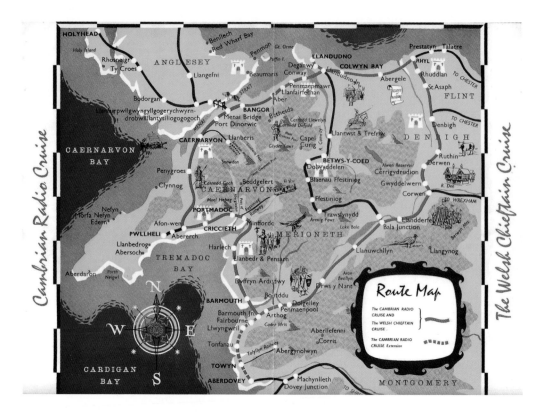

The Cambrian Radio Cruise was a popular way for post-war holidaymakers to take a trip around North Wales, and the special trains operated from 1951 until 1961, when planned closure of the Rhyl to Corwen line meant the circular route was no longer available. In its final year, 1961, the adult fare was 22/6 (£23.50 today), with the train departing Llandudno at 09.45, making a clockwise circuit, with a lunch stop at Barmouth, before arriving back in Llandudno at 17.59.

potential savings were lost. The types ordered did not allow for the significant losses of freight traffic that were occurring, while on the Western Region a fleet of new diesel-hydraulic locomotives – notably the Western, Warship and Hymek classes – were ultimately deemed non-standard when the rest of the network had opted for diesel-electric power, so were all withdrawn after relatively short working lives. The same fate befell huge numbers of post-war steam locomotives, many of which had working lives of ten years or less. Equally wasteful was the development of huge new freight marshalling yards to cater for wagon-load traffic that was quickly being lost to road or to train-load services of container carrying wagons.

Re-appraising the Plan

A reappraisal of the 1955 plan, published four years later in July 1959, re-assessed the cost of the whole programme at **£1.66** billion (equivalent to around **£37** billion today) given additional spending on depots and stations over what the 1955 plan had envisaged. It specifically referred to the need for what it termed 'an economic but judicious pruning of uneconomic services' and also talked about the railways being free to 'compete on less unfavourable terms with other forms of transport' – a reference to unfair competition from road hauliers – as well as being relieved of statutory duties to maintain public level crossings and road over-bridges. In terms of achievements, the re-appraisal document highlighted the **£40** million (£880 million today) already spent on electrifying the routes from Colchester to Clacton and Walton and part of the Kent Coast Scheme. It also singled out the successful introduction of diesel multiple units, which had delivered a 55% increase in revenues since 1957 and a 112% leap on Tees-side.

But for all these initial successes, the financial position of the British Transport Commission (BTC) had worsened on a far greater scale than had been anticipated during this period of reconstruction and development: 'The Commission attributed the worsening of their financial position to the sudden decline in their traffic receipts, particularly the bulk traffics, which was occasioned by the fall in the level of activity in the industries vital to the railways; a fall which was as unexpected by the industries concerned as by the Commission.' The dramatic fall in freight traffic meant that a forecast loss in 1958 of **£55** million (£1.21 billion today) proved to be a loss of **£90** million (equivalent to almost **£2** billion), of which **£42** million (£924 million) represented Central Charges (almost entirely interest costs).

In a prelude to Beeching's subsequent report, the 1959 re-appraisal introduced rationalisation of the network by asserting: 'The essential requirement of the next five years is that a more compact railway system and a more economic scale of operations shall be achieved more quickly… . Competing interests of the former companies left a complex legacy of duplications both of track and installations, while the growth of other forms of transport has greatly changed the picture since the network was constructed.' It drew a contrast between the railways and the new motorways being built: 'The railways are in a very different position…for they have to hold and if possible augment their traffics while at the same time being engaged in major engineering tasks. The motorways often carry no traffic until they are complete.' In terms of closures, the re-appraisal noted that total route mileage had been cut by 300 miles between the end of 1954 and the end of 1958 to a total of about 18,850 route miles, but anticipated a cut in the order of 10% in the period 1959–63, a much greater scale of closures than in the previous four years.

Summing up the 1959 reappraisal, BTC Chairman Brian Robertson described the 1955 Modernisation Plan as 'soundly based' but spoke of the need to accelerate

Regular interval services were a feature of British Rail's Southern Region timetable long before they became the norm across the network. This 1962 poster trumpeting dieselisation across Hampshire features two Beeching victims – the routes from Andover Junction (now Andover) to Romsey and Alton to Winchester.

A group of young enthusiasts gathers on the northbound platform at Ashchurch for Tewkesbury on 27 July 1963 as Jubilee Class 45626 *Seychelles* speeds through the station with an express for the South West. The lines to the right were the branch to Evesham, which had closed the previous month, although a short stub remains open to serve a nearby army base. Ashchurch station closed in November 1971, but was re-opened in June 1997.
Photo: Trefor David

its execution: 'The Government, the bodies representing trade and industry, and public opinion, have only recently re-affirmed that a modern railway system is essential to the prosperity of the country…. Modernisation should therefore be pressed forward at a rate faster, if practicable, than planned hitherto. Any slackening in the pace of modernisation would delay the improvements on which future revenues depend: heavy deficits, loss of morale among the staff, and a loss of confident amongst the general public, would be inevitable.'

But Robertson was fighting a losing battle. At the end of 1959 the first section of the M1 motorway opened and, almost simultaneously, the increasingly powerful road lobby acquired a new Parliamentary champion when Ernest Marples became Minister of Transport in October 1959. His private road building interests, through the family owned Marples Ridgway, represented what today would be seen as a blatant and unacceptable conflict of interest. For all the ambitious modernisation plans these were different times, the railways were seen as outdated and expensive, so under Marples' five year reign as Minister of Transport, Beeching was appointed Chairman of the new British Railways Board – created when the Transport Act 1962 wound up the BTC. The new Chairman's remit, using new powers to implement closures enshrined in the 1962 Act, was to bring forward and implement whatever changes were required to put an end to the railways' mounting losses.

Implementing Beeching

Once Parliament had considered the Beeching report, no time was wasted in implementing the wholesale closure programme it had recommended. A total of 324 miles of line were closed in 1963, but the following year saw that total trebled, as 1,058 route miles were closed in what became the biggest year of line closures in the entire Beeching era. Among more than 70 lines to close in that 1964 purge were the Scottish branch line from Comrie to Gleneagles that was one of the three Beeching case studies, along with the report's second case study, Thetford to Swaffham in Norfolk, and a number of routes featuring elsewhere in this book as successful

Standard Class 9F 92212 departs Medstead and Four Marks on Boxing Day 2015. After passing the nearby summit (652 ft) it will begin its four-mile 1-in-60 descent to Alton.

revivals or re-opening candidates, including Burton-on-Trent to Leicester, Aberystwyth to Carmarthen, Abercynon to Aberdare, Amlwch to Bangor and Barry to Bridgend.

The rate of closures continued at a significant level during 1965, when some 600 miles were lost and 1966, the second largest year for cuts, when around 750 route miles were cut from the passenger network. Notable victims in 1965 were a trio of lengthy routes in Scotland – Aberdeen to Fraserburgh in the north east, Dunblane to Crianlarich on the Callander and Oban line from Glasgow to Oban and Dumfries to Stranraer. In England, significant losses included Hull to York (the third of Beeching's three case studies), Malton to Whitby (since partly re-opened as the North Yorkshire Moors Railway), and two routes in the Midlands which have since re-opened and feature later in this story – Rugeley Trent Valley to Walsall and Leamington Spa to Coventry and Nuneaton. Elsewhere the Guildford–Horsham route and the 'Cuckoo Line' from Eridge to Hailsham were lost, while in the South West the branch lines from Axminster to Lyme Regis, Chippenham to Calne and Lostwithiel to Fowey all fell victim to Beeching.

Two of the most notorious closures of the entire Beeching era took place in 1966, with the slightly delayed demise of the much-loved Somerset & Dorset route from Bath Green Park to Bournemouth West in March, followed in September by most of the Great Central route from London Marylebone to Nottingham and Sheffield – England's last-built and best engineered main line railway. Both routes had been deliberately run down in an attempt to justify closure, with their most famous named trains – the *Pines Express* (Manchester–Bournemouth) on the S&D and the *Master Cutler* (Sheffield–London) on the Great Central, rerouted along with all other express traffic in order to justify the controversial closure decisions. In truth, though, the demise of both routes significantly predated their proscription by Dr Beeching.

In the case of the Somerset & Dorset, the run-down had begun five years before Beeching, in 1958, when control of most of the line was taken over by the Western Region of what was then known as the BTC's Railway Executive. First it was through freight traffic that was diverted away from the line to take a far longer route via Westbury and Southampton, then Sunday services disappeared, to be followed by overnight passenger services in 1962 and finally the *Pines Express* and all other through holiday traffic in September 1962. Two years later, in September 1964, night time freight services were withdrawn and the line closed at night for the first time in almost a century.

Along with his prodigious correspondence on the Cheltenham–Kingham line (see below) my father, Trefor David, gave vent to his feelings when rerouting of the *Pines Express* was announced in June 1962. In a letter to the *Gloucestershire Echo* dated 8 June 1962, following its report on the train's new route and published under the heading *'Pines' Public Outcry*, he wrote:

Sir,

I have rarely seen a more dishonest statement than that from British Railways which was the subject of your leading headline in Thursday's Echo. How much longer will faceless British Railways spokesmen be allowed to talk such rubbish?

Re-routing the Pines Express will in itself save nothing. The 'additional points' of Banbury, Reading and Basingstoke could never compensate for the loss of passengers from Cheltenham and Gloucester, especially as all these places already have several through trains to Bournemouth. And what about Bristol?

Why don't the British Railways admit that the sole purpose of this re-routing is to enable them to close the line from Mangotsfield to Bath and the main line from Bath southwards? Mention is made of just one train, but what about the much greater number of trains which use the route in summer?

In a carefully worded statement, we are assured that it will be possible to get connections from Bristol to the South Coast. But what part of the South Coast? Mangotsfield to Bournemouth is at present 81½ miles by rail; the new 'route' via Bristol, Westbury, Yeovil and Dorchester will be exactly 112¾ miles and passengers (if any) will have to walk between stations at Dorchester.

Why cannot British Railways tell us the facts? Why cannot they tell us that when the latest closures in the county are effected, Cheltenham St. James's Station will close? Perhaps they will also tell us how many trains in future will omit to stop at Cheltenham Lansdown.

It could be that they are not allowed to tell us. In that case it is up to our own elected representatives to demand an answer from the Minister of Transport.

We are told that a public outcry by Gloucestershire people is unlikely to make British Railways have second thoughts on the re-routing of the Pines Express.

If the Minister of Transport and those under him published all the facts, the public reaction would, I am sure, be sufficient to reverse the whole disastrous policy being followed by British Railways.

T. David
53 Shaw Green Lane, Prestbury

Formal announcement of the proposed closure of 104 route miles, comprising the main S&D route from Bath to Bournemouth, the connection from Mangotsfield (near Bristol) to Bath Green Park and a branch line from Evercreech Junction to Highbridge was made in June 1964. It was to take effect in October, but was delayed by objections that were heard at TUCC hearings during that month. Hopes were raised by the election of Harold Wilson's Labour Government in October with a pledge to avoid any more major line closures until national and regional transport plans had been prepared. Nevertheless consent for the closure was finally announced on 10 September 1965. Despite fierce local protests and an appeal by a local Labour party branch to Wilson himself, there was to be no backing down and, after a two month delay in securing rail replacement bus services, the line closed on 7 March 1966.

The Great Central had only been completed in 1899 and was the product of a fiercely competitive era, significantly duplicating the Midland Main Line from St Pancras and the West Coast Main Line from Euston. Its demise had been foretold in Appendix B of the British Transport Commission's 1959 re-appraisal document, discussed above: 'Since nationalisation [1948] the extension to London has become less important because its services are mostly duplicated by other routes, and there has already been a planned reduction in the freight traffic movement to and from London.'

BTC's 1959 document went on to signal the end of express services on the line: 'Because of gradients and distances, the long-distance passenger trains between Marylebone, Sheffield, Manchester and the West Riding cannot provide as good a service as is available on the other routes. It is therefore now proposed to substitute, so far as the London trains are concerned, a service between Marylebone and Nottingham catering for the intermediate traffic of the few stations it is proposed should remain open between Aylesbury and Nottingham.'

Hopes that the Great Central might be revived emerged in the early 1990s when a company called Central Railway unsuccessfully promoted a plan to develop a privately funded freight railway from the Midlands to the Channel Tunnel, using a large part of the former GC route. It was a highly ambitious scheme, championed by a former neighbour and friend, Andrew Gritten, but it aroused significant public hostility, not dissimilar to the howls of protest in the Home Counties over High Speed 2 (HS2), and failed to find favour in Parliament before Andrew's untimely death in November 2004.

While it is too much to hope that the Great Central will ever be revived in its entirety, a number of sections do have a new future. At the southern end of the route, the East–West Railway scheme will return passengers to the section of line from Aylesbury to Calvert Junction; two preservation groups are working to restore a link from the northern outskirts of Leicester to Nottingham once a new bridge over the Midland Main Line at Loughborough has been built, while High Speed Two will follow the former GC alignment for some 14 miles north of Aylesbury.

Fighting the closures

Before every Beeching closure, opponents lobbied the TUCC hearings being held to consider the basis of the closure, almost invariably to no avail. In his seminal work on the Beeching era, *The Great Railway Conspiracy*, David Henshaw catalogues in detail

the stunts that were pulled to ensure that closures went ahead as planned, a practice dating back well before Beeching. In one notable case, he describes a bitter battle which broke out on the Isle of Wight in 1953 when proposals were published to close almost half of the island's remaining 50 mile railway network (a little-used branch to Ventnor West having closed in 1952).

When the alleged losses suggested by the British Transport Commission's Railway Executive were examined by an expert witness hired by the County Council it emerged that the figures had indeed been falsified by ignoring the effects of contributory revenue being generated by the lines up for closure. Besides ignoring this share of income from passengers making longer journeys to mainland destinations (which was enough to show that the lines were covering their direct operating costs) there was a dispute over the inflated cost of maintenance of the track and rolling stock and a disagreement over the level of income from ticket sales. But for all that the closure inquiry did to expose false accounting, it failed to save the island's lines, with two of the three routes (Newport–Freshwater and Brading–Bembridge closing in 1953 and the third (Newport–Sandown) following in 1956.

A delightful early British Railways map of the Isle of Wight shows the full extent of the 55½-mile network, before the rationalisation which started in 1952, with closure of the line from Newport to Ventnor West. This was quickly followed by Newport–Freshwater and Brading–Bembridge (both 1953) and Newport–Sandown (1956). With Ryde–Cowes and Shanklin–Ventnor falling victim to Beeching in 1966, all that remains today is the 8½ miles from Ryde Pier Head to Shanklin, and even this is now threatened by major infrastructure and rolling stock issues.

One man's crusade

In the year before Beeching unveiled his report (1962) my father, Trefor David, became a prolific campaigner against one particular closure – the 24-mile route from our home town of Cheltenham to Kingham. He had numerous letters published on the subject, principally in the *Gloucestershire Echo*, but also raised the matter of closures in a letter to *The Guardian*, and unsuccessfully sought to make personal representation to the TUCC hearing that considered the closure. By some strange quirk of fate his invitation to speak at the hearing was lost in the post.

Looking back at his sentiments – and those of a few others at the time – this correspondence gives a real and fascinating sense of just how this one particular example was pushed through, when no attempt had ever been made to reduce operating costs or make the service more attractive. The Cheltenham–Kingham line closed with effect from 16 October 1962, while Cheltenham's two former Great Western stations, St. James's and Malvern Road, succumbed on 3 January 1966. His correspondence begins with a formal written objection to the Kingham line closure:

> *53 Shaw Green Lane*
> *Prestbury*
> *Cheltenham*
> *Glos*

17th January 1962

The Secretary,
Transport Users Consultative Committee,
South West Area
10 Fairlawn Road,
Montpelier,
Bristol 6.

Dear Sir,

> *Passenger Train Service*
> *Cheltenham – Kingham*

Further to the recent notices concerning the proposed termination of the above service, I wish to put on record my objections.

These are made as a member of the travelling public currently using the railways to the extent of 10,000 miles per annum on a wide number of routes.

My objections are based on:

1. *Withdrawal of these facilities will seriously reduce the train service from Cheltenham to London*

2. *The present service is tabulated below:*

	a.m	a.m	a.m	a.m	a.m	a.m	a.m
Cheltenham	12.05	6.30 K	6.55	8.00	8.30	8.50 K	10.50
Paddington	4.40	9.51	10.26	10.35	12.28	11.55	1.55
Journey time (hrs.mins)	4.35	3.21	3.31	2.35	3.58	3.05	3.05

	a.m	p.m	p.m	p.m	p.m	p.m	p.m
Cheltenham	11.45	2.00	2.50 K	4.00	5.50 K	6.35	6.50 K
Paddington	2.46	5.29	5.48	6.50	9.05	10.15	10.00
Journey time (hrs.mins)	3.01	3.29	2.58	2.50	3.15	3.42	3.10

K – via Kingham

If services giving a journey time of 3½ hours or less are considered, the proposals will cut the daily service from 10 trains to 5.

1. *Withdrawal of the direct link to Oxford will prohibit use of the Oxford–Bedford–Cambridge cross country link, necessitating more expensive journeys via London.*
2. *The alleged savings to be made by closure have not been published.*
3. *Little or no attempt has been made to improve traffic and results by:*
    i. *Improving passenger facilities at Kingham Station in order to attract traffic to this route.*
    ii. *Increasing speeds by omitting stops at Leckhampton and Charlton Kings and possibly also at Malvern Road and Notgrove.*
    iii. *Increasing speeds by using the full potential of the present steam locomotives or by substituting diesel multiple stock.*
    iv. *Exploiting cheap fares and through trains to Oxford.*
4. *Little or no attempt has been made to reduce expenditure by:*
    i. *Singling the main line*
    ii. *Reducing staffs e.g. by selling tickets on the train*
    iii. *Introducing new equipment or methods*

I feel that until a satisfactory answer to all the foregoing points is given, closure should be vigorously opposed.

Would you please let me have details of any official replies or let me have notification of any public meeting when answers may be given.

Yours faithfully,

T. David

On the same day as his formal closure objection, he also wrote the first of many strident letters to the editor of our local evening newspaper, the *Gloucestershire Echo*, correctly anticipating further local closures to come. It was published two days later (19 January 1962) under the heading 'St. James's Station May Be Next':

> *53 Shaw Green Lane*
> *Prestbury*
> *Cheltenham*
> *Glos*

17th January 1962

The Editor,
Gloucestershire Echo,
1 Clarence Parade,
Cheltenham

Sir,

A few weeks ago I suggested in your columns that closure of the Chipping Norton branch would speed up the end of the Cheltenham–Kingham line. Your front page of yesterday confirms that this is now imminent. Officially it is only a proposal to be submitted to the T.U.C.C. but whatever they or anyone else may say, close it will.

What next? Talk of future proposals, although not official, is pretty reliable. This further reduction of traffic should now enable St. James's Station to be closed finally (The fact that the travelling public like a station to be centrally situated won't count for anything). The land should give Dr. Beeching a useful card in the real estate game.

After that, all intermediate stations between Barnt Green and Bristol excepting Worcester, Cheltenham and Gloucester will close. This should enable all the Birmingham – South Wales traffic to be worked via Bromsgrove, enabling the Cheltenham – Stratford upon Avon – Birmingham line to close. This in turn might permit Malvern Road Station to be closed, and all remaining traffic to be concentrated at Lansdown.

The remarkable thing is that we pay Dr. Beeching £25,000 per annum to run British Railways. How refreshing it would have been if your front page news had been of a new through service from Gloucester via Kingham to Oxford or even to Bletchley and Cambridge. That, of course, might have made money and this would have been embarrassing.

(One is reminded of the day return fares to London on the 8.00 a.m. train. These facilities were abolished early last Autumn because, one gathers, too many people were travelling. An enterprising management could presumably have duplicated the train…)

The latest bit of 'running' will effectively reduce the Cheltenham to London service from 10 trains per day to 5 and cut out the earliest and latest trains. The luckless population of Stow and Bourton will, of course, have no train service at all.

Whatever the mere public say or do, a figure will be produced of 'saving' and the Kingham line will close. Figures are interesting. On the previous day, your front page detailed the Gloucestershire Highways estimates for 1962/1963. We are to spend £3.5 million [equivalent to £70 million today] on 3,222 miles of road – something over £1,000 [around £20,000 today] per mile. It is a pity that we cannot afford something for a few miles of railway track and convenience.

Even if we accept the figures to be supplied, the thinking is quite pathetic. In the words of the official spokesman 'on finishing the examination, it has been proved that it (the line) does not pay, and British Railways feel they have a case for closure'. Do they mean that with the present method of working, expenses are more than receipts? That would seem to indicate a case for new ideas and new management – starting at the top.

I trust that your latest news will provoke sufficient reaction from interested parties to at least slow down events. Dr. Beeching is serving only a five year term. There may be some lines left at the end of this period for his successor to run.

Yours faithfully,

T. David

Three days after this letter had appeared (22 January 1962) the *Gloucestershire Echo* published another eloquent reflection on the serious consequences of closing the Kingham route, this time written by a family friend and solicitor in the town, David Lyall. Under the heading 'Trains to London Cut By Nearly Half' he wrote:

Sir,

Do your readers (and indeed yourself) realise how near the truth your remark in 'Today's Gossip' was about losing our train service to London?

Do they realise that this Kingham line proposal actually does mean the loss of not far from half of our London trains already? And do they know that the threatened trains are, on an average, some 20 minutes faster than those remaining?

Is it generally known that London is really only 109 miles away via Kingham, but no less than 121½ via Gloucester, which therefore costs 10 per cent more on the fare? Or that the rail link will be lost not only with Bourton and Stow, but with Oxford too?

Cheltonians have long been dissatisfied with – and visitors surprised at – our town's rail service to London. Now that we are faced with losing almost 40 per cent of even that, it is time we compared our plight with that of lesser towns.

Worcester (pop. 65,000) enjoys nine London trains a day, mostly at two-hourly intervals and taking only 2¾ hours; even Cirencester (pop. 12,000) has eight trains.

Cheltenham, with a population of 70,000 is to be reduced to the same level as Cirencester, and will be only one London train better off than Tetbury (pop. 2,500) which can boast seven London trains linked at some expense by a new railbus on a true branch line which has a road parallel to it! Besides losing our second fastest train and several other good ones, we shall be left with a service averaging nearly 3½ hours.

These are facts which BR omitted to mention when using your columns to announce their proposals. They seek to give the impression that only a few wayside stations on another unimportant 'branch line' (for so they miscall our shortest route to London) are involved, in the hope that the public will once again not realise what has happened until it is too late.

D.B. Lyall
52 Hall Road
Leckhampton

Three months later, on Wednesday 21 March, the South Western Area of the TUCC held a hearing at Cheltenham Town Hall to consider the proposed closure of the Cheltenham–Kingham line. In his written letter of objection on 17 January Trefor had asked to be advised of any hearing, but either he was not advised, or the memorandum advising of the hearing mysteriously got lost in the post. That prompted a furious missive to the Secretary of the TUCC, P.H. Sims – who claimed that a note advising of the hearing had indeed been sent to him – as well as another salvo to the *Gloucestershire Echo*:

53 Shaw Green Lane
Prestbury
Cheltenham
Glos

2nd April 1962

The Editor,
Gloucestershire Echo,
1 Clarence Parade,
Cheltenham.
Glos.

Sir:

When the proposal to terminate the passenger train service between Cheltenham and Kingham was first announced, I placed my objections before the Transport Users' Consultative Committee. On that occasion I specifically asked to be notified of any meeting when the closure would be discussed.

I was therefore surprised to read your account of the subsequent enquiry held at the Town Hall on 21st March. I had received no notification of the meeting, although on taking up the matter with the Secretary of the Committee, I was assured that a notification had in fact been sent. It appears to be one of the fortunately rare cases of mail getting lost. I would be pleased to know as soon as possible if any other objectors were also denied the opportunity of attending the enquiry.

I believe I am correct in saying that a Public Meeting must be held prior to any closure of this kind. In this case the Public Meeting appears to have been completely unadvertised while attendance was by invitation only.

Yours faithfully,

T. David

Not content to let the matter rest, on 21 June 1962 he wrote again to Mr P.H. Sims at TUCC demanding to know more about the organisation's composition and workings:

53 Shaw Green Lane
Prestbury
Cheltenham
Glos

21st June 1962

The Secretary,
Transport User' Consultative Committee,
South West Area
10 Fairlawn Road,
Montpelier,
Bristol 6.

Dear Sir,

I am doing some research into the rapid decline of British Railways. In this connection I would very much like to know:

1. The structure of the TUCC, i.e. its organisation by areas
2. Who appoints the members of the TUCC
3. Who are the current members of the Committee for the South West Area?

I take it that the answers to the foregoing questions are not confidential, and look forward to your reply.

Yours truly,

T. David

Having been given the details he was looking for, another missive to the *Echo* quickly followed:

> 53 Shaw Green Lane
> Prestbury
> Cheltenham
> Glos

2nd July 1962

The Editor,
Gloucestershire Echo,
1 Clarence Parade,
Cheltenham.
Glos.

Sir,

Your notes in reply to Mr Bill Hartley's letter on the constitution of the Transport Users' Consultative Committee are correct as far as they go. However, they should go a little further.

There are 19 members in the Committee for the South West Area. According to the hand-book on the functions of the TUCC, these nominees of the Minister of Transport 'form a cross section of transport users as a whole'. Although they represent various bodies 'their views, though fully representative of such users, are their own….'

The notes go on to say 'the most important work of all Committees…has been the consideration of proposals to withdraw complete train services or to close branch lines or stations'.

The picture is one of a panel of railway travellers giving a considered opinion and, according to their Secretary, having a 'strong voice with British Railways'.

Looking at the Committee, the most surprising thing is the inclusion of Mr D.S. Hart, Divisional Manager of British Railways, Bristol. Here, I would suggest, is someone most unlikely to criticise any proposal made by the British Transport Commission.

Another 'typical traveller' on the Committee is Mr I.R. Pately, Director and General Manager of the Bristol Omnibus Company and a Director of Black & White Motorways [the Cheltenham-based coach operator]. It would be interesting to know what he would say to the proposal to close St. James's Station, particularly as Black & White are popularly tipped to take over the site.

The other members representing Agriculture, Industry and Commerce are a mixed bag, but include the Chairman of the Western Division Trade Road Transport Association and the Managing Director of Nadder Valley Coaches Limited.

The travelling public are in fact represented by two members. These are ladies from Thornbury and Yeovil respectively, each holding an impressive number of positions in public life. I have no doubt that both of these ladies, and indeed all members of the Committee have cars, but dutifully travel on the special train of inspection, which doubtless precedes each closure.

Yours faithfully,

T. David

Broadening the debate from just the Cheltenham–Kingham line to the work Beeching had undertaken prior to publication of his Reshaping report the following year, Trefor wrote to *The Guardian* on 20 July 1962 and his letter was duly published under a heading 'The railway traffic surveys':

Sir,

Dr Beeching's special traffic surveys tell us that 50 per cent of the lines carry only 8 per cent of the total traffic. This is intended to create the impression that closure will result in a 50 per cent reduction of costs and a loss of only 8 per cent in revenue. This, or course, is a completely wrong conclusion. Equipment and staff are largely involved in operating the heavily loaded 50 per cent of the mileage. If closure of the remainder reduced costs by only 10 per cent, then the benefit to anyone other than the road haulage interests would be questionable.

Perhaps a report could be published on the method of costing on the railways. In costing a branch line, are the traffic receipts allocated to that line or are they split on the basis of x miles travelled on the branch line and y miles on the main line?

There is a naïve belief that if local facilities are withdrawn a person is going to ring up a freight depot or travel to a station 20 miles away. This ignores elementary psychology. Closure of 'unprofitable' lines will simply reduce the traffic density on marginal lines and these in turn will become unprofitable.

These surveys would be a little more convincing if the BTC could demonstrate that it was actively interested in carrying traffic. Instead, it is pursuing a deliberate policy of withdrawing attractive fares and facilities.

Branch lines are being 'tried' and condemned although in the majority of cases the method of working has not changed in 40 years. Even so, the figures put forward to support closure will rarely stand critical examination.

The annual accounts of the BTC speak for themselves. Right up to 1955 British Railways could show an operating surplus. In 1961 the deficit increased by £19m to a total for the year of £86m [equivalent to £1.77 billion today]. Why a sudden increase of £19m? Receipts fell by £4m. As the annual report rightly states, a lot of this fall is due to the industrial recession, although the withdrawal of facilities must have an effect. The frightful thing is that operating costs went up by £15m. Of this increase, nearly £11m was solely on the maintenance of rolling stock. This is the department where BR workshops are being closed because private industry is alleged to do the job at lower cost. These maintenance costs were incurred in spite of the investment during the year of a further £74m in new stock, the bulk of this sum going to outside contractors.

Modernisation there must be and on a massive scale. At the same time, the means of doing this should be examined in more detail. May I suggest that it would be far more useful if a survey could be made of BR spending. It would be interesting if their losses could be compared with the profits of their main sub-contractors.

Yours faithfully,
T. David
53 Shaw Green Lane, Prestbury, Cheltenham

Returning to his familiar ground of the Kingham line, Trefor marked its closing with another letter to the *Gloucestershire Echo*, dated 16 October 1962 and published in the same week – here is an extract from it:

Sir,

The thoughtless celebrations are over and the Kingham line is closed. In Cheltenham it is interesting to compare the present 'Improved train services' with those of 12 months ago.

The weekday services to London have been reduced from 14 trains to nine, while those doing the journey in 3½ hours or less have been exactly halved from 10 trains to five.

Fast through trains to Cardiff have been reduced from six to three per day while those to Birmingham have been reduced from 17 to seven.

We have a reduced number of through trains travelling beyond Sheffield, while we have lost our only through trains to Manchester, Bournemouth, Torquay and Penzance.

Locally, we are reduced to a token two trains per day to Stratford while Oxford is now virtually inaccessible.

If anyone can get from A to B substantially quicker than last year, then the point has escaped me. Certainly the populace of Stow, Bourton, Fairford and Witney to name but a few places can get precisely nowhere by rail....

...The BTC did precisely nothing by way of improving facilities, fares or even by economising to save the Kingham line. The Minister of Transport is patently disinterested in running railways, except as a means of awarding lucrative contracts to outside industry.

May I through your columns ask our Council and particularly our Members of Parliament what they intend to do about preserving what few rail facilities we have left? Or do they accept that a bus ride to Gloucester is to be a reasonable prelude to any rail journey from Cheltenham?

T. David
53 Shaw Green Lane, Prestbury, Cheltenham

An interesting postscript to my father's efforts was a letter published in the January 1963 edition of *Railway Magazine* and written by a schoolboy from Cheltenham, Martin M'Caw, who was a pupil at Dean Close School, near Lansdown station. It is headed 'Kingham–Cheltenham Closure' and his comments reflect many of the points made in vain by my father, David Lyall and others:

'I would like to comment on the note on p871 in your December issue, dealing with the closure of the Cheltenham to Kingham line. My school overlooks Lansdown Junction, Cheltenham, where the Kingham branch leaves the main line and I have a good view of it from my study. From what I have seen of the Kingham line over the past four years, I would disagree that the passenger traffic before closure was almost nil. In fact, on several trains there were enough people to warrant an extra coach.

'The only service which was not patronised was the stopping train from Southampton, which ceased running a few months ago [the former Midland & South Western Junction Line which had closed in September 1961]. That service averaged five or six passengers a day. If British Railways had used a multiple unit on the branch (there are plenty in the Cheltenham and Gloucester area) and had planned a more suitable timetable, the line would be used by a considerable amount of people, as it provided a shorter and quicker route to London, as well as a local service.'

That observation on the passenger loading of Kingham trains by Martin M'Caw was a theme Trefor picked up on almost two years after the line had closed, when hopes of a revival had not been completely extinguished and there were suggestions it might be operated as a light railway. Such notions did not find favour with local MP Nicholas Ridley (Cirencester & Tewkesbury), a man who cared very little for the future of railways in his constituency (yet later became Secretary of State for Transport!), and attracted Trefor's wrath in the following letter to the *Gloucestershire Echo*, published on 2 October 1964 under a heading '29 Stations Closed: No Protest by MP':

Sir,

I am not surprised to find that at his recent press conference Mr Nicholas Ridley was sceptical about the use of the Kingham line as a light railway.

His scepticism no doubt explains why 29 out of 32 stations in his constituency have been allowed to close without a word of protest from our Member of Parliament.

He tells us that when the lines were used the trains carried an average of only eight passengers each. Since there were six trains per day we are to infer that only 48 passengers are involved.

Had Mr Ridley at any time seen the first train down in the morning he would have seen this total handsomely exceeded before 9 a.m.

Despite scepticism and distorted figures there is plenty of evidence to suggest that a light railway would not only be feasible but profitable. Such a light railway would work to a timetable to meet local needs, with a fare structure designed to attract passengers....

...Mr Ridley speaks of flexibility. Surely the alternative of a railway across the Cotswolds would increase flexibility when roads are blocked by fog, ice, snow or simply traffic.

The existing facilities offer no choice except a relatively slow journey by bus. Coupled to this is the prospect of paying a perpetual subsidy to a bus operator.

T. David
53 Shaw Green Lane, Prestbury, Cheltenham

One final extract from a letter to the *Gloucestershire Echo* that deserves a mention is from one Trefor wrote on 15 June 1965 after proposals had been published to close St. James's and Malvern Road stations in Cheltenham and, on this occasion, he had been invited to attend the closure enquiry:

Sir,

May I add a few words to the current correspondence on the proposal to close St James's and Malvern Road stations?

I feel that so many of your correspondents have missed the point here. The question is not whether we use this station or that station. It is not whether we put up with old fashioned toilets or demand new ones. It is the fundamental question of whether we are to have a train service befitting the Borough and surrounding area.

May I repeat what I said at the enquiry, namely that these latest proposals are a breach of faith by the British Railways Board. It is less than three years since the Kingham Line closed and we received an assurance that passenger facilities would be retained at St. James's Station [close to Cheltenham town centre]. That assurance was worthless.

In presenting the case for these latest closures the Board produced figures of the alleged savings. These figures I suggest were also worthless. To quote but three, revenue attributable to the Stations is quoted as £900 p.a., direct costs as £31,000 p.a. with an average of something like 400 passengers arriving and departing per day.

One does not need to be a financial genius to work backwards and find that even with existing costs we would need to handle the staggering total of 13,600 passengers per day to make the Stations viable. On this basis St. James's Station was a financial liability even in its heyday and one wonders why the Great Western Railway Company tolerated this loss.

With the closure of Malvern Road we lose the pitiful train service to Stratford and Leamington, but the Board glibly assures us that connections will be made to meet these trains at Gloucester. The Board know perfectly well that within a month of Malvern Road closing they will propose the withdrawal of the Gloucester–Leamington service and total closure of the line between Cheltenham and Stratford. This incidentally means the final closure of Racecourse Station, a fact which did not emerge during the enquiry.

We were assured that the majority of services will simply be diverted to Lansdown Station, but when pressed at the enquiry to say how many of these will survive beyond next year, there was a stony silence.

It is claimed that the through trains to Cheltenham [from London] will be retained, but when one considers the forthcoming 'improvements' to the line between Cheltenham and Swindon (including the singling of the line between Standish Junction and Swindon) the claim becomes thoroughly unconvincing [In the event, only the Kemble–Swindon section was singled, and this was subsequently redoubled in 2014].

Perhaps the qualified approval of the local Council simply means that they are too pre-occupied with re-development schemes to worry about transport. I would suggest that the Borough Council would be better occupied in ensuring a train service rather than getting their Surveyor to report on the obvious deficiencies of Lansdown Station.

Yours faithfully,

T. David

Rounding off the story of closures in the Cheltenham area, a few years after the Kingham line episode, I remember correspondence between my late father and Barbara Castle in 1967, when he fought closure of what was always referred to as the Honeybourne Line – the former Great Western route from Cheltenham Spa to Stratford-upon Avon, whose closure he had correctly anticipated in the June 1965 *Echo* letter quoted above. At the time it finally succumbed in March 1968 the service had been reduced to a twice daily single unit (Class 121) railcar, which ran non-stop for 36 miles from Stratford-upon-Avon to Gloucester, unable to serve Cheltenham after Malvern Road station had closed two years earlier.

This 1966 view of the former Severn Railway Bridge has been taken from the swing bridge at Sharpness, which spanned the Gloucester & Berkeley Canal. The line from Berkeley Road, on the Birmingham–Bristol route, to Lydney Junction on the route from Gloucester to South Wales, served as a useful diversion when the Severn Tunnel was closed, but the bridge was hit by two barges on 25 October 1960 and never repaired. It was demolished between 1967 and 1970. Photo: Roy Taylor

Not much prospect here of Beeching's 10,000 passengers a week, so closure duly occurred, yet the line survived for another eight years as an important freight and diversionary route, while Cheltenham Racecourse station was re-opened for the highly popular race-day special trains. Today much of the line has been revived as the Gloucestershire & Warwickshire Railway, with the Honeybourne–Stratford section being a strong re-opening candidate (see Chapter 8 'Still to Come').

A network for development

By 1966, three years after Beeching's report had been published, and with almost 2,000 route miles of passengers services axed in accordance with the plan, there came the first sign of a change in approach by the Labour Government. Although more than 2,000 route miles were still to be cut in line with Beeching's recommendations over the next eight years, Harold Wilson's Government published a White Paper on Transport Policy in July 1966 which signalled a change in approach by asserting that 'Commercial viability is important but secondary' and acknowledging that the British Railways Board had not been given a proper yardstick for measuring 'the effectiveness of the railway system against the real national requirement'.

It said of the Transport Act, 1962 – which had created the new British Railways Board as an independent entity with a challenge to achieve break even as fast as possible – that 'little account had been taken in the Act of the interrelation of the railways with other forms of transport and of economic and environmental needs, whether national or regional.'

Contrasting the observation that no commercially viable rail network could be developed without 'further extensive closures of socially necessary lines' with management's need to improve rather than reduce the railway system, the Government decided that in order to restore *stability* to the industry, the general shape and size of the system must be determined, including a network of main trunk routes, secondary feeder routes, commuter routes and 'certain lines essential to the life of remote areas.'

Striking a somewhat optimistic note, Clause 20 of the White Paper stated: 'The result will be a considerably larger than seemed likely with the previous policy of widespread closure [the Beeching cuts]. This change reflects a revised assessment by the Board of traffic potential and the associated operational requirements, as well as a recognition of the importance of the contribution of the railways to broader planning for society as a whole. It will, nevertheless involve some further closures beyond those already announced, since there is some pruning still to be done before the system is brought up to date.'

Following the White Paper, the 'stabilised' railway network it spoke of was revealed in a short five-page document published jointly in March 1967 by the Ministry of Transport and British Railways Board. It was entitled *British Railways Network for Development*, signed by Transport Minister Barbara Castle and BRB Chairman Stanley Raymond, and included a map of the British railway network, showing clearly which routes would make up what it called 'the basic railway network...of some 11,000 route miles compared with the drastically reduced system which would result if the Board were to continue to operate under its existing terms of reference.'

Referring to its map, the Foreword described its purpose as being 'to show the stabilised rail network planned to meet social as well as economic and commercial needs.' After repeating the criteria for a rail network outlined in the previous year's White Paper, the document sounded a note of warning: '...on passenger lines the Board may have to review from time to time the type and level of services. In some cases this may lead to proposals for the closure of individual sections, but the Minister's consent will be required and they will then be subject to the full statutory procedures.'

The *Network for Development* map showed those lines to survive as heavy black lines (freight and passenger), thin black lines (freight only) and grey lines to 'represent routes which on present evidence are not proposed for inclusion in the basic network.' The preamble added, however, regarding the grey lines: 'This does not mean that a decision has been taken to close them. Each passenger service at present using these routes will be reviewed by the Railways Board, where this has not already been done. All proposals for withdrawal of services will continue to be dealt with under the provisions of Section 56 of the Transport Act, 1962.'

The early days of preservation on the Severn Valley Railway, with a view of Hampton Loade station in 1968, a year before regular services began. A party from the Gloucestershire Railway Society has arrived from Bridgnorth on former GWR railcar 22, which is owned by the Great Western Society at Didcot, and spent a number of years on loan at the SVR during the early years of preserved operation.
Photo: Roy Taylor

Reviewing the map half a century after it was published, it is clear there are a significant number of 'grey lines' that have escaped and survive to this day. In Scotland, these are the lines from Inverness to Kyle of Lochalsh and the section of the West Highland Line from Fort William to Mallaig, while in Wales the two principal survivors, apart from the Pembroke Dock branch mentioned in my Introduction, are the Heart of Wales Line from Llanelli to Craven Arms and the Cambrian Coast Line from Dovey Junction to Pwllheli. Significant 'grey line' escapees in England are the Settle to Carlisle Line, Whitehaven to Barrow-in-Furness, Leeds to Morecambe, Leeds to Ilkley, Hull to Scarborough, Norwich to Sheringham, the North Warwickshire Line from Tyseley to Wilmcote, Witham to Braintree, Bletchley to Bedford, East Croydon to Uckfield, Ashford to Ore (Hastings), Bristol Temple Meads–Severn Beach, Exeter to Exmouth, Par to Newquay and Truro to Falmouth.

On the debit side, lines shown in bold which failed to survive include Penrith to Keswick and Exeter–Okehampton, both of which feature elsewhere in this book as potential re-openings, Cambridge–St Ives (now converted to a guided bus way), Bangor–Caernarfon, Bridgend–Treherbert (since re-opened as far as Maesteg) Kidderminster/Hartlebury–Bewdley (now partly owned and operated by the Severn Valley Railway), Skipton–Colne and Poulton-le-Fylde–Fleetwood (two other re-opening candidates featured elsewhere in this book). In addition, a large number of freight only lines featured in that map have since closed as their freight traffic disappeared. These included the last remaining section of the former Somerset & Dorset Line from Bournemouth to Bailey Gate and West Moors, the North Somerset Line from

Bristol to Radstock, Oxford–Princes Risborough (now partly operated as a preserved line) and the Leamside Line in County Durham (another re-opening candidate).

A potential lifeline: the Transport Act 1968

After the apparent lifeline represented by BR's *Network for Development* report, the first tangible legislation to safeguard rural lines against closure came in the Transport Act 1968. Besides a planned re-organisation of the bus industry, the railways' historic deficit, totalling £153 million, was wiped out. But its crucial significance to preserving the railway network was contained in Section 39, where the principle of defined subsidies for unremunerative, but socially necessary railways, was first recognised. Grants could be paid 'for a period not exceeding three years' where three conditions had been met, namely that the line was unremunerative, that is was desirable for social or economic reasons for the passenger services to continue, and that it was financially unreasonable to expect British Rail to provide those services without a grant. This progressive new measure was to take effect from 1 January 1969.

One final major closure

Section 39 of the Transport Act 1968 sadly came too late to avert one last major closure, when the 98-mile Waverley Route succumbed only days after the new Act came into effect, on Monday, 6 January 1969, after a bitterly fought campaign against its closure. Like the Great Central, the Waverley Route was seen as a duplicate route, in this case the alternative route from Edinburgh to Carlisle was via Carstairs and then on the West Coast Main Line. Whilst it was a lifeline to those communities it served, this was a sparsely populated area producing limited passenger revenues, and with freight traffic in decline, it was no surprise that its closure was one of the most significant to feature in Beeching's report.

Strenuous efforts were made to draw attention to the social implications of closure. The Scottish Office tried to get publication of closure notices postponed in April 1964, while later that year the future Liberal Party Leader, David Steel, a vehement opponent of closure, came close to seizing the Parliamentary seat of Roxburgh, Selkirk and Peebles from the Conservative, Charles Donaldson, who had voted for the Beeching report. Donaldson died soon after the October 1964 election and, when a by-election was held in March 1965, Steel secured almost 49% of the vote, winning on a manifesto that featured opposition to the route's closure as one of his key election pledges. Despite the lobbying, and the Labour Government's pledge to halt the closure programme, formal closure notices were posted on 17 August 1966, with a planned closure date of 2 January 1967.

That the line survived exactly two more years reflects the strength of feelings aroused by the planned closure. More than 500 objections were submitted to the TUCC and its hearing in Hawick on 16/17 November 1966 attracted representatives from every Scottish town and county along the route. While British Rail estimated that it would make a net financial saving of £232,000 a year (equivalent to around £4.0 million today), and pointed to falling passenger numbers and rising car ownership, opponents highlighted the inadequacies of local roads and the damage which would be caused to the fabric of Borders life. The TUCC reported to Transport Minister Barbara Castle in December 1966 but, after lengthy deliberation, she declared in April 1968 that the annual subsidy needed to keep the line open of £700,000 for the entire 98-mile line (equivalent to £11.4 million today) or £390,000 (£6.3 million today) for just the Edinburgh–Hawick section was not justified.

Barbara Castle was succeeded that same month by Richard Marsh, following a cabinet reshuffle, but he was no more sympathetic than her to saving the line. A meeting of the Ministerial Committee on Environmental Planning (MCEP) held immediately after the reshuffle failed to win over the new minister. Marsh pointed out that passenger numbers between Edinburgh and Hawick had fallen 30% between 1964 and 1967, while car ownership had risen by 120% and the local population had decreased by 9.5%. In reply, those favouring retention argued that closure of the line at a time when government policy was to encourage industry to move to the Borders area would send the wrong message, and asked the Minister not to reach a final decision until publication of a report by a group of University of Edinburgh consultants, on development of the Borders region.

This report – *The Central Borders: A Plan for Expansion* – was delivered on 19 April 1968 and crucially failed to support the line's retention. Its fate was then sealed at another meeting of the MCEP on 21 May 1968, after which its Chairman, Peter Shore (Secretary of State for Economic Affairs) indicated the committee's support for closure, saying that the impact on freight traffic would be minimal, but acknowledging that inconvenience for some passengers was inevitable. Last minute pleadings by Scottish Secretary Willie Ross to Prime Minister Harold Wilson fell on deaf ears and Marsh confirmed closure of the Waverley Route in a statement to the House of Commons on 15 July 1968. One final attempt to halt the closure was a petition containing 11,678 signatures, which was presented to Harold Wilson in December 1968 by a housewife from Hawick, Madge Elliot, along with David Steel and Earl of Dalkeith, MP for Edinburgh North. But it was all in vain, and it would be another 47 years before Madge could once again travel by train to Edinburgh on the revived Borders Railway.

A sad postscript to the Waverley route closure came in an editorial entitled 'Border isolation' published in the February 1969 issue of *Railway Magazine*, which read:

'In the continuing pattern of railway closures in Britain, certain lines form milestones indicating that a new phase has begun. Such a one is the Waverley route from Carlisle to Edinburgh, closed from January 6 despite vocal protest that continued right up to the end. This closure leaves about 30,000 people in Galashiels and Hawick about 40 miles for the nearest station. No communities of anything like this size have been left so far off the railway map before.

'A comparable situation would exist on the coast of Cardigan Bay if all of the Cambrian system west of Shrewsbury was closed, and yet Aberystwyth with 10,000 people seems confident of a social grant for some years to come. Perhaps one difference is that the Borders have only negligible tourist traffic whereas the Cambrian coast is expanding rapidly as a holiday area for the Midlands, despite the serious discouragement of total closure on Sundays. Without doubt the circumstances of the Waverley closure will be repeated elsewhere once the full impact of direct subsidy is felt in the cold hard terms of pence per passenger mile. In the case of Edinburgh to Hawick, every 3d [1.5p] paid by the passenger would have to be matched by 11d [4.5p] from the public purse'

A ticket to Ryde on the network's oldest trains

Fifty years after its unlikely survival and electrification in 1967, the remaining 8½ miles of a rail network across the Isle of Wight that once extended to some 55 miles is under renewed threat of closure, due to a need to replace its ageing rolling stock and the poor state of the rail infrastructure.

Having outlasted Beeching, who had recommended closure of both remaining lines on the island (Ryde to Cowes and Ryde to Ventnor), and succeeded in closing the Ryde–Cowes line and the section from Shanklin to Ventnor, the issue of a future for the remaining line is coming to a head now, due to a lack of suitable replacement stock for the pre-Second World War (1938) rolling stock and the substantial subsidy needed to keep the Ryde Pier Head to Shanklin line open.

A consultation exercise undertaken at the end of 2015, and prior to awarding of a new South Western franchise, pointed out that revenues were running at £1 million a year, but operating costs were over £4 million.

Behind the scenes meetings had taken place between the franchise holder, Stagecoach, and the island's MP, Andrew Turner, in May 2014, at which Stagecoach had suggested replacement of the train service with buses. A number of low-cost alternatives to the

Set 483004 arrives at Ryde Esplanade with a service from Shanklin.

Set 483007 passes the signalling centre at Ryde St John's Road with a Pier Head train.

Sets 483004 and 483007 pass at Ryde St John's Road.

Set 483004 on the remaining section of double track near Smallbrook Junction.

current franchise have also been put forward, including the fanciful one that the service be taken over by volunteers from the Isle of Wight Steam Railway!

Numerous ideas have been put forward in the past for how to rejuvenate the island railway, with longstanding hopes that the 4½ miles of line south from Shanklin to Ventnor might one day re-open, and second-hand trams from the West Midlands being one favoured replacement for heavy rail.

Reading a fascinating account of the launch of new electric services in the May 1967 issue of *Railway World* it is remarkable how much has been rationalised since those early days of electric traction, when there were five signal boxes – although the one at Shanklin was only used a peak periods – double track for the majority of the route, seven coach trains and a frequency of one train every 12 minutes on summer Saturdays.

Whatever the future holds, for the time being it remains a great novelty and pleasure to travel in the aged Class 483 trains. These are the second generation of tube stock to be used on the island since its 1967 electrification, and, like their predecessors, were adapted for use on the island's third rail system because the 386-yard long Ryde Tunnel has a restricted loading gauge that precludes the use of standard-sized trains.

Set 483007 pauses for passengers to alight at 1987-opened Lake.

Nearing journey's end: 483007 approaches the 7½ milepost south of Lake.

Set 483004 enters the passing loop at Sandown.

Set 483004 climbs out of Ryde Tunnel as it approaches Ryde Esplanade.

Chapter 2

THE MAKING OF A MODERN RAILWAY

By the start of the 1970s the Beeching closures had all but come to an end and British Railways entered a period of relative stability that would see the steady decline in passenger numbers reversed in 1983, leading to a golden era in the latter half of the 1980s before the spectre of privatisation loomed and ultimately led to a damaging and costly fragmentation of the network in the mid-1990s. That break-up has been followed by a franchise merry-go-round, where operators have come and gone on a seemingly endless round of new promises and unsustainable financial deals. Meantime, the privatised infrastructure owner, Railtrack, soon collapsed under the weight of its debts and the burden was passed to Network Rail, now struggling itself under the weight of a £40 billion debt mountain. Trying to sum up 50 years of railway progress in one chapter is no easy task, so I have picked what I consider to be ten key developments that have shaped the railway system we have today:

- West Coast Main Line electrification
- Development of the High Speed Train
- Electrification of the East Coast Main Line
- Serpell gets short shrift
- Sectorisation heralds a golden era
- Clapham Junction and the end of Mark I rolling stock
- Privatisation and the franchising model
- Open Access: limited competition but no level playing field
- Rising passenger numbers but rising Government support
- Revived lines and new stations

West Coast Main Line electrification

By the time the Waverley Route closed, the age of steam had ended, reliability of the replacement diesel fleet was getting better and the major electrification programme envisaged in the 1955 Modernisation Plan was well under way. In the south, the Kent Coast electrification scheme had been completed by 1962 and the Bournemouth line electrification, which had spelled the end of steam, was launched in July 1967. On the Eastern Region, electric suburban services had run from Liverpool Street to Shenfield since 1949, with the wiring subsequently extended to Chelmsford (1956) and the branch to Chingford (1960), gradually being extended in later years to Norwich (1986) and finally King's Lynn (1992), while the isolated London, Tilbury and Southend lines from Fenchurch Street had been electrified in 1962. Elsewhere, much of the extensive suburban network in Glasgow had been electrified and the famous 'Blue Trains' launched in 1960.

But the most significant electrification project envisaged by the Modernisation Plan was that of the West Coast Main Line. Over a 15 year period this saw overhead electrification progressively extended along the whole route from Euston to Glasgow, beginning with the section from Manchester Piccadilly to Crewe, on which electric services began in September 1960. Electrification from Crewe to Liverpool was completed in January 1962, with services from the rebuilt London Euston being launched in April 1966. A year later, in March 1967, services were extended to the re-built Birmingham New Street, while wiring finally reached Glasgow Central in May 1974, when the 'Electric Scots' service was launched amid a fanfare of publicity.

Electrification of the West Coast Main Line (WCML) was a transformational event for Britain's railway network. It marked the birth of the InterCity branding and, in the comfort of the new Mark II coaches, passengers on the country's most important trunk route could enjoy new standards of comfort, speed and a regular interval service, hitherto a feature only of suburban services. Indeed, when the initial hourly service to from Euston to Birmingham was later increased to half-hourly, there was a time when it had the distinction of being the world's most frequent InterCity service. For the ultimate in comfort and service, as well as the fastest journey time, the twice-daily all-first class *Manchester Pullman* linked London and Manchester in 2 hours and 30 minutes, from the start of electric services in 1966 until its dedicated Pullman vehicles were replaced by the latest Mark III coaches in 1985.

Since those halcyon days of the 1980s, traffic on Britain's busiest trunk route has grown to such an extent that, even after a massive

Closure notices like this were a feature of the Beeching era, put up at doomed stations after the often farcical TUCC Hearings had dismissed objectors' arguments against closure. The Alton to Winchester route was one of the last Beeching closures, succumbing in 1973, despite the route's importance as a regularly-used diversionary route for main line services from Waterloo to Southampton and Bournemouth.

£10 billion upgrade project that cost far more and took far longer than budgeted, the route is running out of capacity, prompting the planned development of HS2. WCML service frequencies are far greater than in the early days of electrification in the 1960s and 1970s, with the launch of Virgin Trains' High Frequency timetable in December 2008, following completion of the upgrade programme, meaning that Pendolino trains to Birmingham and Manchester run every 20 minutes on weekdays. Journey time improvements have put Manchester only two hours and seven minutes from London, significantly faster than the *Manchester Pullman* timings and in marked contrast to the substantial slowing down of services over the same period on the Great Western Main Line.

Development of the High Speed Train

Besides completion of the WCML electrification project, the other most notable achievement by British Railways during the 1970s was development and launch of the High Speed Train (HST). This was a vital development in passenger train technology as Britain lagged well behind almost every continental country in the rate at which its electrification programme was being implemented. It was not until 1991 that the East Coast Main Line (ECML) electrification was completed to Edinburgh, while electrification of the Great Western and Midland Main Lines remains the subject of continuing delays and escalating costs, as discussed elsewhere in this book, and electrification of a core section of the cross-country route from Doncaster to Bristol is not even on the political agenda at the time of writing.

When the first of the new InterCity 125s (now known as Class 253/254) entered service on the Great Western Main Line

One of the many unsuccessful classes of diesel introduced following the 1955 Modernisation Plan was the North British Type 2, or Class 22. A total of 58 were delivered to the Western Region from 1959, but reliability issues meant the first units were withdrawn in 1967, with the entire class gone by 1971. D6342 is seen here at Bristol Bath Road shed at an open day on 19 October 1968.

A far more successful diesel-hydraulic design for the Western Region was the Class 35 Beyer Peacock Hymek. A total of 101 entered service from 1961–64, but when hydraulic traction was deemed to be non-standard, they were withdrawn between 1971 and 1975. D7007, seen here with two classmates at Bristol Bath Road, was one of a number not to receive a full yellow end. Four have survived into preservation (D7017/18/29/76).

in autumn 1976 they brought about a revolution in speed and comfort to match what had happened with electrification of the West Coast Main Line a decade earlier. A major upgrade of the routes to Bristol and Cardiff had been undertaken to allow the new trains to operate on the fast lines at 125 mph and the faster journey times (London to Bristol Parkway in 70 minutes and London to Cardiff in only 1 hour and 45 minutes) proved an immediate hit with passengers, and revenues grew significantly.

Almost a decade after their first introduction on the Great Western Main Line, at a time when I was working on the business section of *The Observer*, the Welsh Development Agency kindly invited me to join an attempt by an HST to break the speed record for a journey from London to Cardiff. I was unable to join the trip, but my father was welcomed in my place, and was rewarded for his interest in the speed of the journey (most other guests being simply along for the ride) by being interviewed on numerous radio stations! That special train on Thursday, 18 July 1985 – *The Capital Clipper* – covered the 146¼ miles between the two capitals in a time of 80¾ minutes, an average speed of 108 miles per hour, and cutting 20¼ minutes off the previous record. Today, with virtually every train now calling at Reading, Swindon, Bristol Parkway and Newport, the best London–Cardiff time is two hours and one minute.

Two years after their highly successful launch on the Western Region, HST services were extended in 1978 to the East Coast Main Line, once again following infrastructure work to enable high speed running. While the Western Region sets were seven coaches in length, the heavier ECML traffic led to the introduction of eight-coach sets, which took over all services to Bradford,

Leeds, Newcastle, Edinburgh and Aberdeen. Further limited HST services were then added to places such as Cleethorpes, Hull, Middlesbrough and Sunderland, although all but the Hull service eventually fell victim to cost-cutting prior to privatisation of the rail network in the mid-1990s. With further expansion of HST services onto Cross-Country routes from 1981 and the Midland Main Line in 1983, the fleet steadily expanded and, by the time production ceased in 1982, a total of 95 sets had been delivered.

While many HSTs remain in service today, pending arrival into service of the new IEP fleet, that was never the intention back in the pioneering days of UK train development during the 1970s. Instead the HST was fill-in development before introduction of the Advanced Passenger Train (APT), a revolutionary beast whose key feature was an ability to tilt and so travel over the many bends along the West Coast Main Line at far higher speeds than conventional rolling stock. As a hint of what might have been with continued investment and commitment, a new and still unbroken record time of 3 hours and 52 minutes was set by an APT in 1979 for the 401 miles from London to Glasgow.

Tilting trains such as the Pendolino in the UK and similar sets elsewhere in Europe, such as Germany's ICE fleet, have now become commonplace, although their development owes much to the British Rail engineers who developed the APT but could not find sufficient enthusiasm or investment to see the project to a successful conclusion. Of the three sets that were built for service between London and Glasgow, two were scrapped when the project was finally abandoned in 1984, while the final one stands forlornly alongside the West Coast Main Line within the Heritage Centre at Crewe. Like Concorde, it is a reminder to future generations of truly great and pioneering British engineering skills.

Electrification of the East Coast Main Line

Arrival of HSTs on the East Coast Main Line in 1978 spelled the end for one of the most successful diesel classes introduced as a result of the 1955 Modernisation Plan. The 22 Class 55 'Deltics' had been the mainstay of fast services on the route between London, Newcastle and Edinburgh from the end of steam, but their days were numbered with the arrival of the first HSTs and, after a brief period operating semi-fast services, the last of the fleet was withdrawn at the end of 1981. But HST domination of the key east coast artery would not last long, as Transport Secretary Nicholas Ridley (the man my father had chastised in the *Gloucestershire Echo* for allowing 29 of the 32 stations in his constituency to close!) announced on 27 July 1984 that the Government had approved a £306 million (equivalent to £925 million today) electrification of the route.

The line had been electrified as far north as Hitchin during the Great Northern Suburban Electrification Project, which was completed in 1978 and also included the Hertford loop and the section of line from Hitchin to Royston. ECML electrification was a scheme undertaken on the cheap, with far lighter catenary structures than those used on the West Coast Main Line, meaning many instances in subsequent years of disruption due to weather causing damage to the overhead wiring. Progress was rapid, with the wiring completed to Peterborough by 1987, York in 1989, Newcastle in 1990 and finally Edinburgh in 1991. Once the core route had been wired, two further add-ons saw electrification of the short, and once closure-threatened, North Berwick branch, and the line from Edinburgh to Carstairs, a junction with the West Coast Main Line, allowing through electric services to run from Glasgow Central to Kings Cross via the ECML.

While the WCML is beset by a great many curves, which were a key driver behind the work of British Rail engineers to develop tilting technology in the APT and why Pendolinos now operate passenger services on the route, the ECML passes through much easier and flatter terrain and, from the time when A4 'streamliner' *Mallard* set a never-to-be-broken world steam speed record of 126 mph on 3 July 1938 until the opening of HS1 in 2003, it held the distinction of being UK's fastest main line route.

Besides *Mallard's* legendary record, the pre-electrification era saw no less than three speed records broken by HSTs on the ECML: firstly on 12 June 1973, a year after it was built, the prototype HST established a world speed record for diesel traction of 143.2 mph (230.4 kph) between Northallerton and Thirsk; 12 years later, on 27 September 1985, an HST set forming the inaugural *Tyne-Tees Pullman* service covered the 268 miles from Newcastle to London King's Cross in less than 2 hours 9 minutes, at an average speed of 115.4 mph, with its speed averaging 140.1 mph over an 18-mile section of the route near Peterborough. Finally, on 1 November 1987, a shortened HST test train set a new speed record of 148 mph between York and Northallerton.

Since electrification, electrically-hauled services on the ECML have been formed of Class 91 power cars pulling or pushing a set of Mark IV carriages, with an unpowered Driving Van Trailer (DVT) at the opposite end of each nine-coach formation. At the same time, HSTs have continued to operate on the route in order to provide direct links between London and currently unelectrified destinations, including Hull, Harrogate, Aberdeen and Inverness, while 'Open Access' operator Grand Central has HSTs on its services to Sunderland, and both Grand Central and Hull Trains currently use five-car Class 180 diesel units on their services to Bradford and Hull respectively. Speed records have continued to be broken on the ECML in the electric era: shortly after electrification was completed, on 17 September 1989, a Class 91 (91110) set a British locomotive speed record of 161.7 mph (260.2 km/h), while another classmate (91131) set a record time of three hours 29½ minutes on a test run from London to Edinburgh.

Apart from the long awaited introduction of the new IEP fleet to replace the HSTs and IC225 (Class 91) sets currently in use on the ECML, another major development on the horizon is electrification of the 35-mile link from Temple Hirst Junction, north of Doncaster, to Selby and Hull, which has long been demanded by local MPs, Councillors, and by the Open Access operator, First Hull Trains. In March 2014, Transport Secretary, Patrick McLoughlin, confirmed the scheme would go ahead when he announced funding of £2.5m for the next stage of the feasibility process, known as GRIP3. Electrification of the Hull–ECML line, as part of the Government's Northern Powerhouse initiative. Two years later, however, its electrification plan was scrapped in favour of "bi-made" trains.

Serpell gets short shrift

Two decades after Beeching had launched his report, a further attempt to destroy the railway network was launched with publication of a report into the state of the nation's railways from a committee chaired by Sir David Serpell, a retired former civil servant. Under the Government of Margaret Thatcher, no fan of the railways herself, Transport Secretary David Howell had commissioned Serpell's report in May 1982 at a time when British Rail's deficit was spiralling ever upwards. Howell gave Serpell's team a remit of investigating BR's finances, with a clear understanding that some way must be found to keep costs down. At the time of his appointment, the *Daily Telegraph* commented: 'Whether Sir David Serpell ever becomes a household name in the manner of that great railway cost-cutter Dr Beeching will depend greatly on whether the Government favours the more drastic options suggested by his committee.'

The year Howell commissioned Serpell's report (1982) was a low point in the history of our railway network. It was a year in which the lowest number of passenger journeys was recorded in the second half of the 20th century, following a steady decline since 1957 during which time the downward trend was only briefly broken between 1978 and 1980. The network at this time comprised 10,370 route miles, while total revenues were £1.8 billion (equivalent to £6.2 billion today) having slumped from the equivalent of £2.3 billion in 1970 (£7.9 billion today).

Faced with this decline in revenues, and a mounting deficit, Serpell's team produced a report, published in January 1983, which took a slightly different course to Beeching by setting out a wide range of options from retaining the network at 10,300 miles to cutting it to 10,000, 7,610, 6,120 or 2,210 miles. This latter option would have left most of the country unserved, closing every main line except those between London, Bristol and Cardiff, the West Coast Main Line from London to Birmingham, Liverpool, Manchester, Glasgow and Edinburgh, and the East

Coast Main Line from London to Leeds and Newcastle. A minority report from one dissident committee member, Alfred Goldstein, painted an even bleaker picture. He was a consulting engineer close to Margaret Thatcher's economic adviser, Sir Alan Walters, and his report asserted that only if the network was slashed to 1,630 miles, and season ticket holders were stripped of their 40 per cent discount, could the railways ever make money.

While Howell sat on Serpell's report for several weeks before its publication, astute leaking of the contents from within British Railways had rallied public opposition to its draconian solutions, to the extent that any thoughts of implementation had become politically unacceptable, even to a lady who was 'not for turning'. Howell was forced on to the defensive, stating as he introduced the report in the Commons that the Government was not contemplating a programme of cuts, at a time when an election was looming. The Serpell Report left the Government and British Rail where they had been beforehand, and instead of driving through a new programme of unwelcome cuts, BR turned a corner under its new Chairman, Sir Robert Reid, and achieved a notable period of stability and growth through the 1980s, helped by the sharper business focus that 'sectorisation' would deliver.

Sectorisation heralds a golden era

Transforming the structure of British Railways from one formed by geographic regions – based largely on the pre-nationalisation companies that had existing from 1923 until 1947 – represented one of the most significant steps ever taken during the nationalisation era to achieve the holy grail of profitability, which Beeching, Serpell and others had been seeking in vain. From the passenger's point of view, that 1982 shake up created three clearly identifiable businesses – InterCity, London & South East and Regional Railways – that helped deliver the most successful period in the history of British Railways, with bold branding and new marketing initiatives helping to reverse the decades of declining revenues and passenger numbers.

Highest profile of these new businesses – at least until London & South East was rebranded as Network SouthEast in 1986 – was

Last sitting on the Southern Region: despite withdrawal of the famous *Bournemouth Belle* when the route was electrified in 1967, full restaurant service continued for some time after electrification. It sadly came to an end on Friday 2 October 1981 when, having been the only enthusiast travelling aboard the final service, (18.35 from Waterloo), I asked the catering crew to sign my menu.

InterCity. While the name dated as far back as 1950, when an express from London Paddington to Wolverhampton Low Level was given the title 'The Inter-City', and had been adopted when electric services were launched in 1966 from London Euston to Manchester and Liverpool, this was the first time that InterCity had become a business in its own right. At the time the business was formed, InterCity was significantly loss making, as indeed were the other two passenger sectors. But its financial transformation during the 1980s was quite remarkable, with a loss of £196 million in 1982 transformed into a profit of £98 million in 1993/4, its sixth and final year as a profitable standalone business.

A number of factors lay behind the transformation of InterCity into Europe's only profitable rail passenger business. One was a transfer to InterCity of Gatwick Express services from London Victoria to Gatwick Airport in 1985. This dedicated service had only been introduced the previous year, but was an immediate success, with revenue and passenger numbers growing sharply and rail having secured 25% of the passenger market from London to Gatwick Airport by the early 1990s. The mid 1980s also saw the new phenomenon of long distance commuting, as the speeds offered by the IC125 (HST) made commuting to the capital from as far afield as Bristol, Leicester and York a realistic option.

InterCity relaunches the Pullman brand

Typical of management's confidence in the InterCity product was a £5 million relaunch of premium Pullman services at a time in the mid-1980s when the dedicated Mark II rolling stock used on the *Manchester Pullman* service was 19 years old and reaching the end of its working life. On 2 May 1985, during my time on *The Observer*,

British Rail InterCity publicity shot from 1985 shows a Travellers Fare Chief Steward at Euston station, marking relaunch of the Manchester and Merseyside Pullman services following a £5 million refit of Mark III coaches.

I was invited by the InterCity management team to join a preview run from Euston to Liverpool of the *Merseyside Pullman,* one of three new Pullman services being introduced from 13 May 1985, that also included a revamped and enhanced service to Manchester and a *Yorkshire Pullman* from Leeds and Bradford to Kings Cross.

The press release I was given on the trip read:

'In a bid to capture more business travellers, a big expansion of Pullman services and on train telephones was announced today by British Rail InterCity. From Monday 13 May, the present Manchester Pullman service will be more than doubled and new Pullman services between Merseyside, West Yorkshire and London will also be introduced – providing a total of 20 Pullman services a day. Later this year, InterCity plans to reintroduce the Tees/Tyne Pullman service between London and the North East.' [It was the inaugural run of the Tyne-Tees Pullman on 27 September 1985 that covered the 268.6 miles from Newcastle to London in a record breaking two hours nine minutes.]

'On the Liverpool and Manchester routes a new fleet of 22 Pullman coaches – incorporating new, more comfortable seats – will be used. On the Leeds/Bradford route, the Pullman service will be provided in a redecorated and refurbished Intercity 125 high speed train with its seats improved to provide greater comfort...the present Manchester Pullman service of four trains

Merseyside Pullman
Bill of Fare

Prices include 15% VAT, service not included.

Two course meal

This comprises main dish, with sweet, savoury or cheese board.
Coffee is included. The price is governed by the choice of main dish.
Additional items may be selected from the à la carte list.

Steak "Pullman"   £10·95
*Sirloin Steak in a White Wine Sauce
with Tomatoes, Mushrooms and Onions*

Fillet of Sole Maître d'Hôtel   £8·95

Smoked Ham and Roast Chicken with Mixed Salad   £7·95

Celery Hearts, Garden Peas
Sauté and Parsley Potatoes

Raspberry Charlotte Russe

Selection of Fresh Fruit

Selection from the Cheese Board with Salad and Biscuits

Sardines on Toast

Coffee Service

If you prefer, select any of the following dishes:—

A la carte

Asparagus Soup with Fresh Cream	95p	Wholemeal Asparagus Flan with Mixed Salad	£2·95
Choice of Chilled Fruit Juices	60p	Prawn Salad	£3·25
Grilled Grapefruit with Honey	£1·15	Raspberry Charlotte Russe	£1·15
Avocado Vinaigrette	£1·65	Selection of Fresh Fruit	95p
Avocado with Prawns	£2·35	Cheese Board, Salad and Biscuits	£1·15
Smoked Salmon Pâté	£1·65	Sardines on Toast	£1·15
Ardennes Pâté	£1·35	Coffee Service	75p
Sandwich Selection: *Three half rounds chosen from Prawns, Cheese, Ham, Tongue*	£1·60	Pot of Freshly Brewed Tea	75p

LPI 5/85

• A Merseyside Pullman menu from the 1985 relaunch, which saw the introduction of eight Pullman services each weekday (four in each direction) between Liverpool Lime Street and London Euston.

Hard to believe in our digital era, but 30 years ago the 'Trainphone' was a real novelty. Relaunch of the Pullman services to Manchester and Liverpool was accompanied by an announcement from BR that telephone facilities would be available on more than 130 InterCity trains by the end of 1985.

daily [two in each direction] is to be extended to ten trains per day [five in each direction] Mondays to Fridays. The Merseyside Pullman will provide eight trains each day [four in each direction] running between Euston and Liverpool (Lime Street).'

Further expansion of the Pullman network in 1987 saw the revival of a number of famous named trains including *The Master Cutler*, *The Golden Hind* and the *Birmingham Pullman*, giving another boost to the all-important first class ticket revenue. With an ever sharper focus on costs, fleet refurbishment and improved marketing that featured the launch of new ticket types, including heavily discounted advance purchase opportunities, the financial transformation was achieved and the British Rail Board's Annual Report for 1988/9 declared 'in its first year as a fully commercial business, InterCity turned an operating loss of £86m into a profit of £57m.'

A lick of red paint and new trains for London and the South East

Like InterCity, the creation of Network SouthEast in 1986 was a marketing triumph which later became another significant financial success story. Its financial turnaround was even more heroic than that of InterCity, as a loss of £310 million in 1982 was steadily reduced and eventually eliminated, to be replaced by a profit of £71 million in 1993/4. As the excellent account of this iconic brand *The Network SouthEast Story* chronicles in great detail, this was achieved by uniting different railway systems across a large area of southern England from Exeter to King's Lynn, and on each side of the River Thames, under one strong brand.

High standards were set by the new sector in terms of station and train presentation, while new fare offers such as the Capitalcard and Network Railcard helped reverse the decline in passenger numbers and rapidly drove up off-peak travel, the key 'marginal revenue' that filled empty seats outside prime commuting periods and help deliver the holy grail of profitability. Created initially as a product for daily travellers, launch of the Capitalcard in January 1985 – forerunner of today's Travelcard – was transformational in offering for the first time a ticket which gave commuters on overground BR services the freedom of London Underground (LU) services for a modest add-on to the cost of their season ticket.

Equally important was the arrival of a one day off-peak Capitalcard on the day after Network SouthEast (NSE) was formally launched in June 1986. This extended the benefit of integrated BR/LU ticketing to leisure travellers and proved massively popular, with 18 million being sold in the first year, generating revenues of £33 million, and annual sales eventually growing to £100 million. Alongside the new off-peak Capitalcard came the Network Railcard, which was launched in September

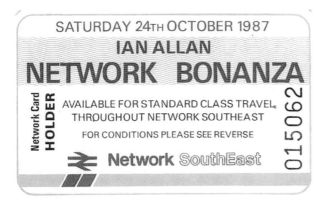

1986 and for an initial price of £10 secured the loyalty of leisure travellers by offering one third off the price of all NSE tickets bought after 10.00am on weekdays and any time at weekends. To make it even more attractive and lure families out of their cars, the discount was extended to three accompanying adults, while up to four children could travel with the card holder for just £1 each.

NSE was the brainchild of Chris Green, the senior BR manager who had been drafted in to run the London & South East sector in 1986 after seven years spent in Scotland, where he had overseen a wholesale transformation the rail system north of the border through creation of the ScotRail brand. The new NSE brand was unveiled 10 June 1986 and was characterised by a distinctive new livery for rolling stock and for stations, most memorable being the extensive use of red paint on all station seating and lamp posts. At the outset, the newly-branded sector did not own the infrastructure it was maintaining, which remained in the hands of individual BR business units, although that was to change in April 1990, when the BR Board announced its intention to abolish the regional management structure, effectively transforming NSE into the UK's 15th largest company, with 38,000 staff and assets of £4.7 billion.

Launch of the Capitalcard (now known as the Travelcard) was one of the most successful and enduring features of the Network SouthEast era, with the one day off-peak variant stimulating huge growth in leisure traffic by rail.

This commemorative medal was given to those attending a celebration to mark completion of the 1.2-mile tunnel under Stansted Airport. Being single track it represents a constraint on further increases in service frequency to the Essex airport.

The NSE sector today is probably best remembered for the Network Railcard, which remains highly popular with leisure travellers in southern England and a major source of off-peak income for the region's franchised operators. But there was far more to the business than merely being a highly astute marketing organisation. In particular, NSE was responsible for a host of major improvements, including the wholesale introduction of new trains, a major electrification programme, the opening of some 23 new stations, linking of rail systems north and south of the Thames through the creation of Thameslink and a total upgrade of the route from London Marylebone to Birmingham Snow Hill to recreate a second major link with England's second city and establish a base from which Chiltern Railways has continued to successfully build post-privatisation.

Among the principal classes of rolling stock to be introduced during the NSE era were the Networker family of diesel and electric multiple units. This comprised the Class 465/6 third-rail electric units, for use on suburban services to Kent, and the diesel Class 165/6 variants, which were used on *Chiltern Turbo* services from Marylebone and *Thames Turbo* services from Paddington. Elsewhere the 24-strong Class 442 'Wessex Electrics' fleet was introduced in 1988 to coincide with the extension of electrification from Poole to Weymouth, while Class 317 and 319 units were delivered from the BREL works at York for the newly launched Thameslink services and suburban electric services from Kings Cross. Other major fleets to be delivered included Class 321 for services to East Anglia and Euston–Northampton and Class 322 units for Stansted Airport services.

Electrification was another major feature of the NSE years and, if privatisation had not intervened, there is little doubt that Green and his team would have achieved their ambition of eliminating diesel operation from all but the main lines from Marylebone, Paddington and the former London & South Western Railway (LSWR) route from Basingstoke to Exeter. Their many successes included Tonbridge–Hastings, Manningtree–Harwich and Hitchin–Peterborough (1986); Bishops Stortford–Cambridge and Sanderstead–East Grinstead (1987); Royston–Cambridge and Poole–Weymouth (1988); Portsmouth–Eastleigh/Southampton (1990); Cambridge–King's Lynn (1992); and Redhill–Tonbridge (1994).

Chris Green on Network SouthEast

Having risen to prominence during his time in Scotland, where he created the enduring ScotRail brand and transformed perceptions of rail with new and re-opened stations and lines, the next task for Chris Green was to repeat the trick on what was then known as the London & South East Sector. Here, in his own words, are how he accepted and addressed the challenge:

Summoned to London

'I got a phone call in late 1985 from Chairman Bob Reid whilst I was working happily in Scotland. He simply asked me to come to London and 'Do a ScotRail'. That was all he said. So I had three words and that was my remit. Well, you don't argue with the Chairman, do you? What he wanted – and he was backed by the Government in this – was a repeat of what had happened in Scotland, where we had revitalised the railway and got 25% more passengers travelling; got lines re-opened and got the population and politicians applauding us. So please could we do the same in London where everyone hates us!

'The problem in London was massively bigger, but I had two lucky breaks. First, the ScotRail experience was a gigantic apprenticeship for London so I had some experience of what was needed. Second, I knew the London railway network intimately. It was at least three times bigger than Scotland, with three times more stations, ten times more trains – and yet was far more run down. Far too little money had been spent on London infrastructure in the shape of trains or track, signalling or tunnels since the 1960s. So we were able to treat the challenge as a cut and paste of the ScotRail experience, including the ability to move fast.'

Creating a new brand

'The need for a single brand was obvious from my ScotRail experience – there we created a clan loyalty around the ScotRail totem pole. We needed a totem pole in London, but it was harder in the South as there wasn't an obvious name. You've got London Underground – but 'London & SouthEast' stretched to Exeter and King's Lynn! We had an agency competition and J Walter Thompson won it – and that was the first time I saw our future name: "Network SouthEast".

'We didn't roll over and say that is absolutely fantastic. We did quite a lot of research on it, but couldn't find a better name – so we decided to run with it. They also brought the bright red, white and blue branding, which we loved, because we had inherited a grey railway! Staff immediately called it "spearmint toothpaste" but that was what we wanted – we were no longer going to be a grey railway, we were going to be bright and cheerful!

'We then gave ourselves 100 days before we made any public announcement – that was a lesson from ScotRail – while we got all our ducks in a row. How were we going to use the brand? How were we going to market it? What were we going to do with the stations and the trains? Then we had a major public launch in June 1986 when we brought all the opinion formers to Waterloo station and announced everything – we deliberately burned our bridges and publicly committed to all the things we were going to do over the next decade.

Delivering improvements

'So we said immediately that we would spend £10 million to upgrade customer service in Network SouthEast. We would modernise all 940 stations, we would modernise all 7,000 coaches; we would upgrade the track and bring in a new "Networker" train; we would recruit 1,700 staff. Some of this was a surprise to the BR Board, but it was all based on the Scottish experience that a smarter product will bring in more income. It was the same formula of creative marketing bringing more income – which is then invested in product improvements. In the background, you also keep on cutting costs without making a big fuss about it. The formula worked just as well the second time around!

'The difference in London was that you couldn't promote the rush hour, as the trains were full already. So you could only promote the off-peak. This led to the launch of the One Day Capitalcard, which became a £100 million product, generating more than the entire income from Scotland. There is almost no cost in running a train off-peak and that £100 million was almost all pure profit, which went straight back into upgrading stations, opening new ones, re-opening lines and electrifying 17 routes.

'I see 1986–1990 as the golden age where everyone was on our side. Growth and expansion were suddenly OK again and funding was available because we were expanding the network. Cecil Parkinson, for example, when he was Secretary of State for Transport, helped us get 642 new coaches authorised – the Networker trains – by going to see Margaret Thatcher at Chequers on a Saturday. Imagine that happening in the Beeching era!

'The net result was that by 1990 we had got 25% more passengers and we had achieved a spectacular increase in income which was going into these investment schemes. So we had a virtuous circle and once again we moved incredibly fast– in fact, we could not have moved any faster. In the case of City Thameslink station, for example, in three weeks we closed and demolished Holborn Viaduct station; removed the famous bridge over Ludgate Hill and built the new underground City Thameslink station. Our reward was to be told off for re-opening the line half an hour late! Nowadays the same project would take six months.'

Station re-openings

'Re-opening stations and lines was hugely symbolic, because the south hadn't had many and people were expecting this, because of the Scottish experience. This was a good example of the power of delegation, with the Route Managers opening 17 stations in close cooperation with their local councils. It began to feel like shelling peas – new stations were opening almost without my knowledge and certainly faster than I had expected. The local councils were hugely supportive with planning permission, and they would fund on the Scottish model, where they would pay to build the station and we would then take it into our care.

'Obviously some re-openings were more successful than others. There were major successes such as City Thameslink in the middle of London, but there were also other successes, such as Templecombe on the Exeter to Salisbury route, and Haddenham & Thame Parkway on the Chiltern Line – it is hard to imagine life without them today.

'What I liked about station openings was that they were major gala events in the local community. Network SouthEast was suddenly being seen as a smart, modern transport system and the local media, local mayor, local politicians and local schools all turned out to celebrate with us. We were always promoting off-peak travel, so the whole investment cycle was self-reinforcing. It did wonders for staff morale and everyone was saying "please can we have a new station?"

Mixed success with re-opening lines

'There were several potential lines for re-opening, but not all were successes. Luton–Dunstable was one that never made it to re-opening. Oxford–Bicester was the first re-opening and that was supported by Oxfordshire County Council to help relieve traffic congestion in Oxford. But these were early days, and we still lacked the bigger vision to see that this line should continue to Bedford and Cambridge.

'Kettering to Corby was a re-opening that didn't work initially. It was re-opened under what is known as the 'Speller Amendment' – a mechanism which allowed lines to be opened experimentally for a three year period and then closed again (if unsuccessful),without going through the full closure process. Corby was not a success, because it was only served by a diesel shuttle service to Kettering, which was a pretty miserable experience. It was then re-opened again, this time by Stagecoach, as the East Midlands Trains franchise holder, with a through service to London. This was what the market actually wanted and it finally proved a success.

'After that came the Thameslink "Snow Hill" tunnel, which can now be regarded as a national success. Then came the Stansted Airport branch to a brand new airport. This was followed by the

Heathrow Airport branch which is now the busiest shuttle service in the country. We tried hard on Luton–Dunstable, but couldn't make it work on cost grounds. It would have been an expensive railway as it was unrealistic to cross the Fast lines to provide a through service to London – so you would have been forced into a change of trains.'

Electrifying the network

'After that there were 17 electrification schemes, with the aim of ultimately electrifying all NSE routes, except for Salisbury to Exeter. The earliest electrification schemes were pooh-poohed by the Treasury, which did not want electrification in 1982 because they felt that it committed them forever to having a railway. If you have diesels, you can always transfer the trains somewhere else! So on Tonbridge–Hastings, for example, Whitehall wanted us to find diesels to replace the old 'Hastings' diesel units – and even suggested Pacers! Imagine commuting from Hastings to London on a Pacer!

'The new sector director at that time, David Kirby, put a stop to these ideas and insisted on making the case for the Hastings electrification on the basis that it won't cost Government a single new train. So the deal was that the DfT paid for the conductor rail and the Sector spread the existing fleet more efficiently, and this was to set a new pattern.

'Dalston to North Woolwich was funded by the Greater London Council, who were wonderful and we missed them badly when they were abolished. We were also lucky with some of the mainline schemes. East Anglia was being electrified to Norwich and we extended that to include Harwich. The East Coast electrification got us to Peterborough and Cambridge – and the Weymouth electrification was one where we finally had to get some new trains.

'On the electrification from Royston to Cambridge, the productivity gains came from introducing driver-only operation of trains with sliding doors, so we could say to government that not only are these trains cheaper, but they also bring the opportunity for driver-only operation. Extending electrification to King's Lynn was a battle because we were in recession by 1990 and the government said "not now, please". So we waited two years and then did it.'

Lines that were missed

'We were going to electrify all the other routes in the NSE region, and we had a strategic vision for the nine other routes, but most didn't happen because of recession and privatisation. Corby and Gospel Oak–Barking are finally about to happen; Reading–Basingstoke has been put back to 2020; Ashford–Hastings is back in the planning process; Reading–Redhill is long overdue and Basingstoke–Salisbury is still only a long-term dream.

'NSE was planning to electrify short branches such as Marks Tey–Sudbury as training exercises for the bigger schemes. It would just have happened! Nowadays we are not that clever and you need business cases, government approval and heaven knows what else.'

Clapham Junction and the end of Mark I rolling stock

The darkest day on Britain's railways in the modern era fell on Monday, 12 December 1988, when at around 08.10 a crash just south of Clapham Junction was to have far reaching consequences for future signalling and rolling stock safety. When the driver of a crowded 12-car train from Basingstoke saw a signal ahead suddenly change from green to red he was unable to stop, but did so at the next signal, where he was told that there was no fault. His train was then hit by a following train – the 06.14 service from Poole – while a third train, running empty in the opposite direction, then ploughed into the wreckage. In the worst UK rail accident since the Hither Green disaster of 5 November 1967, 35 people died, with 69 seriously injured and a further 415 people sustaining minor injuries.

In an official accident report, prepared by Anthony Hidden QC and published in September 1989, the accident was blamed on signal failure due to a wiring fault. New wiring had been installed, but the old wiring had been left connected at one end, and loose and uninsulated at the other. The Hidden report discovered that the signalling technician responsible had not been told his working practices were wrong and his work had not been inspected by an independent person. He had also worked a 7 day week for the previous 13 weeks. Hidden was critical of the Health and Safety culture within BR at the time, recommending that work was independently inspected and that a senior project manager be made responsible for all aspects of any major, safety-critical project. BR was fined £250,000 for violations of health and safety law in connection with the accident.

Hidden recommended the introduction of Automatic Train Protection (ATP), a system that guards against driver error, and also made comments on the crash worthiness of the Mark I rolling stock that made up all 32 vehicles involved in the disaster. Paragraph 15.34 of the official report makes chilling reading:

'In the Clapham Junction accident no-one who had been travelling in the first third of the leading carriage survived: compression of the passenger space was the cause of most of the fatal injuries. In the remaining two-thirds of the coach there were fatalities along the near-side, mostly but not exclusively among those who were sitting next to the carriage wall which was stripped off. The same area in the second carriage, the buffet car, was the scene of similar devastation. Further back in the buffet car the loose seating coupled

*with the hard edges of tables caused fatalities and serious injuries.
Other injuries were caused by direct contact with internal fittings
such as luggage racks or with the luggage expelled from them.'*

But Hidden stopped short of condemning Mark I rolling stock
outright, as was summed up in an Appendix to the official report
(Appendix G, para 35):

*'The inventory of Mark I coaching stock is large, and much of it
has not reached an end of economic life, nor will do so for another
decade or more. Mark I vehicles have good riding qualities, and
are not intrinsically lacking in collision resistance, since the latter
has emerged by a process of natural selection over forty years.
The limited diagonal strength demonstrated for the first time in
this accident could be adequately supplemented in various ways
through attention to structural details, which would be expected to
be revealed in dynamic model tests. Reinforcement of the corners
between headstocks and solebars might be one such improvement.
It is relevant in the best interests of BR customers to point out
that a head-on collision between twelve-coach trains did not occur
during the past half-century, and would be a rare probability in
future. That being the case, it could be forcibly argued that there
are more rewarding candidates for large capital investment in
the railway than would be incurred by early replacement of these
vehicles.'*

Despite their remaining the mainstay of passenger services across
the whole of the former Southern Region post the Clapham
Junction disaster, the writing was on the wall for Mark I rolling

Heritage traction
was marketed as a
feature of the Conwy
Valley Line during the
mid/late-1980s, at a
time when it was fast
disappearing from the
network. Here 101694,
still in Strathclyde livery,
stands at Llandudno
with a service for
Blaenau Ffestiniog.

Even more remarkable was the use on Conwy Valley Line services of the first main line diesel, English Electric Type 4 D200 (40122), which had been repainted in its original green livery, as seen here near Blaenau Ffestiniog with a service for Llandudno.

stock. The newest vehicles had been delivered in 1974, with much of the fleet dating back to the early 1960s, so they were reaching the end of their design life. But it took until 1999 before the Health and Safety Executive declared that all Mark I vehicles were to be withdrawn by the end of 2002, unless modified to prevent over-riding in the case of a collision. That deadline was later extended in the case of units fitted with Train Protection Warning System (TPWS), with the final 'slam door' Mark I units being withdrawn on 7 October 2005. One exception was made in the case of the branch line from Brockenhurst to Lymington Pier in Hampshire, where a dispensation was granted, as there was only ever one train running at any time on the six mile line, so specially adapted three-car units continued to operate until 2010.

Privatisation and the franchising model

Railways Act 1993 – structure and implementation

After the spate of privatisations that were the hallmark of the Thatcher era in the 1980s there was a certain inevitability that once the railways had been restored to a situation of growth and of relative financial stability, Conservative dogma would call for privatisation. So the Conservative government that was unexpectedly elected in April 1992 had a commitment in its manifesto to privatising British Rail, without specifying exactly how this would be done. Many lobbyists backed the BR Board's view that a number of regional companies should be set up, rather like the situation as it was before nationalisation, but the Treasury favoured a model based on the franchising of passenger operations, a structure which was included in the Railways Bill that was eventually passed as the Railways Act 1993.

Under the terms of the new Act, a new infrastructure company called Railtrack assumed control of the physical network and stations, while passenger operating franchises, typically for periods of between seven and 10 years, were let to a wide range of transport undertakings, notably bus operators, but with less participation from former BR management than had been anticipated. The Office of Rail Regulation was established to approve the contractual relationships between the new operators, government and Railtrack, including the complex franchise agreements governing levels of service and setting out the subsidy or premium profile of each individual franchise. Letting of the first franchises, a process which lasted from February 1996 until April 1997, was carried out by the Office of Passenger Rail Franchising (OPRAF), which later became the Strategic Rail Authority (SRA), before it too was abolished and responsibility passed to the Department for Transport.

Upholding a Passengers' Charter

Franchising of passenger rail services had come at a time when the government of John Major was making great play of the Citizen's Charter, an initiative launched in July 1991 that sought to improve public services by making administration accountable and citizen-friendly and ensuring transparency and the right to information. The new private rail operators were quick to jump on the bandwagon with their own Passengers' Charters and it was not long into the new operating regime that I was able to test out the robustness of one such charter. Having begun a daily commute from Haslemere to Waterloo in 1992, one feature of the line I had grown to appreciate was the conviviality of the buffet car, with coffee and toast in the morning and a beer in the evening. It was a welcome break to the tedium of longer distance commuting for many, but one which the new private operator of the South West Trains franchise, Stagecoach Group, quickly sought to end.

Rumours that South West Trains planned to close the buffet cars in its fleet of Class 412 (4-BEP) units began circulating shortly before the summer timetable was to start on 2 June 1996, but were categorically denied by the SWT customer relations team. Days later the threat featured in the *Daily Telegraph* and I felt moved to launch a save our buffet cars campaign. Using my public relations contacts, I persuaded two transport correspondents – one of them a former colleague on *The Observer*, Christian Wolmar – to travel on one of the threatened evening services. This led to excellent features on Saturday, 1 June 1996 in *The Independent* and *The Times* with anecdotes from irate 'regulars', while on the previous night a friendly steward had allowed me to make a PA broadcast to travellers on the busy 18.50 train, warning that this was the last night of buffet cars and urging them to make their views known!

The buffet cars were duly closed but, on 4 June, I had a letter published in *The Times*, headed 'Railway buffet' in which I pointed out that the SWT Passengers' Charter explicitly said that the company will 'keep passengers informed of new developments and their implications' and posed the question 'If charter initiatives are anything more than a cynical public relations exercise, then surely this must open the way for a legal examination of the action being taken by SWT?' In the face of a growing campaign of outrage at the closure, SWT remarkably caved in – on 14 June posters appeared on stations headed 'The Bar is Back', stating that 'due to popular demand' the bar service would be reinstated from Monday 17 June on key commuter services. So for the next seven years, until final withdrawal of the 4-BEP units in 2003, we were able to carry on enjoying our coffees and beers in the traditional manner!

A franchising merry-go-round

Looking back on two decades of franchised passenger services, what is remarkable is how few of the original franchises are still in the hands of their original operators, while others have changed hands multiple times and in some cases boundaries have been redrawn. Among the long distance operators, only InterCity West Coast (Virgin Trains) and Great Western (First Group) have remained with their original franchisees, although in the latter case First Group bought out its former partners (a management team and 3i in 1998) and the franchise was significantly extended in April 2006 to encompass London suburban services and local services in the South West, which had previously formed two separate franchises. Among franchises in the former Network SouthEast area, only Chiltern Railways and South West Trains had remained in constant ownership since 1996 – until Stagecoach lost the SWT franchise in March 2017 to First Group/MTR.

While the West Coast Main Line has remained in the hands of Virgin since privatisation – helped by the protracted upgrade of the route, and later by the botched franchise competition in 2012 when FirstGroup's award of a new 13-year franchise was rescinded after what was described as 'significant technical flaws' in the bidding process, leading to the resignation of three DfT officials involved in the bid evaluation process, the same cannot be said of the East Coast. Here Great North Eastern Railway (GNER) won the initial franchise, which began in April 1996, and successfully built the most highly-regarded of all long-distance franchised operators. Led by its ebullient Chief Executive, Christopher Garnett, GNER sought to bring back a golden age of rail travel, with a classy dark blue livery for its trains and a reputation for standards of service based on providing full restaurant car facilities on the majority of its trains.

But desperation to retain the East Coast franchise prompted Garnett and his team to make a heroic pledge to make a total of £1.3 billion in premium payments over the life of a new seven year franchise, starting in May 2005. It quickly became apparent that this was a step too far and, with the added headache of serious financial difficulties at GNER's parent company, Sea Containers, GNER was forced to throw in the towel and 'hand back the keys' to government at the end of 2007.

The franchise competition was then rerun and won by National Express, led at the time by former Strategic Rail Authority boss Richard Bowker. Failing to learn the lessons of GNER before it, National Express also 'bet the shop' with a promise of unsustainably large premium payments to Government, and it too was forced to hand back the keys in November 2009, after less than two years running the route. This jewel in the franchise crown was then effectively returned to state control under the East Coast brand, before the franchise competition was run again and won by Virgin Trains East Coast, a business 90% owned by Stagecoach Group and 10% by Virgin. Its eight-year franchise began on 1 March 2015. Within a year, however, questions were once again being asked about the viability of its winning bid.

Elsewhere the operator which has seen most churn of its franchise portfolio over the past 20 years has been National Express, the company which failed on the East Coast and is best known for its long-distance coach services. In the initial franchising round, National Express won a host of franchises, including Gatwick Express, Midland Mainline and ScotRail, along with a number of regional and London suburban franchises. It then added to its haul through the July 2000 acquisition of Prism Rail, a business formed to bid for and operate rail franchises, which at the time held four separate franchises, two in the London area and two in Wales and the South West.

But one by one the group's franchises were lost – Gatwick Express became part of the Southern franchise, Midland Mainline went to Stagecoach, while ScotRail went initially to FirstGroup and more recently, Abellio with its focus now on rail opportunities in Continental Europe, National Express sold its last UK rail franchise – the London, Tilbury and Southend network operating from London Fenchurch Street, now branded as c2c. This was acquired in January 2017 by Trenitalia for £70 million.

While the majority of passengers are concerned more with whether they can find a seat and whether their train will arrive on time, than with who actually runs their trains, what has been a remarkable and bizarre feature of our privatised railway is the extent to which it has been taken over by foreigners. In a world where the UK Government is only permitted to step in as an 'operator of last resort', as has previously happened in the case of both the South Eastern and the InterCity East Coast franchises, we seem to have no qualms about inviting the state railway operators of France, Germany and Holland to takeover vast swathes of our passenger services.

So East Anglia and Scotland have been annexed by the Dutch (Abellio), who also had joint ventures with Serco to operate the Northern Rail franchise (since won by Arriva) and the contracted Merseyrail services; Wales, CrossCountry and Chiltern Railways are in German control (Deutsche Bahn, via its Arriva subsidiary) while TransPennine and Southern England are currently run by the French. One overseas player from even further afield is Hong Kong listed company, MTR, which will operate Crossrail services under a concession from Transport for London, having already become operator of London Overground, and the services from Liverpool Street to Shenfield that will become part of the Crossrail network when it opens at the end of 2018.

Good-bye Railtrack, hello Network Rail

While the sometimes colourful demise of franchise holders as a result of their financial or operational failings has added a fascinating twist to the story of our privatised railway, the most serious failure of all was that of Railtrack. This was the infrastructure business created in succession to the British Railways Board to assume ownership and control of track, rail infrastructure and major stations. It came into being on 1 April 1994, was floated on the Stock Exchange two years later (May 1996), when shares were sold at 380p each and, propelled by talk of the huge hidden value of its property assets, saw its shares reach a peak of over £17.00 in November 1998.

A trio of fatal accidents lay behind the eventual downfall of Railtrack. Two of these on the Great Western Main Line at Southall (1997) and nearby at Ladbroke Grove two years later, raised serious concerns about the impact on rail safety of fragmenting the network and leaving safety and maintenance in the hands of a wide range of contractors and sub-contractors. At Southall, seven people died and 139 were injured when an HST with a defective Automatic Warning System (AWS) passed a red signal and ran into the path of a freight train which was crossing the main line. The operator, then called Great Western Trains, was fined £1.5 million for breaches of health and safety regulations, and trains were no longer permitted to run with faulty safety equipment, on which drivers of high speed single-manned services had become significantly reliant.

Two years after the Southall accident, confidence in rail safety was again called into question with the crash at Ladbroke Grove on 5 October 1999, where 31 people were killed and 520 people injured, when a local service leaving Paddington, and formed of a three-car Class 165 Turbo unit, passed a red signal that had limited visibility to drivers and had been passed at danger on several previous occasions. This put it into the path of an HST heading for Paddington, resulting in the deaths of both drivers, along with 24 passengers on the Turbo train and nine aboard the HST, where the leading first class coach H was gutted by a fire caused by fuel that had leaked from the Turbo train. This was another crash that could have been prevented if all trains had been fitted with an Automatic Train Protection (ATP) system, something which had been ruled out on grounds of cost.

While Railtrack was heavily criticised in the light of the Southall and Ladbroke Grove accidents, it was a third accident, at Hatfield on 17 October 2000, that was to trigger its collapse exactly a year later. On this occasion an InterCity 225 train on a service from King's Cross to Leeds was derailed due to a fractured rail as it was travelling at 115 miles per hour. The crash worthiness of the Mark IV coaches used in the IC 225 sets meant only four passengers were killed, but when more than 300 similar cracks were found in rails close to the crash site, Railtrack panicked and imposed more than 1,200 emergency speed restrictions on routes right across the country, before beginning a track replacement programme that cost some £580 million and led to two years of delays to services on many major routes.

Relying on a company that no longer had its own in-house engineering skills to assess the scale of the problem was proving politically unacceptable. This was particularly so as it came at the same time as spending on a huge upgrade of the West Coast Main Line was escalating ever upwards – what had begun life as a £2 billion project eventually cost £10 billion and took ten years to deliver, three years longer than originally planned. In 2001 Railtrack announced that £733m of compensation and costs related to the Hatfield crash meant it had incurred a loss for the year of £534 million, yet still felt able to pay a dividend to shareholders in May 2001 after securing extra funding from Government.

Following serious conflict with Rail Regulator Tom Winsor, who had been appointed for a five year term in July 1999, with Railtrack fighting attempts to use regulation to improve its stewardship of the network, a Government decision was made to call time. On 7 October 2001, Railtrack plc was placed into railway administration under the terms of the Railways Act 1993, following a High Court application by Transport Secretary, Stephen Byers. Government efforts to get the company to live within a budget of £14.8 billion for the period from 2001–2006 failed when the cost of post-Hatfield remedial work became clear, so to get Railtrack out of administration the government had to go back to court, where it was able to assert that the company was no longer insolvent on the basis that Winsor had announced an interim review of its finances, with the potential that significant new funding would be forthcoming.

On 2 October 2002 Railtrack plc came out of railway administration and, after attracting no interest from the private sector, to which it was offered for sale, was immediately acquired by Network Rail, a company formed for the purpose, which paid £500 million for the company and at the same time assumed its £7 billion of debts. Proceeds from the sale of its stake in High Speed One (£295 million) and £370 million of cash it held was used to compensate Railtrack's army of 277,000 small shareholders, who eventually received a total of 262½p per share, not far below the share price of 280p on the day its shares were suspended and, by representing a far better return than had at one time been expected, was sufficient to kill off planned legal action by disgruntled shareholders.

Network Rail has not covered itself in glory in the 15 years since taking over from Railtrack. Like its predecessor it has been repeatedly criticised for its failure to control costs, as evidenced by a trebling in the estimated cost of the Great Western electrification project, and on notable occasions such as the Christmas period in 2014, for its failure to complete major upgrade projects on time. It has come under fire from MPs for apparently losing control of a £38 billion modernisation programme and the debt of £7 billion which it took on from Railtrack in 2002 has since ballooned to an unsustainable, and still growing, £40 billion.

Adding insult to taxpayer injury, a report in *The Sunday Times* on 24 January 2016 revealed the state of profligacy amongst its senior managers, showing that between April 2012 and October 2015 senior staff had used procurement cards – a form of taxpayer-funded credit card – to order luxury hotel rooms, expensive dinners and a host of luxury items including £20,000 of Marks & Spencer hampers and a river cruise for executives. In response, Chief Executive Mark Carne told *The Sunday Times* that there had been a crackdown on such expenses since the organisation had been reclassified as a public sector body in September 2014. 'The expenses this organisation has claimed for in the past are no longer acceptable,' he said. 'I've clamped down, changed and tightened the rules. No more hampers, no more birthday gifts, no more expensive meals or hotels. We're now a public company delivering a vital public service with taxpayers' money and we have to make that money go as far as we can.'

Open Access: limited competition but no level playing field

When the Railways Act 1993 received government approval on 5 November 1993, it not only signalled the break-up of British Rail and launch of the now familiar franchising process, but also contained a clause that was designed to pave the way for new entrants into the passenger market. Just as privatisation of the telephone and power utilities led to a fragmentation of those former monopolies, to the benefit of consumers, so Section 4 (b) of the Act spelled out that the Secretary of State for Transport and the new Rail Regulator had a duty 'to promote the use of the railway network in Great Britain...and the development of that railway network, to the greatest extent that he considers economically practicable. Section 4(d) was even more specific, stating that their duty was 'to promote competition in the provision of railway services'.

As new franchisees set about putting their stamp on the new regional fiefdoms there was little sign in the early years of the privatised railway that competition would help do for fares what it had done for phone, electricity and gas bills. While the newly-launched Heathrow Express was technically an Open Access operation, the first competitive entrant into the market did not successfully get onto the network until Hull Trains was granted a four-year access agreement in December 1999 to enhance the then service of just one daily return train a day between London and Kingston-upon-Hull. Two former BR managers, Mike Jones and John Nelson had astutely spotted a poorly-served point-to-point market and their new company, backed by a newly-formed company called GB Railways which had secured the East Anglian rail franchise, successfully launched a new service, which has since grown and gone from strength to strength.

But Hull Trains was not the only party to have spotted an opportunity on the East Coast Main Line. Another was a railwayman named Ian Yeowart, who I first encountered after reading a short news item in *Steam Railway* magazine in early 1996, stating that he, then Chief Executive of the North Yorkshire Moors Railway, was preparing to bid for not one, but two, of the passenger rail franchises being let by what was then the Office for Passenger Rail Franchising, (OPRAF). As a public relations consultant always on the lookout for new business opportunities, I wrote to Ian offering to help in any way I could. What followed was a close business relationship that weathered more than a decade of effort and frequent disappointment, but reached a triumphant moment on the morning of Friday, 27 January 2006, when the Office of Rail Regulation (ORR) approved his company's (Grand Central) application to launch Open Access services from Sunderland to London.

The Grand Central story began in 1996 with Ian's early attempts to become one of the first wave of franchised operators. At the time we first met, he had already made an abortive bid for the Midland Mainline franchise, but had clearly got the bit between his teeth and was intent on bidding for two huge regional franchises – Regional Railways North West and Regional Railways North East. After he decided that it was only feasible to bid for one of the two franchises – Regional Railways North East – I secured financial and logistical support from a couple of clients. We then put together a bid in which the proposed subsidy profile was remarkably similar to that of the winning bidder (MTL), but based its business plan around growing traffic on the all-important Trans-Pennine route, rather than following the disastrous cost-cutting route favoured by the short-lived MTL team.

With the benefit of hindsight, we were remarkably naïve in believing that our motley management team, chaired by an ageing former Chairman of London Transport – Sir Wilfrid Newton – and supported by a small shipping company called Jacobs Holdings could win the day and take on the management of this vast franchise. But what we did correctly identify was the huge potential for traffic growth on the Trans-Pennine route, a fact reflected in its later separation from Regional Railways North East into a stand-alone franchise. For Ian though, this first foray into the uncharted waters of the privatised railway had given him a taste for more. Through the help of the BBC's Northern Transport Correspondent, Alan Whitehouse, Grand Central secured financial backing from one of the major transport groups in the North East – whose identity we kept secret – and began developing proposals for the operation of inter-city services from Newcastle to Manchester under the Open Access provisions of the 1993 Act.

Two key requirements for success in any application to run Open Access services are the need to demonstrate that the proposed services would provide passengers with genuine new journey opportunities, and to provide evidence that there would be a significant level of new revenue generated by the creation of new direct journeys. In other words, to establish that your proposed services would not simply 'abstract' revenue from the existing franchised operator. At the same time, the would-be operator needs the co-operation of Network Rail in confirming that there is space on the network to run new services.

For four years, Ian and one of the team that had been involved in the abortive franchise bid – Warren Breeze – worked on plans for the Trans-Pennine service and made some notable headway. An agreement to lease a redundant fleet of High Speed Trains from Porterbrook Leasing was signed and viable timetable slots were identified by Network Rail. But we ultimately fell foul of the then Rail Regulator, Tom Winsor, who ruled against the application for track access in July 2004, principally on the grounds that Grand Central had failed to prove it would create sufficient new journey opportunities.

Facing a second rejection, and loss of the financial backer, would have been sufficient for many people to throw in the towel, but not Ian Yeowart. He had yet another plan up his sleeve, and made contact with a former colleague, Kevin Dean, who had moved

Grand Central founder Ian Yeowart had bought a copy of this Marilyn Monroe picture for 50p in a car boot sale, but liked it so much that he negotiated a deal with the late actress' estate to enable its use in publicity material and in the vestibule of GC coaches!

Grand Central achieved the highest rating of any UK rail passenger operator in a 2016 satisfaction survey, a far cry for the early months of its operation, which were beset by failures and cancellations. HST power car 43080 stands at Kings Cross on 21 February 2009 at the rear of a GC service from Sunderland.

out of the railway industry to become Managing Director of a private company in Accrington called Fraser Eagle, best known for organising rail replacement coaches during emergency and planned engineering works.

Kevin had worked for Ian at Regional Railways, and was quick to line up a new funding deal for his former boss, that would give Ian the chance for a crucial third roll of the dice. In October 2004, barely three months after Winsor had rejected the Newcastle–Manchester plan, and after some intensive market research and meetings with the Office of Rail Regulation to learn lessons from the rejection – a reborn Grand Central was announcing plans for services on the East Coast Main Line from Sunderland and Bradford to London Kings Cross.

This time there were to be no shortcomings on the supporting data required by the ORR: extensive work in canvassing public opining was undertaken by consultants through regional focus groups, while another set of consultants set about proving that there were gaps in the current timetable to allow the services to run. The citizens of Wearside and Teesside made it clear that they wanted a direct rail link to the capital and we were determined to see that they got it!

There followed an intensive period of some 15 months up to the end of 2005 during which time increasing awareness of the Grand Central proposals – fuelled in part by a helpful full-page article in *The Times* and Ian's tireless efforts to garner stakeholder support – saw backing for the proposed services from virtually every major regional organisation. An Early Day Motion (EDM) in support of the GC proposals, tabled by Halifax MP Linda Riordan, attracted more signatures than another EDM in support of GNER's bid to retain the InterCity East Coast franchise.

Renewal of that GNER franchise – which took effect in spring 2005 – provided a fascinating backdrop to the GC story as it unfolded over the coming two years. GNER had won the new deal with a heroic undertaking to pay premiums totalling £1.3 billion over the seven year life of the franchise. It was a figure which no independent commentators believed was achievable and was several hundred million more than the next highest bidder.

With GNER's parent company, Sea Containers, facing its own financial difficulties, it was not long before it became apparent that the sums did not add up. Meantime, by the end of 2005 Grand Central's prospects looked finely balanced – on the one hand we felt that we had done all the work asked of us by the ORR to prove the demand for our service, yet Network Rail still stood in our tracks and produced a highly contentious report just before Christmas 2005 in which it claimed that there was insufficient capacity on the East Coast Main Line to accommodate our proposed services, along with the planned half hourly London–Leeds service that GNER had committed to as part of its new franchise. But the ORR decided to boldly ignore Network Rail and approve the launch of services from Sunderland to London.

Having been provisionally approved by the ORR on 27 January 2006, it took until September 2007 before the first of Grand Central's High Speed Trains left Sunderland on a scheduled service for London. In the intervening period the company had survived a legal challenge from GNER to the ORR decision, the business had been sold by Fraser Eagle to a consortium called Equishare, funded by offshore millionaire Eddie Davies, and then there had been lengthy delays in delivering the refurbished HSTs to run the initial three trains a day service.

While Hull Trains and Grand Central have gone from strength to strength, with strong owners in First Group and Deutsche Bahn respectively, and steadily increased and improved services, the fate of a third Open Access operator provided a timely reminder that there was no level playing field when it came to competition on the rails.

The crucial requirement for an Open Access entrant to succeed was to have access to at least one established market, in order to generate enough initial revenue to allow traffic to develop from new or under-served markets. So, in the case of Hull Trains that meant Doncaster to London, while for Grand Central it was sharing revenue from the substantial York to London market that allowed it to build up traffic from Hartlepool and Sunderland. But Wrexham & Shropshire (W&S) was not so lucky when it launched services from Wrexham and Shrewsbury to London Marylebone in April 2008, having been denied access to the key markets of

Wolverhampton and Birmingham by virtue of a 'Moderation of Competition' clause in the Track Access Agreement of Virgin Trains, franchised operator of services between Wolverhampton, Birmingham and London Euston on the WCML.

Lacking a key point-to-point journey that would deliver significant revenue from day one and underpin the service as traffic developed, W&S never really stood a chance. An initial timetable of five return journeys a day was reduced to four just a year after launch, with a final change to the timetable in December 2010 cutting the service back still further to three return journeys per day, before the service was finally withdrawn at the end of January 2011. Operationally, however, W&S was a triumph, achieving a 99% satisfaction score in a 2010 National Passenger Survey, the highest rating any operator had ever achieved.

My own experience of W&S was sadly limited to a first class journey from Shrewsbury to Marylebone on the evening of Saturday, 11 December 2010, which I had contrived to take after seeing my football team, Cheltenham Town, draw 1–1 in a League Two match against Shrewsbury Town, and after being tipped off by a senior insider at parent company Arriva that the end may be nigh. Besides me and my youngest daughter there were only four other passengers in the first class coach for our leisurely four hour trip to London, but we enjoyed an excellent dinner of roast turkey and, like the fan club of regular passengers, were left wondering what might have been if common sense had prevailed and the company had been allowed to compete on a level playing field.

Ten years after Grand Central made its controversial arrival onto the ECML, when the ORR had approved its launch of services from Sunderland to London in early 2006, what has now become the Office of Road and Rail announced another ground-breaking decision on 12 May 2016. This was when it gave First Group the go-ahead to launch a five times a day service of low-cost high speed services from London to Edinburgh. First will begin its services in May 2021, using five-coach high speed trains with capacity for 400 passengers, calling at Stevenage, Newcastle and Morpeth and a commitment that single fares will average just £25.00.

Despite rejecting plans by Grand Central-owned GNER for fast hourly services from Kings Cross to Edinburgh (on the grounds that costs were likely to exceed benefits) and other new services to Ilkley and Cleethorpes (due to the high level of expected revenue abstraction), approval of the First Group application will mean a choice of operators, a challenge to the dominance of domestic airlines such as BA, easyJet and Flybe on the London–Edinburgh route and real competition on fares. However, just like the original GNER a decade before, the current East Coast franchise holder, Virgin/Stagecoach, took a dim view of the ORR decision, immediately threatening to take the regulator to court for a judicial review.

Soaring passenger numbers but rising Government support

Evidence of how marginal Open Access remains in our privatised and franchised railway system can clearly be seen in the data on passenger journeys compiled by the ORR (from 2015, Office of Rail and Road). While the number of passenger journeys reached an all-time record of 1.66 billion in the year to March 2015, no less than 1.65 billion of that total was accounted for by the franchised system, with a mere 2.1 million being accounted for by Open Access operators. Within the franchised railway, passenger journeys were up 4.2% on the previous year and by a staggering 125.3% from the 735.1 million journeys recorded a decade earlier (1994–5).

In terms of the distance travelled by British railway passengers, this also more than doubled over that 10 year period, to reach a record of 62.9 billion kilometres, or almost 40 billion miles, in the year to March 2015, with a rise of 4.5% compared to the previous year. Within this increase over the previous year, growth in franchised passenger kilometres in the Long Distance and Regional sectors outstripped growth in London and South East sector, with the franchised Long Distance passenger kilometres increasing by 5.5% to 20.8 billion kilometres in 2014–15, the first time since 2011–12 that the London and South East sector did not record the highest growth. Growth at the three Open Access operators (First Hull Trains, Grand Central and Heathrow Express) was even more impressive, with total passenger kilometres increasing 13% between 2013–4 and 2014–15.

That golden era of the late 1980s and early 1990s, when InterCity and Network SouthEast achieved profitability, looks a distant dream, in the light of what it costs to run today's privatised network. Figures produced by the ORR show that in the year to March 2015 net government support to the rail industry came to a total of £4.8 billion, a welcome reduction of 11% compared to 2013/4, and significantly less than the peak figure of £7.5 billion in 2006/7. In constant values is still double the level of support (£2.4 billion) received by British Rail in 1985/6 and in stark contrast to the two best financial performances over the past two decades, 1989/90, when Government support at 2014/5 values fell below the £1 billion mark to £926 million and 1995/6, the year before franchising was launched, when the Britain's railways required a paltry £662 million in support from government.

Within this latest government support figure, by far the largest element was a payment of £3.8 billion to Network Rail, a figure which had increased by £349 million compared to the previous year. Crossrail accounted for almost £1.1 billion of government support in 2014/5, while the net amount received from the Train Operating Companies amounted to £802 million, by far the largest total net premium payment received by government in the five years that it has been a net recipient of funds from the passenger train operators.

A total of 13 operators made payments for their franchises, largest of which were South West Trains (£374 million), East Coast (£249 million) and Greater Anglia (£187 million). Of the remaining eight, those receiving the highest subsidy from government were ScotRail (£261 million), Northern Rail (£113 million) and Arriva Trains Wales (£102 million). Looking at those figures in terms of subsidy or profit per passenger kilometre, the biggest subsidy went to Merseyrail (a contracted not franchised operator) which received 12.4p per passenger km, ScotRail (8.6p) and Arriva Trains Wales (8.5p). Of those making payments, South West Trains paid 6.0p per passenger km while at East Coast the figure was 5.1p.

Revived lines and new stations

Amid all that has changed on Britain's railways – from the dark days of Beeching, the end of steam through to widespread electrification, new trains, the revival in passenger traffic and the upheavals of privatisation – what is most heartening has been the extent to which stations have opened and re-opened. Significant stretches of line have been rebuilt for a new generation of passengers and they have flocked to the new services. It took only four months after its opening for the Borders Railway to celebrate its 500,000th passenger, when the so-called experts had only been forecasting 650,000 travellers in its entire first year.

Paying a visit to Cranbrook on Saturday, 19 December 2015 – less than a week after it opened – and it was clear that Devon's newest station was also destined to be a major generator of new traffic for the railway. I counted some two dozen passengers waiting to join the service I alighted from (11.28 to Exeter) while an hour later another 20 or so residents of this fledgling new town were on the platform with me waiting to board the 12.29 service to Exeter. Moving on later that day, I visited the other Devon station to have opened during 2015 – Newcourt, on the ever-busy Exmouth branch. Here again, there was a constant stream of passengers boarding and leaving the half-hourly services, while Sandy Park, on the opposite side of the nearby M5 Motorway, offers the prospect of windfall traffic whenever Exeter Chiefs RFC are playing at home.

At the time Beeching published his report in 1963 there were some 7,000 stations across Great Britain, a number which plummeted through the decade-long closure programme to a low point of around 2,000 British railway passenger stations in 1975. The revival that has taken place since then has led to the opening or re-opening of some 370 stations, as listed in Appendix (ii). These range from what are now long-established and vital transport hubs such as Birmingham International (5.1 million passengers in 2014/5, and Milton Keynes Central (6.6 million passengers in 2014/5) to smaller stations and halts, among the newest of which are Cranbrook and Newcourt in Devon (mentioned above), Coventry Arena and Bermuda Park on the Coventry–Nuneaton line in the West Midlands (opened January 2016) and the seven stations between Newcraighall and Tweedbank on the Borders Railway, which opened (or were re-opened) in September 2015.

Since reaching a low point in the mid-1970s, the line openings and re-openings listed in Appendix (i) have added a total of almost 550 route miles to the national network. As the following chapters describe in more detail, the longest stretch of new or revived line – at least until HS2 has been delivered – is the 68-mile long HS1 link between London and the Channel Tunnel. Of the revived routes, the honours are currently held in England by the Robin Hood Line from Nottingham to Worksop (31½ route miles), in Scotland by the Edinburgh–Tweedbank Borders Railway (35 route miles) and in Wales by the Cardiff–Ebbw Vale Town line (29½ route miles).

What the following chapters try to explain is not only the huge success of virtually every new or re-opened station and route at attracting new passengers to the network, but also the long catalogue of worthy re-opening candidates across England, Scotland and Wales, many of which have been the subject of active re-opening campaigns for 20 years and more. As numbers using newly re-opened stations and lines continue to far exceed initial traffic forecasts, it is a timely moment to ask those that oversee our transport network – the Department for Transport, Scottish Government and Welsh Assembly Government – why so little action seems to be taken and, when it is, why it all takes so long and why it all costs so much?

After they disappeared from everywhere else in the south, dispensation was given for slam door trains to continue being used on the six-mile branch line from Brockenhurst to Lymington Pier, as only one train was ever on the line. Days before final replacement, three-car 1497 waits to depart from Brockenhurst on 16 May 2010, adorned with a commemorative headboard marking this end of an era.

Chris Green on InterCity and today's railway

After the huge success he achieved in launching and delivering the ScotRail and then the Network SouthEast brands, one final challenge for Chris Green before railway privatisation was to take control of the most iconic British Rail sector of all, InterCity. Here he reflects on his time as its Managing Director (1992–94) and on two subsequent decades of a privatised railway network:

'There is absolutely no doubt that in 1982 InterCity was the jewel in the crown of the Chairman's five sectors and the InterCity brand, like ScotRail, was an inspired name. You could go anywhere in the world and say "Intercity" and people would know what you meant. It is ironic that the name is now widely used internationally, but that Great Britain is the only place where we no longer use the InterCity name officially.

'InterCity was already well established as a brand in 1982, but huge effort went into developing it as a professional marketing name. And by that I don't mean just the name and the colour scheme – I mean the fact that we had a consistent InterCity product across Great Britain. If you went on an InterCity train, you knew that it would be a fast, limited stop journey; that there would be a buffet car from the first train to the last train; that there would be restaurant car meal service Monday to Friday. You could also be sure of a simple fares structure with Full fare, Saver and Super Saver. Simple and effective.

'InterCity staff were trained in customer service to a far higher level than Network SouthEast. InterCity was ahead of the game on things like telephone enquiry bureaux and advance purchase tickets at this time.

'But we struggled to get investment in the rolling stock. There just wasn't enough profit to justify new trains. The government refused to back the Advanced Passenger Train and only grudgingly agreed to East Coast Main Line electrification. They refused to agree to any new trains on the West Coast Main Line after the APT was cancelled. They refused any new trains on Cross-Country and they left Gatwick with the most appallingly ancient Class 73s. It was left to private owners to develop new trains on all these InterCity routes.

'The problem with InterCity was that (a) it was not allowed to be subsidised, so they were always having to watch the pennies, and (b) they couldn't raise enough investment without government support to modernise the product. Privatisation was a breath of fresh air in terms of capital investment – a good example being the Gatwick service, which suddenly got a new fleet of trains.'

The need for more capacity

'Today, the privatised intercity routes are facing a very different problem. A doubling of passengers has created serious congestion problems. The issue is no longer how to get new trains funded, but how to create capacity for them to run.

'Inter-city travel has doubled in just 15 years – and all the signs are that it is going to double again. There is no room on the ECML or the WCML for any significant increase in train paths – and both commuter and freight traffic is competing to grow in the same space. The best solution is undoubtedly to build a completely new railway for inter-city travel, and then use the classic network for more commuting and more freight traffic.

'I can't see any alternative – there is absolutely no way to simply double capacity on the existing ECML or WCML. The project problems you are now seeing on the Great Western Main Line would happen on the other trunk routes – it is just not possible to keep a 25kv mainline running whilst trying to double its capacity.

'There are a lot of issues around our current privatised railway, but it is now working well enough for me to say that I would not want to upturn the wheel-barrow again. Yes, the changes were too fast and too radical, and they resulted in a massive loss of experience, which indirectly led to a series of accidents like Hatfield, Ladbroke Grove and Potters Bar. Alastair Morton used to talk about a "collective nervous break-down" when the rail industry went into melt-down after Hatfield.

'But a working compromise has emerged, where we have a fast growing, professional rail industry that is beginning to deliver big results. Huge amounts of capital investment are now flowing into the railways in a way we would never have seen in British Rail days.

'A public industry will always be at the mercy of the Treasury when the national economy hits problems. The Treasury simply stops the money flowing to the railways. In a privatised rail industry, legally binding contracts safeguard the investment in five year packages. Today we are seeing phenomenal growth in demand for rail, which is forcing the Government to support expansion and investment.'

Challenges facing Network Rail

'The weakness is that the fragmented companies, like Network Rail, still depend heavily on contractors who do not have the same experience that British Rail had in-house. If the investment continues to come in stop–go five year chunks, then the contractors are not going to retain experienced railway staff. The discontinuity and inexperience in the industry, and especially amongst contractors, should worry us.

'As Nicola Shaw said in her review of Network Rail, if you want government investment to keep coming Network Rail's way, you had better start finding other ways of attracting it from the outside world. One way of doing this is to lease out the large stations – there are only about 20 of them – so that retailers and property *developers pay a large sum for the income stream they secure from station retailing and property development.*

'I can live with that, and the customers won't see any difference. Electric power supply is another example – does a passenger really care what the contract is on an electric power supply? The alternative is that we don't see investment in projects like re-opening the former Eurostar platforms at Waterloo. The starting point is that there is not enough money, and it is never going to come 100% from the Treasury, so we are going to have to play along with these clever manoeuvres to get it.'

Re-opening lines and stations

'If we are talking about new lines then there are two types. One is a mega strategic route like Crossrail and Thameslink in London, or HS2 and HS3 – these are obviously going to be Central government inspired and I think the National Infrastructure Commission (NIC) is a brilliant idea. In its chairman, Lord Adonis, we have someone who is focused on finding big opportunities – how we make the business case, how we fund them and how we get planning approval. I think that is really good news.

'Lord Adonis is now championing the East–West Rail scheme, which has not had a champion before. This upgrade will be primarily justified on the back of major housing expansion in Buckinghamshire – and for that you need better transport links. The real problem comes with smaller revival schemes, which are more local. If we were Germany we would have 16 Länder [regions] and they would sponsor and fund the developments. But Britain is far more centralised and the local councils don't have that sort of money. Scotland is the exception to that rule, where the Borders Line was enthusiastically supported by the Scottish Government.

'In a perfect world we would hand big infrastructure decisions to funded regional bodies, like the Northern Gateway authorities, to open a new local line or station; to electrify a route; and to create a cohesive Northern rail network. The Department for Transport could also let the franchise on the basis that the franchisee must bid to cover the cost of the new station or new route.

'What doesn't work is where a scheme does not have a clear sponsor. Take the Uckfield–Lewes re-opening proposal for example. Is it a local or a strategic regional scheme? If it's the latter, then it ought to be one for Lord Adonis and it should be addressing a major transport problem between London, Gatwick Airport and Brighton. A national approach would also address the issue of whether the problem is actually at the London end – would it be better to invest in new capacity from East Croydon to Clapham Junction?

'So re-opening schemes do need a national push, and the best way is through the new National Infrastructure Commission. It is part of a bigger picture where you are convinced that you want

to invest in rail, not road, and where you want new railway not old railway and then you have to fund it and it joins a queue. It is important to take the social and economic benefit into account, so we're not just talking about finance.'

Private sector investment

'East–West Rail from Bicester to Bedford is a good example of a route where private sector investment could play an important role. Network Rail is saying that it can't find anyone to sponsor it. It is not their job to open a line, it's their job to deliver it. So who is it that wants a line from Oxford to Bedford?

'I think the line would be opened primarily to support major housing development in the area. If you are going to put thousands of new houses into North Buckinghamshire, then it makes sense to build them along the new East–West Railway around new stations at Winslow etc.

'In terms of getting franchisees involved in developing the network, the best example is Chiltern Railways, which won a seven-year franchise in 1997 and then chose to give it back and gamble on winning a 20-year deal, in return for which they would commit to a whole lot of infrastructure investment, including the Oxford–Bicester upgrade.

'That is the best example yet of a franchisee wanting to commit to the opening of new railway, although Deutsche Bahn, as its new owner, is concerned at the cost of the Chiltern upgrade work. It will always be easier for London Overground, which has a gigantic shareholder in the shape of Transport for London and the Mayor of London.

'Tavistock is an interesting one, because the South West has made so much noise about connectivity and is now part of the peninsular movement. My approach would have been to do it in bite-sized chunks – I would have got a local line to Tavistock to start with and then developed [Plymouth–Okehampton–Exeter] further in time.'

British Rail vs. Network Rail

'Looking back, British Rail was very good at giving value for money. We had virtually no money so we had to make every pound go a long way. We became very ingenious and we had good in-house teams of engineers and project managers who understood how to keep costs down. At the other extreme Network Rail became profligate when it was able to borrow on its 'credit card' as costs were rising.

'HS2 is being planned by contractors and will be built by contractors, so there is a risk of not having enough in-house knowledge. Network Rail did bring maintenance work in-house very successfully, and this has resulted in a railway with

remarkably few temporary speed restrictions. Project Management however, with honourable exceptions, still tends to be the problem area.

'Crossrail is also working well, being on time and on budget and this reflects the fact that it if you plan something well – and don't then change the plan – things tend to happen on time and budget.

'We need a much cheaper way of running rural railways and it needs to become a much higher priority. Standards do need to be changed – having all these rigid standards since privatisation has not been clever. We need engineers who can common-sense the standards into something more appropriate to rural lines for example.

'One way of controlling costs is to evolve rolling programmes for electrification, rolling track, rolling station modernisations etc, so that you retain the expertise within the industry. I'm sure that by the time it is finished, the team electrifying the Great Western Main Line will have acquired real expertise – but what will happen is that they will be disbanded and someone else will win the next electrification contract.'

Chapter 3

RE-OPENINGS ACROSS ENGLAND

I n contrast to Scotland and Wales, where devolved administrations have been a significant factor in driving forward many of the successful rail re-openings that have taken place, the rail revival in England has largely been confined to major urban centres, notably London and the West Midlands, together with the development of tram or metro schemes in places such as Newcastle, Sheffield, Nottingham and Manchester. Elsewhere there have been a significant number of station openings and re-openings, the development of a number of airport links, and major projects such as HS1, Thameslink and Crossrail, which are featured in Chapters 6 and 7.

The rail network in England was devastated by Beeching, with regions such as East Anglia and the South West damaged economically for decades by the scale of cuts that followed the 1963 report. But, as in Scotland and Wales, there were a considerable number of notable escapees, amongst which the best known was probably the Settle to Carlisle (S&C) line. Survival of this strategically important 72-mile main line, both post Beeching and when under further threat in the mid-1980s, means fortunately that the most scenic rail routes in England, Scotland (Kyle of Lochalsh) and Wales (Heart of Wales Line) have all survived into the twenty-first century and are continuing to thrive, both as community links and as major tourist attractions.

After the S&C Line had survived the Beeching report, an attempt to close it by stealth began in May 1970 when eight intermediate stations were closed, leaving Settle and Appleby as the only remaining stations along the route. At its low point, just two return passenger trains a day were left running on the line. But despite the loss of most freight traffic, and a lack of investment in maintaining the numerous tunnels and viaducts along the route, there were glimmers of hope when, in 1974, the eight closed stations were re-opened for use by summer weekend 'Dalesrail' services from Blackpool and Preston, which were run to encourage

Like a number of other stations along the Settle and Carlisle line, Appleby's Midland Railway buildings are immaculately preserved, along with the water tower seen to the left of the departing Leeds-bound service. This supplies the working water column that is used to provide water to steam locomotives using the route.

ramblers to visit the area and promoted by the Yorkshire Dales National Park Authority.

But closure of the line was formally proposed in 1984, prompting a massive campaign against it led by the group Friends of the Settle–Carlisle Line, which had been formed three years earlier. The Government appointed bankers to handle a potential sale of the line, but British Rail appointed a manager to the line, Ron Cotton, who capitalised on proposed closure to promote the line, with the result that the closed stations were re-opened in 1986 and the two trains a day service – which I can recall had been strengthened from four loco-hauled coaches to nine to cope with the number of passengers – was substantially improved. Passenger numbers increased by 500% in the period between 1983 and 1989, the year the Government finally saw sense and reprieved the line.

My own small part in helping to save the Settle & Carlisle line during that late 1980s closure threat came during my time on the business staff of *The Sunday Times*, when I persuaded the paper's Travel Editor, Will Ellsworth-Jones, that I should write a piece on the line's scenic attractions, at a time when the closure issue was coming to a head. So, on Monday, 15 February 1988 and armed with tickets kindly supplied by British Rail's London Midland Region press office, I set off with my future wife, Clare, from London Euston to Carlisle, with the aim of travelling down the S&C line to Leeds and then returning to London Kings Cross. This was in the days long before mobile phones, so at some point in the afternoon I would need to call the copytakers at Wapping and dictate my 1,500 word feature to meet a vital deadline for the following weekend's travel section.

In those days, the trains from Carlisle to both Leeds and Newcastle were all locomotive-hauled and left from adjacent bay platforms at the south end of Carlisle station. My great mistake that day was to board a Newcastle-bound train and only realise the seriousness of my error when I watched the Leeds train pull out from the platform alongside! No matter, though – a visit to the station manager's office assured me that we could travel on the next southbound S&C train as far as Dent, where the station house was occupied by someone working on the railway who would be happy to let me use their telephone, then we could continue south as far as Settle – walk the 1.2 miles to Giggleswick station and from there travel to Lancaster and then take the overnight sleeper back to Euston!

Dent has the distinction of being not only the highest station in England, at 1,150 ft. above sea level, but also one of the most isolated spots in the country, being almost five miles from, and 400 ft. above the village of Dent itself! So arriving there at dusk and finding no one at home in the station house prompted a degree of blind panic on that fateful day! Ever the intrepid reporter, however, I spotted twinkling lights in the valley below the station and after a couple of failures, eventually reached a house belonging to a family where the husband worked on the railway.

Whether or not they really believed my story about being a *Sunday Times* reporter desperate to file a story about the line, we were welcomed into the house, and I sat for a blessed half an hour in their living room, with the family cat on my lap, dictating my feature to the copytakers in Wapping. After that we had just enough time (and daylight) to head back up the steep hill to Dent station, catch the last southbound train to Settle, leg it from there across to Giggleswick station, catch the last train to Lancaster, have a late night dinner, and then finally board the sleeper train to Euston.

After substantial investment in restoring the line's infrastructure, the S&C today is a vital and heavily used freight route catering for major flows of coal, gypsum and other traffic diverted away from the West Coast Main Line. The spectacular route remains a firm favourite with operators of steam specials, is a vital diversionary route when the West Coast Main Line is closed and has buoyant passenger traffic. Meantime, a number of the intermediate stations with original surviving Midland Railway buildings, including Kirkby Stephen, Garsdale and Dent have been restored and found tourist-related uses.

Making a connection with the Settle & Carlisle line at Hellifield, two stops south of Settle, is an important strategic link to Blackburn that survived partly for freight use, but most importantly for diversion of West Coast Main Line services when the line north of Preston is closed for engineering or other reasons. This route through Clitheroe had become a summer Sunday route for the Dalesrail services that run from Blackpool to Carlisle and served all the eight smaller S&C stations that had first closed in 1970, then re-opened for the Dalesrail services in 1974, before the eight S&C stations were re-opened to daily services in 1986.

Clitheroe station had originally closed in September 1962, but began being served by Dalesrail services in 1990 and reopened to regular traffic four years later (1994), with the ten miles from Blackburn becoming an extension of Ribble Valley Line services from Manchester Victoria. When the new hourly service was launched in May 1994, three intermediate stations on the section from Blackburn – Ramsgreave & Wilpshire, Langho and Whalley – were also opened. Passenger numbers have grown substantially – up from 202,000 at Clitheroe in 2004/5 to 287,502 in 2014/5 – and more than doubling at Ramgreave & Wilpshire during that decade, from 47,935 to 111,744, with the line now promoted as a community railway.

Robin Hood: England's longest re-opening
Until re-opening of the Borders Line from Edinburgh to Tweedbank in September 2015, the distinction of being the longest revived route in Britain was held by the 31½ mile long Robin Hood line in the East Midlands, which re-established services on a Beeching victim from Nottingham via Mansfield to Worksop and was the result of a scheme jointly funded by Nottinghamshire County Council, Derbyshire County Council and Nottingham City Council, with assistance from the former Strategic Rail Authority.

On 5 March 2016, East Midlands Trains 158657 approaches the tram and bus interchange at Hucknall on the single track section of the Robin Hood Line, with a Nottingham-bound service.

Services were restored in stages during the 1990s, with re-opening from Nottingham to Newstead in 1993, followed by a further extension to Mansfield Woodhouse two years later. Additional intermediate stations opened at Bulwell (1994) and Kirkby-in-Ashfield (1996), with full re-opening to Worksop taking place in 1998. A basic half-hourly service as far north as Mansfield Woodhouse and hourly to Worksop carries some 3,500 passengers a day, principally commuter traffic to Nottingham, but with the line also serving a number of leisure attractions in Nottinghamshire and Derbyshire.

Development of the Robin Hood line was made feasible by virtue of the numerous rail-connected coal mines in the area, which meant that a route north of Nottingham had survived as far as Linby colliery, near the present day Newstead station, which closed in 1988. There was then a gap as far as Kirkby-in-Ashfield from where a former Midland Railway route from Pye Bridge Junction on the Nottingham–Chesterfield line remained intact all the way to Worksop, having survived as a freight only line to serve collieries along the route at Sherwood, Shirebrook and Creswell, as well as a number of other industrial sites.

A key requirement in the Robin Hood line revival was to keep infrastructure costs as low as possible. That meant retaining an alignment between Sutton-in-Ashfield and Kirkby-in-Ashfield that had been adopted for freight traffic in 1972, so that British Rail could sell a site in the centre of Kirkby-in-Ashfield and, in the case of the missing link from here south to Newstead, it meant a choice

East Midlands Trains 156473 calls at Kirkby-in-Ashfield with a Nottingham-bound service on 5 March 2016. This station is less central than one which previously served the town, but that site was sold prior to the line's 1996 re-opening, in order to offset infrastructure costs.

A sizeable crowd of young people prepares to escape the impending storm and board a Nottingham-bound Robin Hood Line service at Mansfield on 5 March 2016.

between two long buried tunnels under the Robin Hood Hills. Here the former Midland Railway one was preferred to that of the former Great Central Railway as it was considerably shorter, and its re-excavation became one of the iconic images of the whole Robin Hood project.

While weekday services have become a key part of the local transport infrastructure, Sunday services proved less successful. A campaign in support of Sunday services led to their experimental introduction in December 2008, with funding from Nottinghamshire and Derbyshire County Councils. Had traffic built up sufficiently over the following two years then the seven day a week timetable would become part of the East Midlands Trains franchise, but that was not the case at the northern end of the route, so from May 2011 the Sunday service was curtailed to eight return journeys between Nottingham and Mansfield Woodhouse.

Having previously only travelled as far north as Sutton Parkway, to visit a former lingerie-manufacturing client based at Sutton-in-Ashfield, a return visit to complete my journey, on a Saturday in early March 2016, gave a fascinating insight into the importance of the line. Trains were all well-used, with large crowds boarding Nottingham-bound services at intermediate stations. Hucknall, the second station heading north, is a model example of road-rail-tram integration, where local buses connect with trains and the NET trams terminating here. Further north, travelling on the line through the heart of Mansfield reminds you of just how large the town is (population 100,000) and leaves you wondering how on earth such a large population could have been deprived of rail services for more than 30 years?

A feature of particular note is Mansfield's beautifully restored Grade II listed station building, which was returned to railway use in 2000, five years after the station had re-opened. At Mansfield Woodhouse there is a delightful former goods shed over platform 3, which is used by terminating services, while further north Shirebrook station has been restored for commercial use and the one at Creswell is still standing, albeit abandoned. There are two remaining signal boxes, at Shirebrook Junction and at Creswell (Elmton & Creswell), but the latter box was permanently 'switched out' in 2013 and the semaphore signals it controlled are all set in the 'off' position. Elsewhere, the array of rusted and overgrown sidings south of Shirebrook station and the long lines of EWS-liveried coal wagons west of Worksop are a stark reminder of Nottinghamshire's once huge, but recently deceased, coal industry.

Worksop station is a charming survival, whose notable feature is the delightful and multi-award winning Mallard pub within the main station building on the westbound side of the station. A poster on the platform, meanwhile, is a reminder that not everyone is as lucky as those able to use the regular Robin Hood Line service. This is a promotion for the nearby Brigg Line, a 20-mile route from Gainsborough to Brigg and Barnetby which survived a closure threat in 1988, but since 1993 has seen its service reduced to a Saturdays-only service of three return trains from Sheffield to Cleethorpes.

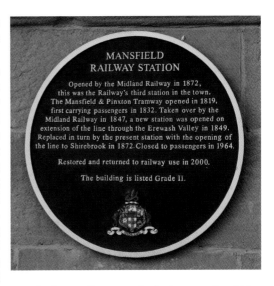

A plaque on the platform side of Mansfield station commemorates the Grade II listed building's return to railway use in 2000.

Journey's end at Worksop for a Robin Hood Line service on 5 March 2016, where most, but not all, the Nottingham-bound services use platform 2. The Mallard pub is at the signal box end of Platform 1.

There is potential for future extension of the Robin Hood Line by making use of a former freight line which leaves the main route at Shirebrook Junction and was used for coal traffic to High Marnham power station until its closure in 2003. In 2009 this 14-mile route became Network Rail's High Marnham Test Track, with Network Rail stating that, as the route of the line would now be maintained (it is cleared for speeds of 75 mph), it might increase the likelihood of being able to restore a passenger service in connection with Robin Hood Line services. At the same time, Nottinghamshire commissioned a feasibility study to consider extending the current hourly service between Nottingham and Mansfield Woodhouse to Ollerton, with new intermediate stations at Warsop and Edwinstowe, the latter being close to a Center Parcs holiday resort.

A distinctly encouraging update on the proposed re-opening to Ollerton came in a report delivered to Nottinghamshire County Council on 11 February 2016, which identified many of the detailed issues needing to be addressed, including construction of the three new stations, and also put a price on both the likely re-building costs and the level of financial support which a new service would require. This report suggested that the total capital cost would be within a range of £18.9m–£24.5m, with the maximum estimated costs being development & design (£2.0m), development of the three stations (£7.741m) track and signalling (£14.756m). The gross operating cost was put at £1.6 million a year, with revenues generated of £840,000 meaning the need for a subsidy of £760,000 a year. The County Council is now hoping to secure various forms of Government funding to meet the infrastructure costs, and for the operating costs to be absorbed as part of a new East Midlands franchise, when it is relet in March 2018.

Nottingham has also established a successful and expanding tram network under the brand name of Nottingham Express Transit (NET), and to make way for the development of its first line, a three-mile section of Robin Hood Line from Bulwell to Hucknall was reduced to single track prior to the opening of NET's route from Nottingham city centre to Hucknall in 2004. Although not the main subject of this book, it is worth noting that in August 2015 a £570 million southern extension of the NET network opened, when service began running on two lines totalling 11 miles of new track from the city centre to Clifton South and Stapleford.

One that got away

While the Robin Hood Line has proved highly successful in providing much needed commuter services into Nottingham, in nearby Derby there is a reminder that not all new rail schemes are going to succeed. In a bold experiment modelled on Birmingham's Lichfield–Longbridge–Redditch cross-city line, Derby City Council promoted the opening in October 1976 of a short branch line south of the city to an industrial area known as Sinfin, with new stations at Sinfin North (which was effectively a private station for Rolls-Royce employees) and Sinfin Central and a re-opened station, Peartree, shortly before the branch junction, on the main Derby–Birmingham line.

Services were run as an extension of the Matlock–Derby route and principally aimed at encouraging public transport use by workers at the Rolls-Royce plant adjacent to Sinfin North station. Patronage did not live up to the Council's hopes and, after a drastic reduction in the service frequency to just four trains a day in January 1978, the service was later reduced to just one train a day in 1992, with all services ending the following year. Today the line remains in use for limited freight traffic, while Peartree, which had re-opened on the site of a station closed in March 1968, is now served by just two trains a day on the route between Crewe and Derby. Passenger numbers remain modest, but have nevertheless risen from just 1,415 in 2004/5 to 5,000 in 2015/6.

Second time lucky for Corby

While rail services came and then went at Sinfin, residents in the former steel town of Corby in Northamptonshire can count themselves lucky when it comes to rail links, having seen services to England's fastest growing town restored not once, but twice. Corby first lost its rail services in April 1966, after Beeching had proposed closure of the route from Kettering via Corby and Melton Mowbray to Nottingham, and for more than two decades the town known had the dubious distinction of being one of the largest places in the whole of Europe without a rail service.

Like so many other revived lines, Corby owes its good fortune to the survival of the route from Kettering (on the Midland Main Line) to Manton Junction, near Oakham as both a freight route and a diversionary route, which sees occasional use for Midland Main Line services when the direct line from Kettering to Leicester is closed. One major feature of this route is the Grade Two listed 82-arch Harringworth (or Welland) Viaduct, the longest structure of its kind in the country. Freight traffic declined considerably when Corby's steelworks closed in 1986 and the section between Kettering and Corby was singled, but the following year a passenger shuttle service was launched with local authority support and operated by Network South East using a single coach Class 121 DMU. Initial success did not last however, and after just three years the service was withdrawn in June 1990.

Fortunately that was not the end of the Corby revival and, second time around the resurrection was to be on a much grander scale. In 2006 bidders for the new East Midlands franchise were instructed to include provision of services to Corby in their tenders to take account of the large scale of residential development that was planned. A year later, in April 2007, Network Rail earmarked

£1.2 million for a new station and two months later the winning franchise bidder, Stagecoach, promised a new hourly service from Kettering to London which could be started at Corby and give a journey time to the capital of just one hour and 15 minutes.

After a somewhat shaky start, due to rolling stock availability issues, and an initial service of just one train a day, the full hourly service from Corby to London St. Pancras began operating in April 2009, with a very limited service north from Corby to Oakham and Derby also being launched. The new single platform Corby station was built on the site of the town's original 1879 station and opposite the short-lived platform that had served as the town's station from 1987–1990.

Passenger numbers at Corby have built up steadily since the second re-opening, more than doubling from 115,000 in 2009/10 to 278,000 in 2015/6, and further expansion is now under way. Electrification, re-doubling of the track from Kettering to Corby and introduction of half hourly services all form part of the planned Midland Main Line (MML) upgrade, whose timing was thrown into doubt following the Government's June 2015 announcement that it was 'pausing' work on the £500 million project. But three months later came welcome news that the pause had been lifted, with wiring as far north as Corby due to be completed by 2019, and electrification of the remainder of the route to Nottingham, Derby and Sheffield due to be completed by 2023.

Heavy rail becomes light rail in the North East

Almost 40 years later it is hard now to appreciate what a revolution in urban transport was launched when the first section of the Tyne & Wear Metro was opened in 1980. It transformed 26-miles of former British Rail branches from Newcastle to the east coast at Tynemouth and South Shields, which had once been part of an electrified Tyneside network, but which had been de-electrified and downgraded in the 1960s, linking them up with new tunnels under Newcastle city centre and seeing construction of the distinctive blue Queen Elizabeth II bridge to take Metro services across the River Tyne.

Since its original opening between 1980 and 1984, the highly successful system has grown to a network of 60 stations and 46 route miles, through subsequent extensions to Newcastle Airport in 1991 and to Sunderland and South Hylton in 2002, with the latter route representing a pioneering use of shared track with heavy rail services between Pelaw and Sunderland. Both the sections of line from Sunderland to South Hylton and the Airport branch use former railway alignments, which is also a feature of a potential future extension to Washington New Town via the mothballed Leamside line (see Chapter 9).

Services today are operated on behalf of the local transport authority, Nexus, by a subsidiary of German state rail operator

Deutsche Bahn, and run along two routes, branded the Green route (Airport–South Hylton via Newcastle Central station) and the Yellow Route, which doubles back on itself on a line from South Shields via Newcastle Central station and the city centre, then loops round via Monkseaton and Tynemouth before returning to the city centre and terminating at St James station. In October 2015 Metro announced that the moving annual total of passenger journeys had reached 39 million, its highest level since June 2010, while DfT figures in June 2015 showed it achieving faster passenger growth than the newer systems in Manchester, Birmingham, Sheffield and Nottingham.

Manchester too turns to metro

Like the Tyne & Wear system, Manchester's successful and expanding Metrolink has its origins in taking over former suburban rail routes, linking them up via a city centre section – street running rather than in tunnel – and transforming their fortunes with the use of passenger-friendly light rail vehicles. A driving force behind selection of the first routes, to Bury in the north and Altrincham to the south of the city, was a wish to create a link between Piccadilly and Victoria stations, each of which is on the fringe of the city. Until opening of the long-awaited Ordsall Chord, as part of Network Rail's Northern Hub, the only direct link between the two stations has been the light rail one, created in July 1992 when Metrolink's Phase One was completed and opened.

Much of the Metrolink network's subsequent expansion has been on new alignments, but there have been two further instances where former 'heavy rail' routes have been converted for use by the Metrolink trams. First of these is what was known as the Oldham Loop line, a route from Victoria station which ran to the centre of Oldham and then joined the Manchester–Leeds Caldervale route at Rochdale. After the opening of a new line to Eccles in 2000 (Metrolink Phase 2), the 14-mile long Oldham/Rochdale line was developed as Phases 3A and 3B, with work beginning when heavy rail passenger services ended in October 2009. Metrolink services first reached Oldham in June 2012 and Rochdale in February 2013, with extensions into the town centres opening in January 2014 (Oldham) and March 2014 (Rochdale).

The Oldham/Rochdale line was one element in a £1.5 billion upgrade programme that was launched by Transport for Greater Manchester (TfGM) in 2008 and designed to triple the length of the network, which is now the UK's largest light rail network, extending to 57 miles and 93 stops. Other elements of that upgrade programme have seen the opening of three new routes to East Didsbury (May 2013) Ashton-under-Lyme (October 2013), and Manchester Airport (November 2014). Of these, the 4.5 mile East Didsbury line is built on a disused railway line, while the other routes are new alignments. Newest of all is a second cross city link via Exchange Square, opened in February 2017, while still to come is a planned line through Trafford Park to serve the 1,300 businesses and 33,000 people working there and provide easier access by public transport to its many retail and leisure facilities.

Both light and heavy rail have been accommodated at Manchester Airport, which has developed into a major destination for Trans-Pennine and other regional services since a branch to the Airport, and a new station, were opened in 1993. The station lies at the end of a mile-long branch which makes a triangular junction with the route from Manchester Piccadilly to Crewe between Heald Green and Styal stations. Since its original opening, the Airport station has been significantly expanded, firstly through the opening of a third platform in December 2008, following a £15 million investment, then more recently with the addition of a fourth platform in May 2015 as part of the Northern Hub programme of rail upgrades around the Manchester area. Another feature of this initiative, the Ordsall Chord, will allow the launch of direct services from the Airport to a range of destinations north of the city, including Bradford, Halifax and Rochdale.

Bridging the gap in Sheffield

While both Newcastle and Manchester have had major success at turning former 'heavy rail' suburban routes into light rail or tram services, and developing new routes well beyond the boundaries of the former rail routes that have been swallowed up, the challenge of rail-based urban transport has been approached slightly differently in Sheffield. Here a Y-shaped tram network was developed that had no significant overlap with existing or former rail alignments, but which is now being linked to an existing heavy rail route serving the nearby town of Rotherham and is pioneering a new generation of 'tram-train' services that could be a blueprint for other UK towns and cities.

During 2018, a 400-yard stretch of line should open near the Meadowhall shopping centre and M1 Tinsley Viaduct to the east of Sheffield city centre, which will create a link between the Sheffield super-tram network and a Network Rail route to Rotherham, on which a new fleet of Spanish-built tram-trains will operate, fitted with special hybrid wheels, enabling them to run on both forms of track, and powered by high voltage electrical current on the conventional rail network, before switching to less powerful overhead lines for the urban section of the route. This long-delayed trial project is seen as a precursor to the launch of similar schemes in other British cities.

A hot-bed of revivals in West Yorkshire

One area of England that has done more than most others to revive its railway network is West Yorkshire. Across the region

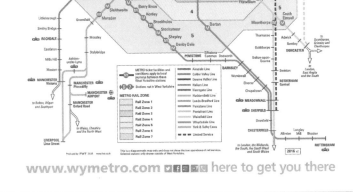

West Yorkshire's Rail Network

www.wymetro.com here to get you there

West Yorkshire has contributed a great deal to the rail revival. There are some 25 new or re-opened stations on this network map, as well as the re-opened routes from Halifax to Huddersfield, and Wakefield to Pontefract. Map courtesy of West Yorkshire Combined Authority

no less than 24 stations have opened or re-opened, partly as a consequence of the huge traffic growth following electrification by British Rail in 1994/5 of the Airedale and Wharfedale routes north west of Leeds to Skipton, Ilkley and Bradford Forster Square. There have also been two notable line re-openings: the 8¾ mile Pontefract Line from Wakefield Kirkgate to Pontefract Monkhill, along with intermediate stations at Streethouse, Featherstone and Pontefract Tanshelf; and a 10½ mile section of the Calder Valley line between Halifax and Huddersfield, along which one new intermediate station has been opened, at Brighouse.

Today these routes see services operated by both the franchised operator, Northern Rail, and by the company I was once a Director of, Grand Central, whose Bradford to Kings Cross services serve Halifax, Brighouse, Wakefield Kirkgate and (occasionally) Pontefract Monkhill. Of all the new stations on the

Brighouse station has been a major success story for West Yorkshire and is mid-way along the re-opened route from Halifax to Huddersfield. On 21 May 2016 Northern Rail 158756 is about to depart with a Calder Valley service to Manchester Victoria.

Passengers from Brighouse wanting to travel to Leeds can travel in either direction to reach the city. On 21 May 2016, Northern Rail 158855 heads north, taking the longer route via Bradford Interchange.

Both re-opened routes in West Yorkshire are served by Open Access operator Grand Central. On 21 May 2016, GC 180905 pauses at Brighouse with the 13.09 departure for Halifax and Bradford Interchange.

two revived routes, the one that seems by far and away the busiest is Brighouse, which has the distinction of being served by trains to Leeds departing in both directions! With regular services also to Manchester via the Calder Valley, Huddersfield and connections at Mirfield for Wakefield, its passenger numbers have soared, increasing from 64,419 in 2004/5 to 416,000 in 2015/16. Paying a first visit on a Saturday in May 2016, I was one of more than 30 people boarding the 13.29 service to Leeds.

Travelling from Wakefield towards Huddersfield and Halifax, on the section of line linking the two revived routes, there is a stark reminder of why railways were so important to the region, as the line splits to pass on either side of the huge and abandoned Healey Mills freight marshalling yard, where eight 150ft high floodlighting towers forlornly stand guard over a 140-acre site that was one of Europe's biggest freight depots, comprising no less than 57 miles of track and capable of handling 4,000 wagons a day. It closed as a freight depot long ago as 1987, but had remained home to dumped rolling stock, including a large number of redundant locomotives, until 2012. Today all that remains, apart from the lighting towers and encroaching vegetation are a few rusting sidings, an abandoned signal box and a few disused wagons.

By contrast with the bustling scene at Brighouse, hourly services on the re-opened section of Pontefract Line seem rather modestly patronised. I was one of less than 10 passengers on the Pacer train forming a Saturday afternoon departure from Wakefield Kirkgate on the day of my visit to the area in May 2016, with no passengers joining at the three intermediate stations and just three of us remaining by the time we reached our destination at Knottingley, 25 minutes later. That level of patronage was in stark contrast to my onward journey to Leeds on the other section of Pontefract Line. Here a large leisure centre called Xscape Yorkshire, built alongside

Northern Rail is one of three UK rail operators (along with Arriva Trains Wales and Great Western Railway) to still rely on the much derided Class 142/3 Pacer units. On 21 May 2016 Pacer 142089 stands at Wakefield Kirkgate with the 14.31 service for Knottingley, which will take it along the re-opened line to Pontefract.

the 2005-opened station at Glasshoughton, near Castleford, is a huge generator of traffic, with at least 60 people joining the mid Saturday afternoon Leeds-bound service I was travelling on.

Four major developments in the West Midlands

Apart from the huge developments that have taken place across London, the other area of England to have seen the most significant expansion of its heavy rail infrastructure is the West Midlands. This can be broken down into four major developments, which began in the late 1970s, continues up to the present day, and comprises the re-opening of Birmingham Snow Hill and the development of cross-city services based on the former Great Western Railway station, the highly-successful cross-city line from Lichfield to Longbridge and soon to Bromsgrove, the Chase Line from Walsall to Rugeley and finally the Leamington Spa–Coventry–Nuneaton axis and new stations along it.

As mentioned in my Introduction, Birmingham Snow Hill, at the heart of England's second city, has been transformed since the early 1970s from the world's largest unstaffed halt into a major commuter hub used by some five million passengers a year. That process began after 15 years of closure with its re-opening as a four-platform station in October 1987, along with re-opening of the Snow Hill tunnel, immediately to the south of the station, to enable local services from Leamington Spa and Stratford-upon-Avon to continue on from Birmingham Moor Street station, at the southern end of the tunnel, to the revived city centre station.

Many of these suburban trains had been diverted into Birmingham's other principal station, New Street, but this was

Chiltern Railways began by using Class 67 diesels on its popular *Mainline Silver* services from London Marylebone to Birmingham Moor Street and Kidderminster. Services now are in the hands of recently-delivered Class 68s, including 68013, seen here after arrival at Moor Street on 23 January 2016.

already suffering from the congestion that has blighted it ever since and Moor Street – only a short walk from New Street – had been used as the terminus for many of the services on these routes after closure of Snow Hill tunnel in March 1968. A further increase in services to Snow Hill came in May 1993 with the launch of direct services to London Marylebone, which later became part of the Chiltern Railways franchise following rail privatisation and where an initial frequency of one train every two hours was increased, first to hourly and now to a half-hourly service throughout the day.

Rebirth of Snow Hill as a through station came in September 1995 when services from Worcester and Kidderminster which had previously been terminating at New Street were diverted to Snow Hill as part of the Jewellery Line development, which saw a connection from Smethwick West – which had closed in 1972 – re-opened. This scheme included three intermediate stations at Smethwick Galton Bridge (a new interchange station with high level platforms on this line and low level platforms on the main Birmingham–Wolverhampton route), The Hawthorns and Jewellery Quarter. Services were then able to operate as a second cross-city route from the Leamington Spa and Stratford-upon-Avon lines through Snow Hill and on to Kidderminster, Worcester or Hereford.

London Midland 172215 approaches The Hawthorns on 23 January 2016 with a southbound cross-city service to Whitlock's End. Note the overhead wiring of the adjacent Midland Metro line from Wolverhampton to Birmingham.

Continuing growth of the cross-city line

The busiest suburban route outside the London area is Birmingham's cross-city line linking Lichfield to the north with Redditch and Bromsgrove to the south. This is a route that has been developed in stages over a period of some four decades, with its origins dating back to May 1978, when an existing diesel operated service from Lichfield City and Four Oaks to Birmingham New Street was extended to Longbridge, following the re-opening of a station at Five Ways, the upgrading of stations at Bournville, Kings Norton and Northfields and the opening of two new stations at University (for Birmingham University) and at Longbridge.

Cross-city services were an immediate success and, two years after launch, they were extended hourly to Redditch, bringing regular commuter services to the New Town, along with the stations at Barnt Green and Alvechurch, with a loop later being installed at the latter station to allow the service frequency to be increased. Prior to Alvechurch's re-build the branch line from Barnt Green could only accommodate two trains per hour, but with completion of the station's re-build the basic weekday frequency was increased from December 2014 to three trains per hour an hour.

Services were extended northwards to make an interchange with the West Coast Main Line at Lichfield Trent Valley in November 1988, while electrification of the cross-city line was undertaken between 1991 and 1993. At this time a number of stations along the route were rebuilt to cope with the longer trains formed of Class 323 electric multiple units, which were introduced on the line to replace the 'slam door' class 116 diesel multiple units which had worked the line until then. The latest development will see an extension of electrification southwards from Barnt Green and down the famous Lickey Incline as far as Bromsgrove, where a new four-platform station has been built to accommodate the vastly improved service that will result from extending services which had previously terminated at Longbridge on to Barnt Green and Bromsgrove.

At the opposite end of the cross-city line, there are hopes that the section of line heading northwards from Lichfield Trent Valley to Wichnor Junction on the main Birmingham to Derby line, mid-way between Tamworth and Burton-on-Trent, may one day see a revival of passenger traffic. It has remained in use as a freight and diversionary route long after the loss of its passenger services, as well as being used for rolling stock movements between Birmingham and the Bombardier maintenance depot at Central Rivers. Revival would be particularly welcome news to the villagers of Alrewas, the only significant settlement along the line. They lost their station in January 1965, but a survey in 2014 showed more than 80 per cent of residents favoured re-opening the station, and substantial planned residential development in this part of East Staffordshire has given added weight to calls for a re-opening of the line and station to passenger traffic.

Chase Line goes from strength to strength

As a major population centre and the West Midlands' largest industrial town, Walsall has always enjoyed a good rail link to Birmingham, with the commuter service electrified in 1966 at the time the West Coast electrification from London to Crewe was completed. But as a passenger station, Walsall had become a terminus the previous year when services northwards from the town on the 15-mile link to the West Coast Main Line at Rugeley Trent Valley fell victim to Dr Beeching. That situation continued for more than two decades until a start was made on one of the major rail re-opening schemes in England, with the restoration in April 1989 of passenger services on part of the route, from Walsall as far as Hednesford.

Like large sections of the Robin Hood Line in the East Midlands, the Chase Line had long outlasted the ending of passenger services in 1965, as it served a number of local coal mines and industrial locations. It also provided access to the two Rugeley Power Stations and saw occasional use as a diversionary route for longer distance freight and passenger services. Re-opening to passenger services proved a protracted process – Hednesford remained the northern terminus of services until the section to Rugeley Town re-opened in June 1997, with the final connection to Trent Valley opening the following year, when services on the line were extended from Rugeley through to Stafford on the West Coast Main Line.

Passenger traffic has developed substantially, with numbers using Hednesford having almost doubled from 95,112 in 2004/5 to 167,000 in 2015/6, while at Rugeley Town the count rose from 89,703 to 141,000 during the same period. But there have been setbacks. In 2008 direct service to Stafford were withdrawn in order to free up vital capacity on the WCML, with services then terminating at Rugeley Trent Valley. Two years later, in December 2010, the half-hourly services which the line had enjoyed was cut back to hourly during weekday off-peak periods, due to a reduction in local authority funding, although remaining half-hourly on Saturdays and at peak times. But the line's future became a good deal brighter when a £30 million plan to electrify the route was announced in July 2012.

Electrification of the route is scheduled to have been completed by December 2017, when the route will also have been re-signalled – with the closure of three remaining signal boxes – and the line speed is being raised from its current 45 mph to 75 mph to reduce journey times. Platforms at intermediate stations have been lengthened to accommodate longer trains once the electrification project has been completed, with hopes being raised by local management that the half-hourly off-peak service frequency can be restored and even that the line might eventually see direct services via Birmingham to London.

New links to Coventry

To the south east of Birmingham are two re-opened lines centred on the city of Coventry, one being the 10-mile link south to Leamington Spa while the other is a 10-mile line heading northward to a junction with the West Coast Main Line at Nuneaton. Local services on both routes fell victim to Dr Beeching in 1965, after which both survived as diversionary routes, with the Coventry–Leamington Spa section re-opened to regular long distance passenger traffic following the opening of Birmingham International station in January 1976. This led to most cross-country services from Birmingham to Oxford and destinations in the south being diverted away from the former Great Western route via Solihull, so that they could serve the new station, which had been built principally to serve Birmingham Airport and the National Exhibition Centre.

Growth of services on the Coventry–Leamington Spa route has been hampered by the fact that most of it is single track, but one major planned development is the re-opening of an intermediate station at Kenilworth, the principal town on the route. This has been on the cards for many years – having first been formally proposed in the in 2008–09 Warwickshire Local Transport Plan, but the project has been beset by delays. In July 2009 construction group John Laing won a 20-year contract to design, build, and operate a new station, but was unable to secure the necessary funding and withdrew its plan two years later. However, in 2013 the Department for Transport approved £5 million of funding towards the £12 million cost of a new station. Work finally got under way, but planned opening has slipped, and is currently scheduled for December 2017.

By contrast to the Leamington Spa route, with its regular long distance trains, but no local service yet established, the line from Coventry to Nuneaton only has a local passenger service, together with freight traffic to a number of locations along the line and is occasionally used as a diversionary route. It was re-opened to passengers in May 1987, 22 years after first losing its passenger services, and a year later a first new intermediate station was opened at Bedworth. More recently, two further stations have opened.

One of these, Bermuda Park, is close to Nuneaton and serves an industrial estate of the same name, while the other, Coventry Arena, is close to the Ricoh Arena station, home of Coventry City FC and Wasps Rugby Club. But in a peculiarly British twist, until services have been enhanced and trains on the line lengthened, visitors to sporting events at the Ricoh Arena were being advised not to try to travel there by train to avoid over-crowding on the single coach Class 153 DMU used on passenger services!

Early revivals north of London – the Hertford and Southbury loops

Two of the earliest examples of successful re-openings in England that pre-date Beeching were lines to the north of London which had survived as diversionary routes. First of these to be revived was a nine-mile long stretch of what is known as the Hertford Loop Line, from Hertford North to Stevenage, which has remained an important diversionary route for the East Coast Main Line, but which had lost its passenger service as early as 1939.

Limited services were revived in the 1950s, but the line came into its own with the first stage of ECML electrification, when regular services from Stevenage to London (Kings Cross and Moorgate) began in 1977 and one of two former intermediate stations, Watton-at-Stone, re-opened in May 1982. A local campaign saw the re-building cost met by a combination of British Rail, local authority and funds raised from villagers. Today the delightful village is served by hourly trains from Stevenage to Moorgate on weekdays and London Kings Cross at weekends. Passenger numbers continue to grow steadily – rising from 102,000 in 2004/5 to 162,000 in 2014/15.

Second of the two routes to re-open was the six-mile Southbury loop from Edmonton Green to Cheshunt, which had been closed in 1919, but was re-opened to passenger services on electrification of the Lea Valley route in November 1960 along with three intermediate stations (Southbury, Turkey Street and Theobalds Grove).

The London Overground phenomenon

London has changed dramatically in the half century since the Beeching closures were at their height across England, Scotland and Wales. While the overall population of Greater London did not increase substantially in that time, travel patterns have altered beyond recognition. Congestion on the roads has encouraged more and more of the capital's workforce to commute daily into the capital, with improved rail links making that feasible, albeit expensive, from an ever-widening swathe of Southern England and the Home Counties. A recent announcement on fare rises, for example, quoted the £9,000 plus price of an annual season ticket to London from my home town, Cheltenham – a two-hours each way journey which no right minded person would have even have contemplated in my youth!

On the face of it, much of the capital's surface level railway network has remained unchanged since the 1960s, with the exception of the progressive development of the Thameslink corridor and, more recently, the construction of Crossrail – both of which feature in Chapter 7. One major development was opening in August 1987 of the first sections of Docklands Light Railway – routes from Tower Gateway to Stratford and North Greenwich.

Since those modest beginnings the DLR has been progressively and successfully developed with a series of extensions and new branches now encompassing Bank, Lewisham, Stratford International, Woolwich and Beckton, with further extension to Barking on the cards.

Principal developments below ground have been significant extensions to the London Underground network, with the Victoria Line opening in stages from 1968–72, the Piccadilly Line's Heathrow extensions in 1977 (Heathrow Central), 1984 (T4) and 2008 (T5), creation of the Jubilee Line from the Stanmore branch of the Bakerloo Line and its opening to Charing Cross in 1979, then its major extension to Canary Wharf and Stratford, which opened in 1999. On the debit side, 1994 saw closure of the Piccadilly Line branch from Holborn to Aldwych and the Central Line extension from Epping to Ongar.

One line which survived Dr Beeching, however, has been transformed out of all recognition over the past half century and is at the heart of what I have called the London Overground phenomenon. This is the North London Line, once a Cinderella route, which took a circuitous path from the former Broad Street station, next to Liverpool Street in the heart of the City, all the way around north and west London to a terminus and interchange at Richmond. In 1976 my first home as a student in London was close to Camden Road station on this route and I fondly remember taking advantage of a special 44p off-peak go anywhere fare to escape what was then a less-than-fashionable part of the capital to visit delightful riverside pubs in Richmond!

Back in those far off mid-1970s the North London was worked by ageing three-car Class 313 electric units running at a 20 minute frequency, the same units that were used on the Euston–Watford Junction services, with which they connected at Willesden Junction. But changes were afoot, the first of these being in 1979 when services on another Cinderella line, the branch from North Woolwich to Stratford, were extended to Camden Road. At the time of its re-opening there were no intermediate stations, but a quartet was to follow, with Hackney Wick and Hackney Central opening in 1980, Dalston Kingsland in 1983 and Homerton in 1985.

Once the line from Camden Road to North Woolwich had been electrified (third rail) in 1985, the service pattern was changed, with all trains running from North Woolwich to Richmond. The City terminus at Broad Street had lost its peak hour services from Welwyn Garden City and Hertford North in 1976, when British Rail took over the former Northern Line branch from Moorgate to Finsbury Park, diverting Welwyn and Hertford services onto this route, and the loss of regular Richmond services left only a limited peak time service to and from Watford Junction via Primrose Hill using the station.

A booming City property market made the Broad Street site ripe for redevelopment and, after the original station was demolished and journeys curtailed to a temporary platform north of the old station, services finally came to an end in June 1986, leading to the closure of Dalston Junction station at the same time. The limited remaining peak time service from Watford Junction was diverted to Liverpool Street station via a connection that had been built from the North London Line just south of Hackney Downs station. But the service was now extremely indirect and was finally withdrawn in 1992, when Primrose Hill station was also closed, amid a significant level of protest.

Electric services on what was called the North London Link were initially operated by two-coach former Southern Region electric multiple units, but their limited capacity meant that they were replaced by more modern three-coach Class 313 units. Big changes began in December 2006 when the eastern end of the route from Stratford to North Woolwich was closed to allow construction of the Docklands Light Railway. But the real transformation was launched the following year (November 2007) when services on this route were transferred to Transport for London (TfL), along

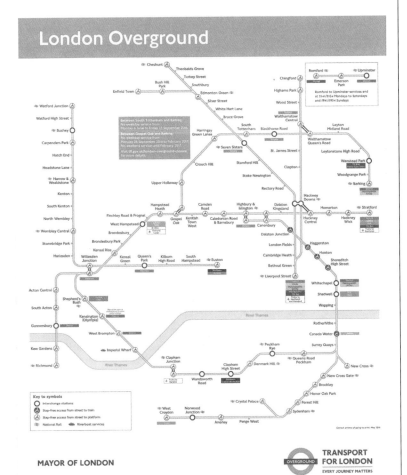

London Overground

MAYOR OF LONDON

TRANSPORT FOR LONDON
EVERY JOURNEY MATTERS

London's successful Overground network incorporates a number of revived routes, including Kensington Olympia to Willesden Junction, Highbury & Islington to Stratford and Canonbury to Shoreditch, as well as a new link from the former East London Line south of Surrey Quays to the former South London Line near Queens Road Peckham. Map courtesy of Transport for London

with those on the routes from Euston to Watford Junction and on another Beeching escapee, the diesel-operated route (now finally being electrified) from Gospel Oak (previously Kentish Town) to Barking. London Overground was born.

For many years there had been talk of creating orbital rail services around the capital, but the opportunity to turn this into a reality came when London Overground swallowed up the East London Line section of London Underground in 2010. It also absorbed another Beeching escapee, the West London Line service from Clapham Junction to Kensington Olympia, which had been extended to Willesden Junction in 1994, to provide both connections and through services onto the former North London Line. Stations were all given a significant make-over and undertakings made that they would be staffed for their entire opening hours, while a new livery was adopted, new rolling stock ordered (the Class 378 units) and the contactless Oyster ticket payment system was extended to the Overground network.

The West London Line is an excellent example of how an entire transport corridor, little served by underground services, has been successfully opened up and developed into a thriving and core part of the capital's public transport infrastructure. Clapham Junction to Kensington Olympia had seen limited services operated, principally for postal workers heading to Olympia, while the exhibition station had also seen use as a Motorail terminal, a diversionary terminus when Paddington had been closed and limited use by cross country services from the north to south coast destinations. But re-opening the route through to Willesden Junction in 1994 created a host of new journey opportunities and, besides electrification, the line has since seen further significant development, with the opening of platforms at

A London Overground Class 378 unit heads across Battersea Railway Bridge on 14 May 2016 with a northbound service from Clapham Junction, which is about to call at 2009-opened Imperial Wharf station.

West Brompton, adjacent to the District Line station, in 1999 and of two new stations – Shepherds Bush in 2008 and Imperial Wharf in 2009.

Absorption of the East London into London Overground was effectively the third part of delivering the holy grail of a London orbital railway. Services from Shoreditch and Whitechapel to New Cross and New Cross Gate had been run by London Underground as an isolated section of the Metropolitan Line, whose most famous structure is the splendid twin-bore Thames Tunnel, which had been built by Marc and Isambard Kingdom Brunel, opened in 1843 for pedestrians and horse drawn traffic, but was taken over by the East London Railway Company and saw its first trains in 1869. As part of the transfer to London Overground, underground trains ceased in December 2007, with the route re-opening in April 2010, having been extended northwards from Shoreditch to Dalston Junction. This utilised the viaduct abandoned since the ending of services from Broad Street station in 1986, with the station at Shoreditch resited onto a new section of viaduct and new stations opened at Haggerston, Hoxton and Dalston Junction.

Less than a month after services were first launched between Dalston Junction and New Cross/New Cross Gate, on 23 May 2010 services were extended at the southern end of the route to West Croydon and Crystal Palace via New Cross Gate, with certain services continuing to serve New Cross, where they connected with South Eastern suburban routes to Dartford and Sevenoaks. At the northern end of the line, the final piece of the jigsaw was put into place in February 2011 when a new curve from Dalston Junction onto the original North London Line was opened, so that trains could run through to Canonbury and Highbury & Islington, an important interchange for Victoria line, national rail services to

Long-awaited electrification of London Overground's Gospel Oak to Barking route will ease pressure on the North London Line, where freight has to compete for paths with the intense passenger service. On 14 May 2016, Freightliner 90042 passes Camden Road with a long container train from Felixstowe bound for the West Coast Main Line.

Hertford North and Welwyn Garden City, as well as westbound London Overground services to Clapham Junction and Richmond.

One final transfer of a former British Rail service completed the circle back to Clapham junction when, in December 2012, the former South London Line service, which had shuttled between London Bridge and London Victoria stations, was replaced by another extension to the London Overground network. A new chord opened between Surrey Quays and Queens Road Peckham stations, which allowed the launch of services from Highbury & Islington directly to Clapham Junction, bringing vastly improved

Camden Junction, just west of Camden Road station, once boasted both third rail and overhead electrification, but the former has now been removed. London Overground 378217 crosses the junction on 14 May 2016 with a Stratford-bound service. The lines to the left lost their passenger service in 1992, but are used by the heavy freight traffic from Felixstowe and Tilbury to access the nearby West Coast Main Line.

Looking west from Hackney Central station on 14 May 2016, the covered walkway to Hackney Downs can been seen on the right as a Class 378 bound for Stratford is passed overhead by a London Overground Class 317 service from Liverpool Street that is about to enter Hackney Downs station.

services to two stations in particular, Clapham High Street and Wandsworth Road, which had for many years been sparsely used due to their limited rail services. The impact of these new services has been dramatic – at Clapham High Street passenger numbers rose ten-fold from 200,000 in 2006/7 to 3.3m in 2015/6, while at Wandsworth Road passenger numbers increased from 164,000 in 2006/7 to 830,000 in 2015/6.

Using London Overground it is now possible to make an entire circuit of the capital from Clapham Junction without changing platform and with one single change of train (at Highbury &

City skyscrapers, including the distinctive point of the Gherkin, form a backdrop as London Overground 378210 approaches Hoxton station on 14 May 2016 with a northbound service to Highbury & Islington. It is travelling on the viaduct which once gave access to the City's former Broad Street station.

The complexity of railway junctions in South West London can be appreciated in this view from the footbridge at Wandsworth Road station on 14 May 2016, where London Overground 378154 approaches from Clapham Junction as a Southeastern Class 377 unit heads north towards Victoria station.

Islington). Travelling on one of the new five-coach Class 378 units from Clapham Junction is an easy way to appreciate just how remarkably passenger levels have grown, with huge numbers travelling on services which run a 15-minute frequency seven days a week, with a 10-minute frequency on the core section from Willesden Junction to Stratford, where the Westfield shopping centre has become a huge generator of leisure travel along the route.

Away from the London Overground network – at least until it swallows up even more of London's suburban rail services – one notable re-opening has been Lea Bridge station on the fringe of Hackney Marshes in north-east London. This saw the return of passengers on 15 May 2016, almost 31 years after it lost its services when a little used route from Tottenham Hale to Stratford was closed in July 1985. The route had re-opened to regular passenger services in 2005 with the introduction of services from the Lea Valley direct to Stratford, but it took another 11 years and £11 million before the re-opening of Lea Bridge. Its basic seven days a week service is a half-hourly train from Stratford to Bishops Stortford, with extras at peak times, and the target is for more than 350,000 passengers a year to eventually be using the re-opened station.

Railways to Runways

As demand for air travel rose inexorably during the 1970s and 1980s there was growing demand for better links to major airports in the London area. While Gatwick had always benefited from its adjacent station on the London–Brighton main line, Heathrow only got connected when the Piccadilly tube line was extended there in 1977 and it still meant a that the world's busiest international was around one hour by rail from Central London. Perhaps surprisingly, then, the first major airport rail link to be built after the Piccadilly Line extension was a branch to Stansted Airport off the main line route from Liverpool Street station in the City to Cambridge.

Stansted Airport had been identified as London's third major airport and a key feature of its expansion was the provision of a dedicated rail link to the capital, 37 miles away. A key feature of the 3½ mile long branch line is a 1.3 mile long single-track tunnel under the airport runway and it was a great pleasure for me, as a business journalist at the time on *The Sunday Times*, to be invited by contractors J. Murphy & Sons and British Rail's Network SouthEast business unit to a celebratory lunch on 23 October 1989 in the middle of the tunnel to mark completion of the tunnelling work! Like the 'topping out' of a building project, there is apparently a long tradition that completion of tunnelling works is similarly celebrated with a major subterranean event for all those involved in its construction.

Services branded Stansted Express were launched in 1991, initially at a half-hourly frequency, but later increased to every 15 minutes, with a less than express journey time to Liverpool Street of around 50 minutes, including two intermediate stops en route. Using a northerly curve from the branch to the main line is an hourly cross country service to Cambridge, Peterborough and Birmingham New Street. Passenger traffic on the branch has inevitably reflected the airports fluctuating fortunes, with the 3.822 million passengers recorded in 2004/5 soaring to 5.522 million in 2007/8, before the impact of recession and financial crisis sent passenger numbers tumbling for the next five years to a 2013/4 total of 3.685 million, recovering to 6.0 million in 2015/6.

Having become London's principal international airport when it opened in 1946, it is remarkable how long it took for rails to reach Heathrow. While the Piccadilly Line arrived in 1977, it was not until June 1998 that the privately-funded Heathrow Express arrived, following completion of a four-mile branch line which connects with the Great Western Main Line from London Paddington to Reading at Hayes & Harlington. Construction of the £150 million link, largely funded by BAA (the privatised former British Airports Authority) had included two five-mile long tunnels and the development of new stations at Heathrow Central and the new Terminal 4.

Heathrow Express is technically an Open Access operator, like Grand Central and First Hull Trains, and has an access agreement for use of the lines into Paddington until 2023. Express services run every 15 minutes and, since 2008 have been diverted at Heathrow Central to terminate at a new station serving the airport's newest terminal, Terminal 5. Passengers arriving on Heathrow Express services can now only reach Terminal 4 by changing onto a shuttle service from Heathrow Central that is open for free inter-terminal transfer by all airport users. A further development of services was the launch in 2005 of a stopping service, branded Heathrow Connect, which offers slightly lower fares that the notoriously expensive Express service and provides an interchange at Ealing Broadway with London Underground services.

While rail links between Heathrow and Central London are now very good, that is not the case for links to the west and south, and has led to numerous proposals being developed for new lines that would significantly improve airport access. After abandonment of the ambitious BAA-promoted Heathrow Airtrack scheme in 2011, the latest attempt to establish better rail links has been a Network Rail proposal for a new rail tunnel to the airport from a junction on the Great Western main line between Langley and Iver, stations. This would give direct services to Heathrow from Reading via Slough, with the proposed new tunnel giving capacity for a service of four trains an hour. If all goes according to Network Rail's timetable, the new link could be operating by the end of 2021.

While London City Airport was once served by North London Link services calling at the now closed nearby Silvertown station, it now has its own station today on the ever-expanding Docklands Light Railway. Meantime, two other airports in the London area to have seen their rail links substantially improved are those at Luton and Southend. Luton Airport is inconveniently located at the top of a hill and was some distance from the town it serves, so in 1999 a new station called Luton Airport Parkway was opened one mile south of the town's principal station and little more than a mile west of the airport itself, to which it is linked by a dedicated shuttle bus service.

More recently, a new station was opened in 2011 to serve Southend Airport. This was privately funded by the Stobart transport group, which had recently acquired the airport and was investing in improving its facilities to attract new airlines as well as passengers. It is rather better located than Luton's airport station, being immediately adjacent to the airport itself, and is served by the three trains an hour running on the commuter route from London Liverpool Street to Southend Victoria.

A trio of successes in the south

Away from the London area, re-openings have been relatively few and far between across Southern England, but a trio of relatively modest successes centred on Melksham in Wiltshire, Chandlers Ford in Hampshire and Yeovil on the Somerset/Dorset border, point the way to what is still to come. The Portishead to Bristol line, the East–West line and a host of other schemes such as Uckfield–Lewes are being actively promoted and are described more fully in Chapters 8 and 9.

Improved services at Melksham station have been a huge success, but the short platform means that when a three-car train calls, only the first door can be opened. On Saturday 2 April 2016, when the station was being served by diverted services from Portsmouth Harbour, Great Western Railway 158961, forming the 11.26 service to Swindon, does good business at the re-opened Wiltshire station.

First up of the trio to be resurrected was Melksham, a town of some 20,000 people that lies ten miles east of Bath and which lost its station when the 12-mile long link from Trowbridge to Chippenham, now branded as the TransWilts Line, fell victim to Dr Beeching's axe in April 1966. Having survived as a diversionary route, it re-opened in 1985 but since that time TransWilts' fortunes have ebbed and flowed: at its low point the route saw its five daily passenger services cut to just two a day and a second closure was a very real possibility. But that position has since been transformed, thanks to diligent campaigning led by a local businessman, Graham Ellis.

The real catalyst for change came in 2013 when financial support from the Local Sustainable Transport Fund was given by the Department for Transport to Wiltshire County Council to substantially improve services on the line for an experimental period of three years. That led to the timetable being massively improved in December 2013, when services were increased to eight return journeys a day on weekdays (since increased to nine) and six on Sundays, a move which led to a dramatic increase in passenger journeys – in the first year of the new timetable passenger numbers had been forecast at 45,000 but were actually more than four times that figure – 183,000.

With many of these passengers not just being commuters making faster or cheaper local journeys, but those discovering the convenience of Melksham to make trips further afield, the future of this line looks bright. Two-car trains are due to replace the current single car Class 153 units in use currently on the route during 2017 and although not yet featuring in Network Rail's forward plans, there is the potential for eventually upgrading the line's signalling and installing a passing loop or double track, which would allow an increase in service frequency to hourly.

Much credit for Melksham station's success goes to Graham Ellis, a local businessman and Community Rail Officer of the TransWilts Community Rail Partnership, seen at the station on 2 April 2016.

Great Western Railway 158953 passes the single coach platform at Melksham with a diverted service from Swindon to Portsmouth Harbour on 2 April 2016. Work to extend the platform is due to take place before the end of Network Rail's Control Period 5 (CP5) in 2019.

Almost 100 miles from Paddington: Great Western Railway 158952 approaches milepost 99¾, north of Melksham on 2 April 2016 with a Swindon–Portsmouth Harbour service. The normal Cardiff–Portsmouth service was being diverted to and from Swindon in connection with track closure for electrification work in the Bath area.

Melksham approaches Meltdown

When rail services between Chippenham and Trowbridge were experimentally and dramatically improved in December 2013, patronage on the route began to grow and grow. Graham Ellis, Community Rail Officer of the TransWilts Community Rail Partnership, explained to me how it has been achieved, what it has meant to the line's intermediate station of Melksham, and his group's hopes for direct trains to Southampton Airport.

Raising awareness of the improved services

'Promotion has been remarkably easy – this has been a line that has been waiting to be done, but it's about coming to the heart of the community. We are looking to reach people in a town with a population of between 20,000 and 30,000, depending on where you draw the line, which hasn't had a decent train service for 50 years. So you are looking at the changing the hearts and minds within this town.

'In Melksham, awareness of the station and service has gone up from 20% of people knowing about it before the improved service was launched to 60% of people knowing about it. Of course knowing about it doesn't necessarily mean you are going to use it. But it is coming along: get people to try it out once and they are hooked!

'You saw the crowds getting on the train you arrived on [around 20 people boarded the 11.26 to Swindon on Saturday, 2 April 2016, when Swindon Town were playing a home match] and I think we are achieving our aims, but to do so you have to have a service which is joined up and which allows people to not only get to where they want to go, but also to get back, and does not just provide half of what they need.

'We have the advantage in having the county town of Trowbridge and the major junction of Westbury at one end of the route and the growing towns of Chippenham and Swindon at the northern end. People commuting by rail from Westbury/Trowbridge to Chippenham/Swindon are typically saving 20 minutes on their journey, plus saving themselves a difficult connection at Bath, and paying a significantly lower fare for the direct service.'

Principal passenger flows on the line

'We did a survey when we spoke to everybody on the train and we found that over a three day period there were over 100 starting and ending destinations, everything from Motherwell to Aberystwyth! The busiest section of the line is from Melksham to Chippenham, with the 17.36 from Swindon on weekdays being full, standing and up the aisle, and the same thing happens on a Saturday match day [Swindon Town home game]. We've also had 84 passengers on a Sunday [in a single coach train] so it's getting a bit silly.

'The current run rate of passengers using the section of route between Chippenham and Trowbidge is around 230,000 a year. At Melksham we have seen station entries rise from 12,000 to 24,000 and then to 58,000 over the past three years. If we look at passenger journeys per head of population for Wiltshire towns, then for that 58,000 to rise to the level of the next worst town in terms of journeys per head of population, would see us at between 300,000 and 400,000 journeys a year from Melksham, so there is potential for five or six fold growth from current numbers!

'The limiting factor now is the trains. Two-coach trains [due from spring 2017] are not enough, but there is a limit to what can be done, and we have said to GWR and to the county council that if they see any tailing off in the level of passenger growth, it will be because they are not providing the capacity.'

Future improvements:

'Lengthening the platform at Melksham [from one to three-coaches] is part of Network Rail's plans for the GW Main Line electrification. It is being done at Network Rail's expense and will certainly happen within the current Control Period [CP5: 2014–19]. If you start stopping trains longer than one carriage at the current platform [as was happening on the day of my visit] you end up increasing your station dwell time because everyone has to use a single set of doors on the train.

'I don't think major infrastructure improvements on the route are necessary. Looking at this fortnight, when diversion of Portsmouth–Cardiff services to Swindon [during work on GWML electrification between Bristol and Bath] means we have an hourly train going up and down the line and, if the experience of similar diversions in August 2015 is anything to go by, it is going to be reliable.

'What we do have is an aspiration for a mid-section signal [there is currently no signalling on the route], line-speed improvement at Thingley Junction [west of Chippenham] where there is a long section of 'wrong line' running, and re-instating bay platforms at both Chippenham and Westbury. These are far more important than re-doubling, or a new passing loop, at the moment.

'We already have two trains a day which run through to Salisbury – although nothing coming back. What we would like to see is our trains linked up to the Westbury–Warminster service, carrying on through to Salisbury and linking up to the Salisbury to Romsey service. That would give you services from Swindon and Chippenham directly to Southampton Airport, with all trains of the same type, so you don't have oddities in capacity.

'The Romsey–Salisbury service currently sits in the bay platform at Salisbury for 40 minutes every hour. If you put six trains onto this service – taking the existing three on this current South West Trains service, two from Great Western and the one

*from Salisbury to Swindon that sits in the bay at Swindon for 75
minutes in every 120 minutes, and you look at some reorganisation
of stock, then you are not far short of having the stock to do it.'*

A second south of England re-opening – this time in the era of a
privatised railway network – was a seven-mile long route from
Eastleigh to Romsey to the north of Southampton in Hampshire.
Having survived largely as a diversionary route, the mainly rural
single-track line re-opened, along with an intermediate station
at Chandlers Ford, in May 2003, almost 34 years to the day since
passenger services had fallen victim to Dr Beeching in 1969.
Services today are operated by South West Trains using Class
158/9 units in an hourly 'lasso' shaped route from Salisbury via
Romsey and Southampton to Chandlers Ford and on to Romsey.
As elsewhere, there has been strong growth in passenger traffic,
with numbers using Chandlers Ford station rising from 155,000 in
2004/5 to 224,000 in 2015/6.

The shortest and newest of re-openings in Southern England
(and one that is particularly dear to my heart) has been the limited
revival in December 2015 of services on the two-mile connection
between Yeovil Pen Mill station on the former Great Western route
from Bristol and Westbury to Weymouth and Yeovil Junction, on
the former London & South Western Railway route from London
Waterloo to Salisbury and Exeter. This has restored a direct link
between the two lines for the first time since the connecting shuttle
service was withdrawn in 1968, and opens up a host of new
journey opportunities.

For almost 50 years passengers using Yeovil Junction have
had to rely on a bus link between the two stations which, as I

On Sunday 1
November 2015,
passengers alight from
South West Trains
158883 at re-opened
(2003) Chandlers
Ford station, between
Eastleigh and Romsey.

discovered on a trip to the town, can sometimes be held up in the town centre, with the result that a vital connection at Pen Mill is missed. The new rail service does not yet compete with the frequency of the bus service, and Pen Mill itself is a brisk ten minute walk from the town centre, but it has established a totally new rail link to London Waterloo via Castle Cary, Bruton and Frome. Once firmly established, one hopes that South West Trains will see the potential in providing a full service to connect with the hourly London Waterloo–Exeter services at Yeovil Junction.

Survivors thriving in the South West

While the South West was hard hit by Beeching, with rail all but eliminated in North Cornwall with the loss of the former London & South Western routes to Bude and Padstow, there were a number of notable escapees which have since prospered. In Bristol, for example, the one remaining suburban branch line from Bristol Temple Meads to Avonmouth and Severn Beach has seen traffic increase dramatically, in part due to a low zonal-based flat fare of either £2 or £3 return which was introduced in 2012. It now forms part of an ambitious metro plan for the Bristol area, which would see an increase in the current service frequency and the eventual extension of services to either Bath or Portishead, once the line to that latter destination has been re-opened (see chapter 8).

Looking further west, another Beeching escapee which goes from strength to strength is the branch line from Exeter to Exmouth, the last remaining part of an East Devon network that once included routes from Exmouth to Sidmouth Junction and another branch off that route from Tipton St. John to Sidmouth, both of which fell

Cheap flat fares have helped stimulate huge growth in passenger numbers on Bristol's only suburban line – the scenic branch to Severn Beach. On 29 May 2010, Pacer 143621 stands at Avonmouth with a service for Bristol Temple Meads.

Newest of the three stations to have opened on the highly successful Exeter–Exmouth Avocet Line, which Beeching had earmarked for closure, is Newcourt. It opened on 4 June 2015 and a little more than six months later was doing good business on 19 December 2015, when 150127 called with an afternoon service for Barnstaple.

victim to Beeching on 6 March 1967. Like the Severn Beach line in Bristol, what is now known as the Avocet Line has developed into a vitally important commuter route into Exeter, with a basic half-hourly service frequency and three new stations opened along the 10-mile branch line – Lympstone Commando (1976), Digby & Sowton (1995) and Newcourt (2015). The latter two stations are not only the site of major residential development, but are also close to Sandy Park, the 12,500-seater stadium that is home to the Exeter Chiefs premiership rugby team.

In another parallel with Bristol, the most recent of this trio of new stations forms part of a proposed Devon Metro scheme that aims to improve rail connectivity across Exeter. Besides another new Avocet Line station at Monkerton, this also envisages a half-hourly frequency on the former London & South Western route from Exeter to Axminster, on which a new £5 million station serving the embryonic new town of Cranbrook finally opened in December 2015, as well as potential new stations on the Great Western Main Line, at Marsh Barton, south of Exeter St David's station and at Cullompton to the north.

The Devon Metro proposal document points out that patronage on the Exmouth route, with its half-hourly frequency, is considerably greater than on the route from Exeter to Torquay and Paignton, known as the Riviera Line, which only has an hourly service. However, a half-hourly frequency of local trains on this route is set to be introduced in December 2018, following the success of a 'Citizens' Rail' project which ran from May 2012 to December 2015 and supported an experimental introduction of a half-hourly frequency on the section of route between Newton Abbot and Paignton.

The remarkable Looe branch line in Cornwall, another Beeching escapee, runs from a platform at Liskeard that is at a right angle to the main line platforms and boasts period features in the form of early Western Region chocolate and cream signage. On Friday, 2 August 2013, passengers wait to board the 16.41 departure for Looe.

Elsewhere in the South West, the delightful Cornish branch line from Liskeard to Looe was a Beeching escapee, as was another remarkably successful line and the most south westerly branch line in England. This is the highly scenic 4¼ mile route along the Hayle estuary from St Erth, the last station on the Great Western main line before Penzance, and the holiday resort of St Ives. As with the other Cornish branch lines, it has benefited from its designation as a community railway and from support by the Devon and Cornwall Rail Partnership, which contributes to publicity for the line's tourist attractions.

St Ives has totally inadequate parking facilities for the many thousands of summer visitors, so a major factor in the line's growing passenger numbers has been development of a large park and ride facility which opened in 1978 at Lelant Saltings, less than a mile from St Erth. Travelling towards the terminus

Journey's end at Looe, 8¾ miles from Liskeard, where holidaymakers alight on Friday 2 August 2013 and day-trippers prepare to join the 17.15 return service.

Britain's most south westerly junction is St Erth, a delightful station complete with signal box, semaphore signalling, and a charming independently-run station buffet. On Saturday 3 August 2013, passengers board First Great Western 150246/249, forming the 11.48 departure to St. Ives.

on a summer Saturday it was amazing to see the hordes of holidaymakers waiting to board the four-carriage train I was on for the short journey to St Ives. Passenger numbers at St Ives have risen from 220,300 in 2004/5 to 658,000 in 2015/6, according to ORR figures, while at Lelant Saltings the growth has been even more spectacular, with a seven-fold rise in passenger numbers over that decade, from 18,281 in 2004/5 to 125,000 in 2015/6.

Hordes of summer holidaymakers alight at St Ives off the 11.31 arrival from St Erth, on 3 August 2013. Most will have joined the train at Lelant Saltings, the huge park and ride facility just ¾ mile from St Erth.

Chapter 4

RE-BUILDING SCOTLAND'S RAILWAY

Within Network Rail's Route Plan for Scotland, which set out its vision for the rail network north of the border for the period 2014–19 (known as Control Period 5) and beyond, there is one sentence which neatly sums up the story of post-Beeching revival in Scotland. It reads: 'We have witnessed some highly successful line re-openings in the past few years, such as Airdrie to Bathgate and the Larkhall branch, and patronage on these lines has *outstripped all expectations*' (my italics).

While Scotland was badly hit by Beeching closures, most notably the now partially re-opened 98-mile long Waverley Route from Edinburgh to Carlisle, the country also benefited from its relatively limited road network. This meant a number of lines identified in the 1963 report as candidates for closure were reprieved and survive to this day. These include the Far North Line from Inverness to Wick and Thurso (168 miles), the famously scenic Inverness to Kyle of Lochalsh route, extending 63½ miles westwards from its junction on the Far North Line at Dingwall, and the 74 miles from Kilmarnock to Ayr and Stranraer.

Closure of the Waverley Route on 2 January 1969, six years after publication of Beeching's report, came as a bitter blow after a long and spirited attempt to avert it. It meant that the Scottish Borders became the only region in Great Britain without a rail service, while Hawick – 56 miles south of Edinburgh and 42 miles north of Carlisle – earned the dubious accolade of becoming the major UK town furthest from a rail service. After closure strenuous efforts were made to secure the route for preservation, but no agreement could be reached with British Rail over price and the line was dismantled in the early 1970s.

Besides the Waverley Route, other notable closures following the Beeching report included the route from Dumfries to Stranraer, the lines from Aberdeen to Fraserburgh and Peterhead, which removed rail services from the whole of North East Scotland, and Aberdeen to Ballater. Another major route closure was a scenic section of the former Callander and Oban Railway from its junction on the Highland main line at Dunblane to Crianlarich, via Callander and Balquhidder, although the line onwards from there to Oban was saved, and is now served by trains using the West Highland Line to reach Crianlarich from Glasgow.

Revival begins

The honour of becoming the first re-openings in Scotland in the modern era is shared between a 9½-mile link between Kilmarnock and Barassie, which re-opened in May 1975 for limited use by Stranraer to London sleeping car services and, later that same year, a 17-mile long link between Perth and Ladybank. This single-track line had been closed to passenger services as early as 1955, but had remained open for freight traffic until 1975, when it was re-opened to re-establish a more direct route between Perth and Edinburgh than via the alternative route through Stirling.

Only a decade after the Waverley Route closure (1979) came the next post-Beeching railway re-opening in Scotland and the first of many in the key Strathclyde region. Glasgow's suburban rail system is by far the most densely used part of Scottish rail system, accounting for two-thirds of Scotland's rail passenger journeys and being the most heavily-used commuter network in the UK outside London, according to the Scottish Government. Much of it had been electrified in the early/mid 1960s when its fleet of 'blue trains' – the Class 303 electric units – made the Strathclyde region a watchword for efficient modern urban transport.

As has since happened in many English cities, there was a need for better cross-city links, which led to development and opening of the Argyle Line in 1979, the first of a number of major upgrades and extensions to Glasgow's rail infrastructure. The Argyle Line re-opened as a joint venture between British Rail and the Strathclyde Passenger Transport Executive (SPTE), and established a new east–west link across the Glasgow city centre by re-opening a subterranean route along the line of Argyle Street that had closed in 1964. This has created a through link between places such as Dalmuir and Milngavie to the north west of the city with places to the south east of Glasgow, including Motherwell, Lanark and, most recently, Larkhall.

Re-opening of the Argyle Line saw the construction of new stations at Argyle Street and at Finnieston, to the west of the city, which became Exhibition Centre in 1986. The route has a frequent train service – the current weekday frequency off peak is nine trains per hour – and was significantly extended when a branch line from a junction near Hamilton Central to Larkhall re-opened in December 2005, almost exactly 40 years after its original closure in October 1965. The Larkhall branch, one of those to have seen traffic far exceed forecasts, is a single-track line, which includes a trio of new stations, Chatelherault, Merryton and Larkhall. Passengers using Larkhall have increased from 269,000 in 2006/7

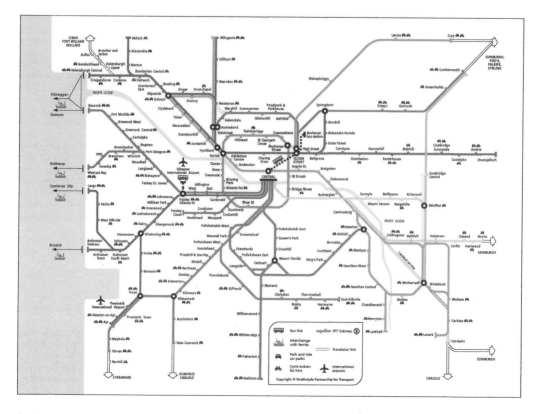

Strathclyde is by far
the most important
rail market in Scotland
and has seen major
development of its rail
network since opening
of the Argyle line in
1979. Map courtesy of
Strathclyde Partnership for
Transport

to 420,000 in 2015/6, prompting suggestions and studies into a
potential further extension to the town of Stonehouse.

To the south-west of Glasgow, another early revival was the
Paisley Canal branch. This formed part of a line which continued
on to Elderslie and terminated at Kilmalcolm, but became one of
the last lines to shut in Great Britain, when passenger services
ceased on 10 January 1983. While the section west of Paisley Canal
was lifted some three years after closure, the section eastwards
from Paisley Canal to Shields Junction was restored by British Rail
and Strathclyde Passenger Transport and re-opened just 7½ years
after its original closure, on 27 July 1990. A trio of intermediate
stations were re-opened – Corkerhill, Mosspark and Crookston,
while two new stations were opened at Hawkhead and Dumbreck.
Further development of the revived route saw its electrification
in 2012 as part of the Ayrshire Coast Line electrification scheme,
with hopes now that the remainder of the route westwards to
Kilmalcolm may one day see trains again.

In the year that the Railways Act paved the way towards a
privatised future (1993), there were two significant openings that
added a total of ten new suburban stations in the Glasgow area.
First up was the Whifflet Line, where trains returned on 4 October
1993 to a route which had lost its passenger services in November
1966, but had survived as a freight and diversionary route until
its revival, along with the opening of new stations at Carmyle,

Mount Vernon, Ballieston, Bargeddie and Kirkwood. Whifflet station, a new terminus for these services, had opened less than a year earlier, on 21 December 1992, being served by services from Motherwell to Coatbridge until the new route was opened. Two decades later the route was electrified in 2014, partly to provide a diversionary route for West Coast Main Line services into Glasgow, while the suburban services have been incorporated into the Argyle Line, to create a new east–west link via Glasgow Central Low Level.

A second significant addition to the all-important Strathclyde network occurred on 2 December 1993, when local services were introduced on the first section of the West Highland Line from Glasgow, with the opening of another five new stations – Ashfield, Possilpark/Parkhouse, Lambhill (renamed Gilsochill in May 1998), Summerston, and Maryhill. This followed a £2.2m investment in the new stations by Strathclyde Regional Council, with a 50% grant from the European Commission, and led to the launch of a new half-hourly weekday service from Maryhill to Glasgow Queen Street (High Level). An extension to the service in 2005 took it to Anniesland, a junction for services on the Argyle and North Clyde Lines, with a further new station opened at Kelvindale. The completed 6¼ mile long route remains diesel worked, but has had seven days a week services since 2014, and in 2015 a new chord was installed at Anniesland to connect with the North Clyde Line in the Glasgow direction, enabling its use as a diversionary route into Queen Street station for services from the north and from Edinburgh.

Creating a Fife Circle

A mere eight miles south of Ladybank and its revived services to Perth came another early post Beeching revival when, in 1989, what is now known as the Fife Circle was created with the reopening of a six-mile stretch of line from Thornton north and south junctions on the main Dundee–Edinburgh line to Cardenden, which at that time was the end of a peak-time extension to local services from Edinburgh to Dunfermline and Cowdenbeath.

By re-opening this section of line, which had remained in use for freight since passenger services were withdrawn in 1969, the present day Fife Circle service was created. It was given a significant new destination in 1992 when Glenrothes with Thornton station was opened along the revived line, to serve both the new town and neighbouring Thornton. The route was further developed with new stations opening at Dalgety Bay in 1998 and at Dunfermline Queen Margaret (the name of a nearby hospital) in 2000 and commuter traffic is so heavy that the route has seen the introduction of peak-time locomotive-hauled trains.

Holyrood backs rail

A real driver of a rail revival in Scotland has been devolution, which was implemented through establishment of the Scottish Parliament at Holyrood in 1999 following the passing at Westminster of the Scotland Act 1998. Rail devolution represented the biggest transfer of power to Scotland from Westminster, giving Scottish Ministers the power to set the vision for the railways in Scotland and the funding to make it happen through Network Rail and the ScotRail franchise, in partnership with other freight and passenger operating companies. Approximately £358 million per annum was transferred to Scottish Ministers to cover all the additional transport responsibilities devolved with effect from 1 April 2006.

The Scottish Government's blueprint for reviving Scotland's railways is the *National Transport Strategy, Scotland's Railways*, a publication designed to set out Scottish Ministers' vision for the rail network over 20 years. Along with the *National Transport Strategy*, it shows how rail can contribute to achieving three strategic outcomes of: improving journey times and connections; reducing emissions; and improving quality, accessibility and affordability.

'Rail is uniquely placed to carry high numbers of people over long distances. It connects people to jobs, links communities and makes services accessible across the country', wrote Tavish Scott MSP, Transport Minister at the time the rail strategy document was published. 'I want to build on the significant improvements we have already made to rail services in recent years – the opening of the Larkhall–Milngavie route; a high quality franchise; and new services. I want to see a successful expansion of the network with delivery of the major investments now underway.'

The strategy document said that by the end of 2006, Transport Scotland's expenditure on public transport was planned to reach £1 billion per year and it singled out seven major rail projects that it wished to deliver:

- Larkhall to Milngavie (delivered December 2005).
- Stirling – Alloa – Kincardine (to be completed during 2007).
- Edinburgh Waverley re-modelling (to be completed by early 2008).
- Scottish Borders Railway (Parliamentary power secured in 2006).
- Glasgow Airport Rail Link (GARL).
- Edinburgh Airport Rail Link (EARL) Bills in Parliament for powers to construct.
- Airdrie to Bathgate Rail Link.

As discussed elsewhere in this chapter, the Larkhall, Alloa, Airdrie–Bathgate and Borders Railway schemes have all been successfully delivered, while the huge £130 million re-modelling of Edinburgh

Waverley station was finally completed in 2014. However, both the Edinburgh and the Glasgow Airport Rail Links fell victim to spending cuts, with the Edinburgh scheme being abandoned in September 2007 and the Glasgow scheme being cancelled two years later, in September 2009. Today, the only Scottish Airport with a direct rail connection is Glasgow Prestwick Airport, some 38 miles south of Glasgow, whose station opened in September 1994 and has the distinction of being the only Scottish station not run by either Network Rail or by the ScotRail franchise holder, currently Abellio.

'Allo Alloa

Following successful re-opening of the Larkhall branch, the next rail revival in Scotland, also destined to be highly successful, was the project to restore passenger services to Alloa, a town seven miles east of Stirling. This was part of a plan to re-open a 13-mile route to Kincardine for use by coal trains travelling from Hunterston Terminal in North Ayrshire to Longannet Power Station in Fife, in order to provide a more direct route for these trains and remove the need for them to cross the congested Forth Bridge.

Much of the track was still intact, but in need of replacement, while new signalling was also required, a passing loop constructed at Cambus, just west of Alloa and a new single platform station in the town. Work on re-building the line began in 2005, with track laying completed by March 2007. The line re-opened on 19 May 2008, with direct services from Glasgow Queen Street and a peak

Stirling, junction for the re-opened line to Alloa, boasts two of the finest remaining signal boxes in Scotland. To the south of the station, Stirling Middle is a Grade A listed building which was built by the Caledonian Railway in the late nineteenth century. Sadly its semaphore signals have since been replaced by colour lights.

In common with so many re-opened lines and stations, passenger traffic at Alloa, terminus of the seven-mile branch from Stirling, has far exceeded initial forecasts. On 22 November 2009, little more than a year after the line's re-opening, Strathclyde-liveried 170471 prepares to depart with the 12.13 service to Glasgow Queen Street.

time direct link to Edinburgh Waverley. Since then, passenger numbers have far exceeded expectations, with 387,000 passengers using the station in 2015/6, compared to a forecast prior to re-opening that the new station would attract 155,000 passengers.

East of Kincardine, the route previously used by coal traffic continues to Dunfermline, where it joins the 'Fife Circle' route south of Dunfermline station. Given the success of the Alloa re-opening there have been calls for this section to be re-opened. In 2010 a report by consultants Scott Wilson for the South East of Scotland Transport Partnership (SEStran) identified the potential of using the route to extend services from Glasgow to Alloa along the line and continuing to Edinburgh via a new chord line south of Dunfermline, with new stations at Clackmannan, Kincardine and Cairneyhill. It put the cost of upgrading the line at £65 million and, although it has strong local support, as well as featuring on a wish list of schemes published by the Railfuture lobby group, the project has not yet won support from the Scottish Government.

Chris Green on ScotRail

One of the most highly respected managers in British Railways' history was Chris Green, who rose through the ranks after joining as a graduate trainee in 1965. Following a wide variety of roles within BR, he moved to Scotland in 1979 and became General Manager of the Scottish Region in 1984, achieving huge success by creating the ScotRail brand, which continues to the present day. Here he sums up his time in Scotland:

Re-organising BR and creating ScotRail

'Scotland in 1980 was a classic British Rail Region. The BR Board was set on managing decline and the mission in the 1980s was still to shut marshalling yards, rationalise tracks, un-staff stations and reduce train services. But everything was to change in 1982, both nationally, and particularly in Scotland, for several reasons.

'First, the Serpell Report had been a major public relations disaster for the Government, who had had to say publicly that it did not wish to close any more lines or introduce bus substitution. Bob Reid was appointed as the new chairman of British Rail, and he told Government that he was going to re-organise the railway into business sectors to make the whole operation more business-like and this led to the creation of the five sectors – InterCity, Provincial Railways etc.

'The result was a more positive government and a railway that was more geared towards being entrepreneurial. In Scotland we saw ourselves as a sub-set of Provincial Railways, but with a lot of freedom. So in 1982 Scotland started exploiting the railway in a way which really hadn't happened since the war.

'We decided to re-brand ourselves and the name was decided in an afternoon, making the point that we could move fast. We chose the name ScotRail which was, and still is, blindingly obvious! It appealed immediately to the staff, the customers and, indeed to the Scottish government, so we suddenly had a new image and purpose. Almost immediately, ScotRail was fighting the deregulation of buses. The Government had decided to pilot the deregulation of buses in Scotland, just to see what would happen, and this was causing us to lose business hand over fist.'

Re-opening to Bathgate

'The buses were under-cutting us by using the new motorways and were charging £1 fares simply to get people off rail. So we decided to play them at their own game. The BR Board in London gave us a lot of freedom to fight bus competition and we quickly realised that to do this we would have to change the image of the product, invest money in upgrading the stations, procure more modern trains and better track and introduce customer service courses for our staff.

'That worked really well, but it led to questions about why didn't we start re-opening stations and lines? We re-opened about five stations at that time, but the most important thing we did was to re-open the Bathgate line, and this was billed at the time as 'rolling back Beeching'. It was the first significant re-opening of a line anywhere in Britain and it happened fast because we had total co-operation from all the planning communities and the funding communities. There were something like ten different bodies involved in the re-opening of the Bathgate line.

'The deal was that the local Councils would fund the capital costs of the re-opening, and then ScotRail would take the line into its ownership and cover the annual maintenance costs – hoping that income would equal costs. So we suddenly found that we had the Scottish Office, Lothian Regional Council, Bathgate and Livingstone District Councils, and a number of other councils, all supporting their local rail services. That made a huge impact nationally and it suddenly became OK to re-open lines and not just stations. I think that ScotRail can honestly claim to have led the way in rolling back Beeching by re-opening stations that had previously been closed and by re-opening the Bathgate line.'

'The Bathgate re-opening was a phenomenal success from day one. It was an easy line to re-open because it was originally a double track line, which had been reduced to a single track freight line – we kept it to single track and we put a diesel unit on and just got it going. The trick with these early re-openings was just to get them going and then to extend them incrementally as you got more income. Today it is a double track main line again – a fast electrified route – and that is something which we never dreamt of and far exceeds our expectations. But it all started in bite-sized chunks.

'From the first day the trains were over-crowded and we were having to put more units on the route. It eventually had to have double track to get more trains through. Then it was electrified as part of the extension to Airdrie and Glasgow.'

Transformation in Strathclyde

'Strathclyde Council was very pro-rail, as you would expect, and strongly supported re-opening of the Argyle Line under Glasgow Central station, to connect up south Glasgow with the Helensburgh Line. Unfortunately at around the same time we discovered massive asbestos problems in the Class 303 'Blue Trains' and Strathclyde Council was faced with a bill that was heading towards £30 million – and they just did not have that sort of money.

'BR was saying take it or leave it – this was in 1980 – and I arrived on the scene to find that Strathclyde wanted to shut a great chunk of the network just because they hadn't got the money. It did shut the Paisley Canal line to Kilmalcolm line, and that was done to frighten BR. For a Labour council that was a very brave thing to do. So we formed a working party with Strathclyde Transport and I attended a steering group meeting every week – I think we had 33 meetings and the mission was to see how we could develop the network, not shut it.

'The understanding was that we had to get something like a third off the cost of the network if we wanted to keep it. We did come up with a solution and it was a nice mixture of expanding income and reducing cost. It included some singling of track; staff productivity improvements; driver-only operation, speeding up the introduction of power signalling to close signal boxes – and open stations where we abolished ticket barriers and transferred the ticket checks onto the trains.

'It worked, and all talk of closures ended. One of the few failures was to get the East Kilbride line electrified and strangely it is still diesel operated to this day. From that point onwards it was a positive relationship that led to other re-openings, like Larkhall, Whifflet, Maryhill and Airdrie–Bathgate of course. Scotland is still leading the way when it comes to railway re-openings The Alloa line was another exciting one and then, of course, came the Borders Line – I never dreamt that we would see that one re-open. Hopefully that will get to at least Melrose and Hawick in the future.

'Scotland is also leading the way in electrification of its network – they are doing what I would have done, which is 'rolling electrification' – which is much cheaper than stopping and starting, by keeping your staff and materials and simply moving them on from one project to the next.'

Re-openings in retrospect

'We couldn't have moved any faster during my time at ScotRail. What we had was one unified organisation where the General Manager of ScotRail controlled everything from engineering to marketing and relationships with local councils to project management. You also had staff inside the industry to deliver the projects, rather than relying on contractors, to do the job. So if you wanted a new station, you went to the railway engineers who knew exactly what you wanted.

'Today you spend six months specifying what you want and then you go out to competitive tender and then you find a lot of mistakes have been made. The beauty of having a unified management is that we could move incredibly fast. We were also mega-focused on keeping costs down, because that's what BR was good at, and if anything we were not far-sighted enough. We never foresaw the Bathgate line becoming an electrified double-track mainline!

'It is interesting to speculate what would have happened if Edinburgh–Bathgate had arisen as a re-opening opportunity today. It would certainly have been a lot more expensive – but *there would probably also have been more funding from Transport for Scotland.*

'Just because lines existed before Beeching doesn't mean that they have to re-open. The trick is to find the best economic cases and in Scotland I would have thought this is the bottle-neck on the existing mainline from Edinburgh into Fife, where there must be a case for investing in the 12-car trains that we take for granted in the London area. You are not going to get the same number of passengers from St. Andrews, and you have to prioritise the investment on the benefits they will bring.

'I would also focus on upgrading the existing Scottish inter-city network, so I would love to see Inverness to Aberdeen as a double track 100 mph main line. I would also like to see the main lines from Aberdeen to Edinburgh and Glasgow electrified and, while that is not as sexy as re-openings, is probably going to benefit more people.'

Borders Line extension

'In the case of the Borders Line, you don't automatically go all the way to Carlisle just because that was where the line originally went: it may have been justified in 1850, but it may not be necessarily in 2017. I would certainly extend the line further to significant population centres such as Melrose and Hawick. The challenge south of Hawick will be the lack of population and the large numbers of level crossings needed for local access. But the lack of passenger demand could be offset by freight traffic, such as timber from the Kielder Forest, to help justify re-opening.'

Re-creating a fourth Glasgow–Edinburgh route: Airdrie–Bathgate

While the Scottish Government can claim to have committed to the creation of a fourth rail link between Glasgow and Edinburgh, credit for establishing the opportunity ought to really go to Chris Green and to the former British Motor Corporation. For it was during his two years as General Manager of the newly-branded ScotRail between 1984 and 1986 that Green identified the potential for restoring passenger services to a line which for the previous quarter of a century had been a freight-only rail link serving the British Motor Corporation's Truck and Tractor Division Factory at Bathgate.

During his two years as General Manager of ScotRail, Green – who then moved on to a larger stage and created Network SouthEast – did a great deal to revive the Scottish rail network and help it recover from the economic downturn of the early 1980s. A £140 million, five year investment programme was agreed for the all-important Strathclyde network, stations and trains were repainted in a bold new orange livery and a total of 11 new stations were added to the network.

Passenger traffic on the line to Bathgate had ended in 1956, but when the new BMC plant was opened in 1961, and Bathgate was designated a Special Development Area, it gave a new lease of life to the Bathgate end of a former through line from Glasgow and Airdrie. Daily services began to use the line to take finished trucks and tractors to the BMC plants at Longbridge and Cowley, while in the reverse direction, train loads of cars were sent to Bathgate from both the two BMC plants and from Ford at Dagenham and Vauxhall at Luton. Imported cars were also sent to Bathgate from ports including Harwich, Felixstowe, Tilbury and Sheerness.

BMC's successor, British Leyland, had hit financial problems by the mid-1980s and the Bathgate plant was closed in 1986. Although cars continued to flow westwards along the line for distribution from Bathgate by road to dealers across Scotland, the future of the railway line was nevertheless in doubt. In 1985, a year before the truck plant closed, ScotRail had secured approval for the reinstatement of a passenger service from Bathgate to Edinburgh, which took place on 24 March 1986. While this had involved some rationalisation of the track – much of the previously double-track branch was split between the new passenger service using one line and the remaining freight services the other – it was an immediate success.

Being single track for much of its length – as is the revived Borders Railway – meant inevitable reliability issues, but traffic growth at Bathgate and at the intermediate stations at Livingston North and Uphall prompted plans for further development of the route. In 2003 the Scottish Executive, forerunner of today's Scottish Parliament, announced plans to improve transport links between Glasgow and Edinburgh by completing the M8 motorway and by re-building the 15 mile 'missing link' between Bathgate and

Drumgelloch station was re-opened as a temporary terminus for trains from Glasgow in May 1989, but this new through station replaced it in March 2011 as part of the Airdrie to Bathgate re-opening project. On 1 August 2015, 334034 heads a six-car formation into the station with an eastbound service for Edinburgh Waverley.

Caldercruix, seen here on 1 August 2015, is the next station east of Drumgelloch and is typical of the four new stations between Airdrie and Bathgate. Along with Blackridge and Armadale, it has only a half-hourly service, with alternate trains running non-stop between Drumgelloch and Bathgate.

Another view of Caldercruix station as 334035 arrives with a stopping service to Edinburgh Waverley on 1 August 2015.

Like Drumgelloch towards the western end of the re-opened route, Bathgate station was resited to the south of the one that was originally opened in March 1986. A good crowd of passengers is on the platform as 334024 arrives in the 2010-opened station on 1 August 2015 with a service for Edinburgh Waverley.

Edinburgh Park station to the west of the capital was opened in December 2003 to serve a growing commercial area, and later provide a link, via the new tram route, to Edinburgh Airport. ScotRail 170396 pauses on 1 August 2015 with a service for Edinburgh Waverley.

Airdrie, which was the terminus of an electrified suburban route from Glasgow. Royal Assent for the £300 million scheme was granted in May 2007 and work began almost immediately.

In contrast to the more recent Borders Railway revival, a key feature of this scheme was that it was to be a double-track electrified route from the day it opened. The re-building process took just over two years, with a new through station built at Bathgate and track relaying completed by September 2010, with the route opened for driver training the following month, at the same time as a new Bathgate station was opened.

Scheduled services on the new route began on 12 December 2010, although construction delays meant that the four new intermediate stations at Armadale, Blackridge, Caldercruix and Drumgelloch were not ready in time for the start of services.

Despite having arrived very late and way over budget, the single-route Edinburgh tram service, linking the Edinburgh Airport with the city centre has proved increasingly popular, attracting 5.3 million passengers in 2015/6, its second year of operation. At Edinburgh Park it offers an important interchange with national rail services.

Services from Glasgow had been extended in 1989 to a new single platform station at Drumgelloch, but this was closed in May 2010 and a new station was built east of the original site, finally opening in March 2011, three months after re-opening of the line to Bathgate. Caldercruix had opened in the previous month, with Armadale and Blackridge also opening in March 2011.

Services today are in the hands of 3-car Class 334 electric units, operating in 3 or 6 car formations, and maintaining a 15 minute frequency, with services running from Edinburgh Waverley to Glasgow Queen Street (Low Level) and on to a variety of destinations to the west and northwest of the city, including Milngavie and Helensburgh Central. The fastest journey time between the two cities is 67 minutes for the half-hourly trains which do not serve three of the smaller re-opened stations – Armadale, Blackridge and Caldercruix – and which also run fast from Airdrie to Glasgow.

The trains are comfortable and fast, with a maximum line speed of 80 mph, and are certainly well used, with Bathgate particularly busy. The new stations are smart, basic structures which are unmanned and have lengthy footbridges to give access for cyclists and the disabled. There is nothing remaining at Bathgate to indicate where the car distribution terminal, which the line owes for its resurrection, ever was, its former location having been taken over as a substantial new depot for the line's passenger train fleet.

The big one: Borders revival

By contrast to the scale of the Airdrie–Bathgate re-opening, the £350 million Borders Railway project has been done on the cheap and, even before its opening on 6 September 2015, concerns were being expressed the line had not been 'future proofed' against a need for subsequent expansion or extension of services, in particular by the re-construction of around half a dozen over-bridges for a single-track only. Taking a first trip on the new line just three weeks after its re-opening, the relatively basic nature of the infrastructure quickly becomes apparent, with long stretches of single track line and only three sections of double track, leaving little capacity for services to recover from any delay or train failure, and minimal scope for enhancing the launch timetable of half-hourly services throughout the day.

While there was clearly a fair amount of traffic from people keen to sample the line for the first time, there were also a great many local users and, travelling on crowded trains with standing room only in a couple of instances, made one really wonder why it had taken 46 years to be brought back to life. There seems little doubt that it will prove a catalyst for significant economic regeneration in a place like Galashiels, where the station has been built on a narrow strip of land across the road from a smart new £5 million bus interchange, whilst places like Stow and Gorebridge

Four miles from Edinburgh Waverley, Brunstane opened in June 2002 when 4¾ miles of former Waverley Route (now Borders Railway) was re-opened, principally to serve a park-and-ride facility at Newcraighall. On Sunday 2 August 2015, shortly after the introduction of Sunday services, ScotRail 158867 arrives with a Newcraighall-bound train.

look set to become increasingly desirable residential locations for commuters into Scotland's capital city.

For all the limitations of its infrastructure, the Borders Railway is nevertheless a huge triumph for all those who campaigned against its original closure and who have campaigned for many years since to get the line re-opened. Those efforts date back as far as 1992, when a local architect named Simon Longland established a company called Borders Transport Futures, to examine the prospects for re-opening the entire route. That initial work led to

All change at Newcraighall, where recently-launched Sunday services were already attracting plenty of custom on 2 August 2015, as ScotRail 158867 arrives with a train from Edinburgh Waverley, just a month before services were extended to Tweedbank.

Galashiels station had once occupied the site now taken over by the road to the left of this picture, but the re-opened station is confined to a narrow corridor, albeit across the road from a smart new £5 million bus interchange. On 24 September 2015, less than three weeks after re-opening, ScotRail 158731 departs with the 11.45 service to Tweedbank.

the formation in 1999 of the Campaign for Borders Rail, while in the same year the Scottish Parliament supported a call to re-open the line as a way of reviving the local economy.

There then followed a feasibility study by consulting engineers Scott Wilson, whose February 2000 report found in favour of the re-opening, identifying 'no insurmountable planning or environmental constraints' to reinstatement of the line as far as Galashiels and Tweedbank, with much of the original line capable

Tweedbank station was provided with platforms long enough to accommodate special trains, but not with run-round facilities. That means steam specials must be topped-and-tailed with a diesel locomotive that pulls the return train. Here DB 67026 passes Stow on 24 September 2015 with the 14.38 return special from Tweedbank.

of being re-built, provided a number of significant obstacles could be overcome. Scott Wilson noted particular problems in the first 12-mile section of the route as far as Gorebridge, where road improvements to the A7 and construction of the Edinburgh city bypass had all taken sections of the former railway, whilst residential development had taken place at Gorebridge on the railway alignment.

As if the £100 million needed to overcome these issues was not enough, the consultants were pretty gloomy about projected passenger traffic on a revived line. None of the options examined produced an adequate cost/benefit ratio, although re-opening as far as Gorebridge was neutral, according to that initial study. Set against that, they recognised that a revived line would benefit the Borders region, with better links to Edinburgh helping create up to 900 new jobs. Choosing to respond to growing popular clamour for the line to be built, rather that the negative tone of the consultant's report, the Scottish Executive committed £1.9 million from its Public Transport Fund to allow a Parliamentary Order for reopening as far as Tweedbank to be taken forward.

What gave real impetus to the re-opening project was the re-introduction in June 2002 of services on a remaining stub of the line, to serve a new park and ride facility at Newcraighall, almost five miles from Waverley station in Edinburgh. This new half-hourly service, with an intermediate station opened at Brunstane, a mile north of Newcraighall, proved successful and meant that when Borders Railway services began on 6 September 2015, they were in effect just a lengthy extension to the well-established and well-patronised Newcraighall service.

A full business case for the line published in summer 2004, and showing a modest benefit-to-cost ratio of 1.01 to 1, was an improvement on the earlier Scott Wilson study and partly based on plans for significant new housing developments along the line of route. The Waverley Railway Joint Committee reported in July 2005 in favour of reopening as far as Galashiels, a Borders Railway bill was introduced at Holyrood in September 2005 and, after lengthy debate and subject to an additional new station at Stow and the line been re-built all the way to Tweedbank, the bill was passed with only one dissenting vote, on 14 June 2006. The Waverley Railway (Scotland) Act 2006 received Royal Assent ten days later, providing for construction of more than 30 miles of railway and seven new stations.

After a fraught tender process in which the three parties which had expressed an interest all withdrew, Network Rail was selected by Transport Scotland in November 2012 to re-build the line, at a cost of £294 million and with a commitment to deliver it by Summer 2015. A month later, in December 2012, BAM Nuttall was appointed as Network Rail's main contractor and in June 2013 a £3.5 million design contract for the route went to engineering consultants URS, who were to design all the new structures needed for the re-building, including the refurbishment of remaining bridges, tunnels and viaducts.

Re-construction of the line took less than two years, beginning in April 2013 following preparatory work that had included land acquisition, removal of vegetation, demolition of certain buildings and remedial works at the site of old mine-workings in Midlothian. After work to re-align the track at Monktonhall, just south of Newcraighall, the first track was laid in Bowshawk Tunnel just a year after the reconstruction began and on 5 February 2015 track installation was completed, with formal completion a week later, when Scottish Transport Minister, Keith Brown MSP, clipped the final rail into place.

Once signalling equipment had been installed and works on the seven new stations completed, a first test train was run on 13 May 2015, with formal handover of the completed line to the ScotRail Alliance, a group formed by Network Rail and Abellio ScotRail, a month later, on 14 June 2015.

The total Borders Railway scheme comprises 31 route miles of which 21¼ miles are single-track and the remaining 9½ miles is double-track, in the form of three extended or 'dynamic' passing loops, which permit operation of the currently scheduled half-hourly service frequency. In terms of structures, there are 42 new bridges, 95 refurbished bridges and two refurbished tunnels along the revived line, as well as seven new stations – from south to north, these are at Tweedbank, Galashiels, Stow, Newtongrange, Shawfair, Eskbank and Gorebridge. Although sections of the route permit speeds of 90 mph, the number of station stops means the end-to-end journey takes an average of 55 minutes.

Since re-opening, the Borders Railway has become the sixth and latest route in Scotland to be promoted for its scenic attractions

Stow station was an afterthought on the revived Borders Railway, included in the project as a result of public pressure and now attracting far more passengers than originally forecast. Here ScotRail 158724 passes non-stop on 24 September 2015 with one of the two trains each hour that is not timetabled to serve the station.

Over-crowding was a recurrent theme in the early months of the revived Borders Railway, prompting use of three and four-car sets on a number of services. On 24 September 2015, three-car 170478 approaches Eskbank with a Tweedbank-bound train.

and leisure traffic will certainly be a hugely important element in determining how successful it becomes in the longer term. Besides its one major town, Galashiels, there is the mining museum close to Newtongrange station, some delightful and wild countryside south of Gorebridge, and at Tweedbank there is only a gap of just over a mile to the splendidly restored and listed station at Melrose. How long it will be before trains return there is the question which campaigners are now asking.

The revived Borders Railway represents a fascinating blend of the new and the old, with a number of major new structures, such

Eskbank is one station on the revived Borders Railway to have attracted less initial passenger traffic than forecast, but, like nearby Shawfair, it is in an area where large scale residential development is taking place, promising substantial traffic growth in coming years. On 24 September 2015, ScotRail 170478 arrives with a Tweedbank service.

The starkness of station architecture on the revived Borders Railway has attracted some criticism. It is all too apparent in this 24 September 2015 view of Stow station, as 158707 departs from platform 2 with a southbound service for Galashiels and Tweedbank. The old station building here has been restored, though not for rail use.

as the bridge carrying the Edinburgh bypass over the line just south of Shawfair station and the lengthy span taking the line over the A7 trunk road south of Eskbank station. There are also many survivals of the old Waverley Route which have been reused as part of the project, most notably the 23–arch Newbattle Viaduct, north of Newtongrange station, and Redbridge Viaduct between Galashiels and Tweedbank, but also including many other tunnels and bridges, a real testament to the quality of nineteenth century railway construction.

Escapees from Beeching

If Beeching had had his way, there would have been no more rail services north of Inverness and later generations would not have been able to appreciate the wild and rugged terrain of either the Far North Line – by far the longest route anywhere in Britain to have escaped the axe – nor Britain's most scenic rail journey, the line stretching westwards from Dingwall to Kyle of Lochalsh.

I well remember my first trip to Thurso, when in March 1981, as part of a British Rail promotion running that month, I had secured a free ticket to any station in the UK by renewing my Young Person Railcard. Working in southeast London at the time, and being young and adventurous I had naturally picked Thurso, so after travelling up to Glasgow from Euston I had then taken the overnight sleeper train from Glasgow Queen Street to Inverness – though not able to afford a sleeper berth myself!

At Inverness I then caught the 06.00 train to Thurso and Wick, which was hauled by a pair of Class 26 locomotives and comprised no less than nine bogie vehicles – five carriages and four parcels/newspaper vans. After lengthy stops to unload newspapers and mail *en route*, the train divided at Georgemas Junction, with arrival into Britain's most northerly station at around midday – some 21 gruelling hours after I had begun my 741-mile journey in Lewisham!

While boasting somewhat less dramatic scenery than the Kyle line, the Far North route is nevertheless a magnificent survival and a vital link to many isolated communities. Despite speeding up of services and no more splitting and joining of trains at Georgemas Junction, however, upgrading of the A9 trunk road has put rail at a significant disadvantage to road in recent years, with the rail journey of four hours from Inverness to Wick at least an hour longer that it is now possible to make the journey by road.

In an effort to speed up the rail journey, proposals have been drawn up and long discussed to eliminate one of the lengthiest detours on the route, the so-called Lairg loop, by building a line across the Dornoch Firth, to create a direct link from Tain over the Dornoch Firth on a new bridge which carries the A9 to

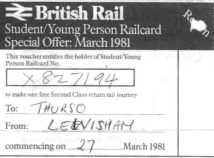

Railcard number on the voucher.
Fill in your journey details before you travel.
See the reverse of voucher for full details.

≩ British Rail
Student/Young Person Railcard
Special Offer: March 1981

This voucher entitles the holder of Student/Young Person Railcard No.

X 827194

to make one free Second Class return rail journey

To: *THURSO*

From: *LEWISHAM*

commencing on _27_ March 1981

Issued subject to the Regulations and Conditions in the Publications and Notices of the British Railways Board. Not transferable.

Not valid unless stamped below by the Railcard issuing office AT THE TIME THE STUDENT/YOUNG PERSON RAILCARD NUMBERED ABOVE IS PURCHASED. Not valid after 31 March 1981. For offer conditions see over.

NO. 358 596

My first venture to the Far North was courtesy of this free ticket, offered in March 1981 to anyone buying a young person railcard that month.

Golspie. This would significantly speed up the overall journey to the Far North, albeit at the loss of four stations on the loop, Ardgay, Culrain, Invershin and Lairg.

One recent feature of the Far North Line has been the development of local services based on Inverness and the re-opening of no less than three stations on the 18¾-mile stretch of line between Inverness and Dingwall, junction for the Kyle of Lochalsh route. First of the trio was Muir of Ord, a village of some 3,000 inhabitants that is roughly halfway between Inverness and Dingwall and boasts the only passing loop on this stretch of the line. It had originally closed in June 1960, but re-opened on 4 October 1976 and has seen significant growth in patronage over the past decade.

Second to re-open was Beauly, a small village which had also lost its station in June 1960 along with numerous other places along the line, due to increasing competition from buses. But a local campaign led to its highly successful re-opening in 2002. Such was its success that 75% of local commuters switched from road to rail and five years after its re-opening, in 2007/8, the village's usage-to-population ratio (the village had a population then of 1,164 people) of 36 rail journeys a year per head was one of the highest in Britain.

The third station to re-open was Conon Bridge, between Muir of Ord and Dingwall, which had been known simply as Conon

Conon Bridge has the distinction of being both newest and smallest of the three re-opened stations along the 18¾ miles between Inverness and Dingwall (the others being Beauly and Muir of Ord).Here 158704 approaches the station on 25 September 2015 with the 12.08 service from Kyle of Lochalsh to Inverness.

Services on the Far North routes from Inverness have been significantly improved to cater for growing passenger traffic to the highland capital. On 25 September 2015, 158709 departs re-opened (2013) Conon Bridge station with the 13.35 Inverness to Kyle of Lochalsh service.

before becoming another of the June 1960 closures. The new station, which opened in February 2013, is another basic structure like Beauly, and also boasts a remarkably short platform, like Beauly only 49 feet (15 metres) in length, meaning only one door of any train can be opened for passenger use at either of these two stations.

Services on the Far North Line today are in the hands of Class 158 'Sprinter' multiple units, with a frequency of four trains each way per day from Inverness to Thurso and Wick. There has been

Britain's most northerly station is Thurso, 154 miles and around 4 hours' travelling time from Inverness, and 722 miles from London Kings Cross. On 25 September 2015, 158716 prepares to depart with the 17.53 service to Wick, which will return south to Georgemas Junction before continuing on to its final destination.

steady development in traffic from the furthest destinations over the past decade, but closer to Inverness there has been far more dramatic growth in passenger numbers, driven both by the station re-openings, but also by the efforts of the Highlands and Islands Strategic Transport Partnership (HITRANS) to develop commuter services called 'Invernet' centred on Inverness.

Invernet was first launched in December 2005 for an experimental three year period, but its initial success has made it permanent, and today there are short workings to Inverness from Lairg, Ardgay and Tain to cater for both commuters, as well as off-peak leisure travellers. Evidence of Invernet's success can be seen in passenger numbers: Dingwall, for example, has seen passenger numbers rise almost threefold in a decade from 34,898 in 2004/5, to 82,500 in 2015/6, according to the figures compiled by the ORR. At Muir of Ord, the growth has been just as dramatic, with numbers up from 24,365 in 2004/5 to 66,500 in 2015/6.

My excuse for paying a return visit to the Far North Line in September 2015 – 34 years after my original visit – was to take advantage of another rail deal, this time a special £10 return 'go anywhere' fare to mark the launch of the 'Club 50' railcard by new ScotRail franchisee, Abellio. What struck me then was the high level of local passenger traffic between Inverness, Dingwall and Invergordon, but also the remarkable scale and splendour of this amazing route. Never mind seeing the A9 head off across the Dornoch Firth and realising that this means an hour-long, 40-mile detour, this trip is about appreciating the beauty and ruggedness of a journey to Scotland's far north.

Both termini of the Far North Line boast attractive Highland Railway station buildings. Wick, Britain's most north easterly station, was built in 1874 and was once the junction for a branch line southwards to Lybster. Passenger numbers at Wick are only around half those at Thurso, with 2015/6 seeing 19,760 users at Wick and 38,426 at Thurso.

There are delightful and restored stations to appreciate – Invergordon station's painted murals, Tain's prize-winning station gardens, Rogart's restored station building, with its private owner also boasting two former passenger carriages and preserved signal box nearby, and the charming listed chalet that serves as the seasonally re-opened station for visitors to Dunrobin Castle.

Forsinard station, 125¾ miles north of Inverness, is one of the quietest stations on the Far North Line, attracting around 30 passengers a week. But it is an important passing place, as seen on 26 September 2015 when 158702 arrives with a Wick-bound service as 158703 waits to depart with the 13.47 service to Inverness. The preserved station is used by the Royal Society for the Protection of Birds for its Flow Country visitors' centre.

Britain's most northerly railway junction is Georgemas Junction, where northbound trains from Inverness will reverse up the line seen diverging on the right to Thurso, before returning to the junction and taking the line in the foreground onwards to Wick. The siding to the left was used by nuclear traffic from the former Dounreay nuclear plant.

An 11-mile run along the wild and deserted coastline from Brora to Helmsdale is then followed by an hour-long crossing of the Flow Country, a 1,500 square mile area of nothingness that is the largest area of what is known as blanket bog or peatland anywhere in the whole of Europe. Midway through this traverse lies the crossing point of Forsinard and then, an hour after leaving the coast at Helmsdale, Georgemas Junction, an occasional source of freight traffic and in whose disused station building a poster advertising train times from October 1984 to May 1985 is a reminder of just how long it is since the station was manned.

Skye's the limit

Another Beeching escapee is the spectacular route from Dingwall to Kyle of Lochalsh, a 64-mile line that shares with the West Highland Line from Fort William to Mallaig the accolade of being one of the world's greatest railway journeys. When the railway finally reached Kyle in 1897, 27 years after it had reached Strome Ferry, the route between the two stations had become the most expensive piece of railway engineering to have been undertaken by that date – costing £250,000 (around £27.5 million today) or £20,000 a mile ([£2.2 million today) due to the need to cut 31 rock cuttings and build 29 bridges. That final 10½ miles completed the route from Dingwall and transformed Kyle from a tiny hamlet into a significant ferry port, which then adopted the name Kyle of Lochalsh. Today the ferry to Skye has been replaced by a bridge, but the UK's most celebrated scenic railway lives on as a vital local service and a magnet for tourists from all over the world.

It not only featured in Beeching's 1963 Report as a candidate for closure, but was also under threat again in 1970. Making reference to a grant of £178,000 (equivalent to around £2.6 million today) being paid to keep the line open at the time, the Minister of Transport, Peter Walker, told the House of Commons in December 1970 that 'on the information available to him he would not be justified beyond 1971 in continuing to pay the grant to maintain the service.' But tourism came to the line's rescue – in 1965 the total number of passengers on the line had been 25,085 – by 1969 it had increase four-fold to 102,000 and that upward trend happily continued.

In a 1971-published pocket guide 'The Kyle Line' author Tom Weir neatly summed up the case for keeping the line:

> 'The present subsidy to keep the railway operating works out at £3,500 per week [£51,500 today] and for this money the Hebrides get a direct link with Inverness, Aberdeen, Edinburgh and Glasgow – cheap at the price, especially when it is reckoned against the £7,400,000 [£109 million today] which British Railways are spending to improve commuter services in Bedfordshire, not to mention the untold millions which may be spent shortening the travel time between London and Glasgow [the West Coast Main Line electrification, completed in 1974] to make the rail service competitive with air travel'

The Kyle line was reprieved a second, and hopefully final, time in 1974. Today the four times a day service is operated by the fleet of Class 158 two-car units based at Inverness and also used on the North Highland and Inverness–Aberdeen routes. Traffic levels have shown a steady increase in recent years, with passenger numbers using Kyle of Lochalsh, for example, have risen from 44,263 in 2004/5 to 65,706 in 2015/6.

Like the West Highland and North Highland Lines, the Kyle route was equipped with a form of radio signalling called Radio Electronic Token Block (RETB) in 1984, to reduce operating costs, while all the line's 12 stations are now unstaffed, with the exception of Kyle of Lochalsh itself. There are three remaining passing loops on the otherwise single track line, at Garve, Achnasheen and Strathcarron, and among scenic highlights is the run along the south shore of Loch Carron where the famous and delightful village of Plockton, which featured in the Hamish Macbeth and Inspector Alleyn Mysteries TV series, can be seen on the opposite shore. In addition to a mixture of tourist and local traffic, the Kyle line also sees visits from a variety of special trains, some steam hauled, although there is no remaining freight traffic.

Struggles on the Stranraer line

My vivid memory of travelling on Scotland's third major escapee from Beeching is of being on a crowded six-car DMU from Stranraer Harbour in summer 1975 – during a 'Freedom of Scotland' holiday with my family – when the train was full of Orangemen fresh off the ferry from Larne in Northern Ireland, who were heading for a rally in Glasgow. Fast forward to the present day and this pleasantly scenic route faced a renewed threat of closure following the 2011 relocation of ferry services to Cairnryan, which has led to the loss of ferry traffic, as foot passengers are now taken by bus between Ayr and the Cairnryan ferry terminal.

Passenger numbers at Stranraer have inevitably fallen as a result of the lost ferry traffic, with the total number falling from 53,190 in 2004/5 to 45,530 in 2013/4, but recovering to 53,968 in 2015/6. Strenuous promotional efforts are being successfully made by SAYLSA – the Community Rail Partnership for Carrick and Wigtownshire – to promote use of the line. One significant victory was to stop a relocation of the existing Stranraer Harbour station to a new location nearer the town centre, but without a run-round loop that would allow for the potential running of special steam-hauled tourist services, which SAYLSA would like to see operating on the line.

Another setback for the line's long term potential and viability came in March 2015, when Network Rail removed freight sidings at what was known as the Stockton Haulage facility. It had lost its freight traffic in the early 1990s, but when Network Rail had been given consent by the Office of Rail Regulation to sell off another strategic site, the Stranraer Town Yard, it had been on condition that the nearby Stockton facility 'and access to it be retained for future use.' Network Rail's response to SAYLSA was that the facility would be reinstated if a potential operator could demonstrate a suitable business case.

The frequency of passenger services on the line was significantly improved in December 2015, when the previous

A 2015 timetable change means most ScotRail services to Stranraer originate at Kilmarnock, meaning passengers to and from Glasgow must change there or at Ayr, where 156508 stands on 28 January 2016 with the 11.31 service to Stranraer.

Stranraer station on 28 January 2016, where 156508 has reached the end of the line with the lightly-loaded 12.56 arrival from Kilmarnock. Loss of Irish ferry traffic to Cairnryan, on the opposite side of Loch Ryan, means the left hand platform and station signal box are 'mothballed', pending the hoped-for development of new tourist traffic.

six return journeys a weekday service was increased to nine. But rerouting these services to Kilmarnock, where the majority of them terminate means the Glasgow–Stranraer journey time, now usually requiring a change at Ayr or Kilmarnock, increased by some 20% – from an average 2 hours 11 minutes in 2007 to 2 hours and 37 minutes in 2015.

Paying a return visit to Stranraer four decades after my first visit I found a lot had changed. The distant sight of an Irish Sea ferry at Cairnryan on the opposite side of Loch Ryan and the large Harbour station signal box 'switched out' – presumably indefinitely – are reminders of how serious a blow it was for the line to have lost its ferry traffic when services were moved away from the town. Passenger numbers seem worryingly low – of the four trains I travelled on, or passed, during my mid-week visit in January 2016, none had more than a dozen passengers on board a two-car Class 156 unit for the hour-long stretch of line south of Girvan. Yet much of this 38¼-mile section of the line is a scenic gem to rival much better known routes like the West Highland and Far North Lines and deserves far more appreciation and patronage.

After a brief glimpse of Ailsa Craig, a rocky outcrop off the coast at Girvan famous for its bird-life and as a source of curling stones, the line heads south through the remote moorland of Carrick and the Galloway Hills before another fleeting glimpse of the coast at Luce Bay, several miles east of Stranraer, followed by a westward run towards Stranraer and the sight of Loch Ryan. From an enthusiast point of view what makes the Stranraer line particularly interesting is that, unlike the Highland and Kyle lines, it was never equipped with RETB signalling. An excellent feature on single-line signalling in *Rail* magazine (No. 796/16 March 2016) notes that this route is the last one in Great Britain to still use large

Barrhill is the one remaining intermediate station on 38¼ miles of route from Stranraer to Girvan. On 28 January 2016 the driver of a northbound service to Ayr and Kilmarnock collects the single-line tablet from the signaller (wearing the high-vis jacket). Note the tiny signal box on platform two.

circular 'tablets' to control access to the longest three signalling sections on this line, between Girvan to Stranraer.

Having taken the single line tablet at Girvan, the drive then exchanges it at the one remaining intermediate station, isolated Barrhill, followed by two further stops to exchange tables at signal boxes located on the site of former stations, both of which featured in Beeching's report and closed in 1965: remote Glenwhilly and finally Dunragit, some six miles from Stranraer. The Network Rail masterplan for replacing every signal box in the UK with 12 control

ScotRail's newest electric units are the Class 380 series, which first entered traffic in December 2010. Here the first of 16 four-car variants, 380101, awaits departure from Ayr on 28 January 2016 with a service that will run to Glasgow Central, continuing on via Carstairs to Edinburgh Waverley and North Berwick.

centres by the year 2050 has set a date of 2021 for elimination of the six remaining signal boxes between Ayr and Stranraer, which would finally bring to an end the use of Victorian single-line tablet instruments on the national railway network.

Looking ahead

Following the huge success of Scottish re-openings to date there have, not surprisingly, been calls for Transport Scotland to continue the process. While the campaigners' hoped for 17-mile southern extension of the Borders Railway to Hawick has been ruled out in the short term, in June 2015, Scottish Infrastructure Minister Keith Brown confirmed that talks were underway on the commissioning of a feasibility study for an extension of the line, not just to Hawick, but all the way to Carlisle. That would open up the route for potential use as a diversionary route for West Coast Main Line services, as well as opening up the previously talked about possibility of timber traffic from the Kielder Forest.

North of the capital, proposals have been promoted for the re-opening of two separate sections of what was once the Fife Coastal Line, linking Thornton Junction, near the new town of Glenrothes, with Leuchars via the towns of Leven and St Andrews. This was slated for the Beeching axe and the central section between St Andrews and Leven was duly closed in September 1965. At either end of the route, however, services survived for another four years until 1969. Remaining passenger services on the five-mile route to St Andrews had been severely hit by the opening of the Tay road bridge in 1966 and were withdrawn in January 1969, while passenger services on the five miles of track at the southern end of the line, between Thornton Junction and Leven, ceased in October the of same year.

A campaign to bring trains back to the famous university and golfing town of St Andrews began as long ago as 1989 when the St Andrews Rail Link (StARLink) Campaign was established. In 2012 a feasibility report by Tata Steel Rail Consultancy put a price tag of £76 million on a reinstated link that would include a triangular junction with the main Edinburgh–Dundee line south of Leuchars, to give direct access from the town to both Leuchars and in the direction of Edinburgh.

Proposals to re-open the route from Thornton to Leven have been promoted by the LevenMouth Rail Campaign, which points out that Levenmouth is the largest urban area (pop 37,000) in Scotland not directly served by rail. Having survived for freight use after the ending of passenger services, the line from Thornton to Leven remains 'mothballed' and the campaign is pushing for the restoration of both passenger and freight services, given poor road links in the area. After the successful Borders Railway re-opening, the case for this re-opening, at an estimated cost of £55 million, seems compelling – not only does it offer rail access to a large population of up to 50,000 people, but there are a number potential freight users for a revived link.

Chapter 5

REVIVAL IN THE WELSH VALLEYS AND BEYOND

Just as is the case in the corresponding document for Scotland, so in Network Rail's *Route Plan for Wales* – outlining its vision and priorities for the rail network in Wales during the period 2014–19 (known as Control Period 5) and beyond – there is a sentence which succinctly sums up the rail revival story to date: 'We have witnessed some highly successful line re-openings in the past few years, such as the Vale of Glamorgan and the Ebbw Vale lines, and patronage on these lines has outstripped all expectations.'

That success raises serious doubts about the wisdom of the extensive closures across Wales which followed the Beeching Report and, in particular, the decision to eliminate perceived duplication and allow only one of the four routes to the Cambrian Coast to survive. This had meant closure of the busy route from Ruabon via Dolgellau to Barmouth, the line south from Bangor through Caernarfon to Afon Wen, near Pwllheli and in the south west of the Principality, the route from Aberystwyth to Carmarthen. It left the route from Shrewsbury to Machynlleth as the only means of rail access to Aberystwyth and the Cambrian Coast route northwards to Barmouth, Porthmadog and Pwllheli.

Now the success in Scotland of the Borders Railway revival has given heart to those campaigning for one of these three lost routes – the 56-mile line from Carmarthen to Aberystwyth – to be rebuilt, at an estimated cost of between £500 million and £600 million. In August 2015 the Welsh Assembly Government committed £30,000 for a study into the viability of re-opening a link which would serve a population similar to that of the Borders region in Scotland, larger than that served by the existing Aberystwyth–Shrewsbury line and, most importantly, would hugely improve links between Aberystwyth and Cardiff as well as putting the university town of Lampeter back on the railway map.

Buffer stops at the north end of Carmarthen station mark the start of the 56-mile route to Aberystwyth, which crossed the River Towy immediately beyond the road over-bridge.

The study into potential re-opening represents a triumph for the lobby group Traws Link Cymru, which has argued that re-opening of a line closed to passengers in February 1965 and to freight in 1973 would strengthen the local economy. But significant obstacles remain as much of the route has been built on, to the extent that a new alignment would be needed in locations like Lampeter, where the former line has been lost to a supermarket and car park and, further south, where a section of the old line has been bought and is operated by the Gwili Railway as a tourist service.

The bay platform at Aberystwyth formerly used by services to Carmarthen has been taken over by the Vale of Rheidol railway. On 22 April 2016 Vale of Rheidol No. 8 *Llewelyn* prepares to depart with the 14.00 service for Devil's Bridge.

On 23 December 2015 the results of this initial study, undertaken by consultants AECOM, were published and were broadly encouraging to those seeking a re-opening, although raising the estimated cost to £750 million. AECOM reported that a remarkable 97% of the original route remains undeveloped, with the most significant development at the Aberystwyth end, adding that the core formation, including tunnels, embankments and bridges has generally remained intact. The consultants also noted that the original route would not necessarily be the optimal one in today's environment, but acknowledged that the topography of the area does not readily lend itself to alternative railway alignments.

In a further encouraging note, Welsh Government Economy and Transport Minister, Edwina Hart commented: 'Improving public transport links is a key priority for this government and this includes increasing access links across rural communities. Carmarthen to Aberystwyth is already connected by a regular Welsh Government funded bus service, but I am open-minded to alternative public transport links and this scoping exercise will help inform the debate. Although funding railway infrastructure is non-devolved, I am pleased the Welsh Government has been able to assist with this first step in the possible re-introduction of rail services between these two locations.'

Like the Borders Railway in Scotland, what is quite remarkable is just how long the potential reopening of such a strategic link has been talked about. As long ago as 1966, only a year after final closure to passenger services, the line was subject to an adjournment debate in the House of Commons when, in the early hours of 21 June 1966, the Member of Parliament for Cardigan, Elystan Morgan, raised the issue of closure. 'This closure, like so many others, was sponsored by the Beeching Report', he began. 'When that plan was published in 1963 the people of Cardigan realised the full significance to them of its provisions. With the exception of the line from Shrewsbury to Aberystwyth and the spur running up along the Cambrian coast, the whole of central Wales was to be a railway vacuum.'

In a rousing conclusion to his speech, Morgan used the sort of language we have become familiar with in far more recent re-opening debates:

'The attitude of the Ministry [of Transport] seems to be that here is a railway which traverses an area of rather thin population and which runs between two towns of 10,000 and 12,000 population. I suggest that that is a narrow view. Here is a vital link between North-West and South-West Wales. There is here a service which has a potential of serving many scores of thousands of people. To the land and nation of Wales there are many divisive forces and factors. Mountain ranges divide us and communications divide us. Some people would even argue that language divides us. Here *is a factor which can unite a large part of North, Central and South Wales.*

'There is a deep and growing feeling in the hearts of many people in Mid-Wales that the closure of this line is the symbol of an inevitable fate. Economic and social decline is the way of life for many hundreds of villages in the Mid-Wales area. There is an instinctive feeling of helplessness which creates a psychology and a malaise. I do not accept this view, but I know this psychology to be a most potent and sometimes damning factor in relation to possible development in that area. Cardiganshire as a community has reached the point of a crucial decision. Either we surrender to this malaise or we challenge it in a bold and determined manner. The reopening of this line could be the forerunner of such a challenge.'

Sadly, Morgan's analysis did not find favour. Responding to his call, John Morris, Joint Parliamentary Secretary to the Ministry of Transport, made no concessions:

'The facts are that this line is 56 miles long and the average number of passengers each way on weekdays in July 1963 was 110. The savings to be effected by closure would be £114,200, less the bus subsidy. My hon. Friend has raised the issue of freight in a number of aspects, and in particular as regards milk.

'Freight is entirely a matter for the Railways Board and it would not do for me to comment on that aspect, but I would say that even if my hon. Friend's figure of £185,000 as coming from milk revenue is right, that is revenue and not profit. The greater proportion of this would be offset against the cost of transporting the milk, and whatever net profit remained at the end of the day would have to be apportioned not only as to the stub-end of the line running between the counties of Cardigan and Carmarthen but to the whole of the distance that the milk is transported through many parts of the country.

'Therefore, my hon. Friend will have to bear in mind that these are not realistic issues to put one against the other. Indeed, this revenue would never come anywhere near meeting the total additional costs of running a passenger railway service on this line. I was glad that he pointed out, so that there is no ambiguity, that this line was closed by a decision of the last Conservative Minister of Transport – a decision taken on 10th September, 1964. The line was actually closed in the following February, although some part of it had been closed earlier because of flood damage.'

For all the damage done by the Beeching closures in Wales, such as Aberystwyth–Carmarthen, there were two remarkable survivors, though for very different reasons. Foremost of these is the 90¼-mile long Central Wales Line – now known as the Heart of Wales Line – running in a north-easterly direction from Llanelli, just west of Swansea, to Craven Arms, a junction to the south of

Shrewsbury which is on the Marches Line route running north from Newport, through Hereford and Shrewsbury to Crewe. The second significant survivor of Beeching in Wales, though for a different reason, was the equally scenic 28-mile long Conwy Valley line from Llandudno Junction to Blaenau Ffestiniog.

Wales' greatest survivor: the Heart of Wales Line

Perceiving another duplicate route across a sparsely populated corner of the Principality, Beeching had wanted to close the lengthy Heart of Wales line, but it was saved on the grounds that it carried a significant amount of freight traffic from industrial South Wales and it also passed through six marginal Parliamentary constituencies.

Going back to that 1966 adjournment debate on the Aberystwyth–Carmarthen line, it was also referred to by Elystan Morgan, who cited it as a model example of how reducing operating costs had transformed its financial performance: 'I draw the attention of the House to the case of the Llanelly–Craven Arms line for, before streamlining, that railway lost £175,000 per annum, and after streamlining that deficit was reduced to £30,000 per annum,' said the MP for Cardigan in his adjournment debate speech.

In November 1969 the *Railway Magazine* reported that the Central Wales Line had been saved from closure:

> 'This decision has been made by the Minister of Transport following a study of the TUCC report and all other relevant factors. He accepts that considerable inconvenience and some hardship would be caused by the closure and that a suggested replacement bus service would not provide and entirely adequate substitute for long distance through passengers.
>
> 'It is the Government's policy to attract industry to Wales and it is consistent with this policy to maintain and improve communications in the Principality. The heavy annual grant of over £300,000 [equivalent to £4.65m today] that must be paid to the Railways Board for the retention of the service is considered, at present, justified on social and economic grounds. The Minister is now examining with the Board whether any modification of the existing service is called for.'

Having survived Beeching, the Heart of Wales Line might yet have succumbed to closure in 1987, when flooding – the cause for premature closure of both the Ruabon–Barmouth and Aberystwyth–Carmarthen routes in 1964/5 – brought tragedy to the line. On 19 October 1987 the Glanrhyd Bridge near Llandeilo, which carried the line over the River Towy, collapsed. The 05.27 train from Swansea to Shrewsbury, formed of a two-car Class 108 diesel multiple unit, fell into the river, which claimed the lives of the train driver and three passengers. But sentiment towards

Having left Pantyfynnon station on the Heart of Wales Line with the 17.27 departure for Swansea on 18 April 2016, the driver of 150281 pauses at the signal box to hand over the token for the section of line from Llandeilo.

railways had change considerably from the dark days of the mid-1960s and, with a strong political will to ensure the line's survival, a new lightweight 6-metre steel span was installed to restore rail services.

Being one of the tens of thousands of commuters to daily pass through the UK's busiest station, London Waterloo, it seemed too good an opportunity, while on a visit to Llandeilo to take a 'peak hour' train to what is officially the least used station in Wales and

Early morning at Llandeilo on 19 April 2016, where ATW 150245 arrives on the recently-introduced commuter service, which has left Llandovery at 06.24 and will depart at 07.03 after passing a northbound service to Crewe.

one of the least used in the whole of Great Britain. So armed with my £4.40 day return to Sugar Loaf Halt (a suffix used on the ticket but not the station, and one I had thought no longer officially existed) it was a something of a thrill to alight at 07.45 from the first door of the first northbound train of the day at a station or halt used by only a handful of passengers a month! Like many other intermediate stations, Sugar Loaf had closed in 1965, but was re-opened in 1987 to cater principally for walkers.

Getting to this remote spot from Llandeilo had taken me along one of the finest stretches of the line, over the new Glanrhyd Bridge, where there is a permanent 20 mph speed restriction, through the delightful station at Llandovery, over the famous 18-arch Cynghordy Viaduct – covered in scaffolding while extensive maintenance was taking place, and finally through the 1,000 yard long Sugar Loaf Tunnel and past the sign indicating Sugar Loaf Summit (820 feet above sea level) just to the south of the diminutive platform. While it may only be a request stop used by around five passengers a month, Sugar Loaf does have a re-assuring digital train time display and can boast direct rail services to places as far afield as Cardiff and Crewe!

Today the Heart of Wales line remains and prospers as one of the UK's most scenic rail routes. Its basic service – currently operated by two-car Class 150 units – comprises four trains a day along the full length of the line, with two additional commuter-orientated weekday services having been introduced in May 2015, one from Llandrindod to Shrewsbury at the northern end of the line and one from Llandovery to Swansea at its southern end. During my April 2016 stay in Llandeilo I took the chance to sample this commuter service, just a year after its introduction, and there seems plenty of scope to promote it better to increase patronage. I was one of only two passengers on board as we left Llandeilo (07.03), with around a dozen on board by the time we reach Llanelli at 07.45, in good time for a Great Western HST service to Paddington, departing at 08.05.

The delightful spa town of Llandrindod Wells is the principal station along the route and one of five passing loops on the otherwise single-track route. Travel on the line is actively promoted by the Heart of Wales Line Travellers' Association, with virtually all of the remote halts along the line having been 'adopted' by local people. By contrast to routes elsewhere on the UK rail network, passenger numbers

At passing places along the Heart of Wales Line drivers will exchange the token for one single line section with one for the next. This is the token machine for the Llandeilo to Pantyfynnon section, which stands in a large cupboard on the southbound platform at Llandeilo.

ATW 150254 slows down to make a request stop on 20 April 2016, in order to pick up the author from Wales' least used station, Sugar Loaf. It is forming the 05.56 service from Shrewsbury, which will run through to Cardiff Central.

have remained fairly static over the past decade – at Llandrindod, annual passenger numbers slipped from 42,992 in 2004/5 to 39,648 in 2015/6 while at Llandeilo that decade has seen a healthy 30% rise in passenger numbers from 13,473 in 2004/5 to 17,562 in 2015/6. Elsewhere though, the picture is less rosy: at Builth Road, for example, the station for the spa town of Builth Wells, passenger numbers slipped from 8,530 in 2004/5 to 8,244 in 2015/6.

For some local people there is a feeling that not enough is being done to promote this remarkably scenic line, with trains such as the morning commuter service timed too early to attract large numbers of passengers. One such critic is Simon Buckley, a prominent member of the 'beerage' and currently boss of the renowned Evan Evans Brewery in Llandeilo. Over a couple of pints of his finest brew in the town's White Horse pub (and brewery tap), he told me of his vision to emulate the success of the Settle to Carlisle line in exploiting its scenic attractions to develop large scale tourist traffic.

Buckley is planning for his retirement from brewing and talks about his establishment of the Towy Valley Steam Company, establishing workshops capable of maintaining steam locomotives at Llandovery and running regular steam services between there and Llandeilo, with the possibility of also operating northwards from Llandovery over the famous Cynghordy Viaduct. He points out that the Heart of Wales Line is actually a main line route, but cannot realise its full potential with the present level of service, and believes that coach operators could bring thousands of tourists a year to patronise his planned steam services.

Nuclear power saves the Blaenau Ffestiniog branch

Flooding has been a common feature of railways in Wales, as noted above, and has been a recurrent feature of recent history on the other major Welsh survivor from the Beeching cuts, the delightful 28-mile long Conwy Valley branch line from Llandudno Junction to Blaenau Ffestiniog. While it may now be thriving like so many other British branch lines – passenger numbers at Blaenau Ffestiniog are up from 25,700 in 2004/5 to 35,826 in 2015/6 – it owes its survival not to its passing through marginal Parliamentary constituencies, but due to construction of a nuclear power station at Trawsfynydd in the early 1960s. That created the need to maintain a rail connection for the safe transport of nuclear waste flasks for re-processing at Sellafield.

Trawsfynydd, six miles south of Blaenau Ffestiniog, is situated on a former Greater Western Railway branch line to Bala Junction, where it had made a connection with the Ruabon–Barmouth line, another Beeching victim. While a short spur from Bala Junction to the town of Bala survived until that route's closure in 1964 the rest of the branch had been closed completely in 1961, so that part of the route could be flooded to create the huge Llyn Celyn reservoir. That led to a short new rail link being laid in Blaenau Ffestiniog between the station serving trains to Llandudno Junction and the former Great Western Branch terminus – a distance of around half a mile – so that nuclear traffic could then travel along the branch from Llandudno Junction to reach a loading point adjacent to the new nuclear facility.

Use of the Conwy Valley Line for nuclear traffic from Trawsfynydd helped ensure its survival through the dark days of the 1960s and 1970s until its true passenger potential was finally realised in 1982. This was the year which saw restoration for tourist services of the narrow gauge Ffestiniog Railway to Blaenau Ffestiniog, where a new joint station was opened on the site of what had been the town's Great Western station.

It meant a rail link had been re-established, albeit a seasonal and narrow gauge one, between the Cambrian Coast and the North Wales Coast and opened up many new journey opportunities. Amongst these, one I remember well and used a number of times was a 'Round Robin' day ticket from Birmingham New Street, offering a full day out by rail, travelling from Birmingham to Minffordd near Porthmadog on the Cambrian Coast, then up the Ffestiniog Railway to Blaenau Ffestiniog, along the Conwy Valley Line to Llandudno Junction, and finally back to Birmingham via Chester and Crewe.

Like the Heart of Wales Line, the Conwy Valley Line is another scenic gem, passing through some delightful terrain from the Conwy estuary, just south of Llandudno Junction, through the two main settlements along the route – Llanrwst and Betws-y-Coed – and a number of other small villages before reaching Blaenau Ffestiniog after going through one of the longest railway

Llanrwst North is the only crossing point on the 28-mile long Conwy Valley Line, with drivers pausing at the signal box here to exchange single line tokens. On 23 April 2016, ATW 150283 departs with a service for Llandudno.

tunnels in Britain and, at 2 miles and 333 yards, the UK's longest single-track rail tunnel.

In the days when it was possible to sit behind the driver of a diesel multiple unit and look ahead along the track in front of the train, it was possible on a southbound train, once past a slight curve at the north end of the tunnel to see a tiny pin-prick of light as the rest of the tunnel is dead straight. For a number of years after their displacement elsewhere, 'heritage' diesel multiple units

The new Llanrwst is a rather more modest structure than Llanrwst North, which stands less than half a mile beyond the short tunnel under the main road.

were marketed as a feature of the line and for at least one glorious summer the line was even operated by the first diesel locomotive to be delivered under the British Railways 1955 Modernisation Plan – English Electric Type 4 D200 (later renumbered 40122), which had been repainted in its original green livery, prior to eventual preservation.

Services today are provided by franchisee Arriva Trains Wales using two-car Class 150 units, with a service of six return trips on weekdays. The first southbound train of the day starts at Llandudno Junction, but all others work through to or from Llandudno. There are also three return trips on Sundays. Passenger numbers were given a major boost in 2007, when the Welsh Assembly Government granted free travel on the line to holders of concessionary bus passes who lived in the local area.

Patronage of Blaenau Ffestiniog branch services seems good, if my trip on a Saturday morning in April 2016 was any guide. With the benefit of a connecting arrival on the Ffestiniog Railway, there were at least 25 aboard on departure from the terminus, with a similar number joining at Betws-y-coed, 14 at Llanrwst and 5 at North Llanrwst, the only passing loop on the line. No services are scheduled to pass at what is now a request stop, so it is good to see that both platforms remain in use at this attractive station, which sees relatively few passengers since the 1989 opening of a new station closer to the town centre. What seems curious about public transport in the Conwy Valley is an apparent lack of co-ordination

A view of Blaenau Ffestiniog station on the afternoon of 23 April 2016 shows the convenient interchange between two railway systems. The Ffestiniog Railway's newest locomotive, 1979-built *Earl of Merioneth* backs onto its train for Porthmadog as ATW 150283 is about to depart for Llandudno.

between the rail timetable and that of the parallel X1 bus service, with two occasions daily in each direction when both rail and bus services leave Bleanau Ffestiniog and Llandudno within minutes of each other.

Five major re-openings in South Wales

Twenty years after Wales had seen the worst of Beeching, the tide began to turn in the late 1980s. Passenger traffic on the Valleys lines running northwards from Cardiff to Treherbert, Merthyr and Rhymney – as well as the southern routes to Penarth and Barry – had always been heavy, and with the demise of coal mining and heavy industry, there were a handful of opportunities to restore passenger services to what had previously been freight-only routes, in order to cater for the steadily growing demand for rail services into the capital.

So, in October 1987 came the first of a quintet of revival schemes when the City Line was re-opened to passenger services. This is a 4¾-mile long loop running west from Cardiff Central station via Ninian Park – a station which had seen football specials but had no regular service despite being in a populous part of the city – and on to Radyr, a station north-west of Cardiff city centre and on the busy route to Pontypridd, Treherbert and Merthy Tydfil. Besides offering regular weekday services to Ninian Park, the new service led to the opening of three new stations, Danescourt, Fairwater and Waun-Gron Park.

Leaving Cardiff Central in a westward direction, the service passes behind Canton shed before its first stop at Ninian Park, whose long platforms are a reminder of its former role as a

Cardiff Central has been expanded to cater for growth in passenger numbers. On 30 April 2016 work to complete the new Platform 8 is about to see track laid onto new concrete sleepers, as 143609 arrives with a City Line service to Radyr.

Ninian Park station is well situated for the new Cardiff City Stadium and stands close to Canton depot, which can be seen to the left on 30 April 2016 as 153303 arrives with a service for Radyr.

destination for football specials to Cardiff City's former home. Yet the club's new home, the Cardiff City Stadium, is a mere 300 yards away, so it seems surprising that more use is not made of the station, particularly as it also has bi-directional signalling to allow trains to terminate there. Beyond Ninian Park the line runs parallel with the GW Main Line for half a mile before crossing it shortly before Waun-Gron Park, on an embankment above a main road and in a major residential area.

Heading north-west the line then passes in a pleasantly wooded cutting through the other two intermediate stops – Fairwater and

Danescourt is one of two pleasantly rural stations on the City Line, and the last stop before Radyr, where services connect with those for the Treherbert, Aberdare and Merthyr Tydfil lines. No passengers are in sight as 153323 pauses with a Radyr-bound service on 30 April 2016.

Danescourt – before terminating in the westernmost of three platforms at Radyr, for onward connections to Pontypridd and beyond. On the day of my visit, a Saturday in April 2016, there was a modest but steady level of passenger traffic, with services in the hands of Class 142/3 Pacer units and single coach Class 153 units.

The current half-hourly service operates almost as a circular service from Radyr via Cardiff to Coryton, a terminus station in a northern suburb of Cardiff that is less than two miles east of Radyr. Future developments will see the unpopular Pacer units replaced by 2019, as they do not meet the access requirements of the 1995 Disability Discrimination Act, while the route should eventually be electrified as part of the Valleys Lines electrification project. Traffic has built up significantly over the past few years – At Fairwater, for example, passenger numbers rose from 18,063 in 2004/5 to 70,910 in 2015/6, while at Danescourt numbers doubled in the decade from 45,943 in 2004/5 to 104,278 in 2015/6.

Next stop Aberdare

A second line to re-open in South Wales prior to devolution was the 7½-mile branch line from Abercynon, a junction on the Valleys Line to Merthyr Tydfil, to Aberdare. This had been a Beeching closure in 1964, but the line had survived as an important freight route, particularly for coal traffic from Tower Colliery at Hirwaun, north of Aberdare, which had earned the dubious distinction of being the last operating deep mine in the South Wales valleys before it finally closed in January 2008. Like the City Line, it was re-opened with support from the local authority – in this case Mid Glamorgan Council.

The Aberdare line re-opening, on 3 October 1988, included four intermediate stations – Cwmbach, Fernhill, Mountain Ash and Penrhiwceiber – and was an immediate success, with passenger numbers having risen year after year. Since re-opening there has been significant further investment in the line. In 2005 the Welsh Assembly Government (WAG) committed funding to allow platforms at all stations on the line to be extended to accommodate four-car trains then, in 2007, the WAG made a further investment in the line, with a two-mile stretch of the line near Abercynon being made double-track in order to permit the introduction of half-hourly services.

Helped by the improved service frequency, passenger numbers have risen steadily over the past decade, with Aberdare itself seeing an increase from 464,026 in 2004/5 to 566,904 in 2015/6. Such has been the success that in November 2009 the Welsh Assembly Government commissioned a feasibility study from Network Rail into a potential extension of services to Hirwaun, which had continued to be used for coal traffic until the previous year. Later, in March 2011, the WAG made a commitment to the re-opening as

Freight traffic continues to use the Aberdare branch to reach Hirwaun and there are hopes that passenger services may be introduced. This 20 March 2016 view, looking north from the current Aberdare station, shows the line to Hirwaun and the remarkably well-preserved former Aberdare High Level station.

part of a local regeneration scheme, but work on the project has not yet begun.

Today well-patronised half-hourly services on the Aberdare line are in the hands of Class 150 Sprinter units and the unloved Class 142/143 Pacer units. The route traces a wooded valley of the Cynon River, with very little evidence left at places like Mountain Ash, the principal intermediate station, of the extensive coal mining activities which ensured that passenger services could be reinstated more than 40 years after they had ended. At Aberdare

Mountain Ash was once one of the most important coal mining centres in this part of South Wales, but today no evidence remains. On Sunday, 20 March 2016, 150259 pauses with a southbound service from Aberdare to Barry Island.

itself, the remains of the former High Level station can be seen just north of the present station, alongside the remaining freight-only section of line towards Hirwaun.

Taking a first ever trip from Aberdare into Cardiff on the Saturday of a Six Nations match in March 2016 aboard one of the reviled Pacer units that still dominate Valleys Line services gave a good impression of how, almost three decades after re-opening, the line has become a well-established part of the local transport infrastructure, while a lengthy pause at Mountain Ash to pass a Class 66-hauled train of empty EWS hoppers provides a brief reminder of the once-dominant freight traffic on the myriad of Valleys routes.

At Abercynon the track layout has been remodelled since re-opening to create a combined junction station controlled by a new signalling centre, but further south there are a couple of notable historic survivals. One is the magnificently restored station building at Pontypridd, The other, with particularly nostalgic memory for me, is the west abutment and a solitary remaining pier of the famous Walnut Tree Viaduct, just south of Taffs Well station, which once carried the Barry Railway over the river gorge. As a child accompanying my father on a trip to seek out surviving and working National Coal Board steam locomotives in South Wales, I vividly remember walking over the viaduct shortly before its demolition in 1969.

This schematic map of the Welsh Railway network shows the five re-opened lines in South Wales, along with stations on the main line from Cardiff to Swansea and Fishguard & Goodwick in West Wales. (*Map courtesy of Arriva Trains Wales*)

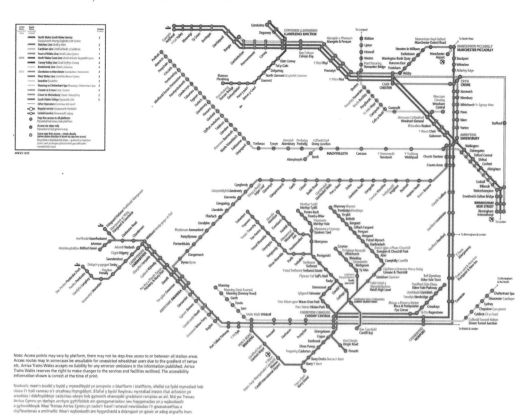

Note: Access points may vary by platform, there may not be step-free access to or between all station areas. Access routes may in somecases be unsuitable for unassisted wheelchair users due to the gradient of ramps etc. Arriva Trains Wales accepts no liability for any erronor information published. Arriva Trains Wales reserves the right to make changes to the services and facilities outlined. The accessibility information shown is correct at the time of print.

Nodwch: mae'n bosibl y bydd y mynedfeydd yn amrywio o blatfform i blatfform, efallai na fydd mynediad heb risiau i'r holl rannau o'r orsafneu rhyngddynt. Efallai y bydd llwybrau mynediad mewn rhai achosion yn anaddas i ddefnyddwyr cadeiriau olwyn heb gymorth oherwydd graddiant rampiau ac ati. Nid yw Trenau Arriva Cymru yn derbyn unrhyw gyfrifoldeb am gamgymeriadau neu hepgoriadau yn y wybodaeth a gyhoeddwyd. Mae Trenau Arriva Cymru yn cadw'r hawl i wneud newidiadau i'r gwasanaethau a chyfleusterau a amlinellir. Mae'r wybodaeth am hygyrchedd a ddangosir yn gywir ar adeg argraffu hwn.

Maesteg rejoins the network

My earliest memory of Wales' third re-opening is of travelling from Bridgend on a Class 121 'Bubble Car' single unit DMU to what was the temporary end of the line at Cymmer Afan, shortly before the line closed to passengers in July 1970. The line had originally continued in a horseshoe shape to Treherbert at the top of the Rhondda valley, but had been severed beyond this remote spot by the disputed discovery of subsidence in the 3,443 yard long Rhondda Tunnel – the second longest in Wales after the one at Blaenau Ffestiniog – in 1968.

Support from Mid Glamorgan County Council and a long campaign to secure its revival led British Rail to re-open the branch line from Bridgend as far as Maesteg in 1992 – freight traffic had once again been the line's saviour, having continued to serve local coal mines until 1988. A new station was built in Maesteg town centre, a short distance from the original Maesteg Castle Street station and five intermediate stations were provided, at Maesteg (Ewenny Road), Garth, Tondu, Sarn and Wildmill.

Following a change in the franchise map that put the line from Severn Tunnel Junction to Gloucester into the Wales franchise, services on the line provide a somewhat improbable sounding hourly link between Maesteg and Cheltenham Spa. As in the case of the Aberdare and City Lines, traffic growth on the Maesteg route has been significant and sustained. At Maesteg passenger numbers have risen from 137,000 in 2004/5 to 184,906 in 2015/6 while at the principal intermediate station on the line, Tondu, the number of users has increased in a decade, from 28,396 in 2004/5 to 41,222 in 2015/6.

Tondu is the principal intermediate station on the eight-mile route from Bridgend to Maesteg, boasting a large signal box and an array of semaphore signals. On 18 April 2016, 150284 departs with a northbound service to Maesteg.

Returning from Maesteg the driver of 150284 is about to hand over the single line token before entering Tondu station with a service to Cheltenham Spa.

Travelling from Bridgend to Maesteg is a pleasant eight-mile trip on a Class 150 unit – no danger of Pacers on this line due to their origin/destination of Cheltenham. After the Wildmill and Sarn on the outskirts of Bridgend, the most interesting point on the line is Tondu, where there is the briefest of reminders of how this was once an important junction for freight traffic with what look like mothballed lines joining from west and east just north of the station. Here too, at least on my visit in April 2016, is a manual signal box

Schoolchildren join the 15.17 service from Maesteg on 18 April 2016 and will alight at intermediate stations on the eight-mile journey to Bridgend.

and a number of semaphore signals, with the signaller handing the driver a token for the five-mile section onwards to Maesteg.

Beyond Tondu the line follows a pleasantly wooded course, with no evidence remaining anywhere of the once extensive mining operations that were the line's saviour and made re-opening possible. A weekday return journey from Maesteg at 15.17 saw the train filled with dozens of school children on their way home – a reminder that, like the Cambrian Coast Line with its school traffic from Tywyn and Harlech, the railway fulfils a vital social purpose. How many of them or their parents, I was left wondering, have ever stayed on their train for its full two hour journey and visited my one-time home of Cheltenham? Indeed, how many Cheltonians have ever availed themselves of the hourly service to visit Maesteg? Precious few, I suspect!

Vale of Glamorgan

Fourth among the South Wales re-openings, and one of the two highlighted in the Network Rail strategy document as where 'patronage has outstripped all expectations' was the 19-mile long Vale of Glamorgan Line from Barry to Bridgend. Barry – or strictly speaking Barry Island – is at the end of a busy Valley Lines route into Cardiff, but the continuation from Barry Town to Bridgend had fallen victim to Beeching in June 1964.

It had, however, remained as an important diversionary route, seeing regular use when engineering work closed the South Wales Main Line between Cardiff and Bridgend. The line had also remained an important freight route, principally for coal to Aberthaw power station and for the transport of completed vehicle engines out of the Ford plant at Bridgend, which opened in 1980 and has a rail connection to the Vale of Glamorgan Line.

The first moves towards a re-opening had come with publication of *Rails to the Vale* by Railfuture in 1997, which claimed that a revived rail service could cover its costs. This was soon followed by a report from the SWIFT (South Wales Integrated Fast Transit) consortium of local authorities promoting the re-opening and, in August 1999, a re-opening proposal was presented to the Welsh Assembly Government by two local authorities, Vale of Glamorgan and Bridgend Borough Councils.

This was accepted and the £17 million revival scheme began in June 2004, including significant track renewal, improved signalling, and the construction of a new platform at Barry station, a new bay platform at Bridgend station, and the re-building of two intermediate stations, at Rhoose Cardiff International Airport and at Llantwit Major. A significant driver of the scheme was expansion of Cardiff International Airport, located around 1.5 miles from Rhoose station, to which a dedicated rail-link bus service from the airport was launched to coincide with the start of the new rail service in June 2005.

When the Vale of Glamorgan Line was re-opened to passenger traffic in 2005, a new bay platform 1A was created at Bridgend for terminating services. On 18 April 2016, 150253 prepares to return to the capital with a Vale of Glamorgan service.

In June 2015, the Vale of Glamorgan line celebrated the tenth anniversary of its re-opening, during which time passenger numbers have risen steadily, to a total of 340,000 in 2014. The occasion was marked by a visit to Llantwit Major from the Welsh Assembly Government's Minister for Economy, Science and Transport, Edwina Hart. Here passenger numbers have risen from 209,000 in 2005/6 – the year since its re-opening – to 304,630 in 2015/6.

A mixture of locals and air passengers prepare to board ATW 142080 at Rhoose Cardiff International Airport on 18 April 2016. This station has staggered platforms, with the down platform on the far side of the level crossing.

This growth has been driven by the parking and cycle storage facilities provided when the station was rebuilt, as well as good bus links with local communities. Meantime, at the line's other intermediate station – Rhoose Cardiff International Airport – the growth in passenger numbers has been even greater, with numbers increasing from 101,000 in the re-opening year to 182,750 in 2015/6. Services on the route currently comprise a basic hourly train from Bridgend to Barry and Cardiff, which then continues to Aberdare, while in the reverse direction, services originate at Merthyr Tydfil.

The service is operated by a mixture of Class 150 and Pacer units and the hourly services are timed to pass near Rhoose Cardiff International Airport station – the longest officially named station in the UK – so that a single bus can connect each hour with the two trains that serve the station and depart within six minutes of each other. Given the cheap and convenient airport bus link, it seems slightly curious that the service faces competition not just from car borne passengers, but also a more frequent direct bus service from the airport to Cardiff city centre.

West of Barry the line crosses the splendid and Grade II Listed Porthkerry Viaduct, from where there are the first views across the Bristol Channel towards north Somerset, which are a feature of much of this line. Beyond the fast expanding settlement at Rhoose there is the well-used freight loop line to Aberthaw power station, which diverges just west of the former station, on whose platform stands an attractive but redundant signal box.

To the north of the line is another rail-connected facility, the cement works, although traffic here looked a good deal less regular. Further on, the remains of a former platform at St Athan

After setting down a large number of passengers at Llantwit Major, ATW 150230 accelerates away from the station on 30 April 2016 with a Vale of Glamorgan Line service for Bridgend.

Llantwit Major is an attractive coastal town on the Vale of Glamorgan Line, where passenger numbers have risen by around 50% since the line's re-opening to passenger services. On Saturday, 30 April 2016, a large crowd waits to board a service for Cardiff and Aberdare formed by two-car unit 150230.

are reminder that here is a significant settlement and important RAF base, which could well justify a future station re-opening, particularly given the 750 new jobs to be created locally when a new $280 million Aston Martin car plant is opened nearby. Second of the two re-opened intermediate stations is Llantwit Major, where there is a steady stream of passengers using the services and another place with a holiday feel about it and more views across the water to Minehead and the Somerset coast.

Ebbw Vale

A fifth, and the most successful of all Welsh re-openings to date, was not even a line closed by Beeching, having lost its passenger service in 1962, a year before his infamous report was released. This is the 2008 revival of services from Cardiff to Ebbw Vale along a 20-mile branch which leaves the South Wales main line just west of Newport. Once again, it was its continued use for freight traffic, in this case for 40 years after the withdrawal of passenger services, which made its revival a feasible proposition.

The route had remained in use to transport production from town's steelworks until its final closure in 2002, sometime after the first proposals for its re-opening to passenger services had appeared. Then, in the year that the steelworks closed down, the Welsh Assembly Government gave its backing to the railway revival plan as one of the measures aimed at helping regenerate the area.

Re-opening of the line on 6 February 2008, represented the culmination of a £30 million project which had been developed by a trio of local authorities – Blaenau Gwent County Borough

Cross Keys station is at the north end of the original double track section of line on the Ebbw Vale route. On 21 November 2015, ATW 150231 is at the rear of a mixed four-car formation on a northbound service for Ebbw Vale Town.

Council, Caerphilly County Borough Council, and Newport City Council – together with the Welsh Assembly Government, South East Wales Transport Alliance (a grouping of ten local authorities in the region), Network Rail and Arriva Trains Wales. Funding for the line came from Welsh Assembly Government, Corus Regeneration Grant and the European Objective One Programme.

At the time of its original re-opening, six new stations were opened – at Rogerstone, Risca & Pontymister, Crosskeys, Newbridge, Llanhilleth, and Ebbw Vale Parkway. Almost 400 car parking spaces were provided at the new stations, along with new signalling and a three mile section of double track installed on the otherwise single track line in order to be able to operate an hourly service from Ebbw Vale Parkway to Cardiff. Since re-opening, another intermediate station at Pye Corner, near Newport, was opened in December 2014, while on 17 May 2015, the line was extended one mile northwards to a new single platform station at Ebbw Vale Town, on the site of the former steelworks, following a further £11.5 million investment by the Welsh Assembly Government.

From the day it re-opened, passengers using the hourly service to Cardiff have far exceeded original forecasts. At the time of re-opening, 22,000 passengers a month had been anticipated, yet by December 2008 the figure had reached 44,000 a month, which was not only double the original forecast but also far in excess of the 33,000 target set for the year 2012. With the monthly total having reached 55,000 by May 2009, over-crowding on trains had become a major problem and longer trains were provided on many services to cope with demand.

Such has been the success of Ebbw Vale's re-opening that there have been repeated calls for an improved service frequency,

Ebbw Vale Town station was the most recent station to open on this highly successful line when a one-mile extension from Ebbw Vale Parkway opened in May 2015. In unseasonal sunshine on Saturday 21 November 2015, 153353 heads a three-coach formation on a diverted service to Newport.

for the establishment of a direct link to Newport and for the rebuilding of a short spur off the existing line from Llanhilleth to Abertillery. In May 2015, WAG Transport minister Edwina Hart said the Government was looking at whether a new station in Abertillery could be built near a Tesco superstore in the town, and also announced that work to allow more services on the Ebbw Vale line, including potential trains to Abertillery, had already started.

Taking my first trip on the Ebbw Vale line in November 2015, on a Saturday when services were operating to and from Newport due to engineering work, it was heartening to see work had indeed begun on extending the current short double track section northwards from Cross Keys through Newbridge and north of Llanhilleth to the former junction of the line to Abertillery, prior to increasing the service frequency to half-hourly. At that stage of the redoubling project no work had started on new platforms at either Newbridge or Llanhilleth, nor was there any work taking place on the branch to Abertillery.

First impressions of the Ebbw Vale line are of a rather scenic route, although not marketed as such, with the lower section reminiscent to me of the Golden Valley line in the Stroud valley. Apart from the pleasant wooded ascent towards Ebbw Vale, there is the impressive Park Junction signal box, where the line from Gaer Junction outside Newport station joins the normal route for passenger trains that have left the main line at Ebbw Junction. West of Park Junction there is the surviving freight-only branch line to Machen Quarry, which once continued to Caerphilly, and was closed to passengers in 1956, but was identified by the

Regular Ebbw Vale Line services pass within a mile of Newport but do not serve the town. Engineering work on 21 November 2015 meant services were running to and from Newport, making easier connections for those heading away from Cardiff.

now disbanded South East Wales Transport Alliance (SEWTA) as another long-term re-opening candidate.

Travelling on a diverted train from Newport is a reminder of just how close the line passes to the town without normally stopping and the potential for a direct service that would give stations on the branch a direct connection to services eastwards for places like Bristol and London. Significant expansion of Newport station, with the recent addition of a fourth platform, would allow regular Ebbw Vale services to terminate, but some re-signalling work is apparently necessary at Gaer junction, where a direct spur from the Ebbw Vale line joins the South Wales main line just west of Newport station.

New stations and two new services

Besides the highly successful quintet of line re-openings, the Welsh rail revival has also included launch of two significant new services, with the opening of yet more new stations. First of these was Swanline, launched in June 1994 to provide new local services between Swansea and Cardiff and included the opening (re-opening) of five stations – Pyle, Baglan, Briton Ferry, Skewen and Llansamlet. Traffic did not develop as fast as had been hoped, however, so the service frequency was reduced to two-hourly in 1999 and remains at that level today.

Despite the limited service frequency – there are additional peak time services, but no Sunday trains – traffic has nevertheless built up steadily. By far the most important of the five stations is Pyle – between Bridgend and Port Talbot – where passenger

The seaside resort of Tenby is by far the most important intermediate station on the Whitland to Pembroke Dock branch and the only remaining passing loop. On 19 April 2016, the driver of 150245, forming the 11.49 service to Pembroke Dock, prepares to retrieve the single line token from the turquoise cupboard near the footbridge.

numbers have increased threefold in a decade, from 48,000 in 2004/5 to 120,732 in 2015/6. Passengers numbers at Briton Ferry (35,224 in 2015/6) Baglan (26,882 in 2015/6) and Skewen (45,172 in 2015/6) have all roughly doubled in that period, with the least growth at Llansamlet, where the increase has been just over 60% to a 2015/6 total of 33,862.

A much more recent revival has been on the line between Carmarthen and Fishguard Harbour, which for many years had only seen two trains a day, both timed to connect with the ferry service to Rosslare and one of them being in the early hours of the morning, so of very little use to local users of the line. Given the potential passenger traffic originating at the West Wales port – and the adjacent town of Goodwick – the Welsh Assembly Government announced in March 2011 that it would fund a re-opening of the station at Fishguard & Goodwick, which is in the town of Goodwick and a mile short of the Harbour station, and finance an experimental five additional local services on the line for a period of three years.

The three year experimental service was launched in September 2011 and proved successful, with passenger numbers at the re-opened Fishguard & Goodwick station rising from 12,072 in 2012/3 to 17,062 a year later and 19,946 in 2015/6. In August 2014, WAG Transport Minister, Edwina Hart, announced that the service would continue until the end of the current Wales rail franchise in 2018, after a review of the three year experimental period had generated positive feedback from the local community, passengers and business, while research showed they had brought economic and social benefits.

'The extra services between Fishguard and Carmarthen have been very popular with passengers, helped improve access

Fishguard & Goodwick on 19 April 2016, where a lone passenger prepares to board 150245, the 09.56 service to Carmarthen. Stena Line's plans to redevelop Fishguard Harbour may see this become the terminus for all rail services to the ferry port.

to services and provided a boost for tourism and other local businesses,' said Ms. Hart. 'The results of surveys with passengers, the local community and businesses point to a need for these extra services.' More than 60% of passengers surveyed said they would not have been able to make their intended journey without the additional services, according to a report in the *Western Telegraph*

The Whitland signaller hands the Whitland–Tenby single line token to the driver of 150285 on 19 April 2016, as the train pauses outside Whitland station with the 14.00 service from Swansea to Pembroke Dock.

After pausing at Narberth, 150285 heads into the 273-yard long Narberth tunnel on 19 April 2016, with a service for Pembroke Dock. Note the HST stop board close to the tunnel mouth and a considerable distance from the platform.

on 11 August 2014, while businesses reported that the extra trains helped attract visitors to the area, leading to increased usage of the Pembrokeshire coastal path and of the ferries to and from Ireland.

Fishguard is a pleasant 35 minute journey from Whitland, junction of the Pembroke Dock branch, with the main items of railway interest being the signal box and token exchange just west of Clarbeston Road station, the remains of Welsh Hook halt, and the long disused passing loop at Letterston Junction, where the track on a short branch line to the former Royal Naval Armaments Depot at Trecwn remains intact. Fishguard & Goodwick station boasts a café and a free car park – a welcome feature common to many stations across Wales that seems alien to someone living in South East England and familiar with ever increasing station parking costs.

But patronage of the new services has significant scope to be improved – I was the only passenger on the 09.10 from Whitland when I visited the line in April 2016 and had only one fellow passenger for company on my 09.57 return from Fishguard & Goodwick. One potentially damaging blow has come from Stena Line, operator of the ferry service to Rosslare, which wants to close the line from Fishguard & Goodwick to Fishguard Harbour and replace the train service with a bus, as part of a planned redevelopment of its harbour facilities.

Revival hopes on Anglesey

Away from the significant rail revival that is taking place in South Wales, on the island of Anglesey there are longstanding hopes that a branch line off the main route to Holyhead will be revived, at least in part. This is the 17½-mile route from Gaerwen northwards to Amlwch, which became another victim of Dr Beeching, when passenger services were withdrawn in December 1964, but remarkably survived almost exactly 30 years more for freight services to the Associated Octel chemical plant, which had been built in 1953 and generated some 70,000 tonnes of freight traffic a year until it was finally lost to road in 1993. The chemical plant itself closed and was demolished a decade later.

Spurred on by the efforts of a local campaigning group, Anglesey Central Railway Ltd, the Welsh Assembly Government ordered Network Rail in 2009 to conduct a feasibility study into the restoration of services from Bangor to Llangefni, some four miles north of the junction at Gaerwen and the principal intermediate station on the branch line. In 2011, as part of its study, Network Rail began cutting away vegetation from the 'mothballed' line and examining structures on the Gaerwen–Llangefni section of line, including the station site at Llangefni. Meantime the campaign group was given the go ahead to clear vegetation along the rest of the remaining route to Amlwch, on which it hopes to run heritage services, if the WAG does not go ahead with a full re-opening of the line.

Behind the re-opening plan is a need to improve communications between the north eastern parts of Anglesey and the mainland, so reducing the pressure on the road bridge across the Menai Strait. At the time its 2009 study was launched, Mike Gallop of Network Rail was cautious about the challenge: 'The Amlwch line has been disused for nearly two decades and bringing it back to passenger use will be tough', he told *Railnews*. 'Today we are taking that first step, working together with the Welsh Assembly Government and the council, to see if it is possible to meet the aspiration of restoring services the line. For passenger trains to run on the line again, we may need to modernise the existing signalling system, repair and replace the disused track, bridges and culverts, which are no longer fit for purpose.'

An electrifying future

Along with Albania, Wales has long been one of the very few countries in Europe without a single mile of electrified railway line. But the Principality is about to lose that dubious honour with keenly-awaited electrification of the South Wales Main Line as far west as Swansea, due to be completed sometime in the next decade, and the equally significant £500 million electrification of the entire Valleys Lines network, including all the re-opened lines such as Ebbw Vale and the Vale of Glamorgan. Overhead wires were due to reach Cardiff in 2017, while the Valley lines scheme is due to take place between 2019 and 2024, in what the rail industry calls Control Period 6, but the whole timetable has been called into doubt by the significant cost over-runs and delays that have beset the Great Western Main Line electrification project. Cardiff should now be reached by 2019, with the extension to Swansea coming during CP6 (2019–24)

An encouraging sign for future rail expansion in Wales came on 15 March 2016, with the signing of a £1.2bn Cardiff Capital Region deal, designed to improve public transport and bring economic growth over the next 20 years. This came shortly after an update to Network Rail's Welsh Route Study forecast that passenger numbers on Valleys Lines services would increase by 76% between 2013–23, with Vale of Glamorgan Line patronage to rise 80% over that period and numbers to more than double (+112%) on the Ebbw Vale Line. A key feature of the deal was funding to the tune of £734 million for the development of South Wales Metro, encompassing the long-awaited Valleys Line electrification project along with bus and light rail developments, which promises to bring a step change in the quality and frequency of rail and bus travel in the capital and valleys. This deal involves 10 local councils and aims to attract 25,000 new jobs and an extra £4 billion in private sector investment to the region.

Chapter 6

A HIGH PRICE FOR HIGH SPEED

Besides the re-openings that have taken place across England, Scotland and Wales, a quartet of major projects have either been completed, are nearing completion or are at an advanced stage of planning. Two of these are new high speed lines – one linking London with the Channel Tunnel (HS1) and one that will eventually link the capital with Birmingham and the North (HS2) – while within London, the other two schemes that are poised to transform the way people cross the capital are the Crossrail and Thameslink developments, both scheduled for completion in 2018 and featured in the next chapter of this story.

High Speed One

Sitting on a Eurostar train as it races through the Kent countryside at 180 mph – passing Ashford barely half an hour after leaving the capital and reaching the Channel Tunnel only five minutes later – it is hard to remember that the tortuous development of what is formally called the Channel Tunnel Rail Link (CTRL) was every bit as controversial and fought over as the current battles being waged by those in Camden and the Home Counties against the development of HS2. With arguments raging over the cost of HS2 and a consultant's appraisal of HS1, published in October 2015, stating that it had failed to regenerate deprived areas in the southeast and had left the taxpayer out of pocket, it is worth considering its rationale, what it was meant to deliver and whether it was all worth the cost.

HS1 cost £5.8 billion to build and the 68-mile line was opened in November 2007, transforming the Eurostar service from London to Paris and Brussels and opening up the potential for new high speed domestic passenger services to destinations across Kent. Three years after it opened the line was sold (or rather a 30-year concession to operate it was sold) to two Canadian pension funds – Borealis Infrastructure and the Ontario Teachers' Pension Plan – for £2.1 billion, a deal which was acclaimed by the then Transport

Secretary, Philip Hammond, as being 'a big vote of confidence in the future of high speed rail.' Presumably the same curious logic will be applied when, in 20 years' time, HS2 is sold off to foreign investors for around one third of what it cost to build it!

What completion of HS1 did mark, however, was the final end to almost 40 years of arguments over the choice of route for a rail link from the Channel Tunnel to London. This began in earnest in 1973 when, with an Anglo–French agreement on the building of a Channel Tunnel nearing completion, British Rail proposed no less than four alternative routes through Kent, reducing this to one preferred route the following year, which broadly followed the existing rail alignment westward from Ashford via Tonbridge to Redhill, after which it would then head for a new terminal on the West London line at White City, where there were good connections to the west and north, as well as underground stations nearby.

This proposal aroused fierce local opposition and there was considerable uncertainty about how much it would cost. Having originally been costed at just £99 million, the price tag quickly rose to £337 million as extras, like provision for freight traffic and a lengthy tunnel in south London, were factored in. By the time the Government responded to the stock market crash and oil crisis, and decided to halt the whole Channel Tunnel project on 14 January 1975, the estimated cost of the rail link had risen still further to £373 million.

Jumping forward 11 years, a key moment in the gestation of the Channel Rail Link came on 20 January 1986 when, flush with her success at securing a budget rebate from the EEC (in June 1984), Prime Minister Margaret Thatcher signed a treaty with French President Francois Mitterrand paving the way for construction of a Channel Tunnel. A winning bidder – Channel Tunnel Group – was chosen, and by February 1987 the Channel Tunnel Act had been passed.

Using taxpayer funds to build a dedicated high speed rail connection to the Channel Tunnel was specifically ruled out in the Channel Tunnel Act (1987), which deemed that the entire Channel Tunnel project was to be funded in the private sector. The key clause in that Act stated: '…. no Minister of the Crown or Government department shall provide funds to the Concessionaires, or guarantees of a financial or commercial nature relating to the performance of any obligations of the Concessionaires, in respect of the construction or operation of the tunnel system or any part of it.'

In his excellent study of the HS1 project *The Right Line,* Nicholas Faith neatly sums up the 1987 Act: 'The Act was a triumph of Thatcherite thinking. It avoided any discussion of wider issues like regional policy, planning or the environment and concentrated almost exclusively on the transport aspects of the project…. Financially it distinguished between the private sector nature

of the tunnel itself and the public-sector funding required for improving the existing rail infrastructure to serve it. It crucially omitted the powers required to build a wholly new rail link to the Tunnel, assuming that construction of such a line could be left to Mrs Thatcher's beloved private sector.'

With no immediate prospect of a dedicated new rail link, British Rail began preparing for the planned Channel Tunnel opening in 1993 by identifying how the £700m fleet of new high speed Eurostar trains could reach London by using what was known as Boat Train Route One, with some investment in making the long straight section of this line from Tonbridge to Ashford suitable for 100 mph running. Victoria station, historic terminus of Channel boat trains, was not large enough to accommodate the new 18-coach Eurostar trains, so another significant slice of the £1.7 billion budget for rail infrastructure improvements related to the Channel Tunnel was the £130m cost of building a dedicated new terminal alongside Waterloo station, which would be reached by a specially-built flyover near the locomotive depot at Stewarts Lane.

Other significant investments made prior to the launch of Eurostar services were £80m spent on developing a new depot at North Pole Junction alongside the Great Western Main Line from Paddington, work to upgrade the West London Line to allow the new fleet to access its depot and a total of some £140m spent on a fleet of 139 'Nightstar' carriages which it had been planned would provide a luxury overnight service to Paris and other continental

A Javelin Class 395 set enters a deserted Stratford International on 14 May 2016 with a service for St Pancras International. Note Platform 1 to the right, which was designed for use by Eurostar services but is currently disused.

destinations from a number of provincial cities as far afield as Glasgow and Plymouth. Sadly the project was abandoned before ever being launched, and the entire fleet of coaches was eventually exported to Canada for a knock-down price of just £12m.

Pressure for a dedicated high speed link began to build up from a number of quarters. Eurotunnel's Chief Executive Alastair Morton was an astute lobbyist and campaigned hard for a new line at a time when Eurotunnel was producing ever more optimistic forecasts of future passenger traffic to support its calls for more investment into the financially struggling Eurotunnel project. Meantime, Kent County Council saw the potential of a new line as a means of regenerating places like Ashford, where it wanted a new station to be provided, while the real catalyst for a dedicated new line came from the French, whose own high speed link from Paris to Lille and Calais had opened in 1993, the year before the tunnel itself was opened.

After several years of fierce wrangling over the route of a new high speed link, a route was eventually identified which avoided the devastating impact of British Rail's proposed options, involved no demolition of residential properties at all and reached a refurbished St Pancras station via a lengthy tunnel through Stratford and East London. While it had long been accepted that public funding would be required to build the link, contrary to the spirit of the 1987 Act, the rules had to be bent and that was done by passage of the Channel Tunnel Rail Link Act 1996.

This was effectively political fudge which meant the link could be built with public funds provided it was used not just for Eurostar services, but also by new high speed domestic services. In February 1996 London and Continental Railways (LCR) was announced as the winning consortium in the race to build the Channel Tunnel Rail Link and in December of that year the Act was passed, providing for a high speed rail link that would be used by both international and domestic services. New stations would be built at Stratford and Ebbsfleet, and St Pancras station would be developed as the London terminus.

The plan was that LCR would finance and build the link under a Private Finance Initiative (PFI) deal, secured by revenues from both the international and domestic services, but crucially the government agreed to provide direct grants totalling £1.8 billion for construction of the line and its use by domestic train services. At the same time, LCR claimed it would spread the benefits from the new line beyond the south-east, by creating a new link north of Kings Cross station to the West Coast Main Line. As asserted in a House of Commons debate on the Bill (29 February 1996) 'That will allow direct and frequent international services from cities such as Manchester and Birmingham, bypassing St Pancras and calling at Stratford. That will cut journey times by up to an hour: for instance, Birmingham will be just four hours from Paris and Manchester five hours.'

On 14 May 2016, one of the original Class 373 Eurostar sets heads down into the tunnel east of Stratford International on its journey towards the Channel Tunnel. These 20-car trains, first introduced in 1993, are the longest and fastest trains to operate in the UK.

LCR quickly came unstuck when at the end of 1997 it became evident that the Eurostar traffic forecasts has proved over–optimistic and LCR was therefore left in a position where it was forced to go cap in hand to the Government for a bail out in order to prevent it going bust. The consortium told the Deputy Prime Minister and Secretary of State for Environment, Transport and the Regions, John Prescott, that it needed a further £1.2 billion in addition to the £1.8 billion already committed. Prescott declared that unacceptable, leading to four months of negotiations, culminating in a deal in June 1998 which saw restructuring of the project and LCR's role.

Under the new deal with LCR and Railtrack, a new management team was installed at LCR, the company agreed to raise new equity to finance the project, and Railtrack agreed to take a major role in managing the project, by overseeing construction of the first section of line, from the Channel Tunnel to Fawkham Junction in North Kent, committing to purchase this section on completion and having an option to build and acquire the remainder of the line. At the same time, a bid to operate the Eurostar service was accepted from a consortium comprising British Airways, National Express and the French and Belgian state railways, SNCF and SNCB.

In announcing the deal, Prescott told the House of Commons on 3 June 1998:

'I have always made it clear that the Government required a fair deal for the taxpayer, consistent with the Government's existing obligations under the contract, and this deal most certainly

achieves that. The basic grant remains at £1.8 billion. There will be no requirement for additional Government support before 2010. Moreover, following intensive negotiations, the extent of the Government's additional contribution will not be the £1.2 billion requested in January, nor the £700 million about which hon. Members may have read in the press this week. It will be £140 million.

'Recognising the unique features of the project and our commitment to strengthen international rail transport links, we have agreed that the Government's credit will stand behind £3.7 billion of bonds issued by LCR privately in the City to fund the project…. That debt will be repaid out of the proceeds of the sale of the completed link. The risk of the Government incurring liability under the guarantees is therefore remote. The Government will support the financing package, which will allow this project to proceed now and at the minimum financing cost.'

Under the new public private partnership (PPP) agreement, LCR was to build the link in two phases, with the project being managed by Railtrack and Bechtel. The first phase from the Channel Tunnel to Fawkham Junction was to be completed by 2003, at a cost of £1.7 billion in 1997 prices, while the more complex phase two from Fawkham Junction via a new Ebbsfleet station to St Pancras was costed at £2.5 billion. Railtrack was committed to acquiring phase one for its construction cost, and had an option to acquire phase two by 2003, with hopes that this would be for a total of £3.3 billion.

So as the construction project finally went ahead, the Government was committed to the original £1.8 billion investment and also agreed to underwrite the track access charges agreed by Eurostar. On top of that, it also guaranteed £3.75 billion of bond issues, with a first £2.65 billion being issued in February 1999 to cover the construction of phase one and the remaining £1.1 billion to finance phase two. Prescott declared that the success of the bond issue meant that the commitment to lend money to Eurostar might be less than £140 million and that this might be repaid on any future sale or further restructuring of LCR.

When the House of Commons' Public Accounts Committee considered a report by the National Audit Office on the CTRL in March 2001, it delivered a blunt warning about the scale of risk now with taxpayers:

'In deciding to restructure the deal rather than pull the plug, the Department put in place complex arrangements that will expose the taxpayer to substantial risk for many years to come. For instance, some £4 billion of bonds were issued by London & Continental subject to Government guarantees, and in addition it is likely that further substantial sums of taxpayer's money will have to be lent directly to the company to keep it afloat. The Department will need

*to ensure that the substantial risks to which the taxpayer remains
exposed are monitored and managed carefully throughout the life
of the project.'*

A further complication to the project arose with the collapse
of Railtrack into administration in October 2001. In June 2002,
Transport Secretary, Alastair Darling, announced the transfer of
Railtrack to Network Rail and, with regard to the CTRL project,
he announced that LCR was acquiring Railtrack's interest in phase
one for £295 million, while Network Rail was paying £80 million
for the right to operate, maintain and manage the CTRL and a
concession to manage St Pancras station.

With the opening of phase two in November 2007 marking a
completion of the construction phase, the Labour Government
wasted no time in bringing forward plans to sell off LCR and the
CTRL. The Channel Tunnel Rail Link (Supplementary Provisions)
Bill 2007–8 set out its aims: 'A separation of LCR's three different
businesses is planned – the infrastructure, including tracks
and stations, the land interests and the UK stake in Eurostar.
Ultimately, as the Secretary of State said last year, we anticipate
that there will be an open, competitive process for any sale, to
secure the best value for taxpayers.'

The Bill was passed in 2008 and the following year, in June
2009, the next Transport Secretary, Lord Adonis, was able to
announce that LCR had again been restructured. This time the
Government assumed ownership of LCR's £5.169 billion of debt,
which had already been guaranteed by the Government, and at
the same time it assumed ownership of LCR. By separating HS1
Ltd (the track-owning entity) and Eurostar (the operator) from

A Class 395 Javelin
set stands at Ebbsfleet
International on 14 May
2016 with a service for
Faversham. This station
is in two distinct parts,
with Platforms 5 and
6 used by Faversham
services and Platforms
1–4 by services to
Ashford and Dover, as
well as the few Eurostar
services to call at the
station.

their past construction liabilities, the aim was for HS1 Ltd to be in a position to charge a commercial rate for track access, while paying a commercial access charge would help put Eurostar on a sounder financial footing.

Once the Government had assumed control of LCR the signal was set for the recouping of at least part of the taxpayer's investment, through the sale of a long-term concession (effectively a lease) on HS1, with the hope that any new owner would then open up the route to competition. After it had been identified as a sale candidate by Prime Minister Gordon Brown in October 2009, just over a year later the new coalition government was able to announce that the two Canadian investment funds had agreed a £2.1 billion deal to acquire a 30-year concession to manage HS1 and its stations, and to sell access rights on a commercial basis.

International services on HS1 began in November 2007, with speeds of 180 mph on phase one and 143 mph on the section from Fawkham Junction to St Pancras. Today it is hard to imagine Eurostar services without the benefit of a high speed link from London to the Channel Tunnel, and the slashing of journey times from London to Brussels and Paris (cut from three hours to two hours 15 minutes) has undoubtedly been a key factor in the build-up of international passenger traffic, albeit at a far slower rate than once forecast.

Commuters across Kent have undoubtedly benefited from the launch of the domestic Class 395 'Javelin' services, introduced in December 2009 as the price for Government funding of the CTRL.

Set 395029 approaches Ebbsfleet International from the east on 14 May 2016 with a service from Faversham on the North Kent Line to St Pancras International.

A total of 23 of the 29 six-car Class 395 Javelin sets were named after famous Olympic athletes following the 2012 London Games. Last in the series is 395029, named David Weir in honour of the Paralympic medallist.

Fares are around 35% higher than for the identical journey on the 'classic' routes, but with the Ashford–London time slashed from around 80 minutes to 35 minutes and an 18-minute journey time from Ebbsfleet International to St. Pancras, compared to the 51 minute journey time from nearby Northfleet to Cannon Street station, it is no surprise that the services have won over passengers from the slower alternatives. Passenger numbers at Ebbsfleet International soared five-fold from 284,000 in its opening year (2009/10) to 1.674m in 2015/6 while nearby Dartford saw numbers edge up only slightly from 3.034m to 3.450m over the same period.

A vast majority of the passenger traffic using the Javelin service are commuters switching from the slower and over-crowded classic services, a pattern evident at Gravesend, the stop after Ebbsfleet on those services from St Pancras to North Kent, where passenger numbers have also only risen modestly, from 2.502m in 2009/10 to 2.932m in 2015/6. Ebbsfleet has a 6,000 space car park – an unimaginable luxury to someone travelling from a Kent commuter hotspot such as Sevenoaks, where there is a wait of more than ten years for anyone seeking a car park season ticket! But the regeneration which Ebbsfleet promised has been slow to get off the ground – planning consent for 6,000 new homes nearby was granted in 2007 and in 2012 that target total was increased to 22,600, yet by the end of 2015 just 300 homes had been built.

That failure of HS1 to deliver the scale of regeneration promised was recognised in a study called 'First Interim Evaluation of the Impacts of High Speed 1' undertaken by a trio of leading consultants – Atkins, AECOM and Frontier Economics – and published in October 2015. This 150-page report concluded that the new line had failed to regenerate deprived areas of the southeast and left the taxpayer out of pocket. The consultants asserted that

A 12-car Class 395 formation enters Platform 2 at Ebbsfleet International with a service from Ashford and East Kent. The few Eurostar services to serve this station call at Platforms 1 to the right and Platform 4.

the net present value of HS1 – when existing benefits are weighed against the cost of building and maintaining the line – represents a loss of up to £5.9 billion over 60 years, before wider economic impacts are factored in. They reported that there was 'evidence of early stage real estate and regeneration' along the route, but said these effects 'could not be considered significant to date'.

An earlier assessment of HS1 by the National Audit Office came to similar conclusions. In this report, published in March 2012, the NAO wrote: 'The HS1 project has delivered a high performing line, which was subsequently sold in a well-managed way. But international passenger numbers are falling far short of

Ebbsfleet International has seen passenger numbers increased substantially since opening in 2007. But few are in evidence on the afternoon of Saturday 14 May 2016 as a service for St Pancras International arrives.

forecasts and the project costs exceed the value of journey time saving benefits… the project went forward on the basis of hugely optimistic assumptions about international passenger numbers. These were not realized….'

The NAO continued 'The line was delivered within the overall funding and timescale available for the project. However, this was at a higher cost and later than its targets. Construction of the line cost £6,163 million – 18 per cent higher than the target costs. Despite missing these targets, this performance compares well with other railway projects. The line has performed well since it opened…. However the number of international passengers using the line is lower than originally forecast. Actual passenger numbers between 2007 and 2011 were, on average, two thirds of the level forecast when the Department guaranteed the project debt in 1998, to enable the line to be built.'

In the light of the October 2015 consultants' report, critics of the grander HS2 proposal were quick to seize on its and the NAO's harsh words about the HS1 project. A story headed HS1 'failed to deliver and cost taxpayer too much' published by *The Times* on 16 October 2015 quoted Richard Wellings, director of the Institute of Economic Affairs, as saying: 'The implications for HS2 are alarming, since similarly flawed arguments are being used to justify this hugely expensive, high-risk scheme.' In response, a Department for Transport spokesman told the paper: 'Despite opening during an economic downturn, HS1 has already had a transformational impact on the areas it serves.'

High Speed One has undoubtedly delivered significant benefits to both Eurostar passengers and those in Kent willing to pay its premium fares. But travel on one of the off-peak Javelin trains

Newest arrivals in the Eurostar fleet are the Class 374 or e320 units. A total of 17 of the 16-car sets are being delivered and, unlike their predecessors, they are designed with electrical equipment that will enable them to operate beyond Eurostar's current destinations. A London-bound service passes Stratford International on 14 May 2016.

towards Faversham in North Kent and there appears, from my limited experience, to be an awful lot of empty seats, while the vast and largely empty stations at Stratford and Ebbsfleet are a real triumph of hope over reality. Another notable sign of what might have been are the disused platforms 1 and 4 at Stratford International – all Javelin services using the island platform 2 and 3 – a reminder of past hopes that some Eurostar services would be calling here.

High Speed Two

On a different scale altogether than the Channel Tunnel Rail Link, the £50 billion+ High Speed Two project looks set to continue dominating the UK railway agenda for the next two decades. It has also polarised opinion on a scale that is reminiscent of controversial motorway building projects such as the M3 Twyford Down, the stationing of US nuclear missiles at Greenham Common Air Base, and the objections of homeowners across Kent and in South London to earlier proposed routes for what was to become HS1. Objectors argue that it is not necessary, too expensive and that the chosen route will cause high levels of environmental impact and damage. Those backing HS2 say that the capacity it delivers is vital to cope with traffic growth and to transform connectivity between London, the Midlands and the North.

After a doubling of total UK passenger journeys to 1.65 billion in the two decades from the mid-1990s to 2014, according to Department for Transport figures, it is clear that serious capacity issues will arise in the not too distant future if this trend continues. In particular, the West Coast Main Line, Britain's busiest rail route, is forecast to reach full capacity sometime between 2025 and 2030, prompting the search for a bold solution. On the basis of an earlier DfT report in January 2009, proposals were developed for a high-speed line to address the long term capacity issue and three years later, in January 2012, plans for the development of a new high speed rail link from London to the Midlands and North, to be known as HS2, were formally confirmed.

A highly ambitious project

Across Continental Europe there has been a huge development of dedicated high speed railway networks since the first 512 km (320-mile) section of France's now extensive TGV network – from Paris to Lyon – opened in September 1981. All we currently have in the UK is the 68-mile Channel Tunnel Rail link, yet by 2033 – in the unlikely event that the project can be kept to its planned timescale – we will have a brand new high speed route from the heart of London to Birmingham and on, in two separate branches northwards, to Leeds and Manchester. Trains travelling at up to 250 mph will reach Birmingham in 49 minutes, Manchester in 68 minutes and Leeds in 83 minutes, with capacity on the line for 18 trains an hour, an hourly passenger capacity of 26,000 people.

Euston station will be extensively remodelled and expanded to cope with the new services. The current, rather unattractive station, opened in 1968 at the time electrification of the West Coast Main Line was completed between London and the West Midlands, is now handling over 42 million passengers a year, more than double the number it was designed to handle, so is in need of significant expansion to cope with the arrival of the first HS2 services in 2026. Under the plans being promoted by HS2 Ltd, a three stage redevelopment will see the initial construction of six new platforms for the use of HS2 services, to the west of the existing station, with five more being built to cope with the second phase services to Manchester and Leeds, due to begin in 2033. Redevelopment of the concourse and existing platforms will also follow if funding can be found.

First stop Old Oak Common

From Euston, HS2 will be in tunnel for most of its route out of the capital, following a number of significant changes to the proposed route in the light of environmental concerns. It will, however, emerge west of Paddington to serve a station at Old Oak Common, which is being developed as an interchange between the new line, Crossrail One (due to open in 2018) and Heathrow Express services. Ever since the high speed line was first proposed arguments have raged over why it was not being designed to serve Heathrow Airport, with a number of options considered for a branch off the main route to serve either a new transport interchange near the airport and the M4/M25 motorway junction, or at Heathrow Central station. But these were finally rejected in March 2015 in favour of the Old Oak Common interchange option.

What remains unclear is the proportion of HS2 services that will stop at Old Oak Common, just minutes after leaving Euston. The principle of high speed services like Eurostar and the TGV services in France is that stops are few and far between – only a handful of Eurostar services, for instance, serve Ebbsfleet, Ashford or Calais because of the time penalty from serving intermediate stations. Critics have argued that much time saving between the promised 49 minute journey to Birmingham on the new line and the 80 minutes it currently takes on the fastest West Coast Main Line services will be lost by the additional check-in time required before boarding high speed services. Adding another five minutes with a stop at Old Oak Common will further reduce the attractiveness of the new services, particularly when passengers are faced with paying a significant premium to existing fares.

Leaving the London area and incorporating a number of environmentally driven changes to the route that was originally proposed, the new line will pass through a number of lengthy tunnels, including a late change to the route in the form of a six-mile tunnel in Ealing, to take the new line beneath the existing rail alignment between Old Oak Common and West Ruislip, another 2.7 mile tunnel at South Ruislip, and a lengthy tunnel from a point near the M25 to Little Missenden. North of Aylesbury the new line will partly follow the route of the former Great Central Main Line, then head in a north-westerly direction across rural Oxfordshire, Northamptonshire and Warwickshire and areas where opposition to the line is at its most strident. More than half (79 miles) of the 140-mile Phase One will now be in tunnels, so the line is unlikely to win any accolades for its scenic appeal!

Environmental concerns

Opponents of the HS2 project, headed by the Stop HS2 campaign group, argue that the new line threatens 350 unique habitats, 67 irreplaceable ancient woods, 30 river corridors, 24 Sites of Special Scientific Interest plus hundreds of other sensitive areas. They also claim that the route adopted for the line breaches what are known as the 'Kent Principles' – which were drawn up in the light of environmental issues arising from the HS1 project and meant that this line avoided the destruction of homes and communities across Kent by following the existing transport corridors of the M2/M20 motorways. By being designed for ultra-high speeds of 250 mph, rather than the 186 mph of Eurostar trains on HS1, the HS2 tracks have to be as straight as possible, so cannot simply curve round environmentally important sites.

One simple example of the environmental damage being caused by the HS2 project emerged in November 2015 when an ancient pear tree in Warwickshire, which was due to be chopped down to make way for the line was voted 'the best tree in England.' The Cubbington pear tree is believed to have been growing near the Warwickshire village for more than 250 years and the Woodland Trust, which runs the Tree of the Year poll, called for it to be preserved, due to its age. Peter Delow, chairman of the Cubbington Stop HS2 Action Group, nominated the tree for the award, and described its award win as sending a clear message to politicians to conserve the country's natural heritage: 'those who voted for our tree clearly care about the protection of our natural environment,' he said. 'It would be perfectly possible to build HS2 without destroying our tree and many others.'

In the same vein, on 3 February 2016, *The Times* reported claims from The Woodland Trust, in its evidence to the Commons HS2 select committee, that dozens of ancient woodlands will be chopped down or damaged to make way for the new route. At least 63 woods dating back more than 400 years could be damaged as part of phase one of the High Speed 2 route from London to Birmingham according to the environmental charity, which accused HS2 Ltd of a cover-up by trying to 'disguise the irrevocable loss and damage this irreplaceable habitat will suffer'.

The trust accused the company of missing out 14 ancient woods while carrying out original environmental assessments on the line and claimed that HS2 Ltd attempted to downgrade the importance of some woods by giving them a low quality rating and failing to state how many trees would be planted to compensate for those lost. According to the Woodland Trust, Broadwells Wood, near Burton Green in Warwickshire, will suffer the largest single loss along the route, with 3.2 hectares chopped down, while John's Gorse near Handsacre in Staffordshire will lose 80 per cent of its total area. A spokesman for HS2 told the paper that ancient woodland was avoided wherever possible. 'Our approach is consistent with Natural England guidance and we have committed to creating replacement wooded areas, which will be managed for up to 50 years,' he said.

Is this railway really necessary?

The fundamental rationale for HS2 is that there is an insoluble capacity crisis looming on the West Coast Main Line, which only a new line can solve. Critics of this view point to the fact that the line is designed to cater for long distance travellers – a large proportion of whom will be business travellers – while the real growth in rail traffic is not in this segment of the market, but in shorter distance commuter journeys. There are unquestionably capacity problems at peak travel times on the West Coast Main Line, but there is capacity for much of the week – it is notable that, having disproved the 'line full' argument put forward by Network Rail on the East Coast Main Line to get its services running, Open Access operator Grand Central has now secured paths for the launch of a Blackpool to London service on the WCML.

When First Group made its fateful bid for the WCML franchise, its bid asserted that 'InterCity West Coast [the formal franchise name] is unique because it has a considerable amount of unused capacity.' In the comment piece I wrote for *The Guardian* on this subject, mentioned elsewhere in this book, I suggested capacity could be created on the WCML by running services from the West Midlands on the Chiltern Railways route via Banbury and High Wycombe and terminating at Paddington, rather than Euston, station in London. That would inevitably require a significant degree of investment in capacity enhancement, but opening of the East–West rail link will alleviate capacity constraints on the Banbury–Leamington section of this route, by allowing north–south freight services to be diverted along the new line from Oxford to the WCML at Bletchley or the Midland Main Line at Bedford. As the Stop HS2 campaigners point out, the East–West link will also provide an alternative commuter route from Milton Keynes to London, using the reopened link to Aylesbury.

Onwards from Birmingham

A second phase of HS2 will see the route extended northwards from the West Midlands in two separate branches that will create a Y shaped high speed network. For Manchester and points in the North West, a branch will run from Birmingham to a junction with the existing WCML south of Wigan, with a branch off it to Manchester's Piccadilly station. An alternative to this has already been proposed, however, after HS2 Ltd Chairman David Higgins put forward the idea in March 2014 of a new high speed junction station being built south of the existing station at Crewe as part of the Phase One construction project and including Birmingham to Crewe in the project's first phase. This would mean many more places being able to benefit from high speed services once Phase One opens, by using the new route to Crewe and then continuing on the existing network to places such as Liverpool, Manchester, North Wales and Scotland.

That acceleration in the construction process was confirmed in November 2015, when plans to open the new line as far as Crewe by 2027 were announced, six years before the full network is completed. At the same time, revised proposals for the new station in Leeds envisage one which is integrated with the existing station, rather than being at some distance from it, which looks to be a major step forward. David Higgins, Chairman of HS2, described the decision to accelerate the second phase of work was a 'significant milestone' in the development of HS2, adding that a 'gratifying consensus' was growing in cities along the northern route over where new stations should be built. But further controversy was stoked up when the HS2 price tag was raised by another £5bn to £55.7bn, at 2015 prices, at a time when welfare and other government spending was being slashed.

For destinations towards Leeds and beyond, the other (eastern) branch of HS2 will head north east from the West Midlands, partly following the line of the M42 motorway, to serve the East Midlands Hub station between Derby and Nottingham and then on to serve Sheffield, with another out-of-town station originally planned at Meadowhall (convenient for the shopping centre, rather than the city centre), and on to the planned new station in Leeds. These grand ambitions were already being scaled back in the light of post-Brexit spending concerns when, in early July 2016, it was announced that the Meadowhall station was being abandoned in favour of a link to Sheffield city centre. This appears a sensible cost-cutting move to save £768 million, giving the citizens of Sheffield a decent connection into the new network, albeit at the cost of losing a direct link between Sheffield and Leeds.

Many organisations in Scotland have been campaigning for the new high speed link to be extended north of the border, but in May 2015 HS2 Ltd declared that there was 'no business case' for building the line beyond Manchester and Leeds, so those new ultra-high speed trains serving Glasgow and Edinburgh will be forced to continue their journeys on the existing network.

A major criticism of the approved HS2 route is that its stations do not serve major towns and cities as well as stations in existing city centre locations. Curzon Street in Birmingham is a good example, being around a mile east of New Street and having no interchange with the rest of the West Midlands rail network – at least until a proposed extension of the Midland Metro is built. Another classic example is the East Midlands Hub station, mentioned above, which is being built at the site of Toton diesel depot, mid-way between Derby and Nottingham, but having no rail link with either city. Stapleford & Sandiacre station nearby closed in 1967, and there is the possibility of a future extension to Nottingham's tram system, but it will inevitably operate as a giant park and ride facility. How HS2 publicity material can therefore claim that 'A new station will help to realise the region's vision of an integrated transport network for commuters, shoppers and visitors' is rather hard to fathom!

Paying a full price

While environmental concerns are inevitable and have in many cases been dealt with by the extensive additional tunnelling now being incorporated into the design, the fundamental question of cost remains a paramount concern. At the time the project was launched in 2009, the whole scheme was costed at £33 billion, but that quickly leapt to £50 billion and some commentators have talked about the eventual bill reaching £80 billion. Evidence from the Great Western Main Line electrification project and the earlier West Coast Main Line upgrade certainly do not give taxpayers much confidence that any major UK rail project can ever be delivered on either time or budget. Politicians have suggested that there will be 'no blank cheque' when it comes to bank-rolling this project, but that is mere empty rhetoric. HS2 is effectively an all-or-nothing option, so once we have started we will have to finish, or be faced with a funding a huge and costly white elephant at a time when there are far more viable rail revival schemes clamouring for support.

Adding insult to injury for those fighting the line was the revelation in December 2015 of just how much of a gravy train HS2 is proving to be. Government figures revealed that 34 officials working on the project were earning more than the prime minister (£142,500), with three on salaries of more than £300,000. The lucky trio is Simon Kirby, the HS2 chief executive, who came top of the 'fat cat' league table of officials with a salary of £750,000, followed by Jim Crawford, managing director of infrastructure, on £390,000, and Alistair Kirk, programme director, on £300,000. The figures revealed that 16 staff working on HS2, out of a total of 626, were on packages of more than £200,000 a year. Such large salaries were attacked by campaigners, including Jonathan Isaby, chief executive of the TaxPayers' Alliance, who said: 'Deep public concerns about the value of HS2 will be compounded by the news that dozens working on the project are already on eye-watering salaries.'

Yet more high speed dreams

While arguments continue to rage about the exact routes and station sites for the second phase of HS2, the government's much talked about Northern Powerhouse initiative has prompted ever more fantastic plans for further new high speed lines criss-crossing the north of England at a cost of several tens of billion pounds. In a report published in March 2016 a coalition of city councils under the banner of *Transport for the North*, unveiled proposals for High Speed 3, and said trains on it could travel from Leeds to Liverpool in just 50 minutes, compared to a current 90 minutes. It called for a new 140 mph route to link Liverpool with the planned HS2 line to Manchester. A second new line would run between Manchester and the HS2 route to Leeds and Sheffield, there should be major upgrades to direct lines between Manchester, Leeds and Newcastle as well as the existing routes between Hull and Sheffield/Leeds, while a new trans-Pennine tunnel should be built to improve connections between Manchester and Sheffield.

There is clearly a real need to improve connectivity between major northern cities, but the danger lies in the scale of these visions – Network Rail has previously estimated that a new line connecting HS2 to Liverpool could cost up to £13 billion and one between Manchester and Sheffield and Leeds would come in at £19 billion. Given the ever escalating cost of HS2, as well as other major upgrade projects, such as the Great Western Main Line electrification, there seems a very real danger that these high profile and big ticket schemes will swallow up whatever funds are available for rail infrastructure projects, at the expense of the many socially-desirable and long-cherished re-openings featured elsewhere in this book.

Chapter 7

RAILS ACROSS LONDON

As the two huge London rail schemes featured in this chapter – Thameslink (£6.5 billion) and Crossrail One (£15 billion) – finally near completion, and another gets off the ground (Crossrail Two) – weighing in at an estimated £30 billion – it is worth reflecting on what a revolution they herald in links across the capital. While Paris invested heavily in developing its RER network of suburban rail services during the 1960s and 1970s, London remarkably went for 72 years without any cross-city passenger rail service, until the Thameslink route was re-opened in 1988.

For many years the little-used West London line through Kensington Olympia, and the Cinderella East London section of London Underground's Metropolitan Line represented the only physical link between the rail systems north and south of the Thames. Yet all this time the length of a vital 'missing link' on what was known as the City Line, between Farringdon station on the underground and British Rail's 'Widened Lines' and Southern Region metals near the former Holborn Viaduct station was a mere 600 yards.

Like Thameslink, the concept of an east–west heavy rail link across London has a long history. Work on Crossrail only began in 2009, but the idea for such a route was first being promoted 70 years ago. During my time writing on transport matters at *The Sunday Times* in the late 1980s I remember David Bayliss, Director of Planning at London Transport, showing me plans from 1948 which foreshadowed not only the current east–west Crossrail One route, Thameslink and also a Chelsea–Hackney alignment similar to the Crossrail Two route now being planned. Interestingly, the only route to have actually been built as a result of this post-war plan was the Victoria Line, the first section of which opened in 1968, 20 years after the plan had been published.

Thameslink

Passenger services on the City Line were withdrawn in 1916 but for more than half a century the route retained a significant level of freight traffic. It finally succumbed to closure, however, in 1969, with the track being removed by 1971. A reminder of what was once there can be seen to this day in the remains of platforms beneath Holborn Viaduct that were once known as Snow Hill (Low Level) station.

The cross-London revolution began in May 1988, four years after the Greater London Council had first proposed to re-open what was then known as the City Line and six years after electrification of the 'Widened Lines' from Moorgate and St Pancras to Bedford. Using electric multiple units equipped with both overhead pantographs and third rail-pick-up, the new services would pause at Farringdon station for the switchover from overhead power to third rail (in the southbound direction) before continuing their journey southwards via Blackfriars and then either London Bridge or Herne Hill towards Brighton and other points south of the capital.

Less than two years after re-opening, the newly re-established link was closed in January 1990, along with Holborn Viaduct station, to allow construction of what was known as the Ludgate Development. This is a series of office blocks stretching from Holborn Viaduct to Ludgate Hill, whose development helped to finance construction of a new underground rail alignment, as well as a new station to replace Holborn Viaduct, City Thameslink,

Thameslink services passing at Farringdon, where 319435 departs with a northbound service on 1 July 2016 as 387123 enters with the 12.24 service to Brighton.

Less than a fortnight after the Class entered service, one of the new 12-car Class 700/1 units for Thameslink services heads north from Farringdon at the start of the 25kv overhead electrification, with a service for Bedford on 1 July 2016.

which has a southern entrance in Ludgate Hill and a northern entrance on Holborn Viaduct. This new route, which sees trains descend sharply as they head northwards from Blackfriars station, opened in May 1990 and quickly developed in to a major north–south rail axis.

Re-opening of the City Line – or Thameslink as it became known – created direct links from stations on the Midland Main Line as far north as Bedford with stations on the Brighton main line, as well as a number of other destinations south of the river, with stopping services to Sevenoaks via Bromley South and others operating on a circular route via Sutton and Wimbledon. Importantly Thameslink gives direct access to two airports, Gatwick and Luton, the latter being served by Luton Airport Parkway station, which opened in 1999.

Thameslink quickly became one of the most notoriously over-crowded sections of the London commuter network and almost as soon as it had opened, plans were being developed for an upgrade that would increase the route's capacity and allow cross-London services to a wider range of destinations both north and south of the Thames. The current upgrade programme started life as Thameslink 2000 and, as the name suggests, aimed to deliver a package of improvements by the Millennium year. But a series of delays, issues over rolling stock procurement and an increase in the project's scope mean it is now arriving a modest 18 years late!

Doubling capacity

The current Thameslink Programme dates back to plans drawn up by Network Rail in 2006 for which funding from the Department for Transport was secured in July 2007, three months before construction work began. In summary, this programme has seen substantial station rebuilds at West Hampstead, Farringdon and Blackfriars stations, the construction of a new two-platform station beneath St. Pancras International, and is concluding with a wholesale rebuilding of London Bridge station and construction of a link north of St Pancras International to allow Thameslink services to run onto the East Coast Main Line (ECML) and serve destinations including King's Lynn, Cambridge and Peterborough.

This link with the ECML is via what are known as the Canal Tunnels, which were built at the time St Pancras station was being rebuilt between 2004 and 2006. This was in anticipation of the future Thameslink programme, and, once track and signalling systems have been installed, the planned new timetable – explained later on in this section – will see eight of the planned 24 trains an hour using the central section of the Thameslink route being services to ECML destinations.

Phase one of the Thameslink programme began in October 2007 when work began at Luton Airport Parkway to extend platform lengths to accommodate 12-coach trains. This was the first of 50 stations where platforms were lengthened over the next four years to cope with the planned longer trains. With the platform extension project completed in 2011, phase two of the Thameslink programme was started in October 2012 with the highly complex remodelling and rebuilding of London Bridge station and the tracks approaching the station, in order to cope with the additional planned services.

Low tech warning! At the south end of Farringdon station a home-made sign reminds drivers that they must switch to dc current collection for the onward trip to Blackfriars and stations to Brighton, Sevenoaks and elsewhere.

DRIVERS

Do not forget to

drop the Pantograph!

One loss resulting from the need to extend platforms at Farringdon station was the final section of the 'Widened Lines' to Barbican and Moorgate stations. This had been electrified in 1982 as part of the 'Bedpan' electrification from St. Pancras to Bedford and had enjoyed regular services until opening of the Thameslink route six years later, when services had been reduced to peak hours only. They were finally withdrawn on 20 March 2009 in connection with the work at Farringdon, a station which has undergone a complete transformation in anticipation of becoming a major interchange between Thameslink service and east–west services on Crossrail One.

In a Government report on progress with the Thameslink programme, published in June 2013, the National Audit Office noted that phase one had been completed on time and to budget, 'despite scope changes to Blackfriars and Farringdon stations and Blackfriars Bridge being in worse condition than expected.' The report underlined the strong need for the Thameslink upgrade, pointing out that services on the route 'have been consistently among the most crowded London routes in recent years at 2.7% above capacity during afternoon peak times.' Not surprisingly, it also noted that passengers travelling on the current Thameslink service 'are among the least satisfied with space on trains.'

Major station upgrades

Given its role as one of the most important rail hubs in central London, Farringdon station has been substantially rebuilt ahead of both the new Thameslink services and Crossrail arriving in

Blackfriars station now spans the River Thames with entrances on both banks. A view of the four-platform station looking north on 1 July 2016.

2018. What was previously a modest intermediate station on the Circle and Metropolitan Lines now boasts a new ticket hall for the Thameslink and Crossrail services, 12-coach platform lengths, refurbished entrances to the underground platforms and new lifts that have made the station step free. One thing that has will not change however will be the switch from 25kv overhead power to 750 volt third rail power, and vice versa, by Thameslink services serving the station.

Blackfriars station is the most visible evidence of the Thameslink programme, with the station becoming the first to span the River Thames and to have entrances on both sides of the river. A £350m redevelopment programme, completed in mid-2012, included extension of the station platforms across the entire length of the bridge, and a completed rebuilding of the adjoining underground station during a two and a half year closure. Walking through the new station offers excellent views of London as well as being a good way to cross the river on a wet day! Among features of the new station are 4,400 solar panels on its roof, which provide up to half of the station's energy needs and apparently reduces the station's CO_2 emissions by an estimated 511 tonnes per year, the equivalent of around 89,000 average car journeys.

Transforming London Bridge

By far the biggest single element of the whole Thameslink Programme is the rebuilding of London Bridge station, a gateway to the City used by some 54 million passengers a year and a major interchange with underground and bus services. The transformation process has been underway since May 2013 and

The dome of St Paul's Cathedral can be seen in the background as 319372/220 approaches Elephant & Castle on 1 July 2016 with the 13.15 departure for Sevenoaks.

Elephant & Castle is an important interchange between Thameslink and London Underground services. An 8-car formation comprising 3193458/319434 pauses on 1 July 2016 with a northbound service.

has been made all the more complex by the need to keep services passing through the station while the work is being undertaken.

To accommodate the much enhanced Thameslink service frequency, the previous six through platforms are being increased to nine (there will then be six terminating platforms). That has meant a two year period during which time trains to Charing Cross were unable to stop while platforms 4–6 were demolished and rebuilt, followed by two years in which Cannon Street services are not able to serve London Bridge while the same process takes place with platforms 1–3.

New trains

From the date that the Thameslink route was opened, the mainstay of services was four-car Class 319 units, but the growth in traffic meant that new capacity was needed. A procurement process for new trains was launched, but pending their arrival, from February 2009 the Class 319 fleet was supplemented by another fleet of dual-voltage units of Class 377. Together with an increase in the size of the original Class 319 fleet, that meant train lengths could be increased to eight cars throughout peak periods.

After a long delay in the procurement process for a new Thameslink fleet, the Department for Transport finally announced in June 2011 that a Siemens-led joint venture company had been selected as preferred bidder for the contract to deliver a new fleet, comprising 1,200 carriages that would enable a doubling of passenger capacity on the route when the upgrade programme had been completed in late 2018. Delivery of this new fleet is allowing existing Class 319/377 units to be progressively 'cascaded' onto newly-electrified routes in the North West and, once completed, onto Thames Valley commuter lines.

Under the terms of the £1.6 billion contract, which was finally agreed in June 2013, delivery of the fleet of Class 700 'Desiro City' units began in July 2015. When completed in 2018, the fleet will comprise 60 eight-car sets and 55 twelve-car sets, being maintained at two purpose-built new depots at Hornsey in North London and at Three Bridges, to the south of Gatwick Airport, on the Brighton Main Line.

New destinations

A blue-print for operation of services on the new Thameslink was the *London and South East Route Utilisation Strategy*. This was published in July 2011 and outlined ambitious plans for a timetable that provided 24 trains an hour on the core central section of the Thameslink route from St Pancras International to Blackfriars. North of London the 24 trains per hour would comprise eight semi-fast trains to Bedford, two stopping and two semi-fast trains to Luton, four stopping trains to St Albans, two semi-fast trains to Peterborough, two semi-fast trains to Cambridge and four stopping trains to Welwyn Garden City. To the south of London, the plan is for four trains to Brighton, as now, and two each to Three Bridges, Horsham, East Grinstead, Caterham, Tattenham Corner, Tunbridge Wells, Ashford International, Maidstone East, Sevenoaks and Bellingham.

Crossrail One (the Elizabeth Line)

Just as High Speed Two is going to cost substantially more than High Speed One, so in the case of the new rail routes across London, the new east–west rail route, known as Crossrail One until being rechristened the Elizabeth Line in February 2016, is expected to cost almost three times the Thameslink price tag, at around £15 billion, including the cost of new rolling stock. Its planned successor, the south-west to north-east London route, originally dubbed the Chelsea–Hackney line, but now known as Crossrail Two, will cost substantially more again, at an estimated £30 billion.

Anyone working in Central London knows all about Crossrail One. For what seems like an eternity the areas around Bond Street, Tottenham Court Road, Moorgate and Liverpool Street have been substantially disrupted by the gigantic tunnelling and construction project. But that decade of disruption, which began in 2009, should soon be forgiven when the new fleet of 1,500-person capacity nine-car trains begins operating between Paddington and Liverpool Street stations.

Crossrail One makes a pleasant contrast to the Great Western electrification fiasco, and looks set to be delivered on time and on budget. The complex 26 miles of tunnelling work was completed by mid-2015 and production of the 66-strong fleet of new trains is well under way at the Bombardier plant in Derby. It will not be long before 24 trains an hour are speeding from Heathrow Airport to Tottenham Court Road in just 28 minutes and crossing London from Paddington to Liverpool Street in just 11 minutes, connecting at Farringdon with those 24 trains an hour that will be operating on the new Thameslink.

That key central portion of the route will allow the RER-style high density suburban trains to speed across London, linking stations from Reading and Heathrow Airport to the west, with those to Shenfield in East London and Abbey Wood in South East London. Serving expanded stations at Bond Street, Tottenham Court Road, Farringdon and a combined Moorgate/Liverpool Street, it will provide long overdue relief to underground services, particularly the Central Line, but also the Piccadilly line from Heathrow Airport.

A long history

While the origins of a new east–west rail link date back to the late 1940s, the origins of the scheme now nearing completion date back more than 40 years to a *London Rail Study Report*, which was published in 1974, sponsored by the Department of the Environment and the former Greater London Council, and looked at a range of new cross-London proposals. These included a Paddington to Liverpool Street line, though on a slightly different alignment to the current Crossrail One, and two schemes which subsequently went ahead, the Jubilee line of London Underground and the Snow Hill tunnel re-opening to create the future Thameslink route.

As development of the Jubilee Line and Thameslink went ahead, nothing came of the east–west route, and it was 15 years until the idea was revived. This time the Central London Rail Study, published in 1989, included Paddington to Liverpool Street among an ambitious range of options that also included a new north–south link from Euston and Kings Cross to Victoria station. Following the Report's publication, London Underground and British Rail promoted a private Parliamentary Bill in 1991. Although subsequently rejected on the grounds that the business case for a new line had not been made, the potential route was at least safeguarded from any developments that would prevent construction of a line in the future.

After further abortive attempts to promote a new link, the deadlock was finally broken when the Crossrail Bill was introduced to Parliament in 2005 and, three years later, became the Crossrail Act when it received the Royal Assent on 22 July 2008. Despite its timing at the height of the banking crisis, there was to be no hold up in the project, and in December 2008 funding was committed

Simon Wright, Programme Director of Crossrail, believes that being run as an independent company has been crucial to its success.

by the Department for Transport and Transport for London, with other finance being secured from Network Rail and the City of London and private sector cash, to the tune of £230 million, from Heathrow owner BAA. While the lines from Paddington–Reading and Whitechapel–Shenfield/Abbey Wood will remain in Network Rail ownership, the central London tunnel section will be owned and operated by Transport for London.

A formal start was made to the construction project at a ceremony on 15 May 2009 attended by Prime Minister Gordon Brown and Boris Johnson, London Mayor. The following year a potential wobble in the project was averted when both major political parties committed to seeing it through to completion, although a spending review by the newly-elected coalition Government pared back the cost of Crossrail One by more than £1 billion through a reduction in the number of tunnel boring machines and a simplified tunnelling process, a decision which put back the planned opening by a year to 2018.

The value of independence

One of the major factors in Crossrail's ability to deliver on time and budget has been its independence, according to Programme Director Simon Wright, who joined the project in July 2014 after previous big project experience with the Olympic Delivery Authority and with Network Rail, where he worked on plans for the redevelopment of Euston station in connection with the HS2 project. During an interview at his Canary Wharf office, he told me:

> 'Crossrail is an independent, publicly-owned company with a clear focus on a very carefully set out series of objectives. We have the Project Development Agreement (PDA) which set out what we are required to do in great detail. It set up a thorough base-line, which had a budget and timeline attached to it. We were then set loose to an extent, although tightly managed, but we are an independent company with our own Chairman and our own Board, with a clear set of objectives. That independence gives us the means and the mechanisms and controls to deliver against our objectives.'

Construction

In the six years between the start of work in May 2009 and the completion of tunnel boring in June 2015 the Crossrail One project had the distinction of being the biggest construction project in Europe, employing over 10,000 people and overcoming numerous technical and historical obstacles to allow eight 1,000 tonne tunnel boring machines to deliver the two parallel 13-mile long tunnels and the four huge new stations at Bond Street, Tottenham Court Road, Farringdon and Moorgate/Liverpool Street that represent the core of this project. Such was the accuracy of the minutely planned tunnelling work that there have only been around 500 claims for damage to buildings during the construction work.

Among historical issues to be addressed, one of the most bizarre was the idea that ancient diseases such as anthrax or bubonic plague might be released by work on the project. This was highlighted by Lord James of Blackheath during consideration of the Crossrail Bill, when he told a House of Lords select committee that 682 victims of anthrax had been brought into Smithfield in Farringdon with some contaminated meat in 1520 and then buried in the area. Allaying such concerns, in June 2009 no traces of anthrax or bubonic plague were found on human bone fragments discovered during tunnelling work.

The eastbound platform at Tottenham Court Road is the only one on the new Crossrail to be built on a curve, as evident in this 3 December 2015 view.

A view of the westbound running tunnel from what is now track level at the eastern end of Tottenham Court Road station, as seen on 3 December 2015.

Crossrail One has the distinction of being the capital's first complete new underground line since the Jubilee Line extension to Stratford was completed in 1999 and one of the most ambitious deep-level tunnel projects since the Bakerloo, Central and Piccadilly tube lines were built in the early 1900s. Besides the four new Central London stations, four other major new stations have been built for the new services at Whitechapel, Canary Wharf, Custom House and Woolwich, with a couple more locations identified west of Paddington for new stations, and a number of potential extensions already being considered.

Paying a visit to Tottenham Court Road station in early December 2015, courtesy of the Crossrail press office and exactly three years before services were due to start, what was immediately apparent was the vast scale of the £1 billion+ station redevelopment, which recently appointed Project Manager Phil Jones described as 'awesome'. Descending around 35 metres (100 feet) to platform level, the size of the two running tunnels and the service tunnel between them becomes apparent. At 260 metres (900 feet) in length, the new platforms are twice the length of the parallel Central Line platforms and will each have 27 platform-to-ceiling doors, in the style of those on the Jubilee Line extension, but reaching the top of the tunnel to create a solid barrier for improved safety in the event of fire.

New trains

Like the Class 378 units in use on London Overground services and the newest sub-surface underground trains on the Metropolitan, Circle and District Lines, the emphasis in the new 66-strong Class 345 Crossrail fleet will be on maximum passenger numbers rather than maximum passenger comfort. With only around 50 seats in each of the nine cars, it means that at maximum capacity of 1,500 people more than two-thirds of them (1,050) will be having to stand. They will, however, be standing in what Transport for London calls a 'welcoming environment' with darker floors, natural colours and plenty of space for wheelchairs, prams and luggage.

Being precise, the new sets will have a total of 454 seats, significantly less than the 632 of the eight-car trains they have replaced on the Liverpool Street – Shenfield section of the new service. These are arranged in a mixture of the side facing seating that are a feature of the Overground sets and seating bays, as in the newest underground trains Like those other fleets operating in London, the new carriages are walk-through and feature free wi-fi and 4G services. They are designed to operate at a maximum speed of 90 mph (60 mph in tunnels) and at 200 metres, are 50% longer than any existing train on the London Underground. The new fleet will be maintained at Old Oak Common, west of Paddington and the site of a potential interchange station with HS2.

Once fully operational at the end of 2019, Crossrail One, which is being run on an eight- year concession from 2015 by MTR Corporation (Crossrail) Ltd for Transport for London, will comprise a 73-mile network connecting 40 stations from Reading in the west to Shenfield in East London and Abbey Wood in South East London. But there is potential for two further new stations, with the likelihood of a new Old Oak Common station to connect with HS2, as mentioned above, and another at Silvertown in East London, where Crossrail One follows the route of the former branch line from Stratford to North Woolwich and provision has been made for a future station to serve London City Airport.

Like the upgraded Thameslink, a key feature of Crossrail One will be a peak time service frequency on the core central section from Paddington to Liverpool Street and Whitechapel of

24 trains per hour or one every two and a half minutes. Starting at the western end of the route, once the full service is in operation at the end of 2019, two trains will start at Reading, a further two will start at Maidenhead, four from Heathrow and two from West Drayton, giving a total of ten services, with a further 14 starting from Paddington, making up the 24 an hour. East of Whitechapel, 12 services go to Shenfield and 12 to Abbey Wood.

Intermediate stations on the route from Reading to Paddington will still be served by Great Western services, comprising two semi-fast trains an hour from Reading, calling at Twyford, Maidenhead, Slough, Ealing Broadway and Paddington; one through train from Henley-on-Thames; and one through train from Bourne End to Paddington. Services on the Greenford branch, however, will become a shuttle service to West Ealing, where they will connect with Crossrail services, and the current stopping service from Heathrow to Paddington – branded Heathrow Connect – will be replaced by new Crossrail services. To the east of London, the route from Shenfield to Liverpool Street will see 6 trains an hour terminating at Liverpool Street, in addition to the 12 Crossrail One services that will continue across Central London to Paddington.

But 24 trains an hour may not be the end of the story, as Programme Director Simon Wright explained to me: 'We have designed the system to run 24 trains an hour in the central section, but we have also future-proofed the engineering and design of the civils to be able to run 30 trains an hour. The platforms are capable of handling an additional coach in the trains, so we can do longer as well as more frequent trains. Of course more frequent trains puts more capacity pressure onto the stations, because you will have more people entering and leaving, so they have also been designed with a capacity for handling 30 trains an hour. It allows for that extra capacity to be relatively simply added at the discretion of TfL, as and when growth demands.'

Future extensions

Besides the additional stations, two potential extensions would greatly extend the reach of Crossrail. Most important of these would be to link Crossrail One to the West Coast Main Line via a very short connecting link from Old Oak Common to Willesden Junction. That would have a number of benefits, freeing up capacity at Euston for the future arrival of HS2, bringing stations between Milton Keynes Central to Watford Junction into the Crossrail One network and making better use of capacity west of Paddington by not terminating so many services there. At the south eastern extremity of the current network, long term provision has been made for an extension to Gravesend.

Completing Crossrail

Chris Binns became Chief Engineer of Crossrail One in June 2015 having previously held the same title on the Thameslink project. Speaking to me in May 2016 at his 30th floor Canary Wharf office, he explained some of the challenges in delivering the £15 billion scheme on time and on budget:

Thameslink was delayed for many years, yet Crossrail is on time and on budget – what is the difference between these two schemes?

'Thameslink was first authorised in 2006 and the plans then only changed once, which was for the Comprehensive Spending Review in 2010, but apart from that there have been no changes to the plan. From when I was there in 2008 through to now, they have stuck to their plan, which is really good.

'The big difference with Crossrail is that Thameslink's pace is governed by access constraints of the working railway, so that when you think about the major stations and all the large scale work that they have done, they are constrained by whenever they can get in.

'During the time I was at Thameslink [2008–2010] we had two years of week-end closures in the core section through Farringdon and those week-ends and nights were the only times we could work on the railway. Then, when you look at the big stations, they were doing them in series, taking major bits apart at a time, but not trying to do it all, because it would have been too disruptive to the flow of passengers.

'What distinguishes Crossrail is its sheer scale, because it is all being done in parallel and because it is a "greenfield" site, so every station is being built at the same pace. The challenge that gives us in technical assurance is that we get huge volumes of work at once, because every site team needs to get on and we don't want to be delaying construction, so we are working on huge amounts of design in parallel, which is great, but challenging.'

Chris Binns, Chief Engineer of Crossrail, says there are many lessons to be learned from the successful construction of Crossrail One and wants these passed on to the builders of Crossrail Two.

What have been the main environmental considerations in carrying out the Crossrail scheme?

'Environmentally we have got quite a number of commitments and undertakings to various people. There are some 400 agreements being administered by my team in terms of settlement so, as we have fed the tunnels through, we are just making sure that we monitor all of the settlement that occurs and putting control measures in place. These specify that we must get to a point where *there is less than a certain number of millimetres in movement and go on for a minimum of two years after the line has opened and, in some cases, for far longer.*

'There is movement all the time, you can't avoid it in tunnelling completely, but you can monitor and control it, so we have movement triggers and a lot of monitoring equipment in place, with teams going out regularly to carry out surveys and take readings. We also have trigger levels when we respond, and various ways of dealing with issues as they arise. We are already closing agreements out and are now in a situation where we are working with developers who are working alongside our railway and having to ensure that they don't disturb us!

'We are also installing two different types of 'floating track' to absorb vibration and noise and in order to isolate the running lines from the ground surrounding the line. The particular instances we have are a concert hall in one place and a recording studio in another, where we can't have the rumbling or noise of trains transmitted into the surrounding ground.

'It is more expensive than conventional track and more complex to build – logistically it is also more difficult to install. In outline you cast the slab in the form of the first stage concrete, then we jack it up and separate it from the tunnel floor, with the slab sitting on elastomeric bearings, which are like rubber pads and being isolated from the surrounding structure in one case, or in the floating track slab (FTS) heavy variant the slab sits on heavy duty coil springs.'

What is the schedule for the new rolling stock and services?

'The first Class 345 trains are due into service in May 2017, when they will be introduced on services from Shenfield to Liverpool Street. The first units will be reduced length because the surface level platforms at Liverpool Street are too short for the length of trains we will be running through the tunnels.

'Then we will start running real trains through the tunnels in November 2017, which is when we will put the first trains through the central section – this is what we call the dynamic testing phase – so we do a lot of pre-testing, bench testing, and then integrated testing and then we put trains into the tunnels.

'When we get to the next stage (Stage Two, May 2018) we will go out on the western side of the route with a shuttle service from the main Paddington station to Heathrow Airport, replacing the current Heathrow Connect service. Next will be Stage Three, the tunnel section, on 9 December 2018, when services are due to start running from Paddington to Abbey Wood. That staging allows us to sequence things, so we are not trying to achieve a 'big bang' opening on a single day.

'All of the new trains are being delivered to Old Oak Common depot and will initially be running empty as far as Westbourne Park, where they will descend to the new low level station and

operate in service to Abbey Wood. That initial service will allow us to bed in the whole operation – not having the complexities of junctions or fitting in with other services out of Paddington to start with.

'Stage Four in May 2019 will be through services from Paddington to Shenfield then finally, in December 2019, Stage Five will see introduction of through services west of Paddington from Reading and Heathrow along the full route to Shenfield and Abbey Wood.'

Based on Crossrail's success, what can be done to keep other major rail infrastructure schemes on budget?

'The only way I know about handling major schemes is to do the detailed design work and create estimates which don't have holes in them. When you look at where we have go to, with well-understood budgets we are sticking to, it is because there is a well-understood outline design agreed before the detailed design work has been tendered and before it has gone too far into production.

'One of the things I am really impressed with in the Crossrail project is that we are already informing both HS2 and Crossrail Two – and anyone who wants to listen – about the lessons we have learned along the way, because there are always lessons to be learned and the learning legacy is a big focus of Crossrail – trying to make sure we pass on all the things that we have been discovering.

'There have not been any major issues that have bust our contingency provisions – we have contingency provisions and contingencies happen all the time – part of the reason I love my job is that one hour I will be doing something relating to concrete and the next hour it will be electronic systems. There are always issues, but we have processes to deal with them as well as contingency funds. We have not had anything hit us that was not already on our risk register.'

How important is it to keep your team together, so that they can move straight onto Crossrail Two?

'It really is important. The worst thing for the rail industry is when we have stop–go type of investment, because then you literally lose the skills. People are more mobile now across global projects and will go and do them. So there is a real win opportunity for Crossrail Two to pick up from Crossrail One and seamlessly move forward.

'I'm also interested to see that there are various moves to extend the coverage of Crossrail One – there is talk of extending to Ebbsfleet in Kent and north from Old Oak Common to connect with the West Coast Main Line and relieve pressure on Euston while HS2 is being built.

'When you look at these ideas along with Crossrail Two, there is a really good opportunity for the tunnel builders and civil engineers to manoeuvre their way onto that project and then there is an opportunity for the railway systems specialists to move onto these potential extensions to Crossrail One. That to me would be the real win, if we can just keep building the skills base, and keep them busy, rather than letting them go away to work on projects abroad.'

Crossrail Two

Like High Speed Two, the second Crossrail project looks set to cost significantly more than its predecessor – approaching double the cost at around £30 billion, according to early estimates – yet just like HS2 there is a strong political will to make it happen and the opportunities it offers to solve a number of major rail capacity issues in the capital seems to make a far more compelling case than that being used to justify high speed rails to the north. Opening will not be before 2030, but the tantalising promise is for 30 trains an hour – one every two minutes – to be running on the core Central London section of the line.

A major step forward for Crossrail Two came on 10 March 2016, when the new line was endorsed in a report from the National Infrastructure Commission (NIC), a body set up by Chancellor George Osborne in 2015 and Chaired by Lord Adonis, a former Transport Secretary. Adonis declared that the line – then priced at £27 billion – was a priority, without which the capital would grind to a halt. 'There is no good reason to delay. Crossrail Two will help to keep London moving, create hundreds of thousands of homes and fire regeneration across the city from north-east to south-west,' he added, 'we should get on with it right away and have the line open by 2033.' The NIC report said the business case for the railway should be rewritten to make sure London contributed its fair share – more than half of the overall cost.

In a similar fashion to Crossrail One, the proposed new line links up a range of suburban routes on opposite sides of the capital. In the case of Crossrail Two, the latest proposals would see services on four suburban routes in South West London that currently terminate at Waterloo (Shepperton, Hampton Court, Chessington South and Epsom) become cross-London services, using the new line to reach two or three destinations in northeast London, partly on new alignment and partly by connecting at Tottenham Hale with the existing (and soon to be upgraded) Lea Valley route towards Broxbourne and Harlow.

Relieving the pressure on Euston station, when HS2 arrives there in 2026, is one key justification for the new route. Others are summed up well in the opening paragraph of an independent report on funding options produced by PricewaterhouseCoopers (PwC) in November 2014. This points out that by 2036, London's population is projected by the Office for National Statistics (ONS) to reach 10.1 million and will rise still further to 11.3 million by 2050. With jobs in Central London increasing by 700,000 over the next 20 years, Transport for London is predicting that even with Crossrail One and Thameslink completed, this new capacity will be insufficient to address the transport needs that London will face.

With net migration to the UK having reached a record 336,000 in the year to June 2015 and showing no signs of slowing, it is not hard to see why TfL has such a strong case in promoting the new line. London's burgeoning population will mean five million more journeys each day on the transport network, it claims, with overcrowding on the tube forecast to double by 2041, and National Rail services will face similar challenges. While Crossrail One will ease the pain short term, only by carrying on and developing Crossrail Two will we be able to cope with the long term growth and have sufficient transport capacity to keep the wider South East working and growing and improve the quality of life in the region.

TfL argues that Crossrail Two would be a transformational development in transport across the South East, supporting 60,000 full-time jobs across the UK during its construction and 200,000 new jobs when it opens. By allowing up to 270,000 more people to travel into London in peak periods, it would relieve crowding and congestion, freeing up space on main lines, to allow more frequent services to run from places including Cambridge, Southampton, Basingstoke, Woking, Guildford and Portsmouth. It would also play a major role in regeneration and planned development of some 200,000 new homes across the region.

Public consultations

A number of public consultation exercises have been organised by TfL in order to gauge public support for the scheme and for a number of possible variances to the route. The strength of support for the principle of Crossrail Two was evident in the first such exercise, in mid-2013, when there was also a choice between an all-underground metro-style route from Wimbledon to Alexandra Palace or the more ambitious regional option now adopted. Support for Crossrail Two was overwhelming (96% of respondents), while the regional option was favoured by 84% of respondents, compared to 73% backing the metro plan.

A further consultation exercise in 2014 proposed some changes to the previous year's proposals, including an extension to New Southgate of the previously planned branch to Alexandra Palace, relocation of the somewhat contentious station planned for King's Road in Chelsea and a change to the location of a junction in North East London. Another set of tweaks were then put forward in 2015, when a planned station at Tooting Broadway was replaced by one at Balham in South London and a variance in the North London route to New Southgate was put forward, to serve Wood Green in preference to Turnpike Lane and Alexandra Palace.

Proposed services

To the South West of London, Crossrail Two would take over all services on the Hampton Court and Chessington South branch lines currently forming part of the South West Trains franchise, with four trains an hour from these branches running towards North East London via the new route. In addition, Crossrail Two services would operate alongside existing services to Waterloo on the branch line to Shepperton, with up to eight trains an hour running as far out as Teddington, four of those continuing to or starting from Shepperton. Finally, there would be up to six Crossrail Two services an hour to and from Epsom, giving an overall service frequency from Wimbledon onto the new line of 20 trains an hour, with a new Crossrail Two station built beneath the existing Wimbledon station.

Having entered a new tunnel south of Wimbledon station, the Crossrail services will then be routed via a new interchange station at Balham, for connections onto the Northern Line of London Underground and South London suburban rail services and on to Clapham Junction. It already enjoys the status of being Britain's busiest railway junction and will become an even more important interchange onto Crossrail Two from longer distance rail services from the South West and the South Coast, as well as suburban services to Waterloo and Victoria from a host of places south and south west of the capital.

Crossing the Thames in a tunnel below the bridge carrying the West London Line, the new route will then serve the new station at Chelsea (see below), before continuing across Central London with major interchange stations at Victoria, Tottenham Court Road (for Crossrail One), a combined Euston–St Pancras station (for both HS1 and 2 as well as mainline and suburban services at Euston, St. Pancras and King's Cross), Angel and finally a station in Dalston connected to both Dalston Junction and Dalston Kingsland stations on separate London Overground routes. From Dalston, between 10 and 15 of the 30 trains an hour would continue to New Southgate, serving Seven Sisters, then either Wood Green or Turnpike Lane and Alexandra Palace. The other 10 to 15 trains an hour would join the Lea Valley route at Tottenham Hale for stations to Cheshunt and Broxbourne.

A controversial new station

Given that the only real opposition to Crossrail Two came from the residents of Kensington and Chelsea, where 16% of respondents to the 2013 consultation strongly opposed the scheme and almost

20% either opposed or strongly opposed the scheme, it is perhaps hardly surprising that a campaign is being fought against locating the one and only brand new station along the entire route on a site in King's Road, Chelsea.

Crossrail Two's promoters point out that their chosen site in King's Road has been safeguarded since first being identified in 1989 plans for a Chelsea–Hackney line. They argue it would improve community access to rail in an area where there is little current provision, improve access to two local hospitals, cut the journey time to Tottenham Court Road by 30 minutes and bring all residents of Chelsea within a ten minute walk of an underground or rail station. Responding to local worries about the location of a new station, the promoters say that their station will avoid affecting Chelsea Fire Station and Dovehouse Green, with the planned ticket hall being 'within existing buildings in order to fully integrate the station and preserve the character of King's Road.'

But such promises do not allay the fears of opponents, who argue that a better and cheaper alternative would be to site the new station at Imperial Wharf, a location which would create an interchange with the London Overground, so relieving pressure on Clapham Junction and West Brompton, the stations either side of Imperial Wharf on the West London Line. Relocating the new station to this site, say the campaigners, would open up the potential for a greater contribution to the new line from developers of residential sites nearby than would be the case with the preferred King's Road site. Opponents of the preferred site also argue that the case for it is based on it becoming a destination in its own right, not just a route elsewhere for Chelsea residents.

In a re-assessment of four potential route options for the section of Crossrail Two between Clapham Junction and Victoria, published by TfL in October 2015, the King's Road site remains a preferred option, although TfL acknowledges that 'finding acceptable worksites in an area of high land values and much development will be challenging'. Running services non-stop from Clapham Junction to Victoria would be quicker and save £0.9 billion, but would increase demand due to a faster journey time between the two stations, and increase interchange pressure at Clapham Junction.

A route via Imperial Wharf would require tighter curves and lengthen the journey time by one minute, say TfL, while an Imperial Wharf station 'would result in small increases in public transport accessibility levels from the walking catchment area.' Finally, the fourth option of an intermediate station at Fulham Broadway is effectively dismissed, as it would result in an even longer journey time (an extra two minutes), increase over-crowding on the Wimbledon branch of the District Line and add to crowd management difficulties at Stamford Bridge football ground on match days, or when other events were taking place there.

Finding the money

While HS2 look set to be an ever-deepening black hole for the next two decades, funding the not inconsiderable cost of Crossrail Two looks far better thought out and set to be borne in significant measure by those who benefit from its opening. Faced with the Treasury Secretary's instruction to London Mayor Boris Johnson of ensuring that 'at least half of the cost of the scheme can be met through private sources, ensuring that it will be affordable to the UK taxpayer', PwC's independent report into funding options suggested that more than half of the cost could be met using existing funding mechanisms.

Following the example of Crossrail One, the PwC report suggests paying back investment through a number of existing methods – a combination of fares revenue, the Business Rate Supplement and Mayoral Community Infrastructure Levy (CIL). The report also suggests that it could see funding raised through retaining the Council Tax contribution for the 2012 Olympic Games, as well as potentially increasing the Mayoral CIL. Funding from developments and land owners adjacent to the line could also help contribute, but the accountants have a blunt message to those who think that a scheme of this scale can realistically attract large amounts of private sector investment:

> '...some commentators cite that a 'wall of money' from Sovereign Wealth Funds, Infrastructure Funds, Pension funds and other similar investors is available to invest in infrastructure and that this provides evidence that projects such as Crossrail Two could be privately financed. While there is no doubt that these investors are keen to invest in infrastructure, Crossrail Two is unlikely to meet many of their investment requirements. The size of the project, the construction risk, the demand risk and the likely reliance on non-patronage revenues to pay the bulk of the project means that, without direct government guarantees, such investors are unlikely to invest in Crossrail Two.'

Chapter 8

STILL TO COME

Highly successful re-opening of railway routes in England, Scotland and Wales has proved time and time again that, if certain criteria are met then the demand is there and passenger traffic will be generated at a level far in excess of what the consultants evaluating potential re-openings could ever have forecast. It is the frequency of service, quality of rolling stock, attractiveness of fares and traffic congestion within the destination town or city that are the key factors behind the steadily increasing popularity of re-opened routes.

In its 2009 Report *Connecting Communities*, the Association of Train Operating Companies (ATOC) noted that in the period since 1995, 27 new lines – totalling 199 track miles – and 68 stations had opened, but added that many other communities had grown, yet still lacked adequate access to the national rail network and pointed out that the process for developing relevant schemes to date had been piecemeal, with the initiative coming in many cases from devolved or local government.

The ATOC report went on to identify 14 places in England with populations in excess of 15,000 that were not currently served by rail and where a new line might be justified, along with a number of places where a new station could be justified. In all cases, the potential schemes had a positive business case to support their implementation, providing direct and indirect access to around a million people, with relatively short construction lead times of between two years and nine months and six years.

East–West Railway

While it only appeared in an appendix to the ATOC report, the most exciting re-opening currently being developed is the first section of what has become known as East–West Railway, a long-awaited link between Oxford and Bedford, and onwards to Cambridge, which ironically was not one of the routes slated for closure by Beeching, along with the re-opening of a connecting

A great deal has changed since this 21 May 2011 view of First Great Western 165132 standing at Bicester Town. This was the last day of FGW operation before the line to Oxford was handed over to Chiltern Railways. Bicester Village as it is now known, has two platforms, regular direct services to London Marylebone via the new south chord, and is set to become a major interchange station on the new East–West Railway.

line north from Aylesbury that was part of the Great Central main line, and which did feature in *The Reshaping of British Railways* and closed to passengers in 1966.

Work on Phase One of the western section of this route has seen substantial upgrading of the line between Oxford and Bicester Village (formerly Bicester Town) – itself a route which re-opened to passenger traffic in 1987 after a 20 year closure. This project, undertaken by Chiltern Railways and Network Rail, saw the construction of a new curve south of Bicester and a doubling of the track prior to introduction of the new service from London Marylebone to Oxford in December 2016, when the service, which had been first launched in October 2015, was extended from its temporary terminus at the newly-constructed Oxford Parkway station into the university city's main station.

A second £1 billion phase of this project encompasses the section of line from Bicester Village station to Bletchley on the West Coast Main Line, an upgrading of the 'Marston Vale' Line onwards to Bedford and a connection there with the Midland Main Line. It will also include the section of former Great Central main line north of Aylesbury Vale Parkway station to its intersection with this route at Claydon Junction. While this section, and that from Bicester to Claydon Junction, has remained in use for freight trains conveying household waste, the section east from Claydon Junction has been 'mothballed' since the early 1990s and is being completely rebuilt, with a major new station planned at Winslow.

At Bletchley, the revived East–West Railway will make use of the 'white elephant' concrete viaduct that was built in the 1960s to take the route across the newly electrified West Coast Main Line, but was little used before the route finally closed to passengers in January 1968. It will now be equipped with high level platforms, with trains on the route then either heading north to terminate at Milton Keynes Central or on to Bedford.

What makes East–West Rail an especially exciting re-opening project is the scale of what is being planned, which is far more substantial than many previous branch line revivals. From its planned opening, this will be a double track electrified route designed to handle both fast and stopping passenger services, as well as freight traffic, particularly flows from Southampton docks to the north which will be diverted along this route to reach the West Coast and Midland Main Lines and to relieve pressure on the heavily used section of line between Oxford and Leamington Spa.

Three separate passenger services will make use of the new route: firstly there will be an hourly fast service from Reading to Bedford, calling at Didcot Parkway, Oxford, Oxford Parkway, Bicester Village, Winslow, Bletchley, Woburn Sands, Ridgmont and Bedford Midland. This will be in addition to the current hourly service shuttling between Bletchley and Bedford and calling at all stations.

Another hourly service from Reading will go to Milton Keynes via Oxford, taking the same route as the Reading–Bedford service as far as Bletchley, before joining the West Coast Main Line as far as Milton Keynes Central, where a new platform (2a) has already been built to accommodate the planned service. Along with the Reading–Bedford service, this will mean a half-hourly frequency along the Oxford–Bletchley corridor.

Finally, there will be an hourly service linking Milton Keynes with London Marylebone, which will run via Aylesbury and High Wycombe, taking around 90 minutes. This will revive the successful Christmas shoppers' specials that were run between Aylesbury and Milton Keynes in the 1980s and, most importantly, give residents in Buckinghamshire towns like High Wycombe and Aylesbury regular and direct access for the first time ever to the fastest growing city in England, as well as direct connections there with West Coast Main Line services to the Midlands, North West England and Scotland.

So much for the western section of East–West Rail, for which the Government has committed £270 million and which could be open in 2019. On a far more ambitious scale is the Central section of route – from Bedford to Cambridge – which will require large scale capital expenditure, as many bridges have been removed or deteriorated since the line closed in 1968, while the Bedford bypass also severs the line.

But the East–West Rail Consortium – a grouping of 16 local authorities from Oxford City Council in the west to Norfolk

County Council in the east – has identified a number of potential routes for the revived line between Cambridge, Sandy (on the East Coast Main Line) and Bedford. The Consortium and Network Rail are working to identify a preferred route, estimated to cost between £250m and £300m and, in a further encouraging signal, work to install a new flyover at Hitchin, which takes Cambridge-bound trains over the East Coast Main Line (ECML), included passive provision for the central section of East–West Rail to link into the ECML.

What gives the Consortium heart that the dream it has been pursuing since 1995 can one day be brought to reality in its entirety and 'brains trains' from Oxford to Cambridge be revived, is the findings of a report it commissioned from Atkins Consulting, which aimed to identify where economic activity and potential growth could be supported through improvements to public rail links and train services. Atkins' report, published in August 2014, showed that improved rail connections and services could deliver sufficient economic benefit to justify the investment.

Further impetus for the East–West Railway came in March 2016, when it became the latest project to come under the scrutiny of Lord Adonis' National Infrastructure Commission (NIC). 'The 67 miles between Oxford and Cambridge could be England's Silicon Valley, but it lacks the transport and housing infrastructure needed, despite its world-class universities and some individually thriving towns and cities,' commented Adonis, who has been charged with reporting on the Oxbridge corridor in autumn 2017.

'The towns and cities between and around Oxford, Milton Keynes and Cambridge could become so much more than the sum of their parts,' he added, 'a high-skilled, high-employment, high-innovation cluster, helping to fire the national economy by leading the world in cutting edge technology and jobs.' The NIC will map out potential sites for new housing and industrial estates, including the use of de-commissioned Ministry of Defence land, while a second stage of the review could finally commit government to fund the revived rail link.

March–Wisbech

North of Cambridge, the ultimate destination of East–West Railway, and also a place to have been identified by the 2009 ATOC report as a scheme with a positive business case, is the town of Wisbech, with a population of some 26,500, but with almost twice that number of people living in the wider station catchment area. It stands at the end of a seven-mile branch line from the town of March, on the route from Peterborough to Ely, lost is passenger service in 1968 and had seen freight services end in 2001.

While re-opening has not been formally confirmed, and re-opening cost estimates have spiralled ever upwards to north of £100 million, a real head of steam is building up for what would be

The seven-mile route from March to Wisbech is nominally mothballed, but precious little evidence remains in the Wisbech area. This view, on 9 August 2015, shows a remaining level crossing gate on the outskirts of the town – a new station would be built somewhere beyond the road.

a relatively straightforward revival. There is even a preservation society, the Bramley Line preservation group, with a base halfway along the route. Like the Bicester–Bletchley section of the East–West route, the line itself is technically 'mothballed' rather than closed, so although the remaining track (now heavily overgrown) will need to be relaid, it remains in Network Rail ownership, meaning that the only real issues will be the need to replace the eight level crossings and find a location for the new Wisbech station.

Besides the preservationists, there is huge support for a re-opening that would bring rail services back to a part of Cambridgeshire blighted by relatively poor road links. It featured in the 2009 ATOC *Connecting Communities* report as having a positive business case, is a prominent campaign for Railfuture and is being strongly promoted by both Wisbech Town Council and the Wisbech Rail Re-opening Campaign. At a national level, the scheme has been taken to Westminster by North East Cambridgeshire MP, Steve Barclay, where at a Rail summit the then Transport Minister, Stephen Hammond MP, acknowledged that the Wisbech re-opening was a strategic priority.

Re-opening campaigners would like to see the line used for a direct train service to Cambridge, where a 40-minute journey time would be significantly quicker than is possible by car or bus. With stops en route at March, Manea, Ely and the new station at Cambridge North (for the Science Park), the link would provide much better access to jobs and education and help connect Fenland with the rest of Cambridgeshire. On a more ambitious scale, if electrified, the route could be served directly from London Kings Cross when the two four-car sets forming existing services to Kings Lynn are split at Ely rather than Cambridge. Instead of terminating at Ely, the second set could continue on to March and Wisbech.

In economic terms, the case for Wisbech is compelling. An economic benefits study by Cambridgeshire County Council, published in April 2014, reckoned that the line would produce benefits of £3 for every £1 spent on the re-opening, while Steve Barclay MP told a meeting of stakeholders that the benefit had increased to £4 for every £1 of expenditure. Meantime, the government had already announced that £10.5 million will be allocated between 2016 and 2020 for further work on key aspects of the route, including the location of a new station in Wisbech, which campaigners want in the town, rather that close to the A47 on the southern outskirts.

Visiting the town on a summer Sunday afternoon in 2015, I saw convincing proof that the line would prove popular when, while waiting to return to King's Lynn from Wisbech bus station, I counted more than 40 people getting off the X1 bus that had arrived from Peterborough, which I was waiting to board, and which is currently the principal public transport route to the town from London and many other parts of the country. Wisbech is a delightful and bustling town with a great many fine buildings – the Georgian terrace of buildings along the North Brink side of the River Nene is one of the finest Georgian streets in England, with Peckover House reckoned to be the finest property in the town, and the classic Georgian Elgoods Brewery at the other end of the street almost as impressive.

Heading to the south side of the town, the dominant feature is the huge Nestle Purina pet food plant, alongside which a site

Wisbech is at the heart of a predominantly agricultural area, as evidenced by the many east European languages to be heard around the town. But it also has significant tourist potential, as this view of the North Brink and its remarkable Georgian architecture clearly shows.

has been cleared close to the factory complex, which appears to be the ideal location for a new station. It was traffic from the pet food plant which had helped keep the line open to freight for more than 30 years after the end of passenger traffic, so there must surely be some prospect of following the trend elsewhere in the country and returning at least part of that traffic to rail, once the passenger service has finally been re-established.

Bristol–Portishead

Like the citizens of Wisbech, the residents of Portishead in North Somerset have been growing increasingly vocal in their quest to see the long-disused rail link with nearby Bristol restored. Passenger services to this important commuter town ceased as long ago as 1964, but freight trains continued to serve the town's docks until 1981 and the line was even used by steam-hauled special trains during celebrations of the Great Western Railway's 150th Anniversary in 1985, when a run-round loop was specially installed at Portishead.

This is a pleasantly scenic line with significant tourist potential, which follows the south side of the Avon Gorge – opposite the route to Avonmouth and Severn Beach on the north side of the river. With shrewd marketing, there seems little doubt that this can in time re-establish its long-lost day tripper traffic to complement the evident demand that exists from daily commuters into Bristol city centre, who have become exasperated by the traffic problems they face every day.

Despite serving a new station in Portishead which had only been built in 1954, at the time of its closure ten years later, the

One day, hopefully by 2020, this will be the site of Portishead's new station. It is less central that the former station, but the site, seen here on 29 November 2015, was selected to avoid the need for a level crossing on Quays Avenue, the road passing beyond the fence.

passenger service had been rationalised to provide a limited morning and evening commuter services only, with no trains at all during the middle of the day. As a prelude to closure there had been a drastic cutting of services in 1962, when Portbury station was closed and the 14 trains daily were reduced to just six – there were no departures from Portishead after a 09.15 train until one at 17.15 – and the popular Sunday service of five return trains a day was axed completely.

Efforts to revive the line began as long ago as 2000, when the Portishead Railway Action Group (a predecessor of the current action group) was formed. Its campaign became a great deal more realistic a couple of years later, when in 2002 the branch line was re-opened from its junction with the main line near Bristol's Parson Street station as far as the Royal Portbury Dock. This £21 million project was undertaken to allow cars to be transported by rail from the docks, but left a disused stretch of just over three miles long from Portbury Junction, near the village of Pill, to Portishead.

Chronic peak hour traffic congestion on the A369 trunk road has been the driving force behind long-running efforts of the Portishead Railway Group and other stakeholders to bring passenger rail services back to the town, with the clock now ticking down to a planned re-opening in 2020, more than a decade after a report by consultants Halcrow that found in favour of re-opening. A long process then began, which included purchase of the disused stretch of track by North Somerset Council from the British Railways Board (Residuary) Ltd (BRB), in order to secure it for the planned re-opening.

Despite not having seen a train for more than 30 years, the Portishead branch remains largely intact, with vegetation having been cut back as part of the long drawn out re-opening process. Here the line passes hundreds of imported vehicles at Portbury Docks, the ideal site for a park & ride station as it is close to M5 junction 19.

A formal public consultation into the re-opening ran from June until August 2015 and the site of a new Portishead station has been selected in Quays Avenue, somewhat short of the previous location, principally to avoid the need for a level crossing in the town centre. Paying a first visit to the town for many years in November 2015, it was slightly disappointing to see that the new station site is a fair walk from the town centre, although very close to significant new retail and residential developments and a reasonable choice, provided a direct path and cycleway to the town centre can be provided on the section of former route to the west of the Quays Avenue station site.

One significant omission from the current revival plan, but something which featured in earlier re-opening schemes, is a park-and-ride station close to Junction 19 of the M5 Motorway, just to the east of the former Portbury station. There seems ample land for such a development here, which would undoubtedly attract commuters from the South-West off the M5 motorway. If rail capacity was an issue, the three over-bridges between this point and Pill are all built for double track, so an extended loop could easily be built between a new station here and Pill, just over a mile away, where the former station is being re-opened as part of the revival scheme and where a loop is already planned.

Another significant omission is a station in the Ashton Gate area, a populous suburb to the south of Bristol city centre and where a former station served the nearby Bristol City football ground, now also home to the city's rugby team. A local campaign by the Friends of Ashton Gate Station to have a station included

A remarkable survival in the village of Pill is this road sign, which points the way to both the railway station, which closed in 1964, and to the Shirehampton Ferry, which ceased a decade later in 1974, when the M5 Avonmouth Bridge was opened.

in the Portishead line re-opening has attracted significant local support, notably from Bristol Sport Ltd, owner of the football and rugby clubs, whose £45 million redevelopment plans include a major conference and events centre in use seven days a week, and the University of the West of England (UWE), which has a 1,000 student arts campus nearby.

Exeter–Okehampton–Plymouth

Looking further south west from Portishead, one of the most exciting and eagerly anticipated rail revivals is the former London and South Western Railway (L&SWR) route from Exeter to Plymouth which, as a through route, was a victim of Beeching and closed in May 1968. However, the section between Plymouth and Bere Alston, along with the short branch to Gunnislake, survived the closure recommendation, due to inadequate road links in the area. The service from Okehampton to Exeter was curiously not recommended for closure by Beeching, but eventually succumbed in June 1972, only to be revived as a seasonal summer Sunday service in 1997.

This revival of Okehampton services was made possible as the line had remained open for access to Meldon Quarry, two miles west of Okehampton, from where there was a daily traffic of ballast trains to various locations on the British Rail network in the south of England until the quarry's final closure. Since 2000 a preservation society has run trains from Okehampton station – restored in 1997 as part of a tourism development scheme promoted by Devon County Council – to a halt at the closed quarry, just to the east of the Meldon Viaduct, a scheduled monument.

Meldon Viaduct, seen here on 26 June 2016 looking north towards Meldon Quarry and Okehampton, is a renowned 'monument to Victorian engineering ingenuity'. Studies into re-opening of the former London & South Western route from Exeter to Plymouth have suggested that it would need to be replaced, although the same was said of Ribblehead Viaduct by those trying to close the Setttle to Carlisle line in the 1980s.

Meldon Viaduct has deteriorated since the line's closure in 1968, so an alternative would have to be built alongside, according to Network Rail, and will represent a significant cost in replacing the 20-mile missing link from Meldon Quarry to Bere Alston. Development has also created obstacles along the closed line in the Tavistock area, but the 5½-mile section from the southern side of Tavistock to Bere Alston has long been talked about as a potential revival for commuter services into Plymouth. This would be funded, at least in part, by a residential property developer, which as long ago as 2008 had offered to rebuild the line if it was granted consent for 800 new homes on the edge of Tavistock.

What has enormously helped raise this long talked about resurrection of the through route high up the public agenda was the devastating storms on the night of 4/5 February 2014, which completed destroyed a section of the famous sea wall at Dawlish, on the only remaining rail link to South Devon and Cornwall. This effectively isolated the South West from the rest of the UK rail network for two months until its re-opening on 4 April 2014, and led to urgent calls for alternatives to be examined and a new route created.

In the aftermath of this devastating sea wall breach, floods minister Dan Rogerson was quoted in December 2014 as saying that it is 'crucial that we protect that link for all those communities across south Devon and southeast Cornwall, and coming down to the west'. He added: 'But I believe there is a real opportunity to do something more imaginative to restore rail connections across the middle of Devon, and also bring it closer to communities like Launceston and Bude, which haven't had it for generations.'

Early morning at Bere Alston on Saturday 3 August 2013, as the driver of the 06.40 service from Plymouth walks to the far cab to take the train on to Gunnislake.

Further strengthening of the case for re-opening the L&SWR route came in the publication of research by Plymouth University, published in December 2015 and sponsored by Network Rail, together with Devon and Cornwall County Councils. This anticipated that rail services through Dawlish could be disrupted for 40 days a year by 2040 and 120 days a year by 2100, due to rising sea levels. *Sea-level rise impacts on transport infrastructure: The notorious case of the coastal railway line at Dawlish England* based its findings on historic sea level data and suggested that Network Rail's current spend of £0.8m a year could rise to between £5.8m and £7.6m by 2040.

At the time of the spring 2014 closure, Prime Minister David Cameron also backed restoration of the Okehampton route as the 'most resilient' alternative to what has so evidently become the increasingly vulnerable Dawlish line in Devon. In an interview with the regional BBC Spotlight news programme in January 2015, David Cameron declared that the UK was 'a wealthy country' that should be making long-term investments in rail. But with the worst flooding in late 2015 occurring not in South Devon but in Cumbria, Lancashire and the Scottish Borders, the impetus for a solution to the Dawlish problem seems to have slipped off the political agenda.

The encouraging ministerial comments came after publication in summer 2014 of Network Rail's *West of Exeter Route Resilience Study* which had been ordered in the light of the sea wall collapse and which examined the costs and feasibility of building a range of alternative routes to the existing line via Dawlish. This study put a staggering £875 million price tag on rebuilding the L&SWR route via Okehampton as a double track main line, including upgrading of the remaining stubs of the route from Exeter to Meldon Quarry and from Plymouth to Bere Alston.

That eye-watering price tag did, however contain a 66% contingency, so a more realistic cost might well be nearer £500 million. But even accepting this inflated figure, it compares well with the report's estimates for alternatives, which ranged from the £470 million cost of rebuilding the former Teign Valley branch line from Exeter to Newton Abbot as a modern double track railway and the £398m – £659m cost of strengthening the existing railway to the cost of between £1.49 billion and £3.1 billion of building an entirely new Exeter–Newton Abbot railway on one of five alternative direct routes.

Network Rail's report did highlight a number of challenges to re-opening the former L&SWR main line: in addition to building on the former line north of Tavistock viaduct and the need to replace Meldon Viaduct, the report said the line did not meet current maintenance clearance standards, the quality of some earthworks was in doubt and a gradient of 1 in 75 crossing the north of Dartmoor was steep in railway terms.

But on a more positive note, the report said a Class 220 'Voyager' train could travel non-stop from Exeter to Plymouth in 53 minutes on a rebuilt line, just 4 minutes slower than on the Dawlish route. There would, however, be a further time penalty for longer distance services of 10–14 minutes by needing to reverse direction at both Plymouth and Exeter. Local stopping trains making seven intermediate stops could do the journey in 75 minutes, said Network Rail, with a journey time of 29 minutes from Exeter to Okehampton.

In an assessment of the report published in February 2015, lobby group Railfuture noted that none of the route alternatives offered a benefit to cost (BCR) ratio of greater than 1 on this basis, let alone the BCR of over 2 that would normally be required for the investment to be made. In fact the highest BCR was 0.29, for

Okehampton station has been delightfully restored and is now shared by seasonal GWR Sunday services to Exeter and the Dartmoor Railway, which operates the two-mile section onwards to Meldon Viaduct. On 26 June 2016, single car units 153361/370 wait to depart with the final train of the day – the 17.59 to Exeter St David's.

the Teign Valley route; however it is not certain that this route is feasible. It was also found that a local service via the Okehampton route would fail to cover its costs, so this was excluded from the appraisal as it would worsen the BCR. The various options for a new direct route between Exeter and Newton Abbot would save between 3 and 6 minutes in journey time for a fast train, but require significant tunnelling, which accounts for their high costs.

While the Network Rail study painted a somewhat sceptical picture of the line's potential viability, it is worth remembering how inaccurate previous studies have been into re-opened lines, and how seriously they have under-estimated the amount of passenger traffic which a new and regular service can generate. Network Rail was only looking at the route as essentially a diversionary and emergency route, but an in-depth study of the line's re-opening prospects *Rural Reconnections: the social benefits of rural rail re-openings* – published by the Campaign to Protect Rural England (CPRE) in June 2015 and based on work by the research group Greengauge 21, paints a rather different picture.

The CPRE report points out that the economic case for creating a long-distance diversionary route can be strengthened by providing a new local rail service. Such a service could mitigate some of the problems faced by remote rural areas in Devon and North Cornwall and would strengthen Tavistock and Okehampton, where additional housing is already planned. It puts an indicative price tag of £650m (again with a 66% contingency mark-up) on a re-opened line, albeit a predominantly single track one, suggesting that the Bere Alston – Tavistock section could be open by 2020/1 while a realistic target for re-opening the full line could be in Network Rail's Control Period 6 from 2019–2024.

Services on the privately-owned route to Okehampton are controlled by a token issued at Crediton, since there is no signal box at Yeoford, three miles to the north where the route parts company with the Tarka Line to Barnstaple. On 26 June 2016 the driver of 150124 accepts the single line token to Eggesford while working the 14.20 service to Barnstaple.

Rural Reconnections concluded that combining the benefit of a resilient diversionary route with those that result from linking up communities and businesses currently cut off from the rail network hugely strengthened the argument for reopening the line. Crucially, valuing these factors properly and taking better account of business losses when a network is temporarily disrupted – as had happened at Dawlish in 2014 and on a number of previous occasions – could have important implications for other lines that are candidates for re-opening elsewhere in the country.

'This report underlines the many benefits that can ensue from reconnecting rural rail lines and have been ignored by previous evaluations', said Ralph Smyth, the CPRE's transport campaign manager. 'Many railways were cut back in the 1960s on the basis that they unnecessarily duplicated other routes. But we need them again now to create sustainable development in our rural communities and to provide resilience against extreme weather', he added. 'Far from being an exercise in nostalgia, rail re-openings are vital to unlocking the potential of rural areas.'

Uckfield–Lewes

By far the longest standing candidate for revived rail services in the south of England is the nine-mile stretch of line linking Lewes, the delightful county town of East Sussex, with Uckfield, a small town of some 14,000 inhabitants, which since 1969 has been the terminus of diesel services from London Victoria and Oxted. This is the Wealden Line, which also included a link from Eridge to Tunbridge Wells Central, before it succumbed to closure on Saturday, 6 July 1985, but has since re-opened as the Spa Valley

Railway as far as the spa town's other station – Tunbridge Wells West.

Efforts to re-open Uckfield–Lewes date back to 1986, but have been repeatedly thwarted by studies that have suggested it is not viable. In 2008, for example, a study was carried out by Network Rail into the case for reinstatement. That report concluded re-opening was technically feasible, but that there was no economic case for re-building the line. Since then, however, re-opening has begun to be looked at in the context of a much wider review into how rail capacity can be improved on the extremely busy London–Brighton or Brighton Main Line (BML) axis.

In its 2009 *Connecting Communities* report, ATOC highlighted its role as a 'potential link line' and in the same year, Network Rail published a draft *Route Utilisation Strategy for Sussex* which acknowledged that a re-opened link would 'provide potential capacity relief to the southern end of the BML.' There was further hope given to the campaign in May 2013, when Patrick McLoughlin, Secretary of State for Transport, announced that the Department for Transport had asked Network Rail to explore the possible re-opening of the Lewes to Uckfield route.

Two signs of progress emerged during 2015. Firstly, in the Spring Budget on 18 March 2015 came a statement that the government will provide £100,000 for a further study into reopening the Lewes to Uckfield rail line. Then, in that year's summer budget on 8 July 2015 came the following hopeful comment: 'The government will extend the scope of the Lewes–Uckfield study to look at improving rail links between London and the south coast, including upgrades to existing routes, consideration of the Brighton Main Line corridor, and re-examination of the DfT's feasibility study on BML2.'

Shortly before the summer budget, a letter from Claire Perry, the Rail Minister, to the newly-elected MP for Lewes, Maria Caulfield, set out the terms of reference for the new re-opening study. In the words of the Rail Minister, these were 'The opportunities that the re-opening of the Lewes–Uckfield line could offer in terms of local journeys… the strategic contribution that re-opening of the line could make during times of disruption to the BML, both planned and unplanned', and 'Consideration of the capital funding options, in the event that a case was identified for re-opening the line. Key to this would be an assessment of the split of local and national funding, reflecting on the findings of the first two elements of the study.'

As with other re-opening proposals, indicative costs have escalated ever upwards. Back in 1974, when a re-opening was discussed in the House of Lords following a serious accident and closure of the BML, the price tag was estimated at just £2 million. By 1987, when the former Network SouthEast sector of British Rail pledged £1.5 million towards re-opening, the indicative cost had risen to £6 million. Then, in 1996 a feasibility study by Kent

County Council into a revived service from Eridge to Tunbridge Wells estimated the cost of that far simpler re-opening proposal at £20–25 million. In the 2008 Network Rail report, the cost of re-building the Lewes–Uckfield line was put at £170 million.

Current proposals for what is now known as BML2 go way beyond merely re-opening the Uckfield–Lewes Line and have assumed a strategic significance matched only by the East–West rail project. Its promoters recognise that the most acute congestion problems are in the London area, so their full proposal is for the creation of a second Brighton Main Line to London, but claim that it is a lot more than relieving pressure on one of the country's most overcrowded rail routes for the benefit of Brighton commuters travelling into London or restoring a rail link between Uckfield and Lewes.

Their three-phase vision – which has already secured widespread expressions of support, including that of Lord Adonis, Chairman of the National Infrastructure Commission – begins in Sussex with re-opening of Uckfield–Lewes, including direct links westwards towards Brighton and eastwards towards Eastbourne. A Kent phase would also see re-opening of the Eridge–Tunbridge Wells line, including a curve from east to north that would allow direct services from Tunbridge Wells towards London and so help relieve pressure on the over-crowded Tonbridge–Tunbridge Wells–Hastings line.

Finally, and most ambitious of all, would be a London phase, including re-opening of a route to the east of Croydon from Selsdon to Elmers End, to relieve pressure on East Croydon station. BML2 would then head northwards to Lewisham on the existing rail alignment, before a new underground section to Stratford, to create a direct connection onwards to Stansted Airport as well as opening up a rail corridor between East Anglia and Sussex, Surrey and Kent, relieving more pressure on the London Underground network and improving links between these counties.

Brian Hart, BML2 Project Manager, says that Brighton Main Line 2 is the only realistic scheme to relieve the chronic overcrowding on both the Brighton and Tonbridge main lines. 'More train paths into London are desperately needed, as well as realistic alternatives. BML2's new link under the Thames between Stratford–Canary Wharf–Lewisham will open up new travel opportunities and help in relieving central London's severe congestion. In March 2017 came a setback, when a long-awaited government report said there was no case for BML2, but invited further work by interested parties, including local authorities and the private sector.

Leicester–Burton-on-Trent
Like Uckfield–Lewes, the 31-mile missing link between Leicester and Burton-on-Trent has been on the re-opening agenda for decades

and remains high on the revival priority lists of campaign groups such as Railfuture and the Campaign for Better Transport. Yet time and again it somehow seems to stumble and fails to find favour with the key local authorities along the line of route, who appear to lack the vision to see that it could be just as much a catalyst for economic regeneration as the successful schemes in Scotland and South Wales, and the Robin Hood line from nearby Nottingham.

The line passes through a heavily-industrialised area and, despite its original closure to passengers in September 1964, had remained an important freight artery giving access to some eight coal mines and a number of important quarry locations along its route. The two principal towns along the line are Coalville, a conurbation with a current population of more than 30,000, and Ashby-de-la-Zouch, an attractive spa town in the centre of the National Forest, eight miles south east of Burton-on-Trent, with a population of around 13,000.

Plans to revive the line date back to the early 1990s when, under British Rail, it was to form the second phase of what was then known as the Ivanhoe Line. This had been launched in May 1994, with the establishment of local services between Loughborough and Leicester and the opening of three new intermediate stations on that stretch of the Midland Main Line, at Barrow-upon-Soar, Sileby and Syston. The second phase of this project would have seen the trains carry on to Burton-on-Trent, serving significant towns en route including Coalville and Ashby de la Zouch, but this fell victim to the upheavals brought about by privatisation of BR.

In its 2009 *Connecting Communities* report, the Association of Train Operating Companies picked the line as a prime re-opening candidate. It put a £49 million price tag on a scheme which would have seen the opening of seven intermediate stations – Kirby Muxloe, Bagworth and Ellistown, Coalville Town, Ashby-de-la-Zouch, Moira and Gresley –with the possibility of another on the outskirts of Leicester, which would have given access to the nearby King Power Stadium, home of Premier League winning Leicester City FC. But in the same year as the ATOC report, a study by consultants Scott Wilson on behalf of Leicestershire County Council painted a less than rosy picture of re-opening prospects.

Scott Wilson said it would cost £53 million to reinstate an hourly service on what is now known as the National Forest route, operating the trains as an extension of an existing service from Lincoln and Nottingham to Leicester. That would include construction of seven new stations and reinstatement of an essential new section of track called the Knighton Chord, which would allow trains direct access from the line to Leicester, without the current need to reverse at what is now a south-facing junction. The April 2009 Report forecast annual operational costs of £4.9 million but said fares would only generate £895,000 a year –

and it was this £4 million annual shortfall which persuaded Leicestershire County Council to reject the planned revival.

But look more closely at the 47-page study, particularly in the light of how successful re-opening schemes have proved to be elsewhere and it is possible to pick big holes in the report and raise doubts about the validity of its findings. Looking at forecast total demand (Page 20 10.4.1), the consultants suggest that Coalville, the most important station on the line, would generate 48,928 trips per year – that is 940 a week or just 157 people per day using an hourly service operating for some 16 hours a day – an average of less than five passengers per train! Ashby-de-la-Zouch would produce 22,814 trips a year, or 73 passengers a day (assuming only six day a week operation) – little more than two passengers per train calling.

Tourism gets a mention, but nothing is factored in for that significant likely source of revenue. There is no mention of the level of passenger traffic that would originate at either Burton-on-Trent or Leicester – a station recording almost 5 million passenger journeys a year – and there is no mention of new passenger traffic being generated from people travelling to London and making a connection at Leicester. With an indicative end-to-end running time of 48 minutes, a passenger travelling from Burton to London would find it quicker to travel on the line and change at Leicester to get to London, rather than take the currently advertised route and change at Derby. London is by far and away the most important long distance rail destination, yet there is not one word in the report on the longer distance traffic that its re-opening would undoubtedly generate.

Seven years after Scott Wilson – and at the same time as the first six month passenger numbers from the Borders Railway showed that pre-opening forecasts been handsomely beaten – came another consultant's report and more bad news for re-opening campaigners. An 80-page report for Leicestershire County Council by AECOM and dated May 2016 suggested that re-opening of the line could cost up to £175 million and could require a subsidy of up to £4 million a year. Together with doubts over where funding would come from to finance the necessary upgrading work, that has been enough to halt further work on the long-awaited project.

Like those of Scott Wilson before them, the latest passenger forecasts stretch credibility in the light of the actual Borders Railway experience. Taking just the example of southbound journeys from Ashby-de-la-Zouch towards Leicester and London, AECOM forecast these for their base year of 2016 at 15,449 – equivalent to 297 per week, less than 50 per day (assuming no Sunday service) or just over three people per train, assuming an hourly service operating 16 hours a day. That is on the basis of a 44 minute journey time for a 23½ mile journey, which is less than half the time it currently takes by bus routes 9A/29A, with a change at Coalville in each direction.

Galashiels is a town of similar size and population to Ashby-de-la-Zouch and in its first six months the station was forecast to attract 20,567 single trips. In the event the first six months to 6 March 2016 saw *five times* that number of passengers (104,593) while just down the road at Tweedbank, the pre-opening forecast of 18,978 single journeys was completely blown out of the water, with *ten times* that number of people actually using the service (183,918). So the experts' forecasts for Ashby-de-la-Zouch and elsewhere deserve to be treated with a massive pinch of salt.

AECOM conclude that the findings of their study suggest that the level of benefits that could be generated by the scheme will not be enough to produce a positive business case, but crucially add that 'this conclusion is based on a set of demand forecasts which we consider may well be understating the level of demand for the scheme', adding another major caveat regarding costs, by stating that these 'are based on an initial high level costing exercise that has been quickly undertaken for the purposes of informing this study.' Nevertheless, this latest study has been enough to take this highly promising re-opening off the political agenda once again.

For those campaigning to get passenger services restored, it seems deeply disappointing that the key local authorities and Leicestershire County Council have based their judgement on two reports which seem to woefully under-estimate the likely level of induced demand for journeys such as Ashby-de-la-Zouch to Leicester, where indirect and slow alternative bus services are inevitably going to be a major limiting factor on current levels of travel between these two points. Factor in tourist traffic, inbound travel and onward journeys via Leicester to London and elsewhere, and the prospects for this route would be totally transformed, if only local Councillors had sufficient vision to see it.

Stratford–Honeybourne

Stratford-upon-Avon is one of the UK's most popular tourist destinations, with Shakespeare's birthplace attracting some five million visitors a year. In railway terms, however, it is the end of the line, being served by a half-hourly local service to Birmingham and a limited service to Leamington Spa and London Marylebone, but completely lacking any connections to the south or west since withdrawal of local services to Gloucester in 1968 and Worcester in 1969.

Six miles south of the town lies the large former Ministry of Defence (MoD) Central Engineers' Depot at Long Marston which, besides being the focus of major redevelopment plans, is also one of the UK's major storage sites for off-lease railway rolling stock. In MoD days there were a staggering 33 miles of track within the 450-acre depot, including a full circle of track around the site. Long Marston is connected to the Worcester–Oxford North Cotswolds route at Honeybourne by a three-mile link that is in regular use for the transfer of stock to and from Long Marston.

Re-building the missing six-mile link between Stratford-upon-Avon and Long Marston would open up the town to services from the south and west via Worcester – stopping at the new Worcestershire Parkway station for connections to the south-west, and, if a north-to-east curve was reinstated at Honeybourne would allow direct services to run from Stratford to Oxford and create a considerably shorter and faster route to London than the current route via Leamington Spa. Not surprisingly, this potential has attracted significant interest and prompted the local authority to commission a full study into the cost and benefits of a revived line.

That detailed study by consultants Arup was published in September 2012 and put a relatively modest (2012) price tag of £76m on their preferred rebuilding option, which would allow the running of two trains an hour along the revived route – a stopping service from Leamington and Stratford to Worcester and a semi-fast service from Stratford to Oxford and possibly London. A new station would be built at Long Marston to serve the significant residential development taking place there and there would be capacity for a limited number of freight and charter trains.

Arup's preferred proposal was for a single line leading three miles southwards from Stratford's existing station, running parallel to a road that has been built on the former rail alignment, but diving under a key junction at Evesham Place on the edge of the town, then a double track from Milcote, the site of a former station, through Long Marston to a junction north of Honeybourne. From there, one track would run westwards to join the North Cotswold Line at Honeybourne station and another chord would go south-east to make a junction with the North Cotswold Line in the Oxford/London direction (provision for such a junction was made when the line was redoubled in 2012).

Signs of encouragement for pro re-opening campaigners came in December 2015, when both Worcestershire and Gloucestershire County Council expressed their support for a reinstatement of the missing link. A report in the *Stratford Observer* (22 December 2015), said the two authorities based their support on the need to provide relief in towns like Stratford from the ever-increasing number of vehicles on rural roads. 'Provision of frequent public transport services to Stratford and Honeybourne would provide a sustainable alternative to the car for residents and employees travelling for the proposed development [of 5,900 new homes at Long Marston]', a Gloucestershire County Council spokesman told the paper.

Campaign group Stratford/Worcester/Oxford (SWO) believes the line is vital in view of the development proposals at Long Marston. 'We are really pleased that both Gloucestershire and Worcestershire County Councils can see the compelling case for reinstatement of the line', declared SWO spokesman Fraser Pithie, 'With the line's reinstatement, Stratford station has the potential to bring in many more visitors direct to the town centre shops and businesses who also surely deserve the support from greater connectivity and infrastructure.'

By far the strongest indication yet that the line would re-open during Control Period 6 (2019–2024) came in February 2016, with the launch by Great Western Railway of a document entitled *A joint Vision for the North Cotswold Line*. This aims to seek a consensus about development of services along the Oxford–Worcester route, including re-opening of the connecting line to Stratford and, when a consensus view has been reached, campaigners hope that the vision will form the basis of a business case by GWR and Network Rail as part of their investment plans. Campaigners for the re-opening warmly welcomed the vision, the first time that re-opening of the line has been formally been proposed.

Re-opening would enable residents of the planned 5,900 new homes at Long Marston to travel directly to Birmingham in less than an hour, with direct connections also to Oxford, London and Worcester. Evesham would have a direct service to and from Birmingham, taking just one hour. Stratford would be just six minutes from Long Marston by rail and would have direct connections to North Cotswolds stations with Moreton-in-Marsh potentially within 17 minutes of Stratford-upon-Avon and under an hour from Birmingham. By connecting with Cross-Country services at the new £22m Worcestershire Parkway station (due to open in 2018), Stratford would also gain connecting services to the South West and South Wales. Unusually, there is some strong local opposition to the re-opening from residents living on the south side of Stratford, close to the route, but their numbers are relatively limited and there seem too many compelling reasons for this scheme not to happen.

Ashington–Blyth

Re-opening closed railway lines, as the earlier examples have shown, is a tortuously long process even when the line in question has remained in use for freight traffic and the business case for its revival seems compelling. Such has been the case with the most clear-cut reopening prospect in the North East, where local authorities, local MPs and a campaign group have all been trying to get passenger services restored between the former mining town of Ashington and Newcastle-upon-Tyne, some 15 miles to the south, in what is called the Ashington Blyth and Tyne (ABT) scheme.

One leading campaigner for the re-opening was Denis Murphy, Labour MP for the local constituency of Wansbeck from 1997–2010. He raised the re-opening issue in a House of Commons debate on 10 January 2007, having previously discussed it in April 1999, and made the following observation:

'More than 200,000 people in south-east Northumberland live close enough to the Ashington, Blyth and Tyne line to use it regularly.

Since my debate in 1999, more than 1,500 new houses have been built. Well over half the population commute to jobs outside Wansbeck, with 65 per cent of them travelling south to Cramlington and Tyne and Wear. The proportion travelling by car is growing, increasing from 60 per cent in 1999 to 74 per cent today.

'The project has the support of all major organisations in the north-east. It does not make sense – for the economy, the environment or local people – for a working railway line, maintained at taxpayers' expense through Network Rail, to run through the county without passenger trains.... The Government's main responsibility is to make the best use of existing resources.

'The line is a classic case of an under-used resource that could be developed cost effectively for both freight and passenger needs. It could also play a major role in contributing to the diversionary route capability of the east coast main line. The synergy of those key issues will ensure that there is a sound business case for the line. When re-opened, it will contribute towards many Government objectives, including reduced carbon emissions, through a modal shift from road transport. It will promote social inclusion, assist in continued regional regeneration and improve regional prosperity.'

In June 2013, *The Journal* (Newcastle's regional morning newspaper) reported that work had started in putting together a funding package for the £60m project, which has been a key local transport priority since the early 1990s. Northumberland County Council had commissioned Network Rail to complete work on examining the best options for re-opening, with £750,000 to pay for further studies and scheme design. At the same time, talks were being held with developers on potential contributions and a bid is being made to the Local Transport Board for major scheme funding. The LTB is the North East body which is responsible for transport project funding devolved from central Government.

County council officials were also holding talks with stakeholders, including the South East Northumberland Rail User Group (SENRUG), said the report, which went on to say that a key aim of the revived rail link was to improve access to employment and the wider regional jobs market for people in southeast Northumberland. Another was providing a genuine incentive for new employers to relocate to the area, and help realise the potential of a local development area known as the Blyth Estuary Enterprise Zone. The aim of campaigners is an hourly service from Ashington to Newcastle, with four new stations – Ashington, Newsham (for Blyth), Bedlington and Seaton Delaval.

Further progress came in November 2014, when Northumberland County Council announced funding of £20m for the re-opening scheme, to cover Network Rail's GRIP (Governance for Rail Infrastructure Projects) 2 & 3 studies and the later GRIP 4 study, together with a significant contribution towards the actual re-opening cost. Just under a year later, in October 2015, the Council announced that it was proceeding with the GRIP 2 study. In October 2016 this study said reopening was feasible, put a £191 million price on it and said trains could be running by 2021.

All the signs are, that after a 12-year re-opening campaign this is a scheme whose time has come. One particularly encouraging pointer is that, thanks to the success of lobbying by SENRUG, there is a requirement in the latest Northern Rail franchise, which began on 1 April 2016, for its operator (Arriva Trains North) to work constructively with Northumberland County Council to progress the re-opening scheme – the only such requirement in the entire Northern Rail franchise.

Kirkby–Skelmersdale

Like so many other re-opening plans, debate over restoring a rail link to Skelmersdale New Town dates back more than a decade. The town, which lies 13 miles north east of Liverpool, lost its rail service on 4 November 1963, with closure of a branch line from Ormskirk to St. Helens, just two years after 'Skem' had been designated a new town. Attracting principally Liverpudlians, it has since grown to a population of almost 40,000, making it one of the largest towns in the North West without a rail service.

Despite strong cultural ties to Liverpool, the current journey by public transport involves taking a bus to Ormskirk for an onward train, a 90 minute bus journey, or travel from the nearest station (Upholland) with a change en route at Kirkby. A local transport plan produced in 2006 proposed re-opening a three-mile section of line from Ormskirk to the town, a suggestion repeated in ATOC's 2009 *Connecting Communities* report.

Subsequent efforts, however, have focussed on building a spur off the route from Kirkby to Wigan. That would allow an extension to Skelmersdale of the existing Merseyrail electric services currently terminating at Kirkby and also allow diversion into the town of diesel services on the Kirkby to Wigan line. In December 2012 a Merseytravel report proposed that an infrastructure study be undertaken by Network Rail in conjunction with local councils to define the scope of the project.

This report noted that extension of Kirkby services would make best use of available capacity on the Merseyrail network, as Kirkby trains carried fewer passengers than other Merseyrail Northern Line services, due to the short distance between Kirkby and Liverpool relative to other branches. In February 2017 a site was sold for its now station, while Network Rail has indicated that services could start in 2023.

Chapter 9

LONGER SHOTS

Successful re-openings, notably those in Scotland and Wales, have prompted a large number of local organisations to jump on the bandwagon and promote schemes that would re-connect their communities to the national rail network. The previous chapter featured those like East–West Railway and Portishead that are definitely happening and others where the head of steam is such that they look odds on to happen sooner or later. In this chapter I have taken a look at a raft of other potential re-openings (including a few wild cards of my own) and assessed their revival potential. As the previous chapters on Scotland and Wales have featured their main potential re-opening candidates, the focus here is principally on lines in England.

The North/Scottish borders

Recreating the Waverley Route

Reviewing longer term re-opening prospects from north to south, the one that strays well outside England is a southward continuation of the re-opened Borders Railway, or the Waverley Route to use its proper historical title. No sooner had the 35-mile link to Galashiels and Tweedbank been re-opened in September 2015, amid fanfare and a huge level of public interest, when campaigners began demanding that the remaining 60 miles of the route southwards to Carlisle via Hawick and isolated Riccarton Junction be re-opened. Such an extension would bring substantial economic benefit to Hawick, some 17 miles from its now nearest railhead at Galashiels, but open up a whole swathe of the Borders country, as well as creating new journey opportunities to the south and a slightly shorter route from Edinburgh to Carlisle than the current one via Carstairs and the West Coast Main Line.

'To meet its full potential, the Borders needs a direct rail link to the South' said Simon Walton, Chairman of the Campaign for Borders Rail in an interview with *Rail* magazine shortly after

A4 60009 *Union of South Africa* attracts plenty of interest as it stands at Tweedbank on 24 September 2015, after arrival on one of the inaugural steam specials from Edinburgh Waverley.

the re-opening to Tweedbank, 'the key benefits of a southwards extension would include social inclusion, economic regeneration and tourism opportunities – and sustainable transport for timber from Kielder and the Border forests,' he added. Political support for the full re-opening is growing – former Scottish National Party leader Alex Salmond expressed his backing in principle at the time of the Tweedbank opening and a spokesman for the Scottish Labour Party, Claudia Beamish, MSP for South Scotland, also spoke out in support. While the population south of Hawick is sparse, the strategic benefits of a full revival have given it real momentum and the promise of long term realisation.

In a situation with parallels to the Dawlish sea wall collapse of February 2014, the potential value of a revived Waverley Route became apparent on 31 December 2015, when the devastating flooding that had affected Cumbria and the Borders region over the preceding weeks led to the near collapse of Lamington Viaduct, which takes the West Coast Main Line over the river Clyde, ten miles south of Carstairs. The damage was so severe that it led to a two-month closure of the WCML, with Virgin Trains forced to operate diesel shuttle services from Carlisle to Glasgow Central via Kilmarnock and Dumfries –adding 90 minutes to journeys from Glasgow to the south, while its passengers for Edinburgh – who would have been able to benefit from a revived Waverley Route – were forced to take a 2 hour 40 minute journey by coach.

RR odds on a start being made within 10 years: 3/1

Penrith–Keswick

If ever medals were awarded for diligence in championing a railway re-opening proposal, and the Gold award had already been scooped by Borders Railway campaigner Madge Elliott MBE, then a strong contender for the Silver would be Cedric Martindale. He has single handedly been promoting a revival of services on the 17-mile long route from Penrith to the Lake District town of Keswick since 1988. Services west from Keswick to Workington had fallen prey to Beeching in April 1966, but the link to Penrith had survived for another six years after huge protests against its original planned closure, until it became one of the last Beeching era casualties in March 1972. It left the branch line to Windermere – 21 miles to the south of Keswick – as the only rail service into the Lake District, despite it being one of the UK's top tourist destinations.

While the Windermere branch goes from strength to strength, with passenger numbers at the branch terminus having risen from 252,000 in 2004/5 to 419,710 in 2015/6 and electrification now opening up the prospect of direct services to London, Keswick has endured more than four decades of isolation from the rail network, despite its significance as a tourist centre and destination. During his long running re-opening campaign, Martindale has undertaken a complete survey of the line, showing that its revival is perfectly feasible and, despite some piecemeal incursions onto the former trackbed, much of it remains intact and has been converted into a cycle path. One major viaduct along the route was even reprieved from demolition in 1997 in view of the line's potential future re-opening.

In one of his quarterly newsletters, Martindale highlighted a comment made in November 2014 by the then Transport Minister, Baroness Kramer, at the time the Government was announcing the £16m upgrading and electrification of the Oxenholme to Windermere line: 'Electrifying this key rail link will support the vital tourism industry in the area, and help us build a stronger economy in the Lake District and beyond,' she declared. While Windermere serves the South Lakes, whose visitors predominantly come from areas further south, Martindale points out that Keswick is a hub for the North Lakes – whose visitors predominantly come from the north and northeast of England and Scotland. 'All studies done to date indicate that re-opening the railway to Keswick would have significant benefits for the area's economy, support regeneration and diversify employment,' said the veteran campaigner.

Martindale puts a price tag of £60–£70m on the cost of reinstating the line so that it would be suitable for a basic hourly local service to Penrith, with scope for the running of additional excursion traffic. His promotional company, CKP Railways plc, has secured support from Keswick Town Council, and the Regional Growth Fund has declared it a 'worthwhile' project, which he says would take three to five years to realise, but so far the re-opening project has not found the vital support it needs from Cumbria County Council. What he now needs is for local politicians to learn the lessons of the many successful re-openings featured in these pages and give the vital endorsement that would allow this very worthwhile scheme to secure funding.

A potentially serious blow to the re-opening plans occurred when heavy rain and flooding over the weekend of 5/6 December 2015 caused havoc in Cumbria, paralysing road and rail transport. Two bridges on the Keswick to Penrith route were badly affected. In one case (Bridge No. 66) which had two spans with arched girders, the flooding entirely destroyed the bridge, while in another case (Bridge No. 71) – one of the iconic bow girder bridges which are a feature of this line – was swept off its abutments. A third bridge (No. 73) suffered damage to some stonework, but Martindale reported that it was relatively undamaged and recoverable.

RR odds on a start being made within 10 years: 25/1

Fleetwood–Poulton-le-Fylde

Rail services to Blackpool are set for a big improvement with the arrival of regular direct services to London operated by Grand Central Railway Company, and by electrification of the route from Preston to Blackpool North station, as part of the same upgrading project as wiring of the Windermere branch line. Losing out to Blackpool, however, has been the fishing port of Fleetwood, northern terminus of the famous Blackpool trams, but without its own heavy rail link since the seven-mile branch connecting the

A quiet afternoon at Poulton-le-Fylde on 15 June 2016, junction for the mothballed route to Fleetwood, which diverges to the right of the signal box beyond the road over-bridge.

A TransPennine service formed by three-car 185144 passes Poulton-le-Fylde's surviving signal box near the end of its journey to Blackpool North. The route to Fleetwood diverges to the right.

town to the Blackpool North–Preston line at Poulton-le-Fylde fell victim to Beeching on 1 June 1970. Fortunately, a large part of the line remained open until 1999 for freight traffic to an ICI chemical plant near the former Burn Naze Halt and a power station at Fleetwood, giving a crucial building block to campaigners who want the whole line re-opened to passenger traffic.

The Poulton & Wyre Railway Society was formed in 2006 to campaign for the line's re-opening and has established a base at the now restored former Thornton for Cleveleys station, two miles south of Burn Naze Halt, while the society has been allowed by Network Rail to clear vegetation from the line and repair lineside fencing. In a further strengthening of the case for revival, the Fleetwood branch featured in ATOC's 2009 *Connecting Communities* report and the case for its re-opening has been described by Lancashire County Council as compelling. With much of the track still *in situ* this looks a very straightforward opportunity to help revitalise a town of 25,000 plus inhabitants at a relatively modest cost – a new station would be needed in Fleetwood and possibly a new platform at Poulton-le-Fylde.

RR odds on a start being made within 10 years: 15/1

Colne–Skipton

Just 13 miles east of Clitheroe – terminus of the revived Ribble Valley Line service from Blackburn that featured in Chapter 3 – stands the charming former mill town of Colne, presently terminus of trains on the East Lancashire Line, a branch running from east of Accrington through Burnley, over which a stopping service operates all the way from Blackpool South and Preston via Blackburn. Colne only became a terminus, however, in January 1970, when an 11½-mile link north eastwards to the Settle & Carlisle line at Skipton was closed, although curiously not as a result of Dr Beeching's efforts.

Restoration of this missing link is being championed by the Skipton–East Lancashire Railway Action Partnership (SELRAP) which has secured strong endorsement from a number of consultancy studies and some significant political momentum. After study by consultants Steer Davies & Gleave in 2003 identified no major physical obstacles to a re-opening and a 2007 study by JMP Consultants concluded that there was a positive benefit/cost ratio, an even more bullish picture was painted by consultants ARUP in a 2014 study for SELRAP. This highlighted the benefits to towns along the line of route from the increased connectivity which a re-opening would bring, and suggested that more than 600,000 passengers a year would be using the line within ten years, putting the benefit/cost ratio at a whopping 6.5/1.

Meantime, revival is backed 'in principle' by North Yorkshire County Council, which sees it as providing a real boost for the area's increasingly important tourist industry, as well as increasing employment opportunities, by vastly improving access via Skipton to Bradford and Leeds. Another to have expressed support is Julian Smith, Conservative Member of Parliament for Skipton and Ripon: 'I support SELRAP because I believe it will bring very positive environmental and economic benefits to Skipton & Ripon, and beyond,' he declared.

While the campaigning goes on and SELRAP looks at sources of funding the £100m+ project, the trackbed is at least protected from being sold off piecemeal for alternative use under local planning policies. SELRAP Chairman David Walsh points out that having a direct rail service to Leeds means the price of a terraced house in Skipton (Jan 2016–£154,936) is almost double that of a comparable property in Colne (£84,038) and more than three times that of a terraced house in Nelson (£48,523) and says his group's priority is to get Network Rail to commit to a study, hopefully to GRIP3 (route evaluation), in its Control Period 6 (2019–24). Walsh says:

'SELRAP believes there is a strong case for re-opening the line from Skipton to Colne. It reconnects two areas of high population that should never have been disconnected – even Beeching had left it in place! The old track bed is still intact and largely in open country, making for simpler and cheaper development.

'A fast rail connection along the Burnley to Skipton corridor and into Leeds will bring more jobs and colleges into commuting range on both sides. It will also greatly add to people's leisure options. The Northern Powerhouse stresses connections between five major cities, but it is important that the major towns that form the hinterland of those cities are integrated into those plans. Skipton to Colne is one of those complementary developments that will contribute to the whole.'

RR odds on a start being made within 10 years: 8/1

Harrogate–Ripon–Northallerton

Like so many other re-opening proposals, the 26-mile link northwards from the spa town of Harrogate through the cathedral city of Ripon and on to the East Coast Main Line at Northallerton has long been in campaigner's sights. It fell victim to Beeching in March 1967, but revival campaigners (The Leeds Northern Railway Reinstatement Group) have been active since the mid-1980s and as long ago as 2006 a consultant's report (Ove Arup) suggested that re-opening of the 11-mile section between Harrogate and Ripon would be viable.

In a consultation on its Local Transport Plan for 2016–2045, North Yorkshire County Council remained positive about a potential revival of rail services, stating in its consultation document: 'The County Council supports, in principle, proposals for rail reopening in the County, on identified routes such as Skipton to Colne and Harrogate to Ripon/Northallerton.' While the Harrogate–Ripon route has been encroached on by development since closure, and a new station site would be needed in Ripon, the 16-mile northern section to Northallerton has long been protected by the County Council in case of a revival. But the Council's consultation document also sounded a note of caution:

> 'In the past many of the line re-openings were considered to be local schemes and therefore required local funding.
>
> 'The Council will only actively support opportunities for line re-openings where these are demonstrated as of National or pan North of England importance. National or pan North strategic importance will be assessed on the basis of the contribution to network resilience, improved strategic connectivity, the delivery of greater capacity or improved rail freight opportunities. In all cases North Yorkshire County Council will only work with railway industry and local stakeholders where there is common agreement to develop a proposal.'

RR odds on a start being made within 10 years: 20/1

Newcastle–Washington

Washington New Town in Tyne & Wear, ten miles south east of Newcastle and seven miles west of Sunderland, has a population of some 70,000 people but no rail service, making it one of the largest places in England with no trains. Washington's station fell victim to Beeching in September 1963, the year before it was formally designated a New Town, yet for almost three more decades a route known as the Leamside Line remained opened for freight traffic, until it was 'mothballed' in 1991. While the track has subsequently been largely lifted – one section having been famously been stolen in 2003 by a gang who worked at removing it unnoticed for almost a week – the route has been periodically considered for re-opening as a diversionary route for East Coast Main Line traffic and the trackbed has been retained by Network Rail.

With significant local support for re-opening, a number of schemes have been considered, most ambitious of which was a planned TyneTees Express proposal. This would have seen the entire Leamside Line re-opened, along with another freight and diversionary route known as the Stillington Branch, which runs from Ferryhill South Junction on the East Coast Main Line, near the southern end of the Leamside route, to a junction with the Durham Coast Line to the north of Stockton-on-Tees. This scheme could have generated more than 700,000 journeys a year, according to a study by consultants AECOM Faber Maunsell, with a significant proportion being generated by a park and ride station serving Washington and one in the mining village of Belmont to serve Durham.

More recently, the scheme that appears most likely to bring rail services back to Washington has been a planned extension of the Tyne & Wear Metro. This would use the Leamside Line south from Pelaw Junction near Newcastle as far as Washington, then head east along another closed railway line to South Hylton, terminus of existing Metro services from Newcastle via Sunderland on the Durham Coast Line. In April 2014 a study into the business case for reviving the Leamside Line was commissioned by the North Eastern Local Enterprise Partnership (LEP).

'The North East Local Enterprise Partnership has commissioned some work to investigate the potential for the re-introduction of rail services between Newcastle and Northallerton, and the role the Leamside Line might play in this,' a LEP spokesman told the *Sunderland Echo*. 'The intention is to inform forthcoming work by Network Rail and the wider rail industry as part of its "long-term planning process", and in particular to provide evidence that can inform Network Rail's planned East Coast route study, North of England route study and 2018 East Coast capacity review', he added.

RR odds on a start being made within 10 years: 8/1

The Midlands

Lichfield–Brownhills–Walsall–Stourbridge Junction

One route offering potential both as a diversionary freight artery and as a supplement to existing commuter and metro services in the West Midlands is the South Staffordshire Line. This now closed route traces a semi-circle around the north western outskirts of Birmingham, from a junction south of the present Lichfield City station to Walsall, then onwards via Dudley to join the increasingly busy Worcester–Kidderminster–Birmingham commuter route to the north of Stourbridge Junction station. It had never been a through route for passenger services, with the southern section of the line losing its passengers in 1962, while the Lichfield–Walsall section became a Beeching victim, with its closure to passenger traffic in 1965.

Despite the early loss of passenger traffic, freight traffic on the route continued for another two decades, being given a new lease of life by the development of a freightliner terminal at Dudley. This was opened in 1967 on the site of the former station at Dudley – close to the town's famous zoo and near the now equally well-known Black Country Museum – and became a major freight hub. It prospered for more than 20 years, but was closed in September 1989 when remaining traffic was transferred to the Birmingham freightliner terminal close to the Saltley diesel depot to the east of Birmingham city centre. The final freight traffic to make use of the route was steel traffic from the former Round Oak steel works at Brierley Hill, which closed in 1982, and traffic from a steel terminal at this site, which kept the line open until 1993.

Since its final closure, and with the route having remained largely intact, there have been numerous proposals for the revival of the route, or parts of it, for passenger use, with its potential also being recognised by ATOC's 2009 *Connecting Communities* report. This focused on the ten-mile section from Lichfield to Walsall and, in particular, the potential to restore passenger services to the important town of Brownhills, mid-way along this section of the line and with a population of 46,000. ATOC suggested that re-opening from Walsall to Brownhills would cost £52 million with Brownhills to Lichfield being a further £70 million (2009 prices and not including the cost of electrification).

Other revival proposals have focused on creating a new branch of the Midland Metro, which would leave the existing Wolverhampton–Birmingham alignment at Wednesbury to create a line to Dudley and the Merry Hill Shopping Centre. Plans have also been developed for re-opening of the route between Walsall and Stourbridge Junction to both freight and metro-style services, being partly funded by the owners of the Merry Hill Shopping Centre. Another idea has featured use of the unique Class 139 Parry People Mover vehicles, currently in use on the ¾-mile branch line from Stourbridge Junction to Stourbridge Town, to operate a service from Stourbridge Junction to Brierley Hill.

Most recently, revival of the route has featured in a long term strategy for the region called *Movement for Growth*, which was approved by the West Midlands Integrated Transport Authority in December 2015, following a public consultation exercise. This wide-ranging strategy envisages re-opening of the entire route, with tram-train services operating between Walsall and Stourbridge Junction and an ambitious range of new light and heavy rail services across the West Midlands, including a revival of the link between Wolverhampton and Walsall, with new stations at Willenhall and Darlaston, and new suburban rail services on what is known as the Camp Hill Line to the south of Birmingham city centre. This sees regular use by cross-country services from Birmingham to Bristol and the south-west, but lost its local services as long ago as 1941. A revival of local services would include the building of new stations at Hazelwell, Kings Heath, Moseley, Fort Parkway and Castle Bromwich.

RR odds on a start being made within 10 years: 8/1

Cheltenham–Kingham

This is a real wildcard entry into the betting, but one that is dear to my heart, as my late father's correspondence in Chapter 1 will have suggested, and based also on my early memories of being taken on day trips from Charlton Kings Halt to Bourton-on-the-Water and Chipping Norton. The 24-mile line from Cheltenham Spa to Kingham, an increasingly important station midway along the recently upgraded North Cotswold Line from Oxford to Worcester, actually closed five months before Beeching published his report, in September 1962, featuring in the report as one of those lines 'under Consideration for Withdrawal before formulation of the Report.'

While the sparse population along the route does not immediately make for a strong re-opening case, with the popular tourist village of Bourton-on-the-Water being the only real population centre served well by the line, what makes the prospect exciting is the creation of a would-be western extension to the revived East–West Railway (see previous chapter), as well as creating a new direct route from Gloucester/Cheltenham to Oxford and a shorter route from these major population centres to the capital. Cheltenham to Oxford via Swindon and Didcot is 77 miles, but via Kingham the distance is just 45 miles; from Cheltenham to London Paddington is 120 miles by rail via Swindon, but only 109 miles via Kingham.

Reviving the line could therefore cut the overall journey time between Cheltenham and Oxford from two hours and 30 minutes, using existing services via Didcot, to around one hour, while the best Cheltenham to London journey time of two hours could be trimmed by 15 minutes. A detailed assessment of the potential re-opening, published on 30 January 2015 by the *Oxford Prospect* online news magazine and written by Alfred Roberts, noted that no less than 19 miles of the line remains largely intact, due to the remote nature of the route. He accepted that the scheme would be hugely disruptive, but identified viable deviations that could be used to create a new route south of Cheltenham, and through the villages of Andoversford and Bourton, where development has taken over the former alignment.

A Facebook group has been formed to promote the re-opening, but with its cost estimated at up to £500 million it has, perhaps not surprisingly, failed so far to find favour with local stakeholders. In a debate on the proposal at a meeting of Gloucestershire County Council in June 2013, as reported in the *Gloucestershire Echo* (21 June 2013), it was backed by one Councillor from along the line of route, Paul Hodgkinson (LD, Bourton-on-the-Water and Northleach), who believed the line would give Gloucestershire a much-needed west–east public transport link and asked the council to consider the bid, despite its current financial challenges.

Councillor Will Windsor-Clive (C, Newent), cabinet member for fire, planning and infrastructure, said the Council was happy to look at ideas that might improve transport in the county, but he questioned if there is enough demand for the service to actually persuade the Government to pay for it: 'Reinstating the Cheltenham to Kingham line would require substantial new track through both Cheltenham and Bourton where the old route has been built over, the rebuilding of the Dowdeswell Viaduct and the recommissioning of the Sandywell Park Tunnel', he added.

RR odds on a start being made within 10 years: 5000/1

East Anglia

Stansted Airport–Braintree

Rail links to Stansted Airport have been an issue ever since the Stansted Express service was launched, with the many intermediate stations and heavy commuter traffic on the double track Lea Valley route meaning frequent delays to a service that already takes around 50 minutes to cover the 37½ miles from Liverpool Street station in the City of London. In autumn 2014 Network Rail put forward a 30-year plan for the rail links in the East Anglian region, but an upgrade of the line to Stansted was not included. London Mayor Boris Johnson had urged an upgrading of the line between London and Stansted and Cambridge, which he says is of national importance, while the Airports Commission report by Sir Howard Davies said Network Rail's plans for the track to Stansted were not ambitious enough.

Former London Mayor Boris Johnson said that the answer is a four-track railway in the Lea Valley, which could see the journey time from London to Stansted Airport slashed to just over 20 minutes. His argument was that the enhanced route has national importance, and is a vital precursor to Crossrail Two, the planned south west London to north east London underground link, due to be built by 2030 (see Chapter 7).

One alternative means of improving access by public transport to the Essex Airport is the £150 million proposal to build a 14-mile link from Stansted Airport to Braintree, currently the terminus of an electrified branch line from Witham on the East Anglian Main Line from London to Ipswich and Norwich. By building a new west-to-north curve at Witham, where the current branch line makes a south facing connection to the main line, it would open up the possibility of fast electric rail services from Norwich and Ipswich directly to the airport and then on to Cambridge. Such a route could partly follow the line of a former branch line from Bishops Stortford to Braintree, which lost its passenger service in 1952, but much of whose trackbed has survived to become a cycle track.

Creation of this new rail route to Stansted Airport, which would allow a station to be built in the growing market town of Great Dunmow, six miles east of the airport, is strongly supported by the Witham and Braintree Rail Users' Association, whose Chairman, David Bigg, told the *East Anglian Daily Times* (27 October 2014) that his association was asking the region's Members of the European Parliament (MEPs) to investigate if it could benefit from EU funding as part of the Trans-European Network. Support was also expressed by Graham Butland, leader of Braintree District Council, who said: 'Braintree to Stansted Airport would have a lot of merit. The airport is the largest single employer of people in the district, with some 1,500 people, and as a district council we are very supportive of the expansion of Stansted.'

RR odds on a start being made within 10 years: 20/1

Cambridge–Haverhill–Sudbury

North of Stansted Airport, another ambitious rail revival plan could ultimately see the revival of a 35-mile direct link between the Cambridge and Sudbury, currently the terminus of a diesel-operated branch line (now known as the Gainsborough Line) from Marks Tey on the East Anglian Main Line. The route lost its passenger service in 1967, but for more than 20 years its re-opening has been championed by the Cambridge–Sudbury Rail Renewal Association, with particularly strong support for the project in the fast growing town of Haverhill, 20 miles south east of Cambridge.

In an interview with the *Haverhill Echo* (9 April 2015), the driving force behind the campaign, Rev. Malcolm Hill (another deserved recipient of a silver medal for persistence) urged local residents to sign an online petition in support of reinstating the line: 'Haverhill Town Council support what we are doing, this would be a great investment for Haverhill and we need it', he said, 'the population is growing dramatically; there are a further 1,150 new homes in the pipeline. Whenever we talk to people in Haverhill, they support a rail link.' Rev. Hill said his association had undertaken a feasibility report and, with a few engineering obstacles across the A11, it was possible to reinstate this section of the line at a cost of around £150 million.

The Association points out that the population of Haverhill has grown from a around 8,500 at the time the passenger service ceased to 27,000 today, and that a rail journey to Cambridge would take only 30 minutes, or half the time it takes to make the journey by bus. Elsewhere in the region there has been dramatic growth in rail traffic, notably on both the Sudbury and Braintree branches and on the Cambridge to Norwich route, where the introduction of regular direct services led to a huge rise in passenger traffic.

RR odds on a start being made within 10 years: 40/1

Wymondham–Dereham–Fakenham

While the Stansted Airport–Braintree and Cambridge–Sudbury schemes would fill important gaps within the ever widening London commuter network, a potential re-opening in neighbouring Norfolk would go some way towards reversing the devastating impact which Beeching had on that county. This is the route from Wymondham, on the Ely–Norwich line to the important town of Dereham and northwards from here to Fakenham, which remains intact, with the section to Dereham operated by the Mid-Norfolk Railway (MNR) and the balance of the trackbed intact and in part owned by the MNR.

Dereham had once been an important railway junction – the line northwards had continued beyond Fakenham to a coastal terminus in the delightful town of Wells-next-the-Sea, while a cross country route headed westwards to Kings Lynn. Despite the early introduction of diesel multiple units and an acceleration of services, the twin pressures of Beeching and road competition meant the 1960s run down was rapid: passenger services north of Dereham were withdrawn in October 1964 with the 11½ miles south to Wymondham being reduced to single track the following

A scene that looks straight from the late 1960s or early 1970s. At Dereham station on 4 April 2010, Brush Type 2 (Class 31) loco D5557 waits to depart with a Mid-Norfolk Railway service to Wymondham.

North Elmham, seen on 4 April 2010, was the only intermediate station between County School and Dereham, and remained open for freight traffic until 1989. The track remains *in situ* south from here to Dereham.

year. Services from Kings Lynn survived four more years, before their withdrawal in September 1968, with the remaining service from Dereham to Wymondham (and Norwich) succumbing a year later, in October 1969.

Freight services on the route survived for considerably longer, with Fakenham remaining rail served until 1980, and final closure of the line from North Elmham and Dereham coming in June

County School, seen here on 4 April 2010, was once an important junction, and the main station building has been restored in anticipation of the time when the Mid-Norfolk Railway re-opens the six miles of line south from here to its current base at Dereham.

1989. Since then, the heroic efforts of the MNR have not only brought tourist rail services from Wymondham back to the town's pleasantly restored railway station, but the preservation group has also acquired the line for a further six miles northwards, to the remote former junction station of County School, where a museum has been established and some items of rolling stock are stored.

Northwards from County School to Fakenham – a distance of some eight miles, the route has been secured by the local authority for future rail use, with a short section on the outskirts of Fakenham having been bought by the North Orbital Railway. This is the promoter of an extremely ambitious plan for a circular rail service originating in Norwich that would continue north eastwards from Fakenham on a former rail alignment via Melton Constable and connect with another preserved railway, the North Norfolk Railway, at Holt. From here, the circular service would continue along the NNR route to its connection with the national network at Sheringham, continuing on what is now known as the Bittern Line via Cromer and back to Norwich.

Like a realisation of the orbital vision, the question of whether services could ever be restored on the route north from Fakenham to Wells-next-the-Sea looks doubtful – there are obstructions in Fakenham itself and a significant part of the route north of the town is now occupied by the Wells & Walsingham Light Railway. But restoring regular passenger services on the 25 miles from Fakenham to Wymondham is distinctly realistic, and would open up a huge area of the county that has been devoid of rail connections for almost half a century. It would offer much improved links with Norwich, from where half-hourly trains will offer a 90-minute journey time to the capital, once timetable and rolling stock improvements have been made.

RR odds on a start being made within 10 years: 40/1

The South
While the outstanding candidate for re-opening in the south of England remains the Uckfield–Lewes line, featured in the previous chapter, there are a couple of other interesting candidates which deserve a place in the betting, both having featured in the ATOC *Connecting Communities* report and both representing relatively modestly-priced opportunities to put large population centres back onto the rail network.

Guildford–Cranleigh
Re-opening the seven miles of track that separates the significant Surrey commuter town of Cranleigh with the national rail network at Peasmarsh Junction, south of Guildford, has been a source of

debate locally for more than 20 years. It forms the northern end of a line from Guildford to Horsham that became the county's only Beeching victim when it closed in June 1965. The prospect of revival was first raised in 1994, when Surrey County Council commissioned a study by consultants Colin Buchanan and Partners to look into rail improvements in the County in order to potentially identify worthwhile new services and improvements which could be made to the rail infrastructure in Surrey to allow new or revised services to be introduced.

Buchanan estimated that some 500 people travelling from Cranleigh would transfer from car to rail per 12 hour day. This did not, however, include new trips which might be generated from a new service or trips diverted from public transport. The consultants came up with a price tag of **£24** million for the civil engineering and related costs, but excluding the cost of acquiring land and the estimated **£750,000** cost of replacing a missing bridge over the River Wey.

They concluded that re-opening was not economically feasible, with first year income estimated at covering just 3% of the capital cost, even without taking into account operating costs. A further study for Railtrack (predecessor to Network Rail) in 1996 put the cost of re-opening at considerably less – **£13.4** million for an electrified line. A second part of this study, published in June 1997, noted in the local survey of public opinion that the level of switch from road to rail would be very low (although rail would attract a large number of bus users) and concluded that a new line would not recoup its total costs, which it put at **£14.24** million.

Despite these previous setbacks, the 2009 *Connecting Communities* report painted a positive picture of the re-opening potential, putting a price tag this time of **£63** million on an electrified single track line to be served by a half-hourly extension of existing stopping services from London Waterloo to Guildford, with re-opened stations at Bramley and Cranleigh. In its favour, the line has been safeguarded as a transport corridor and is currently used as a path and cycleway.

From a practical point of view, new and regular rail users would undoubtedly want a faster connection at Guildford for London than would be offered by staying on a stopping train, as suggested by ATOC (Guildford–Waterloo is around 33 minutes on a fast train and about one hour on a stopping service). At Guildford most fast peak-time services to Waterloo are already 'full and standing' (as I know from my experience as a commuter from Haslemere) so any significant new traffic generated by a Cranleigh re-opening raises the much bigger question about improving overall rail capacity from Guildford into Waterloo.

RR odds on a start being made within 10 years: 50/1

Southampton–Hythe

One other compelling and relatively straightforward re-opening prospect in the south would be a restoration of passenger services along part of what is currently a freight-only link from Totton, west of Southampton, to the Fawley oil terminal. Revival of the seven-mile stretch to Hythe would allow the re-opening of stations there (closed under the Beeching axe in February 1966, and an intermediate station at Marchwood, where a passing loop still in use means that there is capacity for a revived passenger service alongside the limited remaining freight traffic. In its report, ATOC rated this as having the highest benefit/cost ratio of any scheme being proposed and suggested a very modest capital cost of just £3 million.

There is a more direct route from Hythe to Southampton, but it is via the Hythe Ferry, accessed by a famous and historic miniature railway running the length of Hythe Pier – acknowledged as the world's oldest pier train – with a bus connection from the ferry terminal in Southampton to Southampton Central station. The half-hourly ferry service takes 25 minutes, compared to a potential rail journey time for the longer distance of around 20 minutes, with intermediate stops at Marchwood and another new station at Hounsdown near Totton. If the route was to be re-opened without third rail electrification, the logical service would be to link it with the Salisbury–Southampton–Chandlers Ford–Romsey service, as the ATOC report suggested, but third rail electrification would open the route up as the ultimate destination of services currently terminating at Southampton, such as stopping services from London Waterloo or those originating in Portsmouth.

Marchwood station is remarkably well preserved, despite having closed to passengers when the Southampton–Fawley line fell victim to Beeching in February 1966. Oil traffic ceased in 2016 but there is occasional traffic to the nearby port.

The diminutive Hythe Ferry looks on a collision course with the Red Funnel ferry *Red Falcon* as it passes the P&O cruise liner *Arcadia* on 18 June 2016, during its 25-minute crossing from the Town Quay in Southampton to Hythe Pier.

Hampshire County Council has long cherished an ambition to see passenger services restored along what it calls the Waterside Line, but revival hopes were dealt a significant blow by the conclusions of consultants Halcrow in their GRIP (Governance for Rail Investment Projects 3 report), delivered in June 2013. This showed that the cost of preparing the route for passenger services was relatively modest, with development of the three stations, signalling upgrades and installation of a passing loop at the new Hounsdown station being costed at **£11.0** million for a half-hourly train service.

Hythe Pier Railway is recognised by the Guinness Book of Records, as the world's oldest pier railway, having operated continuously since 1922. On 18 June 2016, the three-car train approaches pier head for the connecting ferry to Southampton.

A view from the end of Hythe Pier on 18 June 2016 towards the charming waterfront, with the third rail electrified pier railway to the left of the pier walkway.

But Halcrow concluded: 'The latent demand in the area, overlaid with existing good provision of public transport (bus/ferry) in the area is not sufficient to support the service.' The consultants estimated the benefit to cost ratio (BCR) of a half-hourly service at between 0.7 and 1.1 – well below the 4.8 which ATOC came up with and also below the 2.0 figure which would be expected to trigger financial support from the Department for Transport. As a consequence of the Halcrow report, the county council decided against pursuing the re-opening, but remains willing to review its decision.

RR odds on a start being made within 10 years: 20/1

The South West

Across Devon and Cornwall, an area badly hit by Beeching era closures, the localised promotion of all the surviving branch lines as community railways has been a spectacular success, with substantial growth in passenger numbers on all five remaining routes: Exeter–Barnstaple; Plymouth–Gunnislake; Liskeard–Looe; Par–Newquay; Truro–Falmouth; and St Erth–St Ives. Of these, all but the Newquay and Falmouth lines had been earmarked for closure in Beeching's report and this success adds weight to the arguments in favour of three interesting potential re-openings across the region.

Barnstaple–Bideford

As mentioned briefly in my introduction, the 9-mile link between the railhead at Barnstaple, now terminus of a 39-mile branch from Exeter, and the town of Bideford makes an ideal and feasible re-opening candidate. The former line remains largely intact as a path/cycle-track and this short route – with re-opened intermediate stations at Instow and Fremington – could easily be operated as an add-on to the current Exeter–Barnstaple service, now known and marketed as the Tarka Line. Re-opening featured in ATOC's 2009 report, which gave put a price tag of £80 million on a scheme that envisaged a rail line laid alongside the Tarka Trail path.

Evidence of the surging demand for rail services in North Devon can be seen in the growth of passenger numbers at Barnstaple, which have more than doubled in a decade, from 194,000 in 2004/5 to 421,346 in 2015/6. Besides being an operationally simple re-opening, the Bideford line is a scenic one that would lend itself to use by steam-hauled tourist specials during the summer and so provide a significant boost to local tourism, as well as improving local transport links and easing road congestion. As if that was not enough, Bideford station is already preserved as a heritage centre, with the operators of the centre supportive of the line's re-opening, so there would be none of the high site-acquisition costs that add significantly to price of other potential revival schemes.

RR odds on a start being made within 10 years: 25/1

Lostwithiel–Fowey

One relatively modest opportunity on the south Cornwall coast would be a revival of passenger services on the five-mile branch line running from Lostwithiel, on the Great Western Main Line to the delightful coastal town of Fowey. Passenger services along the branch were withdrawn on the instructions of Dr Beeching in January 1965, but the line has remained open for china clay traffic to a terminal at Carne Point, just north of Fowey. The long-closed bay platform for branch trains remains at Lostwithiel, complete currently with the semaphore signalling that is due to be replaced in the Duchy in 2018. Reinstating at least a seasonal service would require a new station in Fowey, but would otherwise be relatively straightforward and open up another scenic route that could benefit from the growing passenger traffic being seen on all the Duchy's other branch lines.

RR odds on a start being made within 10 years: 50/1

Bodmin Parkway–Wadebridge–Padstow

What is arguably the most exciting of all potential revival schemes in the South West is also one where revival would have to factor in and share a route with a long-established foot and cycle path. This is the line from Bodmin Parkway, on the Great Western Main Line, to Wadebridge and Padstow, fish restaurant capital of the UK and until September 1964 the most westerly destination of the famous *Atlantic Coast Express* from London Waterloo. As with the Wymondham–Dereham line, featured above, a section of this route – from Bodmin Parkway to Bodmin General and westwards to the former Boscarne Junction – is already run by preservationists, with plans already being promoted by a related group to re-build the 4½ miles that would take the line to the town of Wadebridge.

Along with the North Cornwall lines from Okehampton to Bude and to Launceston and Wadebridge (closed in October 1966), the connecting line from Bodmin Parkway (then known as Bodmin Road) closed to passengers a few months later in January 1967. What is needed now is not just the Boscarne–Wadebridge revival, but also a new route through Wadebridge and then a re-building of the scenic six mile link to Padstow, where the former station building still stands and is now used as offices by the Town Council. Since the line closed half a century ago, Padstow has become a massively important tourist centre, and a re-opened station would become only the third rail-served resort on the Duchy's north coast – along with St Ives and Newquay – with the town no doubt reaping the same benefits from being part of the national rail network as the other two resorts.

The six-mile Wadebridge–Padstow section of what was popularly known as the 'withered arm' – the former London & South Western Railway route from London Waterloo to the South West – has become a major part of the Camel Trail but, as in the case of Bideford–Barnstaple, there is no insurmountable reason why railway and cycleway/footpath cannot co-exist. In its plans, the Bodmin and Wadebridge Railway Company recognises the importance of securing the Camel Trail as a popular local amenity, and talks of it being upgraded parallel to a new railway and, in a few places, diverted to a new alignment adjacent to the new railway where the historical railway alignment is too narrow for both trail and rail. If the interests of Camel Trail users can be adequately secured, then this is surely one of the most exciting re-opening prospects in the whole of England.

RR odds on a start being made within 10 years: 40/1

Other preserved lines

In addition to the Bodmin–Wadebridge and Wymondham–Dereham lines, there are a number of other lines which had survived into preservation and make viable candidates for potential re-opening. Scheduled services are run on all but one of my top five selections, and clearly there would have to be agreements struck between the preservationists and the network operators on how track access would be paid for and shared, while there would also have to be agreements reached on ticket prices.

Signalling and track enhancements may also be required to ensure that modern rolling stock was able to run at an acceptable speed to make a regular service viable. But these are relatively minor issues when one remembers that the lines are intact (with one exception) and the costs of making them part of the national rail network once again would be far less than the huge costs of reinstating the other routes featured in this and the previous chapter.

First up, principally because it is a real life test-bed for the potential use of preserved lines for regular traffic, is the six-mile long Wareham–Swanage line in Dorset. Here the £3 million re-signalling of a junction west of Wareham station has allowed trains from the branch line to access the main Waterloo–Weymouth route and bring direct services back to Wareham for the first time since the line closed in 1973. The success of experimental diesel services will determine whether they become a regular feature of the line, but having seen the scale of road congestion on the Isle of Purbeck and huge summer-time queues for the Sandbanks ferry to Poole, it is hard to believe that the experiment will not prove a resounding success.

Longest of all among my selected quintet is the 25-mile long West Somerset Line from Taunton–Minehead, which enjoys a main line connection at Norton Fitzwarren, four miles west of Taunton, but has never had regular access to Somerset's county town, initially due to opposition from local bus drivers and latterly due to re-signalling and re-alignment of the main line when this section was reduced from four tracks to two. Like the Swanage branch, the Minehead line was one of the last Beeching victims, only closing in January 1971, and had enjoyed significant levels of passenger traffic up to its closure – including direct seasonal services from London Paddington catering for tourists heading to the Butlin's holiday camp at Minehead.

One of the finest preserved lines in England is the 16-mile long Severn Valley Railway. While the northern section between Bridgnorth and Bewdley is one for tourists only, the four-mile section from Bewdley–Kidderminster makes an excellent candidate for use as an extension of certain services on the Birmingham Snow Hill–Stourbridge Junction–Kidderminster line. Bewdley is a delightful town on the River Severn, with a population of around 10,000, while Kidderminster, once home to the region's carpet industry, is a major regional centre with a 56,000 population. A good measure of its importance as a commuter town is the doubling of its passenger numbers over the past decade, from 734,000 in 2004/5 to 1,619,928 in 2015/6.

To the north of Manchester, one of the highest ranked schemes in ATOC's *Connecting Communities* report (fifth in terms of benefit/cost ratio) would see regular passenger services operating along the route of the East Lancashire Railway from Rawtenstall–Bury. The route fell victim to the Beeching axe in June 1972, but was thankfully rescued by the preservation society, with support from two local authorities, and services were progressively restored until the whole eight-mile line had re-opened in April 1991. South of Bury, the former route to Manchester was converted to become the first route of Manchester's Metrolink system, but the ELR was fortunately able to bridge the new tram line at Bury and secure continued access to the national railway network via a link eastwards to Heywood, which re-opened to passengers in September 2003.

A direct rail service would require a west-to-south junction onto the Calder Valley route from Rochdale to Manchester, to the south of Castleton station, so that trains from Rawtenstall, Bury and Heywood could run directly on to Manchester along the Calder Valley route. In infrastructure terms, this is a relatively simple and compelling opportunity to put the town of Rawtenstall, which has a population of around 22,000 but a catchment area some three times that size, back on the national railway map.

Last, but by no means least, is a route that is yet to be rebuilt, but where the distance involved is very modest and the strategic potential is very large. This is the missing link of less than two miles between the end of a freight-only branch line serving a stone quarry at Ardingly, north-east of Haywards Heath on the London–Brighton main line, and Horsted Keynes, home of the Bluebell Railway and one of the most splendid preserved stations in Great Britain. Rebuilding this missing link would open up the opportunity for direct services from Haywards Heath–Horsted Keynes–East Grinstead–London.

It might sound far-fetched, but revival and electrification of this route would provide another direct link between London and Brighton, albeit not providing relief to the two-track section south of Haywards Heath. Were that to go ahead, then a trade-off with the preservationists could be to provide funding for a southern extension of the Bluebell Line from Sheffield Park to the former Culver Junction north of Lewes, where the line joined the route from Uckfield to Lewes, featured in the previous chapter as one of the country's hottest and oldest revival prospects. While the Bluebell Railway Preservation Society only sees this as a long term aspiration, it has committed itself to 'protecting the right of way of the track bed, as and when necessary' and 'To challenge development that will compromise the possibility of the re-instatement of the line southwards.'

Chapter 10

ON REFLECTION

Let's meet under the clock at Waterloo! It is a busy Friday afternoon on 1 July 2016 at Britain's busiest station, as weary commuters head for home after a week in which they had suffered a number of signalling related delays.

Looking back to events of 50 years ago, it is ironic that, while countless diesel locomotive classes have come and gone since that time, Merchant Navy 35028 *Clan Line* remains active on main line special trains to this day, having survived far longer in preservation than the 20 years it worked on the Southern Region. Sister loco 35008 *Orient Line* was less fortunate and was cut up in Newport, South Wales shortly after withdrawal, as was West Country Class 34025 *Whimple*. Of the two locos I saw on the Carlisle–Manchester leg of the *15 Guinea Special* a year later

on 11 August 1968, 44781 failed to make it into preservation, but 44871 remains in mainline operational condition, based at the East Lancashire Railway at Bury.

What the past 50 years has shown is the resilience of the railway network, which has bounced back from the traumas of the Beeching cuts and embraced huge changes encompassing, modernisation, widespread electrification, and privatisation, which along with increased road congestion and a trend towards longer distance commuting, particularly as a result of soaring London house prices, have all contributed to a huge growth in passenger numbers, now at their highest level since the 1920s. Coping with this growth has proved a huge challenge for successive governments and for an industry whose key infrastructure provider is saddled with a vast level of debt and a seemingly insurmountable inability to deliver major projects on time and on budget.

Running late and over budget

One theme running throughout this story is the obscenely high cost of rail infrastructure works, whether it is the installation of a new footbridge, the building of a new station, or a wholesale re-opening. There seems a major dichotomy between the frightening cost over-runs and delays to major projects – the WCML upgrade was a glaring past example and the GWML electrification is very much a current issue – and the success and on-budget (usually) delivery of the vital incremental schemes featured in these pages. Take a trip to Alloa, Ebbw Vale, Mansfield, Galashiels or Bathgate – as I have done – and it is almost impossible to believe that these are places that had long since lost their railway services, but where they are now a vital and everyday feature of the local transport infrastructure.

Time and again the industry seems to shoot itself in the foot as the costs spiral and delays mount up. Upgrading the West Coast Main Line was probably the most glaring example – the cost rising from around £2 billion to £10 billion and delays to the project causing wholesale disruption across a wide swath of the country. With mounting concerns about what the final cost of HS2 might eventually be, a worrying omen is the Great Western Main Line electrification project, whose cost has shot up alarmingly from an estimated £874 million in January 2013 to £1.6 billion a year later and £2.8 billion by October 2015 – three times the estimate of just two years before.

When challenged by the House of Commons' Public Accounts Committee (PAC), Network Rail boss Mark Carne put the cost escalation down to 'inadequate planning' and 'scope definition' at the beginning of the project. He pointed out to the PAC that neither NR, nor its predecessor (Railtrack) had undertaken any significant electrification work for the past 20 years, so that the cost base was out of date. One issue encountered has been the uncertain location of underground signalling cables, which has meant that a revolutionary piece of kit bought to plant the overhead electrification masts at a rate of 18 per night had only managed 16 a week.

Under its original schedule, the lines would have been electrified to Bristol, Newbury and Oxford by 2016, Cardiff in 2017 and Swansea by 2018. But this timetable has been missed, as has the one for electrification of the Midland Main Line, where Corby looks like having to wait until 2019 (previously 2017), with wiring to Leicester, Derby, Nottingham and Sheffield slipping from 2019/20 to 2023.

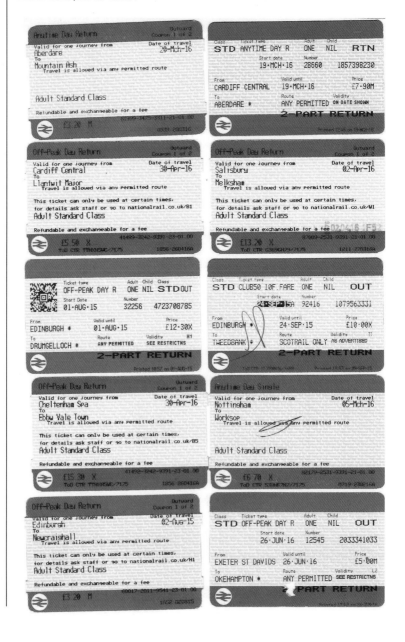

New destinations: tickets to a small selection of places that have been restored to the railway network over the past 50 years.

In the case of the Great Western project, one consequence of this indefinite delay has been suggestions that the fleet of 21 new Hitachi Class 801/0 Super Express Trains, which had been designed as electric-powered only, be fitted with a diesel engine to avoid them having to sit in sidings at the new Filton depot incurring huge leasing costs but earning no revenue. The project delay also has wider rolling stock consequences, since a number of the GWR High Speed Trains are earmarked for further use on long distance services in Scotland, but are likely to still be required for services from Paddington for a number of years, while the 'cascade' of suburban Class 165/6 diesel multiple units from the London area to the South West is also likely to be delayed.

The Public Accounts Committee was scathing of Network Rail over the Great Western debacle, with its final report, published on 20 November 2015, highlighting what it called 'staggering and unacceptable' cost increase to the GW electrification project. The Committee said that there was still 'far too much uncertainty' on costs and eventual delivery dates for the electrification of both the Trans-Pennine route and the Midland Main Line – and warned more projects could be delayed in order to balance Network Rail's budget. In light of its findings, the Committee called for a fundamental review of the regulator's role and effectiveness in planning rail infrastructure.

Meg Hillier MP, Chair of the PAC, declared: 'Network Rail has lost its grip on managing large infrastructure projects. The result is a twofold blow to taxpayers: delays in the delivery of promised improvements, and a vastly bigger bill for delivering them. The potential near-doubling in cost of the electrification of the Great Western Line is a symptom of seriously flawed control and planning. Our inquiry has found that the agreed work could never have been delivered within the agreed budget and timeframe. Yet Network Rail, the Department for Transport and the regulator – the Office of Rail and Road – signed up to the plans anyway. Passengers and the public are paying a heavy price and we must question whether the ORR is fit for purpose.'

Another scathing assessment of Network Rail's shortcomings came in a review of its investment programme for the Transport Secretary by its recently-appointed Chairman, Sir Peter Hendy, and published in November 2015. In it, Sir Peter outlined actions needed to ensure elements of the £12.5 billion improvement programme would not have to be abandoned. These included plans to sell £1.8 billion of surplus property assets, including former depots and station retail units, and said a further £700m would be raised through borrowings – adding further to the company's £37.8 billion debt mountain. At the same time he confirmed that the Trans-Pennine and Midland Mainline electrification projects would be delayed by up to three years.

Faced with this evidence of just how little control there seems to be on costs and delivery of these major infrastructure

Fatal Attraction

Undoubtedly the saddest facet of modern railway operations is the number of people who choose to take their own lives on the track. For a commuter on the South Western Main Line into Waterloo, there are regular instances when total chaos is caused for many hours by a fatality on the line at somewhere like Surbiton or Raynes Park.

Once favoured spots like Wimbledon, as well as many others, such as stations from Paddington the Great Western Main Line, now have fences to prevent access to the edge of platforms used by fast trains, but the problem remains, and the trauma it causes to train drivers affected, as well as relatives and friends, is hard to imagine.

As a daily commuter these incidents can often mean long delays, missed appointments and great frustration, but what we don't ever see is the human side of each one of these tragic incidents. That was brought home for me when I went to take photographs at Norton Junction, just outside Worcester, on Sunday 1 May 2016.

Four days before my visit to photograph the signal box and semaphore signals nearby, a young man named Felix had found his way onto track. He had made his way to the nearby Bristol–Birmingham line, ending his life early on the morning of Wednesday 27 April 2016 near Abbotswood Junction, and causing several hours of delay and diversion to train services, according to the *Worcester News*.

An array of still-fresh floral tributes had been attached to the fence next to the road bridge over the line at Norton Junction in his memory. Reading some of the highly emotional tributes, as I waited to photograph passing trains, was a deeply poignant moment, which brought home how just one of the many hundreds of railway suicides each year had affected friends, family and work colleagues. RIP Felix.

Great Western Railway 166210 passes milepost 117½ as it approaches Norton Junction on Sunday, 1 May 2016, with the 09.20 service from Great Malvern to London Paddington. It is signalled onto the Cotswold Line – the home and distant signals at danger are for the route south via Abbotswood Junction towards Cheltenham.

One of the many floral tributes left on the road bridge at Norton Junction in memory of the young man who had taken his life a few days earlier at nearby Abbotswood Junction.

GWR liveried 166216 comes off the Cotswold Line on 1 May 2016, and passes Norton Junction signal box, three miles south of Worcester, with the 08.03 London Paddington to Great Malvern service. Worcestershire Parkway station will be built nearby, at a point where the Cotswold Line crosses over the Bristol–Birmingham route.

Six months after my visit I read a deeply moving story in *The Times* on 6 October 2016 "Social media bullies killed my son" where Felix's mother, Lucy Alexander, made a heartfelt plea to all young people to be kind always and never to stand by and leave online bullying unreported.

schemes, it is hardly surprising that critics find it difficult to take seriously any figure attached to the HS2 project, even if they do include significant so-called contingency amounts, the padding supposedly designed to cover unexpected extra costs. Evidence of the continuing upward spiral in costs emerged on 15 November 2015, when the *Independent on Sunday* reported that the cost of phase one was approaching £30 billion, a third higher than the previously estimated £21.4 billion (at 2011 prices) and a further indication that the final project bill would be nearer £80 billion than the forecast £50 billion.

Railways is a subject that frequently arouses passions: whether it be the frustration of regular commuters, the devotion of die-hard enthusiasts or the anger of campaign groups fighting in favour of a local re-opening scheme or against a major project such as HS2 or Crossrail Two there are no shortage of emotions. For me the emotional mixture is a blend of nostalgia for the things we have lost – things like steam, restaurant and Pullman cars, and the countless lines and stations that became victims of Beeching's blunt axe – and a fascination with complex timetables and the hardship of being a daily commuter into the capital, with all the challenges it creates to one's mental health.

Over-crowding: scourge of our times

In the two decades between the mid 1990s and 2014 the number of rail journeys made doubled to 1.65 million, according to Department for Transport figures. As London house prices spiralled, there has also been a trend towards longer and longer commuting times, with three million people spending two hours or more commuting in 2014, compared to 1.7 million in 2004, and 880,000 people spending at least three hours a day getting to and from work. Over-crowding on trains is one of the curses of our times, yet I sometimes wonder if politicians really comprehend the scale of human misery it brings.

As one of those two hour plus travellers on my commute from Haslemere to Waterloo, the scale of over-crowding means I now avoid one of the principal peak time departures (07.02) because the stress of trying to find a seat is too much and I cannot face the prospect of spending almost an hour standing. Instead I catch a slower service (07.10) which itself is invariably 'full and standing' before it reaches Guildford, meaning a cramped and uncomfortable 35 minute stand for commuters joining there and at its final stop, Worplesden. If I lived at Guildford, paid over £4k a year to travel and could never find a seat in the morning, I am sure I would be making far more of a fuss than these long suffering travellers I encounter.

Elsewhere it is just as bad, and probably even worse in many cases. On one occasion (14 October 2015) I was travelling in to London at peak time from Bromley South. The 07.58 Thameslink

service to Luton (an 8-coach train) had seats at the time I joined, but soon became so rammed that passengers were unable to join at intermediate stations. I had planned to change at Peckham Rye in order to reach London Bridge, but had no realistic prospect of being able to fight my way to the doors. Finally, as we approached Denmark Hill a poor pregnant lady standing in the packed vestibule fainted and had to be carried off the train to recover. Regular travellers assured me that this was far from being an isolated occurrence.

Nor is it just in the London area that over-crowding on trains has reached crisis proportions. In its endorsement of plans for a new HS3 line from Manchester to Leeds, Lord Adonis' National Infrastructure Commission pointed out in a report published just ahead of the March 2016 Budget that rail passenger volumes have trebled in the North West since 1995–96, up from 39.85 million passenger journeys in 1995/6 to 124.88 million in 2014/5, with more than 24.6 million passengers using Manchester Piccadilly in 2014/5 and 28.8 million passing through Leeds station in that 12 month period. One fifth (20%) of passengers are forced to stand on TransPennine Express trains into Manchester in the morning peak and 6% of trains arriving in Manchester in the morning peak have passenger levels in excess of capacity – close to the equivalent figure of 7% in London (*DfT Rail Statistics 2014*).

One novel solution would be the introduction of double-decker trains, which are a common feature of continental railways, but previously ruled out in Britain on account of our smaller loading

Weymouth is like Pembroke Dock and Newquay in having a seasonal HST service to provide additional capacity during the summer months. On 18 June 2016, HST 43129 (43161 rear) departs Yeovil Pen Mell with the 10.53 *Weymouth Wizard* – a Saturday service from Bristol Temple Meads to Weymouth.

gauge. A report in *The Times* on 16 November 2015 suggested that designers have come up with a way that would create the required space by lowering the floor of passenger carriages so that they are closer to the track. According to the report the Aeroliner 3000 project, led by a Swiss architect, Andreas Vogler, was among three at an advanced stage as part of a £3.5 million project to improve conditions on our railways. The Rail Safety and Standards Board (RSSB), which is running the design competition, said that the new concepts could be introduced between 2020 and 2022 to 'address the challenges facing the UK rail industry'.

A fares jungle

When I was first lucky enough to travel on the *Manchester Pullman* in 1980, I remember that a first class open return from London to Manchester cost exactly £45.00 (there was also a £2.00 Pullman supplement each way and the cost of meals, of course). In 2015 a first class anytime return cost £470.00 – an increase of more than 950% over that 35 year period and almost three times the rate of inflation during that period (353%). In the two decades since rail privatisation unregulated fares such as this have soared, vastly widening the gap between them and fares which were 'regulated' or controlled as part of the privatisation process – principally season tickets and off peak 'saver' fares.

The combination of privatised operators moving to airline-style 'yield management' pricing of tickets – offering huge savings for those in a position to book a journey well in advance of their date of travel – and the huge growth in online sales, has undoubtedly made price comparisons easier for the savvy traveller, yet there is a commonly held view that, despite numerous past efforts at simplification, the fares regime is a still mess and badly in need of reform.

Competition between operators has not been encouraged by the franchise regime, yet the limited areas in which it exists have delivered cheaper fares for passengers. On the East Coast Main Line, the impact of two 'Open Access' operators – Grand Central and First Hull Trains – has meant competitive fares being available to and from a limited number of stations, notably Doncaster and York. One of the few journeys to benefit from the impact of rivalry between franchisees can be seen between London and Birmingham, where competition between Virgin West Coast and London Midland from Euston and Chiltern Railways from Marylebone means that there are often real bargains to be found, with advance single fares for the 110-mile journey regularly being offered from just £6.00.

At the opposite end of the value spectrum is evidence of how a franchise holder's monopoly on pricing a particular flow can artificially inflate prices. One glaring example of this can be seen in the case of an off-peak return from my home town of Cheltenham

Spa to either Bristol or Birmingham – journeys of almost identical length (46 miles). In the case of Cheltenham–Bristol, there are two operators on the route, so the off-peak day return is an attractive £9.10 (2016 price). Head north to Birmingham, however, and with only a single operator, the cheapest off-peak return costs almost three times as much (2016: £24.40). How about that for abusing a monopoly?

Booking a trip to Ebbw Vale threw up yet another anomaly in the price of tickets from Cheltenham Spa, in this case towards South Wales. My day return from Cheltenham Spa to Ebbw Vale Town cost £14.60 (2015 price) a mere 30p more than the cost of a day return to Newport from Cheltenham (£14.30). The cheapest advertised fare from Cheltenham to Cardiff Central, however, was an off-peak day return for £18.60 – yet the normal routing from Cheltenham to Ebbw Vale is via Cardiff, so anyone wanting a day return to Cardiff from Cheltenham could make a significant (21%) saving by buying the Ebbw Vale return and alighting and returning from Cardiff. The rules governing 'break of journey' for an off-peak day return are crystal clear: 'You may start, break and resume, or end your journey at any intermediate station along the route of travel.' Yet more fares madness!

While online ticketing sites have made it easier to compare prices and see whether advance fares are available and whether they are cheaper than a flexible alternative (which is not always the case), a vast array of anomalies exist. Why, for example, do I make considerable savings on journeys to Stansted Airport by

Crediton station on the Tarka Line from Exeter to Barnstaple is one of the finest surviving examples of early railway architecture, with the main station building dating from 1847 and now an acclaimed tea room and with the whole station painted in LSWR livery, thanks to the efforts of the Friends of Crediton station and operator GWR. On 26 June 2016, GWR 150124 is about to depart with the 14.20 service to Barnstaple, while Pacers 143603/612 form the 14.20 service to Exeter Central.

booking to Audley End and breaking my journey at the Airport? Surely that means everyone who buys a full fare or off-peak return from Liverpool Street to the airport is being sold the wrong ticket – remember that booking offices have a duty of 'impartial retailing' and it is certainly not the cheapest fare that is valid to the Airport.

Looking at the cheapest fare I could find for another journey I was making – this time from Haslemere to Kemble – and the cheapest single fare for a journey (not via London) is a super off-peak single for £40.80 (2016 price). But by avoiding a crossing of the franchise boundary between South West Trains and GWR at Guildford, it is possible to almost halve the fare to just £22.50, by buying a super off-peak single from Guildford to Kemble for just £15.80 and starting with a super off-peak single from Haslemere to Guildford for £6.70.

It is not just at off-peak times that obscene fares anomalies can be exploited. In May 2016, I wanted to make a short notice trip from London to Cheltenham Spa, travelling at the busiest time of the week (Friday afternoon) on the 17.42 train from Paddington. Consulting the GWR website showed the only available fare being an anytime single for £80.50, which seemed excessive. However, noticing that this train is first stop Didcot Parkway, I instead bought an anytime single to Didcot Parkway (£20.20, with my Gold Card discount) and then a super off-peak single from Didcot to Cheltenham Spa for £17.60 – a grand total of £37.80, or less than half the through anytime fare.

Forget about 'impartial retailing': in the financial services world I work in, that would be regarded as a blatant example of mis-selling.

Britain's most south-westerly station is Penzance station, 305¼ miles and at least five hours by HST from London Paddington. On 3 August 2013, First Great Western (now Great Western Railway) 150263 has reached journey's end at 10.18, nearly five hours after its 05.24 departure from Bristol Temple Meads.

Re-structuring the privatised railway

Two fundamental aspects of our privatised rail system currently under review are the structure of Network Rail and the franchising system for running the passenger network. Since taking over from the failed Railtrack, Network Rail's debt has ballooned to almost £40 billion, and is set to reach almost £50 billion by 2019. As mentioned above in connection with the Great Western electrification, it has been widely criticised for a persistent failure to deliver major projects on time or on budget.

That prompted a review, undertaken by Nicola Shaw, the Chief Executive of High Speed One, whose initial conclusions, published in November 2015, were that a full or partial privatisation should be looked at, along with stripping Network Rail of control of railway stations and selling assets, including depots and car parks, in order to raise money. The interim report also raised the possibility of Network Rail being broken up into a series of smaller companies, possibly along regional lines.

In her interim report, Ms Shaw declared there was 'genuine consensus' that long-term planning for rail was 'frustrating and time consuming and could be considerably slicker and more effective'. She said that an increased private sector role could 'facilitate risk transfer (albeit partial) away from government as well as potentially reduce the upfront capital demand on the taxpayer'. In reviewing Network Rail's finances and structure, she said that the government should consider 'full or partial privatisation at the parent company level by way of accessing the equity capital markets'.

This assessment of future options for Network Rail came only a month after a scathing report from the Office of Rail and Road,

By the time this book is published another part of our railway heritage is likely to have been swept away, when long-delayed electrification of the Preston–Blackpool North route spells the end of manual signalling. On 15 June 2016 the signaller in Blackpool North No. 2 box has set the road for the departure of a service to York.

Departing shortly

One aspect of Britain's fantastic railway heritage that is disappearing fast is the manual signal box. Among many due for early replacement is Ashwell, a few miles north of Oakham on the busy Leicester–Peterborough line.

Along with the eight other signal boxes on this route, this 1912-vintage Midland Railway box is scheduled for closure in 2017, as control passes to the East Midlands Regional Operations Centre at Derby.

On 9 November 2011, I was invited to spend a day in the box, witnessing the signallers' dying art of using Victorian bell codes to indicate an oncoming train to the next box down the line, and watching the variety of rail traffic that passes this spot.

Ashwell box overlooks a level crossing and controls the barriers, as well as having a phone link to a nearby unmanned crossing, from where users call the signaller to gain permission to cross the line.

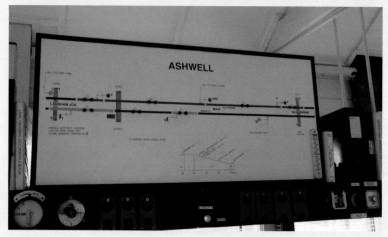

The track diagram showing signals controlled by Ashwell – a mixture of semaphore and colour light – and its neighbouring boxes at Langham Junction to the south and Whissendine to the north.

Cross-Country 170103 approaches the signal box with an eastbound service for Cambridge and Stansted Airport. It is passing the site of Ashwell station, which fell victim to Beeching and closed on 6 June 1966.

Freight traffic is heavy on this route – here 66186 in the former EWS maroon livery, approaches Ashwell with westbound train.

which noted that average delays of more than six months had been recorded on big projects, affecting work on 10 out of 14 routes. The ORR discovered that 36% of targets to complete work, such as new stations, extra track capacity and the electrification of lines, had been missed during the previous year, meaning that train operators did not have the 'confidence they need to plan their businesses effectively'. It concluded that Network Rail was in breach of its operating licence by failing adequately to 'plan and deliver' £13 billion of enhancements over the five-year control period.

Responding to widespread criticism, Network Rail chief executive Mark Carne has already begun to implement reforms, by splitting the company into eight separate businesses based on routes, with a small central function to ensure common standards and three service companies to supply the eight regional businesses.

Anticipating the final conclusions of Ms Shaw's review, *The Sunday Times* reported on 7 February 2016 that she would be recommending the piecemeal sale of certain parts of the network – among them Greater Anglia, Essex Thameside and Wessex – whose new owners would then be free to buy maintenance and other services from Network Rail and other contractors. The paper also suggested that the Shaw Report, due to be published the following month, would recommend creation of a new agency at arm's length from government that would be responsible for strategic rail matters. This new entity, akin to the former Strategic Rail Authority, would handle everything from franchising, big upgrades, control of the system, railway standards and long-term planning of schemes such as High Speed 2.

As a first step in the process of realising value from its assets to provide cash for its huge investment programme, Network

Ashchurch for Tewkesbury station, north of Cheltenham Spa, was an important junction, with lines radiating to Evesham and to Upton-on-Severn, re-opening in 1997 after 26 years of closure. Freight traffic on the Birmingham–Bristol route is sparse, but one regular working is this 'Tesco' container service from Daventry to Wentloog in South Wales, seen here on 1 May 2016 in the hands of DRS-liveried 66433.

Britain boasts many attractively preserved stations. One such example in the North-West is Poulton-le-Fylde, on the route from Preston to Blackpool North, seen on 15 June 2016, as 150119 departs for Blackpool North. The signal at danger is for access to the Fleetwood line, which passes to the right of the signal box.

Rail announced in March 2016 that it was seeking investors to take over the sub-stations, overhead lines and third rails that power electrified sections of the railway network. Having already announced that it was considering selling the 18 main stations that it manages, including Birmingham New Street, London Waterloo, Euston and Paddington, Network Rail also confirmed that it may sell 7,500 properties, freight yards, surplus land for housing, its telecoms network and depots in the hope of raising £1.8 billion.

Mark Carne, Network Rail's chief executive, said that the sales showed it was being 'open and innovative about new sources of finance to fund our growing railway', but the move came under fire from Labour, with Lillian Greenwood, shadow transport secretary, declaring: 'This sale is going ahead because the cost of major projects has sky-rocketed, but Tory ministers kept quiet about the scandal until after the election. They should focus on addressing the chronic fragmentation of the rail network, not on selling off and breaking up Network Rail.'

Meantime, a challenge to the franchise system that has dominated the UK's passenger network since privatisation in 1996 has been mounted by operators Virgin and Stagecoach. Responding to the threat of increased 'Open Access' competition on the East Coast Main Line, the two operators replied to an investigation into the rail market being undertaken by the Competition & Markets Authority (CMA) by declaring that competition should be between two licensed operators on the same stretch of track, rather than the present 'open access' regime that allows independent operators to compete on a limited scale with a franchise holder. This challenge to the *status quo* was not without a strong degree of self-interest, coming shortly after the Rail Regulator began considering bids for new 'Open Access' services between Edinburgh and London from First Group and Arriva.

When its final Report was published in March 2016, the CMA took on board what Virgin and Stagecoach had said and identified a range of benefits that could arise from allowing other operators to run competing services against existing franchised operators. 'Examples of such "on-rail" competition in Great Britain (GB) have mainly occurred on the East Coast main line where "Open Access" operators like Grand Central and First Hull Trains have been able to run competing services', noted the report. 'Although these services represent less than 1% of passenger miles, the evidence of resulting benefits has been underlined by examples of competition between passenger rail operators in other European countries and in other transport markets such as the GB rail freight sector, air transport and airports.' In order to grant more operators access, the CMA proposed that, to cover any fall in premiums paid to government, Open Access operators should make more of a contribution than at present in terms of track access charges and through a Public Service Obligation (PSO) levy in order to help fund important but unprofitable services, such as those in rural areas.

The CMA noted that the benefits of competition in passenger rail services are currently secured primarily by the award of franchises to operators through competition 'for' the market, and asserted that an increase in on-rail competition could result in benefits for passengers and taxpayers, including lower fares, growth in passenger numbers, greater incentives for operators to improve service quality and innovate, greater efficiency by train operators and more effective use of network capacity. It suggests that increasing the number of Open Access services or splitting franchises offers the most immediate benefits from increased competition, but that a move towards a system of multiple licensed operators replacing franchises could also be worth consideration in the future, adding that the potential for such competition exists predominantly on the three main intercity routes – the ECML, WCML and the Great Western Main Line.

Responding to the CMA report, and its suggestion that two or more train companies to run on lines such as the ECML, WCML and Great Western Main Line, Transport Secretary Patrick McLoughlin told Parliament on 17 March 2016 that more Open Access operators may be introduced on to Britain's railways, if reforms to the track access payment system can be pushed through. 'These reforms include fairer charges and robust protections for taxpayers and investment,' he commented, 'I will now explore options for potentially implementing the CMA's recommendations, including legislation if required.' The CMA said more Open Access operators could be introduced onto the network by forcing them to pay higher track access charges,

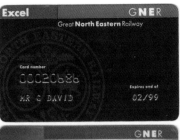

A number of franchised operators in the privatised railway era have run schemes to secure the loyalty of regular travellers. For generosity, none can match the scheme run for many years by GNER, originally known as Excel and later GNERTime, which offered holders benefits including free first class tickets and restaurant car meals.

covering the cost of any fall in premiums paid to the government by the franchise holders. However, the Department for Transport indicated that the government would effectively reject a more radical option spelled out by the CMA to tear up the franchise system altogether, in favour of up to three operators being given equal access to the same route.

Within a fortnight of the CMA report's publication came the first signs of potential fall-out. A comment column in *The Times* (29 March 2016) by seasoned rail industry watcher Robert Lea suggested that Stagecoach, as operator of the Virgin Trains East Coast franchise, had been warning the Department for Transport that its commitment to pay £3 billion in excess profits over the

An early post-Beeching opening was Southampton Airport in 1966, just a year before completion of the Waterloo–Bournemouth electrification and the end of Southern steam. The station was significantly upgraded in 1986, when the Parkway name was added and a new station building provided. On 18 June 2016, Cross Country 221136 calls with the 17.27 service to Manchester Piccadilly.

eight year life of its East Coast franchise could not be delivered if the Office of Rail and Road gave a green light to the Open Access applications from First Group and Deutsche Bahn to run competing services between Edinburgh and London.

If true, it had echoes of dire warnings which GNER was making to MPs a decade earlier, about how the prospect of competition from Grand Central would massively devalue the plum East Coast franchise, only for GNER to collapse before Grand Central even got onto the network! A further warning signal came in July 2016, when a report in *The Times* 'East Coast payouts derailed' (3 July 2016) pointed out that actual annual revenue growth to date at the Virgin/ Stagecoach franchise of 5.2% was well short of the forecast 8–12%, but suggested that it was not just the fault of economic uncertainties, but also of Network Rail's 'spending squeeze, which has slowed work on planned upgrades and hurt routine maintenance', words which had all the hallmarks of another franchisee getting the excuses in quick before s*** hit the fan!

Threats remain

For all that has been achieved over the past few decades in terms of successful re-opening of lines and stations, the spirit of Beeching and Serpell lives on, in certain quarters at least. In a Discussion Paper *Without Delay – getting Britain's railway moving* published by the Institute of Economic Affairs in February 2016, Dr Richard Wellings made highly critical comments about the privatised railway structure, laying the blame on what he called a 'complex web of state-subsidised firms operating in a heavily regulated market, meaning the sector is neither fully public nor properly private.' He points out that state support for the rail sector is now equivalent to £180 per family in the UK, despite the majority of Britons hardly ever travelling by train.

Wellings adds that the true level of government support has been disguised by large increases in Network Rail's debt, which he says is likely to surpass £50 billion by 2020, representing a major long-term burden on future generations. His answer is a liberalised regime that would 'wean the industry off state support and allow its structure to evolve to more cost-effective organisational forms through mergers and demergers.' This anti-rail agenda concludes that 'Private railways should be free to cut costs by closing loss-making lines and services, to introduce "super-peak" fares to tackle overcrowding, to offer cut-price "economy class" options such as standing-only carriages and to determine an appropriate level of safety expenditure.'

Patience, persistence and deep pockets required!

The over-riding passion aroused in me by researching and writing this book, however, is one of impatience and incomprehension at the time and cost even the most straightforward of revival schemes seems to involve. Why does it take years and years to resurrect a three mile spur that would give the citizens of Portishead the rail service they obviously need? Can a seven-mile 'mothballed' link across level ground to Wisbech really cost north of £100 million? Can anyone really be sure that Meldon Viaduct is beyond economic repair when the same was being said of the Ribblehead Viaduct at the time closure of the Settle & Carlisle line was being pursued?

Alas, I am not the expert who can provide definitive answers to these and many other similar questions. The sad fact is that no matter how much anecdotal evidence emerges to support re-opening schemes, the whole mechanism of securing support, overcoming planning issues, the whole GRIP evaluation process, and then getting the scheme adopted within the appropriate strategic plan or Control Period takes an inordinate amount of time. Looking through a pamphlet called *Fighting for Rail* marking the first ten years (1978–88) of what was then known as the Railway Development Society (now Railfuture) it is sobering to see the number of schemes which we are still talking about as revival prospects.

Jumping ahead to another Railway Development Society document, this time one called *Bring back our tracks* which was published in 1996, and it is telling that almost all the revival schemes featured are the ones still being talked about. Happily, though, there are two of the 26 routes it puts forward where re-opening has taken place and another, the East–West railway, where a start has been made. Tellingly, though, neither of the two lines featured which have now re-opened are in England – both are in

Summer Saturday in the South West: HST 43086/43131 stands at St Erth with the 11.11 departure for London Paddington on 3 August 2013. Beeching wanted to close the branch to St Ives, which diverges to the left, while Serpell wanted to shut all lines west of Plymouth. Thankfully they were both ignored and passenger traffic continues to grow on lines throughout the Royal Duchy.

Scotland, with the Bathgate–Airdrie line at No. 7 and Edinburgh–Galashiels, the new Borders Railway, featuring at No. 12.

Researching this book has given me an excuse to visit and re-visit places as far afield as Penzance and St Ives in the South West to Thurso and Wick in the Far North of Scotland. It has taken me to rail-revived communities ranging from Alloa, Bathgate and Galashiels in Scotland to Mansfield, Rugeley and Melksham in England and to Ebbw Vale, Maesteg and Aberdare in South Wales. It has also taken me to places like Wisbech and Portishead, whose citizens patiently await the long overdue return of rail to their towns, while the noise being made nationally is about the all-dominating construction of HS2, which seems to be in real danger of swamping all talk about other rail re-openings.

Trying to assess where we are in terms of railway revival, it seems that we have two ends of the spectrum well-covered, but a big gap in the middle. At the mega-project end, we have government committing seemingly infinite amounts to deliver HS2 and the subsequent HS3 links across the north of England, while the National Infrastructure Commission can hopefully find favour with significant strategic schemes like East–West Rail. On a much smaller scale, the New Stations Fund is a commendable initiative, which has already helped deliver a number of new stations, with more in the pipeline. What we lack is a mechanism for evaluating and taking forward the many other schemes featured in this book, for which – as Chris Green points out – our county councils simply do not have the resources and there is no other obvious source of funding.

If Network Rail sees itself simply as an evaluator and deliverer of new infrastructure schemes that are funded by others, then there is a strong case for involving rail franchisees in the business of promoting and bringing forward re-opening schemes. If the new Northern Rail franchise can contain a requirement that the franchisee works to help deliver the long-awaited Ashington–Blyth re-opening, and if Great Western Railway can strongly support the Stratford–Honeybourne re-opening, then why is there not a catch-all clause in all franchise tenders, inviting prospective operators to set out their plans for 'Network Development'? The Nicola Shaw review of Network Rail talked about the need to attract more private sector investment into the railways, so here would be one easy way for many more franchise bidders to do what Chiltern Railways has been successfully doing for a number of years – putting in real investment in return for a longer franchise.

So what would a wholesale re-opening programme cost? Taking up the theme of my 2013 *Guardian* comment (suggesting there were better ways of investing in rail infrastructure than committing £50+ billion to HS2), the starting point must be to come up with a reasonable estimate of average re-opening costs. While those simply involving the upgrade of an existing freight route will be relatively inexpensive (the range of costs on the

Burton–Leicester route in the latest study was between £3.3m and £5.8m per mile), let us assume a cost of £15 million/mile – the Borders Railway came in at around £10m per mile for example, but this figure is roughly the estimate for March–Wisbech, and many may cost more. It means we could buy 100 miles of revived railway for £1.5 billion, meaning that every single project featured in Chapters 8 and 9 (around 450 route miles) could be delivered for a total of around £6.7 billion, or just 12% of the cost of HS2. A no brainer, many would argue.

If I could hope for anything from the publication of this volume is that it will spur on those like the former Railway Development Society (now Railfuture) and the many other campaign groups across Britain to draw strength from the success of past re-openings and re-double their campaigning efforts. Time and again all the economic and traffic modelling of the experts has proved woefully inadequate in establishing one glaringly simple truth about people's pre-disposition to take rail journeys: make the service regular and the fares attractive and the passengers will be there, not just for the novelty, but because rail offers a superior journey experience and is a real catalyst to improved social mobility, development of tourism, employment and job prospects.

Gazing into the RR crystal ball, there seems a lot to look forward to in the coming decade, particularly with imminent completion of both the Thameslink and Crossrail One (Elizabeth Line) projects and real progress being made in preparing Crossrail Two, so as to avert a transport log-jam at Euston station when HS2 arrives. The HS2 project will continue to escalate in price – reaching the worst case £80 million figure which opponents had come up with by 2015 unless more significant changes to the scope of the project

It is the end of the line, for now at least. This view of newly-opened Tweedbank station, terminus of the Borders Railway, was taken on 24 September 2015, three weeks after its opening. ScotRail 158734 prepares to return to Edinburgh Waverley while the maroon-liveried coaches of the special train, hauled by 60009 *Union of South Africa*, stand in Platform 2.

are made. Electrification will finally reach Swansea and Sheffield, albeit late and well over budget, as well as the Welsh Valleys, and there will be good news on a number of long-cherished re-opening projects featured in the previous two chapters. But the real winners will be the citizens of Hawick, whose 50 year isolation from the rest of the UK rail network will end when a commitment is made to full re-opening of the Waverley Route!

APPENDIX I: LINES OPENED OR RE-OPENED SINCE BEECHING

This list shows lines which have opened or re-opened since Beeching and remain open to regular scheduled passenger services (Summer Sundays only in the case of Crediton–Okehampton). It excludes services which opened and were subsequently withdrawn, such as Walsall–Wolverhampton and Derby–Sinfin and lines such as the Selby Diversion on the ECML which were built to replace an existing alignment.

Distances are shown for the services operated, or from the nearest calling point, so the total distances shown are somewhat greater than the net amount of "new line" – for example Ebbw Vale Line services normally originate at Cardiff Central (29.5 miles from Ebbw Vale Town), but the distance from Ebbw Junction (near Newport) is only 20 miles.

ENGLAND		
Route	Length (miles)	Opened/Re-opened
Barnsley–Penistone	7.50	16/05/83
Bicester South Curve	0.75	25/10/15
Bicester Village (Town)–Oxford	11.75	11/05/87
Birmingham Moor St–Langley Green	5.50	24/09/95
Blackburn–Clitheroe	9.75	29/05/94
Camden Road–Stratford	6.25	17/05/83
Chippenham–Trowbridge	11.75	13/05/85
Corby–Kettering	7.50	23/02/09
Corby–Oakham	14.25	27/04/09
Coventry–Leamington Spa	10.00	02/05/77
Coventry–Nuneaton	10.00	11/05/87

Route	Length (miles)	Opened/Re-opened
Crediton–Okehampton	18.00	01/06/97
Eastleigh–Romsey	7.25	18/05/03
Farringdon–Blackfriars–London Bridge	2.00	29/05/90
Halifax–Huddersfield	10.50	28/05/00
Hayes & H–Heathrow Airport	4.00	23/06/98
Kensington Olympia–Willesden Junction	2.75	12/05/86
Lichfield City–Lichfield Trent Valley	1.25	28/11/88
Liverpool (Merseyrail underground sections)	3.00	03/02/77
Liverpool Central–Garston	5.75	02/01/78
London St Pancras–Folkestone (HS1)	68.00	14/11/07
Manchester Airport spur	1.50	17/05/95
Manchester Airport spur – south curve	0.50	15/01/96
Middlesborough–Northallerton	14.50	20/02/96
Morecambe–Heysham Port	4.25	11/08/87
Nottingham–Newstead	10.75	08/05/93
Newstead–Mansfield Woodhouse	7.75	20/11/95
Mansfield Woodhouse–Worksop	13.00	25/05/98
Ordsall Chord (Manchester)	0.50	[12/17]
Peterborough–Spalding	16.50	07/06/71
Stansted Moutfitchet–Stansted Airport	3.75	19/03/91
Todmorden West Curve	0.25	17/05/15
Wakefield Kirkgate–Pontefract Monkhill	8.75	12/05/92
Walsall–Hednesford	10.00	10/04/89
Hednesford–Rugeley Town	4.00	02/06/97
RugeleyTown–Rugeley Trent Valley	1.50	25/05/98
Yeovil Pen Mill–Yeovil Junction	2.00	14/12/15
England Total	**317.00**	
SCOTLAND		
Barassie–Kilmarnock	9.50	05/05/75
Bathgate–Airdrie	14.50	12/12/10
Coatbridge Central–Greenfaulds	5.50	27/05/96

Route	Length (miles)	Opened/Re-opened
Cambuslang–Partick (Argyle Line)	7.00	05/11/79
Cardenden–Kirkaldy	13.75	15/05/89
Dalmeny–Linlithgow	4.25	03/06/96
Edinburgh Waverley–Bathgate	18.50	24/03/86
Edinburgh Waverley–Newcraighall	4.00	03/06/02
Glasgow Queen Street–Maryhill	4.75	02/12/93
Maryhill–Anniesland	1.50	26/09/05
Glasgow Central–Paisley Canal	7.00	28/07/90
Rutherglen–Whifflet	7.25	04/10/93
Hamilton Central–Larkhall	5.25	12/12/05
Ladybank–Perth	20.00	06/10/75
Newcraighall–Tweedbank	31.00	06/09/15
Stirling–Alloa	6.75	19/05/08
Scotland Total	**161.25**	
WALES		
Abercynon–Aberdare	7.75	03/10/88
Barry–Bridgend	19.00	12/06/05
Bridgend–Maesteg	8.25	28/09/92
Cardiff Central–Ebbw ValeTown	29.50	06/02/08
Cardiff Central–Radyr (City Line)	4.75	04/10/87
Wales Total	**69.25**	
GRAND TOTAL	**547.50 MILES**	

APPENDIX II: STATIONS OPENED OR RE-OPENED SINCE BEECHING

This list shows stations on the national railway network that have opened or re–opened since the Beeching Report was published in 1963. It therefore excludes any re–opening prior to that date, such as those on the Southbury Loop (Southbury, Theobalds Grove and Turkey Street stations) which re–opened on electrification of the line in November 1960.

The listing also excludes stations on preserved lines, London Underground and those on metro and tram systems not served by national rail services. Stations shown as proposed are those where definite re–opening schemes have been adopted – in some cases these stations are already under construction and, hopefully, some will have been opened by the time this book is published.

Station	Closed	(Re)–opened	Note
Abercynon (North)	–	03/10/88	1
Aberdare	13/06/64	03/10/88	
Adwick	06/11/67	11/10/93	
Aigburth	17/04/72	03/01/78	
Airbles	–	15/05/89	
Alfreton	02/01/67	07/05/73	2
Allens West	–	04/10/71	3
Alloa	07/10/68	19/05/08	
Alness	13/06/60	07/05/73	
Anderston	03/08/59	05/11/79	
Apperley Bridge	20/03/65	13/12/15	
Ardrossan Town	01/01/68	19/01/87	
Argyle Street	–	05/11/79	
Arlsey	05/01/59	03/10/88	

Station	Closed	(Re)–opened	Note
Armadale	08/01/56	04/03/11	
Armathwaite	04/05/70	14/07/86	
Ashchurch for Tewkesbury	15/11/71	01/06/97	
Ashfield	–	02/12/93	
Auchinleck	06/12/65	12/05/84	
Aylesbury Vale Parkway	–	14/12/08	
Baglan	–	02/06/96	
Baildon	29/04/57	05/01/73	
Ballieston	05/10/64	04/10/93	
Bargeddie	–	04/10/93	
Barking Riverside	(proposed)		
Barrow upon Soar	04/03/68	27/05/94	
Basildon	–	25/11/74	
Bathgate	09/01/56	24/03/86	4
Beauly	13/06/60	15/04/02	
Bedworth	18/01/65	16/05/88	
Bentley (S. Yorks.)	–	27/04/92	
Bermuda Park	–	18/01/16	
Berry Brow	02/07/66	09/10/89	
Bicester Village (Town)	01/01/68	11/05/87	
Birchwood	–	06/10/80	
Birmingham International	–	26/01/76	
Birmingham Snow Hill	06/03/72	05/10/87	
Blackpool Pleasure Beach	–	13/04/87	
Blackridge	–	12/12/10	
Bloxwich	18/01/65	17/04/89	
Bloxwich North	–	02/10/90	
Bow Street	14/06/65	(proposed)	
Braintree Freeport	–	08/11/99	
Bramley (West Yorkshire)	04/07/66	12/09/83	
Branchton	–	05/06/67	
Bridge of Allan	01/11/65	13/05/85	

Station	Closed	(Re)–opened	Note
Bridgeton	05/10/64	05/11/79	
Brighouse	05/01/70	28/05/00	
Brinnington	–	12/12/77	
Bristol Parkway	–	01/05/72	
British Steel Redcar	–	19/06/78	
Briton Ferry	02/11/64	01/06/94	
Bromborough Rake	–	30/09/85	
Brunstane	–	03/06/02	
Brunswick	–	09/03/98	
Buckshaw Parkway	–	03/10/11	
Bulwell	(1964)	24/05/94	
Burley Park	–	28/11/88	
Burnley Manchester Road	06/11/61	13/10/86	
Caldercruix	09/01/56	13/02/11	
Carmyle	–	04/10/93	
Cam & Dursley	04/01/65	14/05/94	5
Cambridge North	–	21/05/17	
Camelon	–	27/09/94	
Canada Water	–	27/04/10	6
Cannock	18/01/65	10/04/89	
Carno	14/06/65	(proposed)	
Cathays	–	03/10/83	
Chafford Hundred Lakeside	–	26/05/95	
Chandlers Ford	05/05/69	18/05/03	
Chatelherault	01/01/1917	09/12/05	
City Thameslink	26/01/90	29/05/90	7
Clitheroe	10/09/62	29/05/94	8
Coleshill Parkway	04/03/68	18/09/07	
Conon Bridge	13/06/60	18/02/13	
Cononley	22/03/65	21/04/88	
Conway Park	–	22/06/98	
Conwy (Conway)	14/02/66	29/06/87	

Station	Closed	(Re)–opened	Note
Corby	18/04/66	23/02/09	9
Corkerhill	10/01/83	28/07/90	
Cottingley	–	25/04/88	
Coventry Arena	–	18/01/16	
Cranbrook	–	13/12/15	
Cressington	17/04/72	02/01/78	
Creswell	–	25/05/98	
Crookston	10/01/83	28/07/90	
Crossflats	–	17/05/82	
Crosskeys	–	07/06/08	
Curriehill	31/03/51	05/10/87	
Cwmbach	13/06/64	03/10/88	
Cwmbran	–	12/05/86	
Dalgety Bay	–	27/03/98	
Dalmarnock	05/10/64	05/11/79	
Dalston Junction	30/06/86	27/04/10	
Dalston Kingsland	01/11/1865	17/05/83	
Danescourt	–	04/10/87	
Deighton	28/07/30	26/04/82	
Dent	04/05/70	14/07/86	
Digby & Sowton	–	23/05/95	
Dodworth	29/06/59	15/05/89	
Dolgarrog	02/11/64	14/06/65	
Dronfield	02/01/67	05/01/81	
Drumfrochar	–	24/05/98	
Drumgelloch	09/01/56	06/03/11	10
Dumbreck	–	28/07/90	
Duncraig	07/12/64	05/01/76	
Dunfermline Queen Margaret	–	26/01/00	
Dunlop	07/11/66	08/06/67	
Dunrobin Castle	29/01/65	30/06/85	
Dunston	–	01/10/84	

Station	Closed	(Re)–opened	Note
Dyce	06/05/68	15/09/84	
Eastbrook	–	24/11/86	
East Garforth	–	01/05/87	
East Midlands Parkway	–	26/01/09	
Eastham Rake	–	03/04/95	
Ebbsfleet International	–	19/11/07	
Ebbw Vale Town	30/04/62	17/05/15	
Ebbw Vale Parkway	–	06/02/08	
Edginswell	–	(proposed)	
Edinburgh Gateway	–	11/12/16	
Edinburgh Park	–	04/12/03	
Energlyn and Churchill Park	–	08/12/13	
Eskbank	06/01/69	06/09/15	
Euxton Balshaw Lane	06/10/69	15/12/97	
Exhibition Centre (Finnieston)	03/08/59	05/11/79	11
Fairwater	–	04/10/87	
Falls of Cruachan	01/11/65	20/06/88	
Falmouth Town	–	07/12/70	
Featherstone	02/01/67	12/05/92	
Feniton	06/03/67	05/05/71	12
Fernhill	–	03/10/88	
Filton Abbey Wood	–	11/03/96	13
Fishguard & Goodwick	06/04/64	14/05/12	14
Fitzwilliam	–	01/03/82	
Five Ways	02/10/44	08/05/78	
Flowery Field	–	13/05/85	
Frizinghall	22/03/65	07/09/87	
Galashiels	06/01/69	06/09/15	
Garsdale	04/05/70	14/07/86	
Garston (Herts)	–	07/02/66	
Gartcosh	–	09/05/05	
Garth (Mid Glamorgan)	–	28/09/92	

Station	Closed	(Re)–opened	Note
Gilsochill	–	02/12/93	15
Glan Conwy (Conway)	26/10/64	04/05/70	
Glasgow Central (Low Level)	03/10/64	05/11/79	
Glasgow Prestwick Airport	–	05/09/94	
Glasshoughton	–	21/02/05	
Glenrothes with Thornton	–	11/05/92	
Godley	–	07/07/86	
Goldthorpe	–	16/05/88	
Gorebridge	06/01/69	06/09/15	
Green Park (Reading)	–	(proposed)	
Greenfaulds	–	15/05/89	
Gretna Green	06/12/65	20/09/93	
Gypsy Lane	–	03/05/76	
Hackney Central	15/05/44	12/05/80	
Hackney Wick	–	12/05/80	
Haddenham & Thame Parkway	–	05/10/87	
Hag Fold	–	11/05/87	
Haggerston	06/05/40	27/04/10	
Halewood	–	16/05/88	
Hall i' th' Wood	–	29/09/86	
Hattersley	–	08/05/78	
Hawkhead	14/02/66	12/04/91	
Heathrow Central	–	23/06/98	
Heathrow Airport T4	–	23/06/98	
Heathrow Airport T5	–	27/03/08	
Hedge End	–	06/05/90	
Hednesford	18/01/65	10/04/89	
Heysham Port	06/10/75	11/05/87	16
Homerton	23/04/45	13/05/85	
Honeybourne	05/05/69	22/05/81	
Hornbeam Park	–	24/08/92	
Horton-in-Ribblesdale	04/05/70	14/07/86	

Station	Closed	(Re)–opened	Note
Horwich Parkway	–	02/07/99	
How Wood	–	24/10/88	
Howwood [Renfrew]	07/03/55	12/03/01	
Hoxton	–	27/04/10	
Hucknall	12/10/64	17/05/93	
Humphrey Park	–	15/10/84	
IBM	–	09/05/78	17
Ilkeston	02/01/67	02/04/17	
Imperial Wharf	–	27/09/09	
Islip	01/01/68	15/05/89	
Ivybridge	02/03/59	15/07/94	
James Cook University Hospital	–	18/05/14	
Jewellery Quarter	–	24/09/95	
Kelvindale	–	26/09/05	
Kempton Park	–	(05/06)	18
Kenilworth	–	(under construction)	
Kentish Town West	18/07/71	05/10/81	
Kilmaurs	07/11/66	12/05/84	
Kings Cross Thameslink	–	11/07/83	19
Kingsknowe	06/07/64	01/02/71	
Kirkby–in–Ashfield	–	17/11/96	
Kirkby Stephen	04/05/70	14/07/86	
Kirkstall Forge	–	19/06/16	
Kirkwood	–	04/10/93	
Lake	–	11/05/87	
Lambhill	–	03/12/93	
Landywood	–	10/04/89	
Langho	07/05/56	29/05/94	
Langley Mill	02/01/67	12/05/86	
Langwathby	04/05/70	14/07/86	
Langwith-Whaley Thorns	–	25/05/98	

Station	Closed	(Re)–opened	Note
Larkhall	04/10/65	12/12/05	
Laurencekirk	04/09/67	18/05/09	
Lazonby & Kirkoswald	04/05/70	14/07/86	
Lea Bridge	08/07/85	15/05/16	
Lea Green	–	17/09/00	
Lelant Saltings	–	27/05/78	
Lichfield Trent Valley (High Level)	18/01/65	28/11/88	
Lisvane and Thornhill	–	04/11/85	20
Liverpool Central (Deep Level)	–	02/05/77	
Liverpool Lime St. (Low Level)	–	30/10/77	
Liverpool South Parkway	–	11/06/06	
Livingston North	–	24/03/86	
Livingston South	–	06/10/84	
Llanfairpwll	14/02/66	07/05/73	
Llanharan	02/11/64	10/12/07	
Llanhilleth	30/04/62	27/04/08	
Llanrwst	–	29/07/89	21
Llamsamlet	–	27/06/94	
Llantwit Major	15/06/64	12/06/05	
Loch Awe	01/11/65	10/05/85	
Loch Eil Outward Bound	–	06/05/85	
Lochwinnoch	04/07/55	27/06/66	
London Fields	13/11/81	29/06/86	
Longbeck	–	13/05/85	
Longbridge	–	08/05/78	
Lostock	–	16/05/88	
Lostock Hall	06/10/69	14/05/84	
Low Moor	14/06/65	02/04/17	
Luton Airport Parkway	–	21/11/99	
Lympstone Commando	–	03/05/76	
Maesteg	14/07/70	28/09/92	

Station	Closed	(Re)–opened	Note
Maesteg (Ewenny Road)	–	26/10/92	
Maghull North	–	(proposed)	
Manchester Airport	–	17/05/93	
Mansfield	12/10/64	20/11/95	
Mansfield Woodhouse	–	20/11/95	
Marsh Barton	–	(proposed)	
Martins Heron	–	03/10/88	
Maryhill	02/03/64	02/12/93	
Matlock Bath	06/03/67	27/05/72	
Meadowhall Interchange	–	05/09/90	
Melksham	18/04/66	13/05/85	
Melton	02/05/55	03/09/84	
Merryton	–	09/12/05	
Metheringham	11/09/61	06/10/75	
Metrocentre	–	03/08/87	
Milliken Park	18/04/66	15/05/89	
Mills Hill	–	25/03/85	
Milton Keynes Central	–	17/05/82	
Mitcham Eastfields	–	02/06/08	
Moorfields	–	02/05/77	
Mosspark	10/01/83	28/07/90	
Moss Side	26/06/61	21/11/83	
Moulscoomb	–	15/05/80	
Mountain Ash	13/06/64	03/10/88	
Mount Vernon	16/08/43	04/10/93	
Muir of Ord	13/06/60	04/10/76	
Musselburgh	–	03/10/88	
Narborough	04/03/68	05/01/70	
Needham Market	02/01/67	06/12/71	22
Newbridge	30/04/62	06/02/08	
Newbury Racecourse	–	16/05/88	
Newcourt	–	04/06/15	

Station	Closed	(Re)–opened	Note
Newcraighall	–	03/06/02	
New Cumnock	06/12/65	27/05/91	
New Pudsey	–	06/03/67	
Newstead	–	08/05/93	
Newton Aycliffe	–	01/01/78	
Newtongrange	06/01/69	06/09/15	
Ninian Park	–	04/10/87	
Okehampton	05/06/72	25/05/97	
Outwood	13/06/60	12/07/88	
Oxford Parkway	–	25/10/15	
Paisley Canal	10/01/83	28/07/90	
Peartree	04/03/68	04/10/76	
Penally	15/06/64	28/02/72	
Pencoed	02/11/64	11/05/92	
Penrhiwceiber	13/06/64	03/10/88	
Pill	07/09/64	(proposed)	
Pinhoe	07/03/66	11/05/83	
Pontefract Tanshelf	–	12/05/92	
Pontyclun	02/11/64	28/09/92	
Portishead	07/09/64	(proposed)	
Portlethen	11/06/56	17/05/85	
Possilpark and Parkhouse	10/09/62	02/12/93	
Prestwick International Airport	–	05/09/94	
Priesthill and Darnley	–	23/04/90	
Pye Corner	–	14/12/14	
Pyle	–	27/06/94	
Ramsgreave & Wilpshire	10/09/62	29/05/94	23
Rhoose Cardiff Int. Airport	15/06/64	12/06/05	24
Ribblehead	04/05/70	14/07/86	
Robroyston		(proposed)	
Risca & Pontyminster	–	06/02/08	
Rogerstone	–	06/02/08	

Station	Closed	(Re)–opened	Note
Roughton Road	–	20/05/85	
Rugeley Town	18/01/65	02/06/97	
Runcorn East	–	03/10/83	
Ruskington	11/09/61	05/05/75	
Rutherglen	05/10/64	05/11/79	
Ryder Brow	–	04/11/85	
Salford Crescent	–	11/05/87	
Saltaire	20/03/65	09/04/84	
Sampford Courtenay	05/06/72	(2002)	25
Sandal and Agbrigg	04/11/57	30/11/87	26
Sanquhar	06/12/65	27/06/94	
Sarn	–	28/09/92	
Shawfair	–	06/09/15	
Shepherd's Bush	–	28/09/08	
Sherburn-in-Elmet	13/09/65	09/07/84	
Shieldmuir	–	14/05/90	
Shirebrook	12/10/64	25/05/98	27
Shoreditch High Street	09/06/06	27/04/10	28
Shotton Low Level	14/02/66	21/08/72	
Sileby	04/03/68	27/05/94	
Silkstone Common	29/06/59	14/05/83	
Skewen	02/11/64	27/06/94	
Slaithwaite	07/10/68	13/12/82	
Smallbrook Junction	–	21/09/91	
Smethwick Galton Bridge	–	24/09/95	
Smithy Bridge	02/05/60	19/08/85	
Southampton Airport	–	01/04/66	29
South Gyle	–	09/05/85	
South Wigston	–	10/05/86	
Southend Airport	–	18/07/11	
St. Michaels	17/04/72	02/01/78	
Stansted Airport	–	19/03/91	

Station	Closed	(Re)–opened	Note
Steeton and Silsden	22/03/65	14/05/90	
Stepps	05/11/62	15/05/89	30
Stewarton	07/11/66	05/06/67	
Stone	(2004)	14/12/08	
Stow	06/01/69	06/09/15	
Stratford International	–	30/11/09	
Stratford-upon-Avon Parkway	–	19/05/13	
Streethouse	–	12/05/92	
Sugar Loaf	(1965)	21/06/87	
Summerston	–	02/12/93	
Sutton Parkway	–	20/11/95	
Swinton	01/01/68	14/05/90	
Syston	–	27/05/94	
Tame Bridge Parkway	–	04/06/90	
Tees-Side Airport	–	03/10/71	
Telford Central	–	12/05/86	
Templecombe	07/03/66	03/10/83	
The Hawthorns	–	02/04/95	
Thurnscoe	–	16/05/88	
Tiverton Parkway	–	12/05/86	31
Tondu	22/06/70	28/09/92	
Tutbury & Hatton	07/11/66	03/04/89	
Tweedbank	–	06/09/15	
Ty Glas	–	29/04/87	
University [of Birmingham]	–	08/05/78	
Uphall	09/01/56	24/03/86	
Valley	14/02/66	15/03/82	
Wallyford	–	13/06/94	
Walsden	06/08/61	10/09/90	
Watlington	09/09/68	05/05/75	32
Watton-at-Stone	10/09/39	17/05/82	
Waun-Gron Park	–	06/11/87	

Station	Closed	(Re)–opened	Note
Wavertree Technology Park	–	13/08/00	
Welham Green	–	29/09/86	
West Brompton	21/10/40	01/06/99	
Wester Hailes	–	11/05/87	
West Ham	–	(1979/99)	33
Wetheral	02/01/67	05/10/81	
Whalley	10/09/62	29/05/94	
Whifflet	–	21/12/92	
Whinhill	–	14/05/90	
Whiston	–	01/10/90	
Whitwell	12/10/64	25/05/98	
Wildmill	–	12/12/92	
Willington	04/03/68	26/05/95	
Winnersh Triangle	–	12/05/86	
Winslow	01/01/68	(proposed)	
Woodsmoor	–	01/10/90	
Worcestershire Parkway	–	(under construction)	
Worle	–	24/09/90	
Yarm	04/01/60	20/02/96	
Yate	04/01/65	11/05/89	
Ynyswen	–	29/09/86	
Ystrad Rhondda	–	29/09/86	34

Notes
1. Combined with Abercynon South and temporary N station closed May 2008.
2. Alfreton & Mansfield Parkway at opening; renamed November 1995.
3. Date of opening to public; private halt first opened 1940.
4. Re–sited Bathgate station opened 18/10/10.
5. Closure date for Coaley Junction; new station located west of original site.
6. Date London Overground service started; first opened on 19/08/99.
7. Closure of Holborn Viaduct; new station St Pauls Thameslink until 06/11/91.
8. First re–opened 08/04/87 for seasonal Dalesrail services.
9. Corby first re–opened 13/04/87 then closed again 04/06/90.
10. First re–opened 15/05/89; resited on this date to become through station.
11. Finnieston at re–opening; name changed 05/89.
12. Sidmouth Junction at closure.

13. Replaced Filton (earlier Filton Junction) station nearby.
14. Served by Motorail trains only from 1965–1980.
15. Opened as Lambhill; re-named 24/05/98.
16. Heysham Harbour at closure; Heysham Sea Terminal until 28/09/92.
17. Date opened as unadvertised halt; public station from 12/05/86.
18. Race day services only until this date.
19. King's Cross Midland City at opening; platforms closed and re-sited 09/12/07.
20. Replacement for Cefn Onn station; closed 27/09/86.
21. Existing Llanrwst station renamed Llanrwst North (later North Llanrwst).
22. Needham at closure.
23. Wilpshire at closure; new station re-sited south of original.
24. Rhoose at closure; longest official UK station name!
25. Seasonal (summer Sunday) services only.
26. Sandal at closure.
27. Shirebrook West at closure.
28. Start of London Overground services; replaced closed LU station.
29. Expanded and re-named Southampton Airport Parkway 29/09/86.
30. Stepps Road at closure.
31. Replaced Tiverton Junction, which closed on this date.
32. Magdalen Road at closure and re-opening; re-named 03/10/89.
33. North London Line platforms 1979–2006; LTS line platforms opened 1999.
34. Previous Ystrad Rhondda station now called Ton Pentre.

APPENDIX III:
BIBLIOGRAPHY

A–Z of Railway Re-openings, Alan Bevan, Railway Development Society, March 1998

The Banbury and Cheltenham Railway 1887–1962, J.H. Russell, Oxford Publishing Company, 1977

The Barnstaple & Ilfracombe Railway, C. Maggs, Oakwood Press, 1978

Bring back our tracks, Railway Development Society, June 1996

British Railways Network for Development, Ministry of Transport/British Railways Board, March 1967

The case for a renewed rail–link between Cambridge and Colchester, Cambridge to Colchester Rail Project, 2011

Complete British Railways Maps and Gazeteer 1825–1985, C.J. Wignall, Oxford Publishing Company 1985

Connecting Communities, ATOC, June 2009

Crossrail 2 – Funding and financing Study, PwC, 27 November 2014

Fighting for Rail – Railway Development Society 1978–1988, Trevor Garrod, RDS, 1988

First Interim Evaluation of the Impacts of High Speed 1, Atkins/Aecom/frontier economics

From the Footplate – Atlantic Coast Express, Stephen Austin, Ian Allan, 1989

The Great Railway Conspiracy, David Henshaw, A to B Books, 2013

The InterCity Story, Mike Vincent/Chris Green, OPC 1994

Investigation into the Clapham Junction railway accident, Anthony Hidden QC, HMSO, November 1989

Ivanhoe Line Stage II Scheme Re-Appraisal, Scott Wilson, Leicestershire County Council, April 2009

The Kyle Line – An illustrated History and Guide, Tom Weir, Famedram Publishers, 1971

Leicester–Burton Rail Passenger Service – Final Report, Leicestershire County Council and North West Leicestershire District Council, May 2016

Management Today, Profile of Chris Green, Managing Director InterCity, 1 May 1990, Chris Blackhurst

Mayor of London: letter from Boris Johnson to Rt. Hon. Greg Hands MP, 23 October 2015

Modern Railways, July 1963 (Vol XVIII, No. 178), Ian Allan

Modernisation and Re-equipment of British Railways (the 1955 Modernisation Plan), British Transport Commission, December 1954

Movement for Growth: The West Midlands Strategic Transport Plan, West Midlands Integrated Transport Authority, December 2015,

National Transport Strategy, Scotland's Railways, Scottish Executive, 2006

Network Rail's 2014–2019 Investment Programme, House of Commons Committee of Public Accounts, The Stationery Office, 20 November 2015

The Network SouthEast story 1982–2014, Chris Green & Mike Vincent, OPC, 2014

Report to Transport and Highways Committee – Possible re-opening of the Robin Hood Line to Ollerton, Nottinghamshire County Council Agenda Item 7;11 February 2016,

ORR's annual report on HS1 Ltd 2014–2015, Office of Rail and Road, July 2015

Passenger Rail Usage 2015–6 Q2 Statistical Release, Office of Rail and Road, 10 December 2015

Passengers no more (second edition), Gerald Daniels & LA Dench, Ian Allan, 1973

The Pembroke and Tenby Railway, M.R.C. Price., Oakwood Press, 1985

Progress in the Thameslink programme, National Audit Office/Department for Transport, 5 June 2013

Re-appraisal of the Plan for the Modernisation and Re–equipment of British Railways, British Transport Commission, July 1959,

Reflections on the Portishead Branch, Mike Vincent, OPC, 1983

Rail Finance 2014–5 Annual Statistical Release, Office of Rail and Road, 27 August 2015

Rail magazine, numerous issues

Railway Disasters, Stanley Hall, Bookmark Lt,. 1989

Railway Magazine, numerous issues

Railway Finances: Report of a Committee chaired by Sir David Serpell KCB CMG OBE, Department of Transport/HMSO, 1983

Railway World, May 1967: p178 "Single line to Exeter"

Railway World, May 1967:p206 "By underground to Shanklin"

Railways: Channel Tunnel Rail Link (HS1), Louise Butcher, House of Commons Library (SN267), 24 March 2011

Railways of the Eastern Region Volume 1: Southern operating area, Geoffrey Body, Patrick Stephens Ltd, 1989

Railways to Exmouth, C. Maggs, Oakwood Press, 1980

Railways in the Lake District, Martin Bairstow, 1995

Report from Sir Peter Hendy to the Secretary of State for Transport on the re–planning of Network Rail's Investment Programme, Network Rail, November 2015

The Reshaping of British Railways, British Railways Board/HMSO, 1963

Reviving Britain's Railways, Elizabeth Anderson, Bow Group, July 2015

The Right Line, Nicholas Faith, Seagrave Foulkes, 2007

Rural Reconnections, CPRE/Greengauge 21, June 2015

Scoping study for full feasibility study for re–opening a heavy rail railway between Aberystwyth & Carmarthen, Aecom Transportation/Welsh Government, October 2015

Scotland Route: Summary Route Plan, Network Rail, 2013

The Somerset and Dorset Railway, Robin Atthill, David & Charles, 1985

Southern Steam Sunset, John H. Bird/Runpast Publishing 1997

The Story of Bathgate's Railways 1849–2010, Bathgate Historic Conservation Society (website)

The Times Mapping the Railways, David Spaven and Julian Holland, Times Books, 2014

Transport Act 1968, HMSO

Transport Policy, Ministry of Transport, HMSO, July 1966

Wales Route: Summary Route Plan, Network Rail

Waterside Rail Study, Halcrow/Hampshire County Council, June 2013

West of Exeter Route Resilience Study, Network Rail, Summer 2014

Wikipedia, numerous entries

Without Delay – getting Britain's railways moving, Dr Richard Wellings, Institute of Economic Affairs, February 2016

APPENDIX IV: CAMPAIGN AND PROMOTIONAL GROUPS

General

Campaign for Better Transport	www.bettertransport.org.uk
Railfuture	www.railfuture.org.uk
Railway Reinstatement Association	www.railwayreinsatementassociation.co.uk

Routes/Stations

England

Ashington–Blyth	www.senrug.co.uk
Bodmin–Wadebridge (Padstow)	www.bodminandwadebridgerailway.co.uk
Bristol–Portishead	www.portisheadrailwaygroup.org
Bury–Rawtenstall	www.eastlancsrailway.org.uk
Cambridge–Haverhill (Sudbury)	www.railhaverhill.org.uk
Carno (station)	www.carnostation.org.uk
Chippenham–Trowbridge	www.twcrp.info/corridor
East–West Rail	www.eastwestrail.org.uk
Exeter–Okehampton	www.dartmoorrailway.com
	www.Prg2day.uk
Fleetwood–Poulton-le-Fylde	www.pwrs.org
Gainsborough–Brigg–Barnetby	www.grab.eavb.co.uk
High Speed Two	www.hs2.org.uk
High Speed Two (opposition to)	www.stophs2.org
Haywards Heath–Horsted Keynes	www.bluebell–railway.co.uk
March–Wisbech	www.bramleyline.org.uk
Penrith–Keswick	www.keswickrailway.com
Radstock–Frome	www.northsomersetrailway.com
Settle–Carlisle	www.foscl.org.uk
Skipton–Colne	www.selrap.org.uk
Stratford–Honeybourne	www.shakespeareline.com
	www.suawoox.com
Stratford–Honeybourne (opposition to)	www.noavonline.co.uk
Uckfield–Lewes	www.bml2.co.uk
Wareham–Swanage	www.swanagerailway.co.uk
Windsor Link	www.windsorlink.co.uk

Wymondham–Dereham (Fakenham)	www.mnr.org.uk
	www.norfolk-orbita-railway.co.uk
York–Beverley (Minster Rail)	www.minsterrail.net

Scotland

Ayr–Stranraer	www.saylsa.org.uk
Borders Railway	www.campaignforbordersrail.org
Dingwall–Kyle of Lochalsh	www.kylerailway.co.uk
Leuchars–St Andrews	www.starlink-campaign.org.uk
Thornton–Leven	www.lmrc.action.org.uk

Wales

Aberystwyth–Carmarthen	www.trawslinkcymru.org.uk
Gaerwen–Amlwch	www.leinamlwch.co.uk
Heart of Wales Line	www.howlta.org.uk

ACKNOWLEDGMENTS

Embarking on a project of this breadth was a daunting task, bearing in mind the huge amount of scholarly work that has been published over the years on topics such as Beeching, modernisation and privatisation. But by making liberal use of personal anecdote and talking to numerous campaigners, I hope I have managed to bring a fresh perspective to the remarkable transformation of our railways since the dark days of the 1960s, and to have reflected the almost universal success of re-openings to date.

My sincere thanks go to the many people who have taken the time to speak to me, let me interview them, or updated me on their campaigns. In particular I would like to thank Chris Green for his unique insights into ScotRail, Network SouthEast and InterCity, as well as Simon Wright and Chris Binns for telling me in fascinating detail about delivering the Thameslink and Crossrail One projects.

Special thanks also to the Northern Rail gate-line supervisor at Blackpool North, for escorting me to the end of platform 5/6, so that I could photograph the signal box and magnificent array of semaphore signals, as well as all the other railway staff who have been willing to speak to me and answer my questions. Other special thanks go to Graham Ellis (TransWilts Community Rail Partnership), David Walsh (SELRAP), John Morgan (Stratford–Honeybourne), Brian Hart (BML2/Uckfield–Lewes), and Dennis Fancett (SENRUG).

I must also thank friends and colleagues for their support, including John Cormack, Nick Fletcher, Adrian Quine and Ian Yeowart, and not forgetting the drinking club on the 18.00 Waterloo to Portsmouth Harbour train (pictured), for their feigned interest in this project (!) and all those unsung campaigners fighting the good fight to get lines and stations re-opened. Finally, sincere thanks to my long-suffering wife, Clare, who has supported and encouraged my efforts, and was even persuaded to stay at the Premier Inn in Aberdare, just so I could travel the Aberdare branch line, while we were on a Six Nations rugby weekend trip to South Wales!

Fellow drinkers on the 18.00 Waterloo to Portsmouth Harbour service, celebrating the end of another working week, on Friday 1 July 2016.

INDEX

Abellio 74–5, 135, 148, 153

Abercynon 28, 174, 176

Aberdare 3, 6, 28, 173–7, 181–2, 298

Aberdeen-Fraserburgh 28, 130

Aberystwyth-Carmarthen 28, 49, 123, 161–5

Adonis, Lord 88, 197, 226, 234, 247, 285

AECOM 163, 199, 249–50, 262

AECOM Faber Maunsell *see* AECOM

Aeroliner 3000 286

Airports Commission 265

Alloa 3, 6, 134–6, 139, 279, 298

Amlwch 28, 189

Anglesey 189

Argyle Line 6, 131–3, 138

Arriva (Deutsche Bahn) 10, 75, 82, 254, 294

Arriva Trains Wales 84, 105, 171, 176, 183

Arup 251, 260–1

Ashby-de-la-Zouch 248–50

Ashford 46, 68, 191–4, 197, 199, 200, 203, 216

Ashington 253–4, 298

Ashington-Blyth - *see* Ashington

Ashington Blyth and Tyne (ABT) *see* Ashington

Ashton Gate 239

Association of Train Operating Companies
(ATOC) 231, 234–5, 246, 248, 254, 259, 263,
269–71, 273–6

Atkins (WS) 199, 234

Atlantic Coast Express 275

Audley End 288

Automatic Train Protection (ATP) 69, 76

Automatic Warning System (AWS) 75

Avocet Line 127

Axminster-Lyme Regis 28

Aylesbury Vale Parkway 232

Ayrshire Coast 132

BAA 119–20, 218

BAM Nuttall 147

Bangor-Caernarfon 161

Barclay, Steve MP 235–6

Barnstaple *see* Bideford

Barry-Bridgend (Vale of Glamorgan)

Basingstoke 1–2, 29, 64, 68–9, 227

Bath Green Park 28–9

Bathgate 6, 130, 137–44, 279, 298

Bayliss, David 209

Beaconsfield 16

Beamish, Claudia MSP 256

Bedpan (Bedford-St Pancras-Moorgate) 213

Beeching, Dr Richard (Report, axe) 1, 3–9, 14,
17–28, 30–32, 34–5, 39, 44–5, 47, 50, 52–3,
58–9, 66, 84, 91, 94, 99, 109–12, 114, 121, 125–
8, 130–1, 133, 138, 140, 150, 155–7, 159–61,
163–5, 169, 172, 174, 179, 182, 189, 231, 240,
243, 257, 259–64, 267, 270–1, 273–4, 276, 279,
284, 291, 295–7

Bere Alston 16, 240–4

Bewdley 46, 276, 279

Bicester North 16

Bideford 8, 273–5

Binns, Chris 223–6

Birmingham International 84, 110

Birmingham New Street 53, 108, 119, 169, 293

Birmingham Pullman 62

Birmingham (Snow Hill) 7, 64, 106, 276

Blackfriars 210–16

Blaenau Ffestiniog 14, 70–1, 165, 169, 171, 177

Blaenau Gwent County Borough Council 182

Bletchley 16, 34, 46, 205, 232–5

Bluebell Railway 277

Blue Trains (Class 303) 53, 131, 138

Boat Train Route One 193

Bodmin Parkway *see* Padstow

Bombardier 108, 217

Borders Railway 3–6, 48, 84–5, 134, 141–50,
160–3, 249, 255, 257, 298–9

Borealis Infrastructure 191

Bournemouth West 28

Bow Group 16

Bowker, Richard 74

Bowshawk Tunnel 148

Brading-Bembridge 31

Braintree 46, 265–7

Braintree District Council *see* Braintree

Bramley Line 235

Breeze, Warren 79

Bridgend 6, 28, 46, 177–81, 185

Brighton Main Line (BML) 118, 211, 216, 246–7,
277

Bring back our tracks 297

Bristol-Portishead *see* Portishead
Bristol Parkway 4, 55
British Airways 195
British Leyland 141
British Motor Corporation (BMC) 141
British Railways Board 17, 23, 26, 42, 44–5, 75, 238
British Railways Network for Development (1967 Report) 9, 44–5, 47
British Transport Commission 23, 25, 30–1, 38
Broad Street (station) 112, 115, 117
Brown, Gordon MP 198, 218
Brownhills 262–3
Brown, Keith MSP 148, 160
Buchanan, Colin & Partners 270
Buckley, Simon 168
Burningham, Richard 8
Burton-on-Trent 28, 108, 247–9
Bury *see* Rawtenstall
Byers, Stephen MP 76

Caernarfon 9, 46, 161
Caerphilly 183–4
Calder Valley 103–5, 277
Calne 28
Cambrian Coast 46, 49, 161, 163, 169, 179
Cambridge North 235
Cambridgeshire County Council 236
Camel Trail 275
Cameron, David MP 242
Campaign for Borders Rail 146, 255
Campaign to Protect Rural England (CPRE) 244–5
Canal Tunnels 212
Canary Wharf 112, 218, 220, 223, 247
Capitalcard 62–3, 66
Carne, Mark 77, 279, 292–3
Castle, Barbara MP 43, 45, 48
Central Borders: A plan for expansion (The, report) 48
Central London Rail Study 217
Central Railway 30
Central Rivers 108
Central Wales Line *see* Heart of Wales Line
Chandlers Ford 120, 125, 271
Channel Tunnel 4, 6, 30, 85, 191–8
　Channel Tunnel Act 192
　Channel Tunnel Group 192
　Channel Tunnel Rail Link (CTRL) 194, 197, 202
　Channel Tunnel Rail Link Act 1996 194
Chase Line 106, 109
Chelsea-Hackney 209, 216, 229

Cheltenham-Kingham 28, 32, 34, 36, 39, 264
Cheltenham 1, 7, 28–9, 32–44, 82, 111, 177–9, 264–5, 282, 286–8, 292
Chiltern Railways 7, 16, 64, 73, 75, 89, 106–7, 205, 232, 286, 298
City Line (Cardiff) 6, 172–4, 177
City Line (London) 209–11
City Thameslink 66–7, 210
CKP Railways 257
Clan Line 1, 278
Clapham High Street 117
Clapham Junction 52, 69–70, 88, 114–8, 228–9
Class 220 (Voyager) 257
Class 319 215
Class 345 (Crossrail fleet) 221, 224
Class 378 (London Overground fleet) 114, 117–8, 221
Class 395 (Javelin) 193, 197–200
Class 412 (4–BEP) 72
Clitheroe 93–4, 259
Club 50 153
Coalville 248–9
Colne 16, 46, 259–61
Competition & Markets Authority (CMA) 293–5
Comrie-Gleneagles 27
Connecting Communities (ATOC Report) 231, 235, 246, 248, 254, 259, 263, 269–70, 276
Control Period 5 (CP5) 122, 124
Control Period 6 (CP6) 190
Conwy Valley Line 70–1, 165, 169–71
Corby 6, 67–8, 99, 100, 280
Cotton, Ron 92
Coventry 16, 28, 85, 106, 110
Cranbrook 13, 84–5, 127
Cranleigh 269–70
Crawford, Jim 207
Cross-City Line (Birmingham) 8, 98, 106, 108
Crossrail One (Elizabeth Line) 5–6, 15–6, 75, 83, 88, 90–1, 111, 191, 203, 209, 213–28, 299
Crossrail Two 209, 216, 223–30, 267, 299
Cuckoo Line 28
Cullompton 127
Cumbria County Council 258
Custom House 220
Cymmer Afan 177
Cynghordy Viaduct 167–8

Dalesrail 91, 93–4
Dalkeith, Earl of, MP 48
Darling, Alastair MP 197
David, Trefor 28, 32–43
Davies, Eddie 81

Davies, Sir Howard 265
Dawlish 241–5, 256
Dean, Kevin 79
Dent 93
Dereham 267–8, 275
Deutsche Bahn (see Arriva)
Devon and Cornwall Rail Partnership 8, 128
Diesel Multiple Unit (DMU) 99, 110, 157, 177
Disability Discrimination Act 1995 174
Docklands Light Railway 111, 113, 120
Donaldson, Charles MP 47
Dornoch Firth 151, 153
Dovey Junction-Pwllheli 46
Dumfries-Stranraer 28, 130
Dunblane-Crianlarich 28, 131

Early Day Motion (EDM) 81
East Anglian Daily Times 266
East Coast (ECML) 15, 23, 52, 54–6, 68, 73–5,
    78, 80–2, 84, 86, 111, 205, 212, 234, 253, 261–2,
    286, 293–6
East Lancashire Railway (ELR) 260, 276, 279
East London Line 113–4
East Midlands Hub Station 206–7
East-West Railway 30, 89, 231–4, 255, 264, 297
Ebbsfleet 194, 196–200, 202–3, 225
Ebbw Vale 3, 6, 85, 161, 182–5, 190, 279, 287,
    298
Edinburgh Airport Rail Link (EARL) 134
Elizabeth Line *see* Crossrail One
Elliot, Madge 48, 257
Ellis, Graham 121–3
Equishare 81
Eridge 28, 245, 247
Eskbank 3, 148–50
European Commission 133
Eurostar 88, 191–6
Eurotunnel 194
Exmouth 46, 84, 126–7

Faith, Nicholas *see Right Line, The*
Fakenham 267–9
Far North Line 130, 150–4, 158
Farringdon 209–13
Fawkham Junction 195–6, 198
Fawley 271
Feniton 13
Ffestiniog Railway 169, 171
Fife Circle 133, 136
Fife Coastal Line 160
Fighting for Rail 297
FirstGroup 73, 74
First Hull Trains 58, 83, 119, 286, 294

*First Interim Evaluation of the Impacts of High
    Speed 1* 199
Fishguard 6, 176, 186–9
Five Ways 8, 108
Fleetwood 46, 258–9, 293
Flow Country 154–5
Fort William-Mallaig 46, 155
Fowey 28, 274
Franchising 52, 71–4, 77–8, 83, 289, 292
Fraser Eagle 80–1
Fremington *see* Bideford
Frontier Economics 199
Fulham Broadway 229

Gainsborough Line 266
Galashiels 3–4, 49, 144–50, 250, 255, 279, 298
Gatwick Express 60, 74
GB Railways 78
Gerrards Cross 16
Glanrhyd Bridge 165, 167
Glasgow Airport Rail Link (GARL) 134–5
Gloucestershire County Council 251, 265
Gloucestershire Echo 28, 32, 34–6, 38, 40–2, 56,
    265
Great North Eastern Railway (GNER) 15, 73–4,
    81–2, 295–6
Golden Hind, The 62
Goldstein, Alfred 59
Grand Central (Railway Company) 3, 15, 57,
    78–83, 103–4, 119, 205, 258, 286, 294, 296
Great Central 28, 30, 47, 96, 204, 232
Great Dunmow 266
Great Railway Conspiracy, The 30
Great Western (Railway, franchise) 12–3, 73,
    105, 121–2, 124, 129, 167, 224, 232, 243, 252,
    282, 288, 298
    Great Western (pre-1948 company) 7, 12, 32,
        43, 106, 110, 125, 169, 237
    Great Western electrification 77, 90, 190, 216,
        279, 281, 289
    Great Western Main Line 54–5, 75, 87, 90,
        119–20, 127–8, 190, 193, 207–208, 274, 279,
        282, 294
    Great Western Society 46
    Great Western Trains 75
Greater London Council 68, 210, 217
Green, Chris 63, 65–9, 86–90, 137–40, 298
Greenwood, Lillian MP 293
Gritten, Andrew 30
Guardian, The 15, 22, 32, 39, 205
Guildford 28, 227, 269, 270, 284, 288
Gunter, Ray 21
Gwili Railway 162

Halcrow 238, 272–3
Hammond, Philip MP 192
Hammond, Stephen MP 235
Hampshire County Council 272
Hart, Edwina 163, 180, 184, 186
Hatfield 76, 87
Haverhill 266
Haverhill Echo see Haverhill
Hawick 48–9, 130, 139–40, 160, 255–6, 300
Healey Mills 105
Heart of Wales Line 10, 14, 46, 91, 164–9
Heart of Wales Line Travellers' Association 167
Heathrow 16, 68, 112, 118–20, 203, 217–8, 222,
    224–5
    Heathrow Airtrack 120
    Heathrow Connect 120, 222, 224
    Heathrow Express 78, 83, 119, 203
Hellifield 93
Hendy, Sir Peter 281
Henshaw, David 30
Hertford Loop Line 57, 111
Heywood *see* Rawtenstall
Hidden, Anthony QC (Hidden Report) 69–70
Higgins, David 206
High Marnham 98
High Speed One (HS1) 57, 85, 91, 191–2,
    197–204, 228
High Speed Three (HS3) 88, 285, 298
High Speed Train (HST) 5, 10, 54–8, 60, 75–6,
    80–1, 167, 188, 285, 288, 297
High Speed Two (HS2) 6, 15–6, 30, 54, 85, 88–9,
    191–2, 201–8, 218, 221–2, 225–6, 230, 279, 284,
    298–9
High Wycombe 16, 205, 233
Highlands and Islands Strategic Transport
    Partnership (HITRANS) 153
Hill, Rev. Malcolm 266
Hillier, Meg MP 281
Hirwaun 174–6
Hitachi 281
Hither Green 69
Holborn Viaduct 66, 209–11
Honeybourne 16, 43–4, 250–1, 298
Howell, David MP 58
Hull-Scarborough 46
Hull-York 28
Hythe 16, 271–3

IEP (Intercity Express Programme) 56, 58
Ilfracombe 8, 11
Ilkley 46, 82, 103
Imperial Wharf 114–5, 229
Institute of Economic Affairs 201, 296

Instow *see* Bideford
InterCity 53–4, 59–62, 83, 86
    InterCity125 54
    InterCity225 76
    InterCity East Coast 75, 81
    InterCity West Coast 73, 205
Isle of Wight 31, 50–1
Ivanhoe Line 248

Jacobs Holdings 79
James, Lord (of Blackheath) 219
Javelin (Class 395) 193, 197–202
Jewellery Line 107
JMP Consultants 260
Johnson, Boris 218, 230, 265
Jones, Mike 78
Jones, Phil 221
Journal, The 253
Jubilee Line 112, 217, 220–1

Kemble 5, 15, 43, 288
Kent County Council 194
Keswick 9, 46, 257–8
Kettering-Corby *see* Corby
Kidderminter *see* Bewdley
Kingham 28, 32–6, 39–43, 264–5
King's Road 227, 229
Kirby, Simon 207
Kirk, Alistair 207
Kirkby-Skelmersdale *see* Skelmersdale
Knighton Chord 248
Kramer, Baroness 257
Kyle of Lochalsh 14, 46, 91, 150–2, 155–6

Ladbroke Grove 75–6, 87
Lamington Viaduct 256
Lampeter 161–2
Larkhall 130–1, 134–5, 139
Lea Bridge 118
Lea, Robert 295
Lea Valley 111, 118, 226, 228, 265
Leamington Spa 16, 28, 106–7, 110
Leeds-Ilkley 46
Leeds-Morecambe 46
Leeds Northern Railway Reinstatement
    Group 261
Leicester 28, 30, 60, 99, 247–50, 280, 290, 299
Leicestershire County Council 250
Lelant Saltings 128–9
Levenmouth 160
Liverpool Street 53, 75, 112–3, 117, 119–20,
    216–9, 221–2, 224, 265, 288
Llandeilo 165–8

Llandrindod Wells 167
Llangefni 189
Llantwit Major 179–82
London Bridge 116, 210, 212, 214–5, 285
London City Airport 120, 221
London and Continental Railways (LCR) 194–8
London & South East (BR sector) 59, 63, 65
London & South Western Railway (LSWR) 9, 64, 125–7, 241, 275, 287
London Midland (franchise) 107, 286
London Overground 6, 75, 89, 111–8, 221, 228–9
London Rail Study Report 217
Longbridge 8, 98, 106, 108, 141
Longland, Simon 145
Long Marston 250–2
Lostwithiel *see* Fowey
Ludgate Development 210
Luton Airport Parkway 120, 211–2
Lyall, David 35, 41

MTL 78
MTR 73, 75, 221
McLoughlin, Patrick MP 58, 246, 294
Maesteg 6, 46, 177–9, 298
Mallard 57, 97
Malton-Whitby 28
Malvern Road station (Cheltenham) 32–4, 42–3
Manchester 1, 4, 6, 23, 28, 30, 40, 53–4, 58, 60–1, 79–80, 91, 101–2, 105, 194, 202–2, 206, 208, 276–8, 285–6
    Manchester Airport 101–2
    Manchester Piccadilly 53, 102, 206, 285, 295
    Manchester Pullman 53–4, 60–1, 286
    Manchester Victoria 94, 104
Mansfield 3, 6, 94, 96–7, 279, 298
Mansfield Woodhouse 95–8
Marches Line 165
Marchwood 271
Mark I (rolling stock) 52, 69–71
Marples, Ernest MP 20, 26
Marsh Barton 127
Marsh, Richard MP 48
Marston Vale 232
Martindale, Cedric 257–8
Marylebone (station) 7, 16, 28, 30, 64, 81–2, 106–7, 232–3, 250, 286
Master Cutler 28, 62
Mayoral Community Infrastructure Levy (CIL) 230
Meldon (Quarry/Viaduct) 240–4, 297
Melksham 3, 120–4, 298
Merchant Navy (loco class) 1–2, 11, 278

Merseyside Pullman 60–2
Merseytravel 254
Metrolink 101, 277
Midland Metro 7, 107
Midland Main Line 16, 30, 54, 56, 99–100, 205, 211, 232–3, 248, 280–1
Midland Railtourer 2, 7
Mid-Morfolk Railway (MNR) 267–8
Milton Keynes Central 4, 84, 222, 233
Minehead 182, 276
Ministerial Committee on Environmental Planning 48
Mis-shaping of British Railways (The, NUR report) 21
Mitterrand, Francois 192
Modern Railways (magazine) 23
Modernisation and Re-equipment of British Railways (1955 plan) 17, 23–5, 52, 54, 56, 171
Morgan, Elystan MP 163–5
Morris, John MP 164
Morton, Alastair 87, 194
Moses Gate 1–2
Movement for Growth 263
Munby, D.L. 22
Murphy, Denis MP 252

Narberth 9–10, 188
National Audit Office 196, 200, 213
National Express 74, 195
National Forest route 248
National Infrastructure Commission (NIC) 88, 226, 234, 247, 285, 298
National Transport Strategy, Scotland's Railways 134
National Union of Railwaymen (NUR) 21
Nelson, John 78
NET (Nottingham Express Transit) 98
Networker (trains) 64, 66
Network Rail 15, 52, 75, 77, 79, 81, 83, 87, 89, 98–9, 101–2, 120–4, 130, 134–5, 147–8, 157, 159, 161, 174, 179, 183, 189–90, 197, 205, 208, 212, 218, 232, 234–5, 241–7, 252–4, 259–60, 262, 265, 270, 279, 281, 289, 292–3, 296, 298
Network Railcard 62, 64
Network SouthEast 59, 62–3, 65–7, 73, 83, 86, 119, 140, 246
Newbattle Viaduct 246
Newcastle (upon Tyne) 6, 23, 56–7, 59, 61, 79–80, 82, 91, 93, 100–102, 208, 252–3, 261–2
Newcourt 84–5, 127
Newport City Council 183
Newport-Freshwater 31
Newport-Sandown 31

Newquay 10, 46, 273, 275, 285
Newton, Sir Wilfrid 79
Newtongrange 3, 148–50
Nightstar 193
Ninian Park 172–3
North Cotswold Line 15, 251, 264
　A joint vision for 252
North Eastern Local Enterprise Partnership
　(LEP) 262
North Llanrwst 171
North London Line 112–6
North Orbital Railway 269
North Pole Junction 193
North Somerset Line 46
North Warwickshire Line 46
North Yorkshire County Council 260–1
North Yorkshire Moors Railway 28, 78
Northern Powerhouse 58, 208, 260
Northern Rail (franchise) 75, 84, 103–5, 254, 298
Northumberland County Council 253–4
Norton Junction 282–3
Norwich-Sheringham 46
Nottingham-Mansfield-Worksop *see* Robin
　Hood Line
Nottinghamshire County Council 94, 98
Nuneaton 28, 85, 106, 110

Office for National Statistics (ONS) 227
Office for Passenger Rail Franchising
　(OPRAF) 72, 78
Office of Rail Regulation (ORR) – now Office of
　Rail & Road 78, 80–3, 129, 153, 281, 292
Okehampton 16, 46, 89, 240–5, 275
Old Oak Common 16, 203–204, 221–5
Oldham Loop 101
Olympic Delivery Authority 218
Ontario Teachers' Pension Plan 191
Open Access 15, 52, 57–8, 77–9, 81, 83, 104, 119,
　205, 286, 293–4, 296
Orient Line 1, 278
Osborne, George MP 226
Ove Arup *see* Arup
Oxford Parkway 232–3
Oxford Prospect 264
Oyster 114

Paddington (station) 5, 7, 9, 16, 33, 60, 64, 75–6,
　114, 119, 122, 167, 193, 203, 205, 216–8, 220–5,
　264, 276, 281–3, 288, 297
Padstow 11, 126, 274–5
Paisley Canal 132, 138
Par-Newquay *see* Newquay
Passengers' Charter 72–3

Peartree 99
Pembroke Dock 9–11, 46, 186–8, 285
Pendolino 54, 56–7
Penrith *see* Keswick
Perth-Ladybank 6, 131, 133
Perry, Claire MP 246
Pines Express 28–9
Pinhoe 13
Plymouth University 242
Pontefract Line 103, 105
Pontypridd 172, 174, 176
Porterbrook Leasing 79
Portishead 5, 16, 120, 126, 237–40, 255, 297–8
Portishead Railway (Action) Group *see*
　Portishead
Poulton-le-Fylde (see Fleetwood)
Prescott, John MP 195
PricewaterhouseCoopers (PwC) 226, 230
Prism Rail 74
Private Finance Initiative (PFI) 194
Privatisation 52, 56, 64, 68, 71, 73, 84, 86, 90,
　107, 248, 279, 286, 289, 293
Public Accounts Committee (PAC) 196, 279,
　281
Public Private Partnership (PPP) 196
Public Service Obligation (PSO) 294

Radio Electronic Token Block (RETB) 156, 158
Railfuture 136, 179, 235, 243, 248, 297, 299
Railnews 189
Rail Safety and Standards Board (RSSB) 286
Railtrack 52, 72, 75–7, 195–7, 270, 279, 289
Railway Development Society (see Railfuture)
Railway World (magazine) 11, 51
Railways Act 1993 71–2, 76–7
Rawtenstall 276–7
Raymond, Stanley 45
Redbridge Viaduct 150
Redditch 7–8, 98, 108
Regional Railways 59, 80
　Regional Railways North East 78–9
　Regional Railways North West 78
Reid, Sir Robert 59, 65
Re-shaping of British Railways (Beeching
　Report) 3
Reviving Britain's Railways (Report) 16
Rhondda Tunnel 177
Rhoose Cardiff International Airport 179–81
Ridley, Nicholas MP 41, 56
Right Line, The 192
Riordan, Linda MP 81
Roberts, Alfred 264
Robertson, Brian 25

Robin Hood Line 94
Ross, Willie MP 48
Round Robin (ticket) 169
Route Plan for Scotland (Network Rail) 130
Route Plan for Wales (Network Rail) 161
Rugeley-Walsall 6, 28, 106, 109, 298
Rural Reconnections (Report) 244–5

Salmond, Alex MP 256
SAYLSA 157
St. Andrews Rail Link Campaign
    (StARLink) 160
St. Ives (Cambridgeshire) 9, 46
St. Ives (Cornwall) 128–9, 273, 275, 297–8
St. James's Station (Cheltenham) 29, 34, 38,
    42–3
Scott, Tavish MSP 134
ScotRail 63, 65–6, 74, 84, 86, 134–46, 148–9, 153,
    157, 159, 299
Scott Wilson 136, 146–7, 248–9
Scottish Executive 141, 147
Scottish Office 47, 138
Scottish Parliament 134, 141, 146
Sea Containers 74, 81
Sectorisation 52, 59
Serco 75
Serpell, Sir David 52, 58–9, 137, 296–7
Settle-Carlisle 14, 46, 91–3, 168, 259, 297
Severn Beach 46, 126–7, 237
Shaw, Nicola 87, 289, 298
Shaw Report (see Shaw, Nicola)
Sheffield 6, 28, 30, 40, 91, 97, 100–102, 206, 208,
    280, 300
Shore, Peter MP 48
Sinfin 99
Skelmersdale 254
Skipton *see* Colne
Skipton-East Lancashire Railway Action
    Partnership (SELRAP) 260
Smith, Julian MP 260
Smyth, Ralph 245
SNCB 195
SNCF 195
Snow Hill (see Birmingham Snow Hill)
Snow Hill (London) 67, 210, 217
Somerset & Dorset 11, 28, 46
South East Northumberland Rail User Group
    (SENRUG) 253–4
South East of Scotland Transport Partnership
    (SEStran) 136
Southall 75–6
Southend Airport 120
South London Line 113, 116

South Wales Integrated Fast Transit
    (SWIFT) 179
South West Trains (franchise) 12–3, 72–3, 84,
    124–6, 228, 288
Southampton-Hythe *see* Hythe
Spa Valley Railway 245
Stagecoach (Group) 13, 50, 67, 72–4
Stansted Airport 64, 67, 119, 247, 265–7, 287,
    291
Steam Railway (magazine) 78
Steel, David MP 47–8
Steer Davies & Gleave 260
Stobart 120
Stow (Borders Railway) 3–4, 144, 146–8, 150
Stranraer 28, 130–1, 157–160
Strategic Rail Authority 72, 74, 94, 292
Stratford International 112, 193, 195, 201–202
Stratford-upon-Avon 16, 43, 106–107, 250–2
    Stratford Observer 251
    Stratford-upon-Avon-Honeybourne 16, 250
Strathclyde Regional Council 133
Strathclyde Passenger Transport Executive
    (SPTE) 131–2
Sudbury 69, 266–7
Sugar Loaf 167–8
Surrey County Council 270
Swanage 276
Swanline 185
Swindon 5, 11, 15, 19, 43, 55, 121–5, 264

Tarka Line 9, 245, 274, 287
Taunton *see* Minehead
Tavistock 89, 241, 243–4
TaxPayers' Alliance 208
Templecombe 11, 13, 67
Templeton 9
Tenby 9–10, 186–7
TGV 202–203
Thameslink 6, 15, 64, 66–7, 88, 91, 111, 191,
    209–17, 221, 223, 227, 284, 299
Thatcher, Margaret MP 58–9, 66, 192
Thetford-Swaffham 27
Times, The 18, 20, 72–3, 80, 201, 204, 283, 286,
    295–6
Tondu 177–9
Tower Colliery 174
Towy Valley Steam Company 168
Train Protection Warning System (TPWS) 71
Tram-train 102, 263
Trans-European Network 266
Trans-Pennine 78–9, 102, 208, 281
    TransPennine Express 285
Transport Act 1962 19, 26, 44–5